W9-ANA-076

World Anthropology

General Editor

SOL TAX

Patrons

CLAUDE LÉVI-STRAUSS
MARGARET MEAD
LAILA SHUKRY EL HAMAMSY
M. N. SRINIVAS

MOUTON PUBLISHERS · THE HAGUE · PARIS
DISTRIBUTED IN THE USA AND CANADA BY ALDINE, CHICAGO

International Congress of Anthropological and Ethnological Sciences, 9th, Chicago, 1973

Language and Man
Anthropological Issues

Editors

WILLIAM C. McCORMACK
STEPHEN A. WURM

MOUTON PUBLISHERS · THE HAGUE · PARIS
DISTRIBUTED IN THE USA AND CANADA BY ALDINE, CHICAGO

P
35
I5
1973

Copyright © 1976 by Mouton & Co. All rights reserved.
No part of this publication may be reproduced,
stored in a retrieval system, or transmitted,
in any form or by any means, electronic, mechanical,
photocopying, recording or otherwise without the
written permission of Mouton Publishers, The Hague
Distributed in the United States of America and Canada
by Aldine Publishing Company, Chicago, Illinois
ISBN 90-279-7839-5 (Mouton)
0-202-90035-5 (Aldine)
Jacket photo by Cas Oorthuys
Cover and jacket design by Jurriaan Schrofer
Indexes by John Jennings
Printed in the Netherlands

General Editor's Preface

Language is so important a characteristic of the human species that its study has necessarily been integral to anthropology. Linguistics and anatomy are probably the oldest of the human sciences; and the former — humanistic as it is — may nevertheless be the oldest of our comparative sciences. This book concerns not so much linguistics, however, as language as part of human communication, studied as "species behavior" in the sense of study in a naturalistic framework. Thus human communication is presented here in its human developmental, multi-channel, bilingual, and interspecific interactive contextual transformations, and for its role in constituting personal evaluative and social-cultural norms. As discussed in the international congress which was its occasion — and as seen in the Introduction to the book and its Summary of Discussion — the development of new knowledge about human communication has been so rapid in our generation that this book becomes a record of basic theory at a crossroads.

Like most contemporary sciences, anthropology is a product of the European tradition. Some argue that it is a product of colonialism, with one small and self-interested part of the species dominating the study of the whole. If we are to understand the species, our science needs substantial input from scholars who represent a variety of the world's cultures. It was a deliberate purpose of the IXth International Congress of Anthropological and Ethnological Sciences to provide impetus in this direction. The *World Anthropology* volumes, therefore, offer a first glimpse of a human science in which members from all societies have played an active role. Each of the books is designed to be self-contained; each is an attempt to update its particular sector of scientific knowledge and is written by specialists from all parts of the world. Each volume should be read and reviewed individually as a separate volume on its own given subject. The set as a whole will indicate what changes are in store for anthropology as scholars from the developing countries join in studying the species of which we are all a part.

The IXth Congress was planned from the beginning not only to include as many of the scholars from every part of the world as possible, but also with a view toward the eventual publication of the papers in high-quality volumes. At previous Congresses scholars were invited to bring papers which were then read out loud. They were necessarily limited in length, many were only summarized; there was little time for discussion; and the sparse discussion could only be in one language. The IXth Congress was an experiment aimed at changing this. Papers were written with the intention of exchanging them before the Congress, particularly in extensive pre-Congress sessions; they were not intended to be read aloud at the Congress, that time being devoted to discussions — discussions which were simultaneously and professionally translated into five languages. The method for eliciting the papers was structured to make as representative a sample as was allowable when scholarly creativity — hence self-selection — was critically important. Scholars were asked both to propose papers of their own and to suggest topics for sessions of the Congress which they might edit into volumes. All were then informed of the suggestions and encouraged to rethink their own papers and the topics. The process, therefore, was a continuous one of feedback and exchange and it has continued to be so even after the Congress. The some two thousand papers comprising *World Anthropology* certainly then offer a substantial sample of world anthropology. It has been said that anthropology is at a turning point; if this is so, these volumes will be the historical direction-markers.

As might have been foreseen in the first post-colonial generation, the large majority of the Congress papers (82 percent) are the work of scholars identified with the industrialized world which fathered our traditional discipline and the institution of the Congress itself: Eastern Europe (15 percent); Western Europe (16 percent); North America (47 percent); Japan, South Africa, Australia, and New Zealand (4 percent). Only 18 percent of the papers are from developing areas: Africa (4 percent); Asia-Oceania (9 percent); Latin America (5 percent). Aside from the substantial representation from the U.S.S.R. and the nations of Eastern Europe, a significant difference between this corpus of written material and that of other Congresses is the addition of the large proportion of contributions from Africa, Asia, and Latin America. "Only 18 percent" is two to four times as great a proportion as that of other Congresses; moreover, 18 percent of 2,000 papers is 360 papers, 10 times the number of "Third World" papers presented at previous Congresses. In fact, these 360 papers are more than the total of ALL papers published after the last International Congress of Anthropological and Ethnological Sciences which was held in the United States (Philadelphia, 1956).

The significance of the increase is not simply quantitative. The input of scholars from areas which have until recently been no more than subject matter for anthropology represents both feedback and also long-awaited theoretical contributions from the perspectives of very different cultural, social, and historical traditions. Many who attended the IXth Congress were convinced that anthropology would not be the same in the future. The fact that the next Congress (India, 1978) will be our first in the "Third World" may be symbolic of the change. Meanwhile, sober consideration of the present set of books will show how much, and just where and how, our discipline is being revolutionized.

In this *World Anthropology* series are three companion volumes also edited by Professors McCormack and Wurm: *Language and thought, Language and society,* and *Approaches to language.* Other related titles in the series include books on human biology, the origin of man, cognitive and psychological anthropology, and communication in a variety of social and cultural contexts.

Chicago, Illinois SOL TAX
March 24, 1976

Preface

A general session on "Language in Anthropology" of the IXth International Congress of Anthropological and Ethnological Sciences (Chicago, Fall 1973) was organized by Dr. McCormack at the invitation of Professor Sol Tax, President of the Congress. It evolved over more than a year on the basis of relevant papers volunteered to the Congress and an equal number of papers solicited by McCormack, notably at international linguistics congresses in Europe in 1972, under the gratefully acknowledged travel support from The Canada Council of Ottawa and The Wenner-Gren Foundation for Anthropological Research of New York City. What started out as a single session ultimately divided into subsessions, of which four major topical ones have yielded the World Anthropology volumes entitled *Language and man, Language and thought, Approaches to language,* and *Language and society.*

Dr. Wurm joined this undertaking at the invitation of Professor Tax upon the recommendation of McCormack and assumed full responsibility for the conduct and written summary of the session discussions at Chicago. Those were based on precirculated papers. Wurm chaired essentially all subsessions of this general session, i.e. an opening informal subsession, the four formal topical subsessions plus a fifth one on language in anthropology at large, and four *ad hoc* gatherings of self-selected membership. In this, and at his invitation, he was accompanied by Dr. Nguyen Dang Liem of The University of Hawaii, acting as his assistant and discussion coordinator throughout. Wurm's subsequent provision of written summaries of discussions was aided by the prepared texts of formal discussants and tapes of most proceedings.

For three years, from mid-1972 until the finalization of the resultant books, Anna Pikelis McCormack acted as administrative and editorial associate to McCormack for this general session. All operations behind the scenes have carried the stamp of her extraordinary competence. For further and efficient assistance in this regard, she joins me in thanking Mrs. Charlotte Stewart, secretary for the Department of Linguistics of the University of Calgary.

The subsession on "Language and Man" had for its discussion theme "language capacity and acquisition as paradigmatical for man as a species." Only an hour of time was available for it; thus discussion was restricted to its three formal discussants and the authors of papers in the subsession. However all Congress members were explicitly free to contribute additional comments, verbally or in writing, on other occasions.

Editorial discretion for the present volume on *Language and man* rested solely with McCormack. Some papers included for discussion at the subsession in the interests of a maximized basis for discussion have found publication in other volumes of the World Anthropology series, notably *Organization of behavior in face-to-face interaction*, edited by Dr. Adam Kendon and others, and *Socioecology and psychology of primates*, edited by Dr. Russell Tuttle. The paper by John G. Bordie in the present volume was solicited after the Congress and could therefore not be discussed at the Congress.

The University of Calgary   WILLIAM C. MCCORMACK
Calgary, Alberta, Canada
January 15, 1975

Table of Contents

SECTION SIX: DISCUSSION

SECTION ONE

Introductory

Introduction

WILLIAM C. McCORMACK

Language and man is about human communication, verbal and non-verbal, and emphasizes a view that research on this subject must reach out beyond the confines of scientistic linguistics and psycholinguistics to involve all relevant achievable understandings about small-group social interaction and expressive culture.

The speed with which research approaches in psycholinguistics have been changing in recent years is little short of remarkable. Only ten years ago, a prevailing conception of *New directions in the study of language* (Lenneberg 1964) was informed by Noam Chomsky's theoretical assertion of a biological "innate schematism" of cognitive and associated linguistic organization in man (Chomsky 1968: 63–69). It was held that language was reconstructed speech and was species-specific to man, that study of language acquisition could proceed in terms of linguistic concepts and experimental psychological techniques with monolinguals for subjects, and that research on human communication, as opposed to language, should employ the systems approach of information and communications theory. Culture was admitted only symbologically in the abstract. Social interaction was ignored, unless — as with the idea that language might be learned through behavioral conditioning — it was mentioned to be rejected.

Today, the newer directions in the study of language found in the present volume almost overturn the priorities of the Lenneberg book. Here, the subject of inquiry is redefined from "language" to "human communication," and research designs have been made as broadly interdisciplinary and as inclusive of observations on social interaction and sociocultural context as need be. The reasons for this dramatic change are many.

For one, psychologists and ethologists have been energetically conducting research highlighting facts of animal communication, and have come up with findings on kinesics and "paralanguage" that have demanded comparative attention from students of language in *Homo sapiens*. For example, research on the capacity of apes to use American Sign Language for the deaf, to communicate interspecifically with humans, has led the psycholinguist Brown (1973a: 43) to conclude that "the evidence that [the chimpanzee] Washoe has Stage I language (i.e. purposeful concatenation of two symbols) is about the same as it is for children." In these situations, questions have arisen about the species-specificity of human "language," and it has grown difficult not to sensitize to a perspective on human "communication" which assesses itself to be "so successful and powerful just because it relies to such a high degree on extra-linguistic channels" (Bar-Hillel 1972: 126; cf. Birdwhistell 1970 and Hewes 1973; but contrast Spiegel and Machotka 1974: 86–88). Whether we should actually redefine "language" — e.g. to disallow cross-species differentiality in respect of semantics, knowledge, or intent of "speakers" (cf. Stephenson 1974) — remains to be seen.

Second, previous study of language acquisition by monolingual children has been extensified by substantial study of bilingual language acquisition, with results which, again, have invited reexamination of the idea of universals in the ordering of linguistic phenomena in man. Evidently, humans communicate in terms of complex processes such as mixing and code-switching as among forms of both verbal and nonverbal behavior, and, moreover, do what they do in a given case in response to perceived social and cultural context of the communicative act. The complexity is observably there and is not presently reducible conceptually to simple variations of "performance" on some assumed universal base. For now, much more research on the mechanisms and mainsprings of the complexity itself is felt to be necessary.

Finally, recent years have seen more and more scientists explicitly concerned that their research should have applied value for improving the condition of man. Since we live in a world of increasing institutional breakdown and precipitous reorganization — not to mention politicization — generalizations in the social sciences tend to be easily counterable with true allegations of exception. One result is that scholarly quest for truth, these days, seems to many to be served best — and certainly most "safely" — by a strongly empirical approach to human behavior. Empiricism tacitly strengthens an approach to human communication as a complex, contextual, and dynamic phenomenon.

These newer directions in the study of human communication have not yet achieved the stage of formal theory. Progress, to date, has been marked more by the development and testing of valid and productive methodologies for research (cf. Argyle 1969; Hall 1959; Sebeok 1972; Slama-Cazacu 1972). In this, the perspective on interaction and sociocultural context tends to be that of the disciplines of comparative psychology and social psychiatry more than that of social anthropology or of sociology.

For anthropology, the objective of modern psycholinguistics to develop axioms for the observation of human communication and its negotiation of rules for social encounters in culturally meaningful contexts relates most to issues in the theory of culture, approached systematically as semiotic.

The present volume opens with Section 2 on "Human Communication" in which authors support the hypothesis that language is species-specific to man but not without reexamining it in the light of recent research on ethology and early human development. Crystal underscores Lenneberg's view (1967: 265) that "the biological history of language cannot be revealed through a random comparison with animal communication," for he asserts that "any suggestion of a real similarity between human paralinguistic phenomena and animal vocalization is premature, and in the present state of our knowledge, misleading." Bordie's tip in the opposite direction is slight: "There is apparently an overlapping of language and language-like elements in the behavior of adult primates and humans during early development. . . . What has been done so far indicates only that we have a long distance to travel before we know whether primates other than man can use human language."

For a case study on interspecific communication, there follows a paper on domestic animal calling in a Berber tribe, in which Bynon argues that early man accommodated to animal modes of communication, but that after the Neolithic Revolution this vector was reversed. In this regard, discussant Sebeok's comment on animal domestication is of interest for general anthropology in hinting that the term "domestication" may be definable as an end product of a process of mutual "code-switching" during interspecific communication over time.

Focusing squarely on humans, Bullowa, Fidelholtz, and Allan Kessler present results of a longitudinal study of early infant vocalizations which is noteworthy for the methodological sophistication with which it applies an ethological perspective to research on humans. Employing new laboratory techniques for psychological testing of individual differences, complete with instrumentative control against observer bias, this study is one which continues in the tradition of psychological testing and maturational perspective on behavior characteristic of the Lenneberg symposium (cf. also Suppes 1974).

On the other hand, and as a rare direct exploration into the nature, development, and linguistic plus cultural significance of human protolanguage, Halliday provides and interprets an ethnography of communication of a child from the ages of six to eighteen months. Defining the learning of language as learning how to mean, he hypothesizes that learning a mother tongue consists in mastering certain specified functions of language and developing a meaning potential in respect of each, and argues that an infant naturally accomplishes a system of meanings for himself "sociosemantically" in keeping with his own needs but also, analytically, as a necessary and sufficient condition for the learning of adult language. By the age of about 22½ to 24 months "the child has learned how to mean, in the sense that he has mastered the adult linguistic system," and thereafter he can and does use language to share meanings and participate in the transmission of culture. Halliday suggests that presumably the functions he specifies "are universals of human culture, and it is not unreasonable to think of them as the starting point not only for linguistic ontogeny but also for the evolution of the linguistic system." However, he allows that it remains unclear which of a child's moves toward his system of meanings represents universal patterning of human development and which are idiosyncratic and no necessary part of the semogenic process.

Section 3 turns to "Language Acquisition" by persons participating in patterns recognizable from the linguistic system of adult language, and deals with methodologies for study of more advanced language learning, reading skills, and acquisition of bilingualism.

Here, Slama-Cazacu has sounded a keynote by critically surveying methodological errors in previous psycholinguistic and sociolinguistic research on language acquisition, asserting that none of that research has explained early bilingualism, and arguing that, in the interests of a cross-cultural and cross-sectional basis for generalizations, we sorely need — from the world over — many studies of language and communication as a whole, in social context, and conceptualized at several levels including attention to the "social-historical moment." Roeper and McNeill (1973: 132, 135) have recently independently put stress on current need for additional case studies for cross-cultural testing of theories of language acquisition.

Söderbergh reports success in teaching reading to very young Swedish children by means of carefully preselecting teaching materials and organizing instruction by referring to the stage of a child's language development and cultural experience. Since "the written language will then begin to influence the child's spoken language and his way of thinking and reasoning," Söderbergh's work seems to support Brown's contention that teaching devices such as correction, reinforcement, and punishment leave substantially untouched what may be a kind of natural imperative for "children to bring their speech into line with adult models" in their own society (Brown 1973b: 105). At the same time, Söderbergh's pragmatic finding that "exactly as the syntactical complexity of the reading material may be successively increased even beyond the oral capacity of the child, so the contents of the books may gradually extend beyond the immediate [cultural] experience of the child," seems to support Slama-Cazacu's claim that experimental interventions can facilitate language acquisition and language-related learning.

With Miller's paper, we find evidence of social factors predominating over biological factors in matters of "acquired competence" for language learning in primary school. To compare monolingual and bilingual American Indian schoolchildren with respect to school-enhanced learning of English language over a period of time, Miller formulated a competence scale on the basis of both syntactic and morphological markers, sampled the schoolchildren, and isolated causal variables to account for her finding that the older bilingual children achieved lower scores for enhanced competence in English than did younger children initially monolingual in their Indian language. Having ruled out age as a causal variable, Miller calls for a review of those standard theories of competence which endorse age as a significant variable in acquisition of language competence per presumed "innate" maturational scheduling (for speculation about possible revisions, cf. Brown 1973a: 163, 388–389, 408–409).

Researching on bilingualism *per se*, Carolyn Kessler dissents from Slama-Cazacu's keynote on complexity, for Kessler discovered from a study of twelve bilingual children, aged six to eight years, that their acquisition order of marked features was predictable from a simplicity metric based on Fillmore's case grammar (Fillmore 1968). Kessler, then, proposes that attempts be made to formulate "bio-genetic" linguistic theory which would link monolinguals and bilinguals in respect to rule acquisition and thus also explain a presumably epiphenomenal "code-mixing."

Also researching on bilingualism, however, sociopsycholinguists

Oksaar and Hatch again stress complexity. Oksaar's paper on a young boy's speech habit of marking situation and role content has implications for processes of his Swedish/Finnish bilingual language acquisition, in motivating the propositional content and frequency of his "mixed-code" utterances. As a side issue, Oksaar queries Jakobson's allegation (1971) of universals in the acquisition of phonemes, precisely on the ground that without more case studies such an allegation is premature. Hatch gives us a critical survey of studies in language mixing and switching, which stands in support of Oksaar by documenting that a bilingual's mixed code is somehow reflexive of his rhetorical emotive intent, or "tone," in social situational context.

Section 4 on "Mixing and Sequencing" consists of case studies of small-group communication as analyzed with new techniques and methodologies to probe in depth the interactionist and negotiatory process of human discourse including its feature of largely unconscious speaker processing of verbal and nonverbal components of messages. After a general paper by Slama-Cazacu on nonverbal components in the sequence of message, reduced to "linguistically" analyzable units, there are case studies from von Raffler Engel and Duncan that emphasize kinesic cues, and from Martirena that emphasizes paralinguistic markers. Finally, Handelman explores a disjointed adult conversation to show that face-to-face interaction proceeds dynamically via a series of more or less promising "frames," but, as in the course of bridge play, some openings may never allow a definition of the situation to be negotiated.

The papers of Section 4 severally speak for themselves in sensitizing readers to the presence of nonverbal channels of communication and socially relevant, albeit preconscious, boundaries in discourse sequencing. These papers also bear directly or indirectly on possibilities for greater objectivization of anthropological fieldwork. Regarding motivations for interpersonal behavior between subjects of fieldwork, for example, Handelman shows that "by indicating the pattern of offer-response between them, and concomitantly whether they are expanding or limiting their interaction, it is possible to generally avoid the problem of inferring the motivation of participants while recognizing that their negotiations do acquire some measure of directionality and coherence."

Section 5 on "Language and the Science of Man" consists of papers which ground cultural theory in studies of social-interactional communicational processes such as those analyzed in Section 4. This idea of the explanatory value of social perceptions and acts for theory of various kinds is not itself new, for example, it has found adherents among students of phenomenology, ethnomethodology, and symbolic interactionism (cf. Denzin 1970: 28). However, the perspective proffered here is programmatic specifically for culturolinguistic anthropology and encompasses three different approaches to this subject.

In the first paper, Poyatos presents a unique and comprehensive variation on the familiar theme of "emic" description — i.e. the theme of "cognitive calculus by which relevant actors judge the entities [to be] similar or different, real, meaningful, significant, or in some other sense 'appropriate' or 'acceptable' " (Harris 1968: 571) — by putting his own stress on visual and kinesic semiotic systems. These latter he explicates in terms of speaker-actor orientating reflexes, analyzed as occurring sequentially over four successively less global phases, of which the last allows specification of subcultural signaling systems and ritual behavior.

The Leodolters start from the widely accepted premise that the language process is central to human socialization for culture, but they advance relevant theory (e.g. that of Bernstein and Henderson 1969) by explicitly positing that cultural norms are learned via performative utterances, including "reflexives" or "permissions" elicited in the course of face-to-face interaction by which actors must negotiate a definition of the "situation."

In one of the closing papers, Oprescu forthrightly claims for cultural-linguistic anthropology the highest of positions from which to program a broadened scope of future research on human communication, verbal and nonverbal. Maintaining that anthropological perspective is the key to understanding "human creations ... full of explicit or implicit significances which ask only to be brought to light," Oprescu's paper expresses the unity of the anthropological endeavor as a semiotic endeavor uniquely mindful "of the dialectics existing between the biologic, the social, and the cultural."

REFERENCES

ARGYLE, M.
  1969   *Social interaction*. Chicago: Aldine.
BAR-HILLEL, Y.
  1972   "Language," in *Scientific thought: some underlying concepts, methods, and procedures*. Edited by UNESCO, 107–128. Paris and The Hague: Mouton/UNESCO.
BERNSTEIN, B., D. HENDERSON
  1969   Social class differences in the relevance of language to socializa-

tion. *Sociology* 3(1). (Reprinted 1973 in *Class, codes, and control*, volume two. Edited by B. Bernstein, 24–47. London and Boston: Routledge and Kegan Paul.)

BIRDWHISTELL, R. L.
1970   *Kinesics and context: essays on body motion communication.* New York: Ballantine Books.

BROWN, ROGER
1973a   *A first language: the early stages.* Cambridge, Mass.: Harvard University Press.
1973b   Development of the first language in the human species. *American Psychologist* 28(2):97–106.

CHOMSKY, NOAM
1968   *Language and mind.* New York: Harcourt, Brace and World.

DENZIN, N. K.
1970   *The research act.* Chicago: Aldine.

FILLMORE, C. J.
1968   "The case for case," in *Universals in linguistic theory*. Edited by E. Bach and R. T. Harms, 1–87. New York: Holt, Rinehart and Winston.

HALL, E. T.
1959   *The silent language.* New York: Doubleday.

HARRIS, M.
1968   *The rise of anthropological theory.* New York: T. Y. Crowell.

HEWES, G. W.
1973   Primate communication and the gestural origin of language. *Current Anthropology* 14(1-2):5–24.

JAKOBSON, R.
1971   *Studies on child language and aphasia.* The Hague: Mouton.

LENNEBERG, E. H.
1967   *Biological foundations of language.* New York: J. Wiley.

LENNEBERG, E. H., *editor*
1964   *New directions in the study of language.* Cambridge, Mass.: M.I.T. Press.

ROEPER, T., D. MC NEILL
1973   "Review of child language," in *Annual review of anthropology*, volume two. Edited by B. J. Siegel, A. R. Beals, and S. A. Tyler, 127–137. Palo Alto, Calif.: Annual Reviews.

SEBEOK, T. A.
1972   *Perspectives in zoosemiotics.* The Hague: Mouton.

SLAMA-CAZACU, T.
1972   *La psycholinguistique.* Paris: Editions Klincksieck.

SPIEGEL, J., PAVEL MACHOTKA
1974   *Messages of the body.* New York: Free Press.

STEPHENSON, P. H.
1974   On the possible significance of silence for the origin of speech. *Current Anthropology* 15(3):324–326.

SUPPES, P.
1974   The semantics of children's language. *American Psychologist* 29(2):103–114.

SECTION TWO

Human Communication

Paralinguistic Behavior as Continuity Between Animal and Human Communication

DAVID CRYSTAL

To both layman and scholar, that area of nonverbal vocal behavior generally if vaguely referred to as "tone of voice" is held to be a significant point of overlap between human and animal communicative systems. One does not need a batch of references to support the assertion that factors such as pitch, loudness, and speed of speaking are relevant in the elicitation of differentiated responses by many domestic pets; and the implication that this is accordingly an area of communicative behavior that animals and man share is widely found in the literature on zoosemiotics and communication. Sturtevant, for example, expressed the general view (1947: 45) that "the exclamatory parts of language, like many animal cries, are characterized by extreme variations of pitch and loudness.... There is abundant proof that other animals of the same species respond to these calls roughly as men respond to the highly emotional features of languages."

Following Trager (1958), Hockett (1960), and others, this area is generally labelled as PARALANGUAGE in the context of human communication and considered analogous to the expressive vocalizations of various animal species. Abe (1967: 55), for instance, talks of "the universality of animals' use of symptomatic signs which belong to the field of paralanguage," and Thorpe uses the term PARALINGUISTIC to refer to both human and animal communication (1972: 27, 33). In the search for continuities between animal and human communication, then, it would seem that paralinguistic phenomena provide evidence of a particularly compelling kind. The author suggests, however, that positive conclusions on this topic are probably false and at best premature.

The term "paralanguage" has in many ways been more of a hindrance than a help to progress in our understanding of nonverbal vocal behavior. The appealing simplicity of the dualism "language-paralanguage" led very early on within linguistics to an interpretation of paralanguage as a communicational residue; whatever features of vocal behavior could not be coped with by one's model of language were labelled paralinguistic. Paralanguage came to be used as a convenient cover term for a miscellany of unanalyzed phenomena, whose theoretical homogeneity was uncritically assumed. The dualism became institutionalized when paralanguage was classed along with nonvocal modes of communication under the general heading of "semiotics" (see Sebeok, Hayes, and Bateson 1964).

The reasons for this state of affairs would lead us into detailed consideration of the history of ideas in linguistics, and cannot be considered here (a fully referenced discussion can be found in Crystal 1974); but, briefly, what seems to have happened is the following. Trager's influential characterization (1958) of paralanguage was a part of his overall descriptive framework, and the term received its definition and status from its relationships with other categories of the theory, in particular from the view that only phonemic and morphemic analysis was the domain of linguistics proper. As soon as alternative accounts of linguistic structure developed, in the mid-sixties, the status of paralanguage inevitably became unclear. Fields such as psychotherapy, anthropology, and language teaching took over and developed many of the DESCRIPTIVE insights of the approach, and found the notations and *ad hoc* classifications of great value. But there was little examination of the theoretical basis of the description, and no discussion of how a notion of "paralanguage" could be made to fit in with the new concepts of language which were developing at this time.

One thus finds the development of a situation in which a widely used descriptive framework rests on a largely implicit theoretical foundation. And in the absence of explicit analytic criteria, one naturally finds arbitrary descriptive decisions, ambiguous cases being forced into one or another of the set of choices provided by the framework, and, following this, inconsistency in the use of terms by various scholars.

It is possible to distinguish seven main viewpoints as to the range of phenomena which might be subsumed under the heading of paralanguage, and I list them briefly here (for a referenced discussion, see Crystal 1974):

1. including both nonhuman and human vocalization;
2. human communication only, but including nonvocal (kinesic) as well as vocal;

3. vocal communication only, but including some segmental phonation as well as nonsegmental;

4. nonsegmental phonation only, including voice quality ("voice set," in the sense of Trager [1958] — the nonlinguistic, background, person-identifying characteristic);

5. nonsegmental phonation, excluding voice quality;

6. nonsegmental phonation, excluding voice quality and the prosodic phonemes (of intonation, stress, and juncture) found in the approach of Trager and others; and

7. a small subset of (6).

I propose to use a broad linguistic definition as the basis for discussion, as in sense (5). In other words, paralanguage is defined as meaningfully contrastive, institutionalized, nonsegmental phonation. This therefore excludes kinesic and other nonvocal phenomena — a desirable distinction, in my view, until such time as it can be shown that there are sufficient parallels between paralinguistic and kinesic structures to warrant a conflation. Likewise, this sense postpones any discussion of whether intonation and related features are sufficiently different from other types of nonsegmental linguistic behavior to warrant their being given a totally different theoretical status. The point at issue is whether sense (1) is a legitimate conflation and it is this which I hope to throw some light upon.

From an operational point of view, paralanguage is defined with reference to one or more of the following parameters: pitch, loudness, speed, pause, and rhythm (all these sometimes being classified separately as "prosodic features"); and laryngeal, pharyngeal, oral, and nasal articulations. All of these effects are classed as nonsegmental when they cannot be described with reference to a single segment, or phoneme, in the sound system of the language but continue over a stretch of utterance to segments in different parts of an utterance that are all affected by a single configuration of the vocal organs (e.g. when the labialization of adult "baby talk" produces a cumulative impression and interpretation that affects the whole of the utterance).

Each articulatory variable produces a range of effects that can be studied in terms of a system of contrasts, of varying degrees of discreteness and systematicity of function. Examples include contrasts in articulatory tension, degrees of resonance, types of whispered or breathy articulation, spasmodic articulations (as in giggled speech), degrees of nasalization or labialization, variations in the center of gravity of the tongue (advancement or retraction, as in palatalization and velarization respectively), register contrasts (e.g. falsetto versus chest voice), types of pharyngeal constriction (such as huskiness), contrasts in pitch direction and pitch range, and gradual or sudden changes in loudness or speed of speaking.

The question is: given this range of phenomena in man, to what extent is it a major area of overlap with animal vocal behavior? Certainly, while we are speaking in operational terms, there does seem to be an overlap. While accepting that there is an absence of comprehensive descriptive studies (cf. the lament of Sebeok, Altmann, and others, e.g. Altmann 1968: 501), the partial accounts we do have are couched in terms that are remarkably similar to those used for the study of human paralinguistic behavior. Brief examples are the tentative functional classification of neighing in terms of height, loudness, and length (Tembrock 1968: 379), and later in the same paper, the identification of a wide range of vocalizations in terms of pitch direction and range, loudness, rhythm, tonal quality, and various laryngeal, spasmodic, and other contrasts (see especially the discussion of Felidae, Tembrock 1968: 367); and of course there are the classical analyses of bird vocalization by Thorpe (1961, and elsewhere).

In this area, as in human paralinguistic studies, a great deal of effort has been expended on the problem of terminology, both for formal labelling (e.g. croak, grunt, hiss, shout) and its semantic interpretation (e.g. happy, surprised, intention to frighten), though it is strange that such "human-oriented" terms as "intonation" and "paralanguage" receive no attention at all in the otherwise admirably full terminological preamble and index in Busnel (1963). From a functional point of view, the threefold classification of paralinguistic phenomena into emotional, social, and grammatical roles also has parallels in zoosemiotics (the first two are obvious; by grammatical, I am referring to the view — held, for example, by Thorpe [1972: 33, 54] — that certain animal vocalizations display a definite "syntax"). For such reasons, then, one might expect the notion of paralanguage to be readily applicable to both human and animal vocalization and a conclusion about continuity made accordingly.

But I think we would be wrong to draw such a conclusion, at least, for the present. I wish to argue that any suggestion of a real similarity between human paralinguistic phenomena and animal vocalization is premature and, in the present state of our knowledge, misleading. The essence of the argument is that paralanguage was given an inadequate analysis when the question of its potential relevance for the study of animal communication was first raised, namely, in the design-feature approach to language of Hockett (1960; see also Hocket 1968; Altmann

1968). In terms of the criteria used there, paralanguage did seem to be intermediate between human language (in the sense of phonemes, morphemes, syntax, etc.) and the various kinds of animal communication illustrated. Now that a great deal more paralinguistic study has taken place, it is possible to reevaluate its status *vis-à-vis* human and animal communication and to conclude that paralanguage is much closer to the rest of language than was originally anticipated. The overlap with animal communication is minimal and trivial.

In terms of the sixteen design features of human language recognized by Hockett, paralanguage emerged as follows:

CLEARLY POSITIVE

1. Broadcast transmission and directional reception
2. Rapid fading
3. Openness (new linguistic messages are coined freely and easily)
4. Tradition (language conventions are passed down by teaching and learning)
5. Prevarication (ability to lie or be meaningless)
6. Learnability (possibility of foreign language learning)

QUERY POSITIVE

7. Specialization (the direct-energetic consequences of linguistic signals are biologically unimportant; only the triggering consequences are important)
8. Semanticity (the existence of a denotative relationship between signals and features in the world)

PARTIALLY POSITIVE

9. Vocal-auditory channel
10. Interchangeability (adult speakers are both transmitters and receivers)
11. Complete feedback (speaker is able to perceive everything relevant to his signal production)
12. Arbitrariness (no dependent physical interrelationship between signals and referents)
13. Discreteness (repertoire not continuous)
14. Displacement (can refer to things remote in time and space)

NEGATIVE

15. Duality of patterning (meaningless signal elements combine into meaningful arrangements)

16.   Reflectiveness, or reflexiveness (ability to communicate about the system itself).

The design feature listing has its weaknesses, as is readily admitted (Altmann 1968: 64). In particular, not all the features have the same degree of importance, and thus it becomes difficult to establish the status of a type of behavior such as paralanguage. But there are certain specific problems with this characterization of paralanguage as it stands, such that it is possible to argue that of most the negative points (9-16) arise from an inadequate understanding of the formal complexity and functional significance of paralinguistic effect. This is very clear in relation to points 15 and 16.

Of all the design-features, duality of structure (or "double articulation") seems to be the most important with regard to the specificity of its claims about linguistic structure (cf. Lyons 1970: 12). This is the property whereby a set of signal elements, themselves meaningless, produce meaningful results when used in patterned combinations. Language, therefore, has duality of patterning, and the same is said of various animals, including primates, Canidae, and birds.

But paralanguage is said to have no duality. This seems unreasonable. Whatever definition of paralanguage one takes, Thorpe's comment about birds would seem to be equally applicable to it: "A bird's song may . . . be made up of anything from half-a-dozen to several hundred 'notes' . . . . Most of these 'notes' are quite meaningless if sounded alone; but grouped in the correct pattern of the song they can convey a great deal of information both as to the species and the individual involved" (1972: 33). For example, it is well known that the nonsegmental characteristics of a single syllable (e.g. a pitch, a stress, a duration, an instance of nasalization, a whisper) are uninterpretable until they are put into sequences and related to the voice norms of individuals in specific contexts.

In intonation, the fundamental concept of a "contour" or "tone unit" is recognition of the fact that, characteristically, semantic interpretations can only be assigned to "complete" syllable sequences; and the same applies to variations in tempo, loudness, rhythm, and other effects. In each case, the minimal variable element is generally meaningless. (The qualification "generally" is important, because there are usually a few cases within a language where, assuming a known speaker, there are effects which can be interpreted semantically on the basis of minimal occurrence: in other words, the signal elements are meaningful and their sequential combinations do not produce a different kind of meaning.

Examples would be the "voice qualifications" of Crystal and Quirk [1964]: laugh, giggle, tremulousness, sob, and cry. But there are not many examples of this kind in language.) The need to take into account rules of sequence and of hierarchical structure is well recognized in intonational studies (e.g. Halliday 1967; Pike 1945); and one needs to adopt a similar point of view in accounting for the meaningfulness of most other paralinguistic phenomena.

"Reflectiveness" is the property of language by which we can communicate about the system in which we are communicating. (It is a better term than "metacommunication," used for instance by Altmann [1967], as this is readily confusable with the linguists' and philosophers' use of the term "metalanguage." (Reflectiveness is in effect the recognition of context-dependence in language, the fact that certain signals alter the significance of other signals. In their recent discussion, Hockett and Altmann illustrate "metacommunication" in the following way: it is

... communication that is some sort of commentary on other communication. ... In human speech we can have "primary" communication and metacommunication in the same system, as when we interrupt what we are saying with "You're not listening!" or with "I guess I expressed that badly." But we also carry on, in paralinguistic and kinesic form, a virtually uninterrupted running commentary on what we are saying in words. Something much like this seems to be the case with many other animals: virtually all social messages are accompanied by contextual or "framing" cues that affect the interpretation or response (Altmann 1968: 67).

But this approach gives rise to problems. I do not wish to go into the question of whether reflectiveness operates in animals, about which there is a difference of opinion (e.g. Thorpe, following Hockett, says there is not [1972: 33], whereas Cullen cites cases to the contrary [1972: 108]). Purely on the human side, one must ask: How valid is this notion of "commentary"? To what extent is it possible to take an utterance in a given situation and determine what within it is "central" and what "modulation"? As Birdwhistell says (1970: 86, and see further, 188-189): "It is all too easy to assure ourselves that there is in any social interchange a CENTRAL, a PRIMARY or a REAL meaning which is only modified by a redundant environment. ... Our temptation to classify certain aspects of a transaction as the central message and other aspects as serving only as modifiers rests upon untested assumptions about communication." I would agree. To say that X changes Y to Z presupposes that we have criteria for isolating X as "basic" or "primary." And how does one make such a distinction in practice?

The more one examines speech in its full interactional context (and not simply in its written representation), the more one finds examples of utterances in which the primary determinants of the speaker's identity and purpose and of the listener's response are paralinguistic ("Say it as if you mean it," "You don't SOUND as if you're a clergyman," and the unavoidable "It wasn't what he said, but the way that he said it . . ."). In such cases, paralanguage has played a central, not a peripheral role. Another example would be the phonological exponent of emphasis. The emphasized word in "He NEVER said that" may be produced in a variety of ways — with very high pitch range, very low pitch range, fortissimo loudness, pianissimo loudness, extra-long duration, whisper, husky, or creaky voice — and it is difficult to see how any of these effects in this context can be said to be "merely modulating" in function (this phrase being taken from the discussion of Cullen's paper in Hinde [1972: 124]).

If we grant paralanguage a communicative status in its own right, it follows that we must alter our opinion about its ability to display reflectiveness. But we must first take account of the objection of Lyons (1972: 54), who considers it debatable whether intonation has this property, "since the repetition by the listener of some part of what the speaker has just said with a different and distinctive intonation (and stress) may have the effect of querying, not what has been said, but the appropriateness of the words chosen to describe it." This ambiguity does exist; but it can be avoided, with the contrastive intonation involved having a clearly reflective function.

One example is in the use of high pitch range plus rising tone to express echo-utterances (Quirk, et al. 1972: 408 ff.), as in:

(A) John's CÒMING.   (B) He's h CÓMING?
(A) It's JÒHN on the phone.   (B) h JǑHN?

Another example is the intonation which indicates the use of a "softened" connecting phrase, such as "you know," "I mean," "you see," "sort of," where the phrase in the appropriate intonation conditions the stylistic force of the accompanying sentence and contrasts with the "literal" meaning of the words, as in:

you h KNÓW/I think he's RÌGHT   (= let me tell you, I think . . .)
you KNÒW I think he's right (= you are aware that I think . . .)

Examples using other paralinguistic effects would be the use of husky or whispered voice on the word "not" in the following:

(A) John's coming to the meeting.   (B) He's not!

On grammatical words, it seems unlikely for anything other than a reflective function of paralinguistic effects to be present. And as a final example, there is the allegro tempo used on a phrase to indicate that the preceding structure was an error, as in the emphasized phrase following:

You're not getting the bus GETTING THE TRAIN are you?

Now given such examples, I think we must argue that the reflectiveness involved is a property of the paralinguistic system itself. It would be misleading to relate the marked intonational or speed contrasts involved directly to the verbal context preceding, as the "commentary" notion suggests, viz.,

John's COMING.   John's COMING?
Rather it should be:

John's COMING.   John's COMING?

This seems to be typical of intonation, where the "meaning" of a tone cannot be judged in isolation. It is of course partly dependent on the nature of the accompanying verbal language, but it is also very much dependent on the perceived contrast with the intonation of the previous utterance. I do not know how much of intonation is a commentary on previous (or subsequent) intonation in this way, but the potential importance of this function must surely be recognized. The same applies to paralanguage in general.

If we now move on to the design-features which are said to be PARTIALLY positive in respect to paralanguage, it also seems possible to indicate a rather more central role for the phenomenon than in the original analysis. The question of VOCAL-AUDITORY CHANNEL is clearly a matter of definition, which I have excluded from consideration by the definition adopted in this paper. (A comparison of the structural differences between paralinguistic and kinesics warrants a separate study.) INTERCHANGEABILITY, whereby adult speakers are transmitters and receivers of the same range of linguistic signals, would seem to apply almost totally to paralanguage, as long as we realize that by linguistic signals here we are referring to relative, and not absolute, contrasts. The fact that a female voice is higher in terms of fundamental frequency than that of a male is not a relevant consideration; the point is that the relative differences beween, say, high and low pitch contours or between normal and allegro speed are isomorphic between men and women (cf. Crystal 1971b for further discussion). COMPLETE FEEDBACK states that the speaker is able to perceive everything relevant to his signal production. If the emphasis is on ABLE, I can see no difference between paralanguage and language here.

DISPLACEMENT is the ability to refer to things remote in time and space. This property, as Hockett and Altmann accept (Hockett 1968: 64), is not clear, as it is not an all-or-none matter but one of degree. "Just how far away from the site of a communicative transaction must the topic of the message be before we will speak of displacement? And ... do we measure the distance of the topic from the transmitter or the receiver?" There is no intrinsic reason, of course, why pitch, and the other variables, should not be used with a displaced, cognitive role: witness the use of tone in some languages to distinguish between present and past tense, for example (as in Twi). But even with respect to paralanguage in general, it is perfectly possible — and perhaps even normal — if someone has been frightened, for instance, for the vocal indications of the fright (e.g. tremulousness, high pitch range, short tone-units) to remain for some time after the event. *Contra* Lyons (1972: 54), then, it would seem that intonation, and probably paralanguage as whole, is in principle capable of displacement. We are therefore left with DISCRETE-NESS and ARBITRARINESS as partially positive design features, and these are more debatable.

The question of the arbitrariness of paralinguistic features is nowhere near solution, but one thing is clear: there can be no total dependency of paralinguistic effect on the nervous state of the organism. The view that there is an endogenous basis derives from the widely held assumptions that the sole function of paralanguage is emotional and that such features are, as Bastian puts it, "linguistically insignificant" (1964: 144). But the existence of numerous "structural" or "cognitive" uses of para-language, especially of pitch, loudness, and speed, demonstrates the opposite (see above, and Crystal 1969: Chapter 6), as does the range of social or stylistic "roles," where paralanguage is introduced into a discourse in a controlled manner (as when one "adopts" a persuasive tone of voice or an authoritative voice: see the classification of social roles in Crystal 1971a).

But even in relation to the purely emotional role, there are considerable differences between the paralinguistic norms of various languages and the function of the formal contrasts found. Comments about the "liveliness," "monotony," or "speed" of different languages suggest the former; misinterpretations of abruptness or sarcasm in learning a foreign language suggest the latter. There are, of course, cases where the para-linguistic effect is certainly correlated with nervous tension, e.g. degrees of increasing intensity of excitement correlating with increased pitch height, degrees of increasing intensity of disparagement correlating with increased pitch depth or huskiness. But to what extent these are universal remains unclear. Certainly, when one considers the range of functions which paralinguistic effect enters into and the range of differences which cross-linguistic comparisons have already indicated (e.g. in Sebeok, Hayes, and Bateson 1964), it would seem premature to be talking of universals. Referring to paralanguage as "partially positive" in respect to the design feature of arbitrariness thus seems to be reasonable, though it is perhaps something of an understatement, as there is far more arbitrariness involved in paralanguage than in other modes of semiotic behavior.

The issues concerning discreteness have been clouded somewhat by a tendency to confuse physical and linguistic notions of discreteness. As Altmann points out (1967: 341), it is not enough to claim that a communication takes place analogically rather than digitally by showing a continuous gradation in a signal; there must also be functional continuity — a one-to-one mapping of the signals onto a continuous array of denotata — and the difficulty lies in demonstrating this. Thus to say that a falling and a rising tone are at opposite ends of a continuously graded scale is true in a trivial, physical, or perceptual sense, but by no means self-evidently true in a semantic sense, and it is in fact extremely difficult to state the "meaning" of the contrasts in terms which demonstrate a continuous semantic gradation.

Even with examples in context, judges tend to give semantic interpretations of paralinguistic features using a wide range of labels (e.g. a rise in pitch may be understood as "sympathetic," "interested," "puzzled," 'ironic" ...), and these labels often have little in common with those used for the interpretation of the other features with which they are supposed to be in continuous gradation (e.g. a drop in pitch MAY be interpreted as "unsympathetic," "uninterested," etc., but one will also find a fresh set of labels used, such as "serious," "matter-of-fact," "sad"...). It is clearly a complicated situation, which will only be sorted out once the semantics of the various labels have been given some separate clarification, for instance, establishing the meaning-relations (of antonymy, hyponymy, etc.) which operate between them. And meanwhile, all one can safely say about paralanguage, from the point of view of discreteness, is that whereas it is obviously not discrete in the same sense as the phonemic and morphemic systems of verbal language, it is not at all obvious that it is analogic either, in Altmann's sense.

My own view is that the amount of discreteness to be found in paralanguage has been seriously underestimated, as a result of the assumption that the only kind of discreteness which matters is that associated with phonemes and morphemes. This was the assumption which permitted certain aspects of nonsegmental phonation to be given a linguistic description (as "pitch-phonemes," etc.), related aspects being classed as "extra-" or "metalinguistic." The arbitrariness of this demarcation is but one criticism among many which have been made of the phonemic model of intonation (e.g. by Bolinger 1949, 1951), and the dangers of defining significant contrastivity in language solely in terms of a model set up for the analysis of one kind of linguistic patterning only (i.e. the phonemic kind) has been criticized by others (e.g. Sebeok 1968: 9).

The point is that to show that paralinguistic features lack phonemic-type discreteness is not to say that they have no discreteness at all. Discreteness is itself a "more-less" phenomenon: some contrasts, even within phonemics, are more discrete than others. In paralanguage, one may show that certain features are highly discrete, others not, and between them one may plot a gradient of linguistic contrastivity, along which the various systems of paralinguistic features can be placed. This, at least, is the approach of Crystal (1969).

But whether this approach as a whole is valid or not, what is important here is the recognition of the existence of a wide range of paralinguistic contrasts that are quite comparable to the morphemic or syntactic discreteness operating elsewhere in language. The grammatical contrastivity expounded by intonation, between restrictive and nonrestrictive clauses in English, would provide one example; the variations in tonicity which alter the "presuppositions" of an utterance provide another; and many other "grammatical" uses of pitch have been noted (e.g. in Crystal 1969: Chapter 6; in Bolinger 1972).

I am not denying the difficulty of setting up discrete units in the area of paralanguage, of course (cf. Diebold 1968: 544-545); rather, I am admitting that this is very different from denying paralanguage any discreteness at all. It might be, then, that future discussion of this issue would fare better if more attention were paid to our techniques of measurement, and other aspects of our research design. If, as Saussure said, it is the point of view which creates the object, then it is about time we looked more closely and critically at the former. (See Sebeok [1962], especially on the questions of gradience and expressiveness in language.)

On the basis of these remarks, it seems that at best paralanguage can be disassociated from language only with respect to a partial difference under the headings of discreteness, arbitrariness, and duality. There are therefore few grounds for considering it to be "midway" between human language and other modes of communication, human or animal. It may be that with further study a comparable structuring will emerge in animal vocalization; but in the meantime I would agree with Marler (1961: 303) that the notion of paralanguage is not readily applicable to animals. It is as potentially misleading to talk about animal vocalizations in terms of pitch tunes, etc. as it is to talk about vowels and consonants, unless it is made clear that the descriptive terminology has a quite different status. (An identical problem faces the student of infant "prelinguistic" vocalization, see Crystal i.p.).

There seems to have been a pendulum swing in comparative studies, whereby an original emphasis which attempted to make a complete differentiation between language and animal communication (e.g. Hebb and Thompson 1954) has now moved to one in which there is a desire to show as much in common as possible. To go into the relative merits of these approaches is hardly a matter for linguists; but it is important that in any such discussions, for instance those concerning paralanguage, we should keep the limitations of our theoretical constructs clearly in mind.

REFERENCES

ABE, I.
1967　On bio-phonetics. *Bulletin of the Tokyo Institute of Technology* 79:53–57.
ALTMANN, S. A.
1967　"The structure of primate social communication," in *Social communication among primates*. Edited by S. A. Altmann, 325–362. Chicago: University of Chicago Press.
1968　"Primates," in *Animal communication*. Edited by T. A. Sebeok, 466–522. Bloomington: Indiana University Press.
BASTIAN, J.
1964　"The biological background of man's languages," in *Georgetown round table on languages and linguistics* 15. Edited by C.I.J.M. Stuart, 141–148. Washington, D.C.: Georgetown University Press.
BIRDWHISTELL, R. L.
1970　*Kinesics and context: essays on body-motion communication.* Philadelphia: University of Pennsylvania Press.
BOLINGER, D. L.
1949　Intonation and analysis. *Word* 5:248–254.
1951　Intonation — levels v. configurations. *Word* 7:199–210.
BOLINGER, D. L., *editor*
1972　*Intonation.* Harmondsworth: Penguin.

BUSNEL, R.-G., *editor*
1963   *Acoustic behaviour of animals.* Amsterdam: Elsevier.

CRYSTAL, D.
1969   *Prosodic systems and intonation in English.* London: Cambridge University Press.
1971a   "Prosodic and paralinguistic correlates of social categories," in *Social anthropology and language.* Edited by E. Ardener, 185–206. London: Tavistock.
1971b   Absolute and relative in intonation analysis. *Journal of the International Phonetic Association* 1:17–28.
1974   "Paralinguistics," in *Linguistics and adjacent arts and sciences,* 265–295. Current Trends in Linguistics 12. Edited by T. A. Sebeok, et al. The Hague: Mouton.
n.d.   "Non-segmental phonology in language acquisition: a review of the issues."

CRYSTAL, D., R. QUIRK
1964   *Systems of prosodic and paralinguistic features in English.* The Hague: Mouton.

CULLEN, J. M.
1972   "Some principles of animal communication," in *Non-verbal communication.* Edited by R. A. Hinde, 101–122. London: Cambridge University Press.

DIEBOLD, A. R.
1968   "Anthropological perspectives," in *Animal communication.* Edited by T. A. Sebeok, 525–571. Bloomington: Indiana University Press.

HALLIDAY, M. A. K.
1967   *Intonation and grammar in British English.* The Hague: Mouton.

HEBB, D. O., W. R. THOMPSON
1954   "The social significance of animal studies," in *Handbook of social psychology.* Edited by G. Lindzey, 532–561. Reading, Mass.: Addison-Wesley.

HINDE, R. A., *editor*
1972   *Non-verbal communication.* London: Cambridge University Press.

HOCKETT, C. F.
1960   The origin of speech. *Scientific American* 203:89–96.
1968   "A note on design features," in *Animal communication.* Edited by T. A. Sebeok, 61–72. Bloomington: Indiana University Press.

LYONS, J.
1970   *Chomsky.* London: Fontana.
1972   "Human language," in *Non-verbal communication.* Edited by R. A. Hinde, 49–85. London: Cambridge University Press.

MARLER, P.
1961   The logical analysis of animal communication. *Jounal of Theoretical Biology* 1:295–317.

PIKE, K. L.
1945   *The intonation of American English.* Ann Arbor: University of Michigan Press.

QUIRK, R., S. GREENBAUM, G. LEECH, J. SVARTVIK
1972   *A grammar of contemporary English.* London: Longman.

SEBEOK, T. A.
1962 Coding in the evolution of signalling behavior. *Behavioral Science* 7:430–442.

SEBEOK, T. A., *editor*
1968 *Animal communication: techniques of study and results of research.* Bloomington: Indiana University Press.

SEBEOK, T. A., A. S. HAYES, M. C. BATESON
1964 *Approaches to semiotics.* The Hague: Mouton.

STURTEVANT, E. H.
1947 *An introduction to linguistic science.* New Haven: Yale University Press.

TEMBROCK, G.
1968 "Land mammals," in *Animal communication.* Edited by T. A. Sebeok, 338–404. Bloomington: Indiana University Press.

THORPE, W. H.
1961 *Bird song: the biology of vocal communication and expression in birds.* London: Cambridge University Press.
1972 "The comparison of vocal communication in animals and man," in *Non-verbal communication.* Edited by R. A. Hinde, 27–47. London: Cambridge University Press.

TRAGER, G. L.
1958 Paralanguage: a first approximation. *Studies in Linguistics* 13:1–12.

A Consideration of Language
Acquisition Rates and Possible
Interspecies Relationships

JOHN G. BORDIE

Considerable interest has been aroused as a result of recent studies on the acquisition of language by animals other than man. These studies have concentrated on the general development of communication among animals (whether conveyed through visual, auditory, tactile, or other senses) in an endeavor to determine universals of behavior within the animal kingdom. Such universals, if found, could help in separating those items which are genetically based from those which are culturally derived and in the process would also indicate a hierarchy of relations among the species. Additionally such universals would also help isolate those characteristics solely associated with man and through a development of species-specific characteristics might thereby provide insight into the nature of mankind.

Such interest is of considerable antiquity, but though the interest has been of long standing, true insights derived from inquiry have been very sparse. Within the past few years a number of animal experiments have provided information of a kind not previously encountered: some animals have been trained to produce behavior which appears remarkably like language as it is commonly understood. The resultant controversy has become extensive and partisanship both pro and con has appeared and hardened. Whether such behavior is language this paper will not attempt to answer. It will consider what light may be shed on language by language acquisition rates in humans and by the acquisition of "language-like" behavior among chimpanzees.

A number of separate features must be considered during the investigation of language acquisition, features which though separable from the body of the material are investigational constructs having validity in themselves only as they relate to the material from which they have been derived. These features are related to the natural use of language by individuals functioning as members of a larger group. The language of individuals functioning outside a particular group or separated from it by one or another reason may also be investigated but such investigations require relational techniques or means for the translation of collected data to observations derived from larger group concerns. It is apparent that the language isolable in an investigation of individual production must be considered not just on its own terms but on terms deriving from characteristics of use by the larger group. To do otherwise would be to investigate idiosyncratic production, possibly of intrinsic interest but specialized to the point of esthetic creation, instead of attempting a statement of general knowledge. Both insights are necessary for they are not polarities. The result is a kind of "tridimensional understanding" of human behavior instead of a "flat etic [or emic] one" (Pike 1966: 12).

The larger group in turn must also be considered from these two vantage points: the first restricted to its internal characteristics and rules by which its structure is formalized and enlarged, the second comparing and relating the group to other larger and more inclusive groups or to groups no more inclusive than the object of inquiry but rather equivalent in terms of complexity or structure. For investigational ease it is useful to set limits on the size, variety, or number of the characteristics which are to be explored for the specific inquiry. By delimiting the area available, resources and investigational techniques may be concentrated on a task no longer diffuse or inchoate. Such focus can help to prevent irregular random investigation. It is worth noting that irregular random investigation is not as a result excluded from consideration. Miller (1969: 167) suggests that haphazard (noncyclic) general exploration strategies are a natural response to the manipulation of a large variety of symbols required in a general search. Through the outlining of characteristic limits of the area under consideration, the direction of subsequent investigation and the establishment of a rationale for formal constructs may be eased.

Such a procedure promising enlightenment through the investigational validation of a theoretical requirement needs logical justification if its findings are to be more than trivially acceptable. Such justification is readily found and depending on the procedure emphasized may be stated in terms of economy, efficiency, convenience, simplicity, or other *a priori* considerations. Yet although experimental law can be proposed and asserted as inductive generalizations based on the relations established in the acquired information, a similar proposal is not possible for theory. Those basic terms of a theory do not require their meaning to be established by definite experimental procedure, for theoretical adequacy is possible even though supportive experimental evidence is necessarily indirect. Experimental law on the other hand requires evidence of a direct and more immediate variety for its support (Nagel 1961: 85–86). One consequence of this consideration is that the language of theory formulated through construct usually has other connotations than the language of experiment. Where both languages attempt to describe or account for an indefinite area, such connotational incongruity will cause considerable discomfort to proponents of one or the other procedure, a discomfort which is usually not allayed by the awareness of difference of purpose.

To avoid this difficulty, we may specify a definitional sequence whereby items occurring in context are formally described and sharp limitations placed on their applicability. Such definition may be either implicit or explicit. When implicit, these definitions derive from the postulates used within the theory in the sense of predicate variables within an abstract calculus such that the general meanings associated with an item are prevented from inhibiting the validity of proof within a system. Explicit definitions, by using language in a less restricted sense, require the manipulation of a variety of connotations not usually recognized as properly belonging to the goals of the investigation. Thus a definition derived from theory, as, for instance, a relationship derived from the fortuitous association of meaning and term rather than from an inherent relationship, may be only marginally related to a definition derived from experiment. Correspondence statements can be established for the translation of experimental observation to theoretical observation but these statements are usually inexact and loose if they are even formulated at all (Nagel 1961: 99).

Such considerations must be explored, for they are fundamental to exploration of the topic inquiry. One of the more perplexing aspects of inquiry into language and its acquisition is the lack of agreement regarding the subject. As the literature is examined the diversity prevents a synoptic view of the investigational area. Compounding this diversity is the frequent confusion between theory and experiment. Meanings are assigned in a variety of ways by investigators. Chomsky (1957: 12) uses a formal definition, ". . . Language a set (finite or infinite) of sentences each finite in length and constructed out of a set of elements . . . similarly the set of sentences of some formalized system of mathematics can be considered language." Thus also Bloomfield (1926: 154) writes,

"The totality of utterances that can be made in a speech community is the language of that speech community." Such definition may also be made contrastively: "Human speech differs from the signal-like actions of animals, even of those which use the voice, by its great differentiation" (Bloomfield 1933: 27). Operational statements are common in a specific sense. "A language is a system of arbitrary vocal symbols by which members of a social group cooperate and interact" (Sturtevant 1947: 2); or in a more general sense: "Language is a purely human and non-instinctive method of communicating ideas, emotions, and desires by means of a system of voluntarily produced symbols" (Sapir 1949: 8). Other definitions derive from consideration of features of the system as in Hockett's "Origin of speech" (1960), its comprehensibility (Lenneberg 1962), its physiological structure (Tubbs 1969), and its anatomical basis (Kelemen 1948).

Throughout these investigations, the use of "language" as a descriptive term is extraordinarily variable and to a considerable degree quite inconsistent with usage. Such a situation causes considerable difficulty in the application of findings in one area to another and even to extrapolation within one defined area. Vygotsky uses apparently strongly divergent meanings for the term in his work: "But chimp and human phonetics have so many elements in common that we may confidently suppose that the absence of human-like speech is not due to any peripheral causes" (1962: 34). Speech contrasts with language: "The chimp has a fairly rich language of his own. Yerkes' collaborator Learned compiled a dictionary of thirty-two speech elements or 'words' which not only resemble human speech phonetically but also have some meaning" (1962: 39–40). Language may also be non-speech, "... the chimpanzee ... might be trained to use manual gestures rather than sounds. The medium is beside the point; what matters is the FUNC- TIONAL USE OF SIGNS ... play [ing] a role corresponding to that of speech in humans" (1962: 38).

Further conflicts arise regarding the possibility of a physiological basis for language interpreted as speech. "The teeth, tongue and larynx of a chimpanzee are adequate for speech but his brain is not" (Burling 1970: 198). "The structure of the larynx in the chimpanzee forms a basis for a rich vocal production with wide variation within a characteristic limit. On the other hand, in spite of its high mental qualities, this animal is unable to 'imitate' human speech as its own voice is made up of entirely different phonetic elements" (Kelemen 1948: 254–255).

These conflicts regarding physiology become more complex when psychological ordering is presented as a distinguishing factor. "No one has demonstrated that a subhuman form can acquire the principles of speech perception ... of understanding. ... There is no evidence that any nonhuman form has the capacity to acquire even the most primitive stages of language development" (Lenneberg 1966: 67). "Patients with an IQ as low as 25 to 35 have a wide repertoire of sounds and frequently use a vocabulary of 50 or more words" (Lenneberg 1962: 424). "By the time Washoe was about four years old, she had been taught to make reliably more than 80 different signs" (Bronowski and Bellugi 1970: 669).

An inspection of such views indicates the great variability in expectation and connotation associated with "language." Apparently almost every conceivable feature associated with the term has been used as a definitional criterion for invalidating the inclusion of animal communication within the category of human language. Marler addresses himself to the problem of single versus multiple features as specifying characteristics: "Perhaps the most striking generalization that can be advanced from this survey of the communication signals of monkeys and apes is the overwhelming importance of composite signals. In most situations it is not a single signal which passes from one animal to another but a whole complex of them ... the potential for some degree of independent reassortment of signal elements is one of the basic characteristics of human language and it is intriguing to find it in animals even though only in primordial form" (Marler 1965: 583).

Given the difficulty of arriving at a definition of language which may be used by theorist and empiricist it may prove more practical to approach the question from another direction. Is it possible to decide what PROFICIENCY in language might be, and by retracing the stages by which proficiency is reached to come to some acceptable starting point? This point need not be the fundamental source from which all subsequent development derives. Without being discursive about the issue, it can be shown that proficiency for individuals within a group has been as difficult to determine as a definition of language itself. Bloomfield (1926: 439) commented, "... that by a cumulation of obvious superiorities both of character and standing as well as of language some persons are felt to be better models. ... This may be a generally human state of affairs, true in every group and applicable to all languages." Such proficiency requires mastery of an extensive variety of related artifacts both part of language and external to it. In several studies of language mastery, the true measure of proficiency was that measure supported by a variety of skills derived from several areas rather than one or another measure derived from a precisely specified and closely articulated area. Even though no single one of the variety of inquiries can be reliably accepted as the indicator, the aggregate composite measure can be more readily used to indicate areas of capability. Subjective investigation of this variety, while not always completely satisfactory due to its lack of consistent replicability, must be used because of the absence of any acceptable alternative with a similar degree of correspondence to theory or experimental inquiry. Such an aggregate measure has been used by Marler and Hockett. The Premacks state, "We tend to assign definitional weight to every aspect of human language yet it is equally reasonable to suppose that only certain features are critical and should be given definitional weight" (Premack and Premack 1971: 822). To date no satisfactory compilation of features specific to human language proficiency has been widely accepted and efforts to determine such features have been viewed as only partial approximations of ability (cf. Loban 1967; Bellugi-Klima 1968). One suggestive feature, attractive for its simplicity (although equally treacherous because it is simple to misuse), is that of numeric frequency. This may be the aggregate number of items, whether types or tokens, actual length of performance, frequency of performance, or other similar features amenable to arithmetic count. Such measures have demonstrated inherent psychological limitations of performance and serve to differentiate human and nonhuman capabilities. Miller has argued for an inherent processing capacity among humans which is directly related to the specification of content size in bits and chunks of information. "Our language is tremendously useful for repackaging material into a few chunks rich in information. . . . By organizing the stimulus inputs simultaneously into several dimensions and successively into a sequence of chunks we manage to break . . . this informational bottleneck" (Miller 1956: 93–94).

Chunking appears to be significant as a memory factor among humans and primates. Several investigations suggest the validity of a process where content is categorized in a variety of manners to facilitate handling, learning, and recall. Most specific to our current interests is the observation that "a critical factor . . ." in the processing of information by experimentally modified animals "is the proper division or chunking of the stream of stimulation to which the organism is subjected" (Pribram and Tubbs 1967: 1766). Such chunking ability allows the establishment of limits on language ability and the concurrent ability to compare a variety of apparently unrelated perceptual and responsive phenomena. The general advantage of a neutral measure is the feasibility of measuring a variety of items with a standard unit. This unit derived from characteristics of information transfer allows for a wide range of evaluations without translational problems of measuring unit shifts from one standard to another. Simon (1974) argues that the ability of a grand master in chess to visualize the number of alternative positions on a chess board is akin to the ability of an individual within his native language. The characteristics of the chess board can be seen as parallel to the characteristics of language in many respects: finite set of elements, finite set of rules, indefinite number of possible responses, even a strong tradition for one or another response. Permutational variation within chess is of the same order as permutational variation within the limits of language, yet not all possibilities are realized for either the chess player or the speakers of a particular language. The number of possible items available to a speaker of any language at any moment is approximately 50,000–100,000 words. Simon argues that the number of possible moves available to a grand master is of the same order as that in language and that the chunks within chess approximate in size the chunks of speech. Fixation of a chunk based on word list studies, the analysis of chess patterns on a board, and similar items takes place at a general rate of five to ten seconds per chunk (Simon 1974: 487). The proficiency of an individual varies in direct proportion to the number of chunks which an individual has within his command. Storage size is thus a major factor in proficiency. If such conclusions are accurate, then language is one of a number of related behaviors sharing motor and cognitive skill with such diverse areas as chess, tool making, and perhaps general life style.

If these observations are accurate, is language something which man shares with other species, particularly the primates, but not limited to them only? Language then is to be considered not as the exclusive property of man but a behavior sequence which extends across species boundaries although it may be more characteristically used by one or another species. One means of checking this is to consider observations of language-like behavior as examined by such investigators as the Gardners, the Hayes, the Premacks, and the Kelloggs. These experimenters attempted to raise the chimpanzee in a normal human situation and, by virtue of such a process, to teach the chimpanzee to communicate. These attempts have been only partially successful. The Hayes' Viki and the Kelloggs' Gua were taught to speak. For reasons of human-chimpanzee phonation incompatibility, Viki was able to produce only four words and Gua only three. Both however, did respond to a larger number of verbal inputs. The Gardners taught American Sign Language for the Deaf to Washoe and the Premacks used manipulable plastic symbols with Sarah. These attempts were more successful and both animals mastered approximately 130–150 symbols by the end of 1972 when they were six and four years of age respectively. Another chimpanzee being trained by Duane Rumbaugh had in June of 1973 mastered 35 to 40 lexigrams displayed on a typewriter computer keyboard (*Science News* 1973). These numbers lend themselves to remarkable permutation and new string generation as can be seen in the individual creations of Washoe and Sarah but the total number in no way resembles the number of items which must be mastered by the average human adult in order to function within a society.

Learning rates appear to differ for humans and chimpanzees where specific items must be committed to long-term memory and then retrieved at least 70 to 80 percent of the time. Learning rates for discrete items are quite different for the two species with humans being the more adept by a factor of approximately 10 (Fouts 1973). Chunk capacity can be inferred from a variety of evidence to be greater by a factor of approximately 150 for humans at puberty compared to the chimpanzee at the same physiological age. Such differences can be seen in the observations by the Kelloggs of the performance of Gua who at the age of eleven months was ahead of her human companion Donald in number of observable correct responses to verbal communication. At age sixteen months she was slightly behind him indicating that the child, though starting later than the chimp, had accelerated in learning at a far higher rate (Kellogg 1968: 425).

Such considerations begin to establish the limits on that type of behavior we call language and in the process help to determine species characteristics. Although it seems unlikely that further investigation will discover a lost sibling among present-day higher primates, we must consider that the difference between primates and man is not so great as between primates and other mammals. There is apparently an overlapping of language and language-like elements in the behavior of adult primates and humans during early development. It would be useful in this conjunction to determine at what point in the acquisition of symbolic usage, a leveling of the learning curve takes place. We require additional information regarding development stages among humans before conclusions can be drawn with relative safety about any one of these stages, yet certain work is provocative. Some acquisition of language, particularly a second or foreign language, appears to have as its best fitting curve that curve defined by a Fibonacci sequence where any increment requires as much time or effort to achieve as the two preceding stages. Further work remains to be done in this area before we can safely determine the strength of the genetic relationship. What has been done so far indicates only that we have a long distance to travel before we know whether primates other than man can use human language or, for that matter, whether we can define language at all.

REFERENCES

BELLUGI-KLIMA, URSULA
  1968   *Evaluating the child's language competence.* Urbana: University of Illinois, National Laboratory on Early Childhood Education.
BLOOMFIELD, LEONARD
  1926   A set of postulates for the science of language. *Language* 2:153–164.
  1927   Literate and illiterate speech. *American Speech* 2:432–439.
  1933   *Language.* New York: Henry Holt.
BRONOWSKI, J., V. BELLUGI
  1970   Language, name and concept. *Science* 168:669–673.
BURLING, ROBBINS
  1970   *Man's many voices.* New York: Holt, Rinehart and Winston.
CHOMSKY, NOAM
  1957   *Syntactic structures.* The Hague: Mouton.
FOUTS, ROGER
  1973   Acquisition and testing of gestural signs in four young chimpanzees. *Science* 180:978–980.
HOCKETT, CHARLES F.
  1960   The origin of speech. *Scientific American* 204(3):88–96.
KELEMEN, GEORGE
  1948   The anatomical basis of phonation in the chimpanzee. *Journal of Morphology* 82:229–256.
KELLOGG, WINTHROP N.
  1968   Communication and language in the home-raised chimp. *Science* 162:423–427.
LENNEBERG, ERICH L.
  1962   Understanding language without the ability to speak. *Journal of Abnormal and Social Psychology* 65(6):419–425.
  1966   "A biological perspective of language," in *New directions in the study of language.* Cambridge, Mass.: M.I.T. Press.
LOBAN, WALTER
  1967   *Language ability — grades ten, eleven, twelve.* Berkeley: University of California Press.
MARLER, PETER
  1965   "Communication in monkeys and apes," in *Primate behavior.* Edited by Irven DeVore. New York: Holt, Rinehart and Winston.
MILLER, GEORGE A.
  1956   The magical number seven: plus or minus two. *Psychological Review* 63(2):81–96.

1969   *Psychology of communication.* Baltimore, Md.: Pelican Books.

NAGEL, ERNEST
1961   *The structure of science.* New York: Harcourt, Brace, and World.

PIKE, KENNETH L.
1966   *Language in relation to a unified theory of the structure of human behavior.* The Hague: Mouton.

PREMACK, ANN J., DAVID PREMACK
1971   Teaching language to an ape. *Science* 172:808–822.

PRIBRAM, K. H., W. E. TUBBS
1967   Short-term memory, pausing, and the primate frontal cortex. *Science* 156:1765–1767.

SAPIR, EDWARD
1949   *Language.* Harvest Book Edition. New York: Harcourt, Brace.

Science News
1973   *Science News* 103(June):360–361.

SIMON, HERBERT A.
1974   How big is a chunk. *Science* 183:482–488.

STURTEVANT, E. H.
1947   *An introduction to linguistic science.* New Haven: Yale University Press.

TUBBS, WALTER E.
1969   Primate frontal lesions and the temporal structure of behavior. *Behavioral Science* 14(5):347–356.

VYGOTSKY, LEV S.
1962   *Thought and language.* Cambridge, Mass.: M.I.T. Press. (Reprinted 1966.)

Domestic Animal Calling in a Berber Tribe

JAMES BYNON

1. The medium of sound is employed as a channel for the transfer of information by the great majority of higher animal species, mankind being in no way exceptional in this respect.[1] The acoustically based communication systems of the higher animals and of man have in common the qualities of being two-way (the roles of sender and receiver are reversible) and intraspecific (the code is limited to the members of a single biological or cultural group).[2] They also share to a large degree the feature of conventionality, that is to say, the signals of which they are composed bear an arbitrary rather than a natural relationship to the messages they carry.[3] Beyond this point, however, the nonhuman and the human systems diverge, in particular with regard to their more detailed structure and the way in which they are acquired by the individual.

Those systems used by animals would seem to be limited to simple sets of discrete signals which operate on a single plane of articulation, being capable neither of ordered combination to form more complex messages at a higher level[4] nor of analysis into smaller opposable units at a lower level. Among the most characteristic universal features of human language, on the other hand, and crucial to its remarkable efficiency as a means of communication, are its various levels of articulation. Thus the

---

[1]   See in particular Sebeok (1968).
[2]   On the interspecificity of certain alarm calls, however, see Thorpe (1961: 23, 28, 33). On the interspecific calling of honey guides, see Friedman (1955, 1958).
[3]   Except in the case of mimicry, where the arbitrariness of the relationship is at one remove and the primary message is false.
[4]   Animal cries are certainly sometimes combined, but there is no evidence that the result is other than a purely cumulative one (summation). Compare, however, the results of experiments described in Gardner and Gardner (1969).

minimal meaning-bearing signs of all known human languages are built up from a finite set of smaller contrasting units which are themselves meaningless and which are related to one another in a systematic way, while at a higher level of organization the ordering of the minimally meaningful signs in a message, or the marking of their interrelationship in some more complex manner, itself carries information. As regards the mode of acquisition of the system, animal cries are largely instinctive, that is to say, genetically transmitted,[5] while human language is a purely cultural phenomenon, a faculty acquired by the individual after birth as the result of a process of learning.[6]

Occupying an intermediate position between the relatively simple sets of genetically transmitted animal cries and the highly complex culturally transmitted systems of human speech — and sharing certain of the features of each — is an area of human acoustic activity which can conveniently be called ANIMAL CALLING. Like both animal cries and human speech, its primary function is the transmission of information (not necessarily true information) by acoustic means, but it differs from either in two respects: it is interspecific (for the communication is between humans and animals) and it is unidirectional (for only a human being can be the transmitter and only an animal can be the normal target of the message). Animal calling may, then, be defined as the transfer by acoustic means of information from a human being to an animal for the purpose of influencing its behavior,[7] and it falls naturally into two main subdivisions, WILD ANIMAL CALLING and DOMESTIC ANIMAL CALLING, corresponding broadly to the food-gathering (hunting-fishing) and the food-producing (farming) levels of human economy.

The first of these, WILD ANIMAL CALLING, is indeed found at its most highly developed in hunting communities, among the commoner aims being that of tricking the quarry into approaching the hunter or causing it to remain where it is while he approaches it. To this end a wide range of natural animal cries are imitated — so-called approach-eliciting calls,

---

[5]   A small element of tradition is, however, sometimes present, particularly in the case of the higher animals (birds and mammals), but it would appear that such learned behavior is always grafted onto some inherited pattern which it does no more than modify (cf., for example, Armstrong 1963: Chapter 3).

[6]   "Innateness" concerns at best a potential which is only realized in the environment of a traditionally transmitted language. What is innate is a set of predispositions, capabilities, and constraints, not a communication system.

[7]   This definition, if accepted, obliges us to include under the heading of animal calling the use of instruments such as whistles, etc. for the purpose of attracting animals, and of drums, rattles, etc. for scaring them away. The situation is, of course, a clinal one and even more marginal cases may be cited — for instance, that of the Ayt Hadiddu shepherd who whistles to his sheep in order to keep them happily browsing.

cries of young members of the species in distress, etc. The means of production is often purely vocal, but use may also be made of additional articulators, such as the hands, a stretched blade of grass, or even some artifact especially developed for the purpose, so that the field of study overflows into that of organology.

The production of calls of this type comes under the heading of mimicry, and we may expect that any structuring that they may possess will belong to the signaling system of the species whose cry is being imitated rather than to that of the caller. The aim of the mimic is in fact to produce, by whatever means he has at his disposal, a sound having the maximum degree of acoustic similarity to the model — the ideal being identity. Because, however, the sounds are to a large extent produced by means of the same articulators as the performer's speech, it is reasonable to expect some measure of interference. The essential fact, however, is that whereas the sounds produced may not form any part of his culture, the method of their production, which is to a large extent traditional, does, and as a result demands investigation by the anthropologist.

In addition to calls which explicitly seek to imitate the natural cries of wild animals are others which appear to have a more arbitrary basis. These include particular noises used to scare away wild birds and animals or believed to otherwise influence their behavior in some predictable way.[8] Calls of this latter type belong to the repertory of farmers rather than of hunters, and lead naturally to our other major subdivision of animal calling.

It is, in fact, only with DOMESTIC ANIMAL CALLING that the present study is concerned, and more particularly with the set of traditional calls employed by the members of a Berber community of central Morocco for the purpose of communicating with their farm and household animals. Because it is based almost entirely upon the experience of a single individual and has not yet been backed up by systematic observation in the field, it should not be taken as constituting much more than a preliminary survey.

A few points do, however, emerge clearly. These calls to domestic animals differ fundamentally from wild animal calls of the mimicry type

[8] Examples from the community under consideration of calls to wild animals having a more or less arbitrary basis include a number of scares: *hay!* (repeated alternately on a high and a low note) for wild boars damaging the corn; *hušš!*, *kkušš!*, and *kkšš!* for birds in general; *ẓukk!* for sparrows; *aylahušš!* for locusts; as well as the call used by children when playing to try to make a fly settle on their hand, *ɛzzbizi(wizi)ⁿ!*. As examples of those probably having a natural basis may be cited a whistled call used to make small birds alight near a trap, and a call produced by blowing into the cupped hands (mimicking a bird of prey?) used to make a hare remain crouched down until it can be caught.

in that they appear almost without exception to be purely arbitrary signals having little or no connection with any naturally occurring sound and in that they exhibit a high degree of systematic structuring. Furthermore, it is evident that the structuring which they display owes a very great deal to the caller's language, many of these calls being indistinguishable on formal grounds from a normal verb stem used as an imperative, and even capable of taking this latter's plural suffixes. There are therefore good arguments for treating them as constituting no more than a subsystem of the language, so that animal calling can be thought of as a register for use when addressing domestic animals, just as nursery language is a register used when addressing small children.

II.   The data here dealt with comes entirely from the Ayt Hadiddu, a tribe located in the High Atlas mountains of Morocco towards their eastern end, the principal informant being a young man from the village of Ayt Lghazi near Imilchil.[9] All forms were either provided by or checked with him and, unless otherwise stated, any linguistic comparisons relate to his idiolect.

The Ayt Hadiddu possess ten varieties of domestic animal, namely, the horse, mule, donkey, camel, cow, sheep, goat, dog, cat, and domestic fowl.[10] Of these, only the camel is not actually bred within the tribal area and does not play more than a marginal role in the local economy. All have been established in North Africa at least since antiquity and all have names in Berber which are pre-Arabic in origin. The name of the domestic fowl (*tafullust*) is a loan from Latin (*pullus*), although this does not necessarily mean that the species was introduced to the area by the Romans, for it was already widely distributed throughout the Greek world, including Sicily, by the 5th century B.C. (see Zeuner 1963: 446–447). From this point of view at least, therefore, there is no *a priori* reason why any of the calls should be of recent introduction or creation.

A.   HORSE   Formerly horses were employed for warfare, traveling, and mule breeding; today only the latter role persists.
1.   To make it advance from rest or go faster when already in motion:

---

[9]   Aaddou Zayd ben Moha, or Zayd ou-Aabbou. The dialect spoken by the Ayt Hadiddu belongs to the Tamazight group.
[10]   An additional three species are very occasionally kept today, namely, the turkey, the domesticated pigeon, and the domesticated rabbit. All are probably of recent introduction. The climate is too rigorous in winter for beekeeping to be practiced. No calls appear to exist for the pigeon; for the rabbit, one click (Click Number 1) is used to make it come to eat, and in the case of the turkey, the only call noted is a tease used by children in order to make it put up its feathers and gobble at them: *ggiṭṭ!* (repeated).

xiyy![11] Also the slightly more emphatic expanded forms *xiyy-a!* (with intensifying suffix *-a,* also used when addressing humans; e.g. *a-ddu-d!* 'Come here!' but also *a-ddu-d-a!*) and *xiyy-ddu!* (the second element being identical with the imperative of the verb *ddu* 'to go'). Although *xiyy!* can perfectly well be used when addressing more than one horse, a masculine plural form *xiyyat!* may also occasionally be used (for example, when attempting to separate two stallions that want to fight one another), as well as a feminine plural *xiyymt!,* and the more emphatic *xiyymt-a!* (addressed, for instance, to mares on the threshing floor).

2.   To make it come to the caller: *ttɛay!* (repeated). Also a series of labialized retroflex velaric clicks (Click Number 1). One way of making these clicks[12] is by sucking the blade of the tongue along the roof of the mouth until it curls backwards and implosion occurs, the cheeks being kept hollow and the lips protruded.

3.   To make it slow down or stop when in motion, remain still when at rest: $(s)^n(š)^n!$[13] or $(s)^n\text{-}hd(a)^n!,$ $(s)^n\text{-}hda\text{-}y\text{-}a!$ (the element *hda* functions as an imperative with the meaning "Stop! Halt!" when used in addressing humans).

4.   To make it get up: *xiyy-nšr!* (the second element being identical with the imperative of the verb *nšr* 'to arise').

5.   To make it put itself straight when, for instance, its owner wishes to get past it in its stall in order to put food in its manger: *xiyy-sšr!* (the second element being identical with the imperative of the verb *sšr* 'to put right').

6.   To make it advance into its stall to be tied up: *xiyy-qqn!* (the second element being identical with the imperative of the verb *qqn* 'to tie, be tied').

---

[11]   The system employed for the transcription of the Berber is as follows: *x* and *ɣ* are voiceless and voiced uvular fricatives respectively; *qq* is a voiceless uvular plosive; *h* is a voiced glottal fricative; *ɛ* and *ɛ* are voiceless and voiced pharyngeal fricatives respectively; *čč* is a voiceless alveolar affricate; *ṣ, ṛ, ḍ,* and *ṭṭ* are emphatics; *a, i,* and *u* are open, front close, and back close vowels respectively; the remaining symbols have approximately their International Phonetic Alphabet (IPA) values. A few sounds supplementary to the normal system are described in Section IV. Gemination, which is realized phonetically as lengthening when the sound is a nonplosive and as delayed plosion with increase of tension when it is a plosive, is indicated by doubling the symbol.

[12]   The informant was also able to produce it by using what appeared to be a sideways or diagonal movement of the tongue; this was not observed in detail. In the description and labeling of this and the remaining clicks I have relied largely on the criteria employed in Beach (1938: see Chapter 4).

[13]   Round brackets with the letter *ⁿ* in index means that what is contained between the brackets may be prolonged indefinitely if it is a single segment, repeated an indefinite number of times if it is two or more segments. Thus, for example, $(s)^n(š)^n! = sssssššššš!,$ $(ps)^n! = pspspspspsps!,$ etc.

7.   To make it drink: a series of short bilabial whistles with glottal onset; the notes may be slightly separated, with each having sharply falling pitch, $P \searrow !$ (repeated), or they may be produced all on the same level in the form of a chain, the final note being longer and having falling pitch, $(P-)^n P \searrow !$. The two processes are often used alternately.

8.   To make it roll: $(kk\check{s})^n !$ or $kk\check{s}\check{s}!$ (repeated).

9.   To warn it and calm it when about to carry out some manipulation (such as catching it, allowing a stranger to mount it): a short series (four or five) of velaric clicks with unilateral influx (Click Number 2), implosion taking place between one side of the tongue and the palate. Often combined with $(s)^n$-$hd(a)^n !$

B.   MULE   The product of the crossing of a male donkey with a mare, the mule is the most important beast of burden in the region.

1.   To make it advance from rest or accelerate when already in motion: *ušt!* A masculine plural form *uštat!* is sometimes used, for example, when ploughing with two male mules, as well as a feminine plural form *uštmt!* Another call for the same command, often used in combination with *ušt!*, is a sharp velaric click with prepalatal influx (Click Number 3) made by withdrawing the front of the tongue downwards and forwards from the roof of the mouth. More intensive forms, if the animal fails to respond satisfactorily, are *ušt-a!*, *uštat-a!*, *uštmt-a!*, *ušt a-wa!*, *uštat a-wi!*, and *ušt-ddu!* Finally, if really annoyed, the rider may insult the mule[14] by resorting to a call which is normally only used when addressing a donkey, $(r)^n a!$, $(r)^n a$-y-$a!$

2.   To make it come to the caller: *ttzay!* (repeated). Also, commonly in combination with this, retroflex velaric clicks (Click Number 1), as for the horse.

3.   To make it slow down, stop, remain stationary: $\check{s}\check{s}t(a)^n !$ or $(\check{s})^n t !$
More intensive forms are *šta-bdd!* and *šta-bdd-a!* (in which *bdd* is identical with the imperative of the verb meaning "to stand, stay put, come to a halt"). The informant also felt $\check{s}\check{s}t(a)^n$-*bdd!* to be a perfectly acceptable form.

4.   To make it get up: *šta-nšr!* or *ušt-nšr!*

5.   To make it put itself straight: *šta-sššr!* or *ušt-sššr!*

6.   To make it advance to be tied up: *šta-qqn!* or *ušt-qqn!*

7.   To make it drink: as for a horse.

8.   To make it roll: as for a horse.

9.   To warn it before handling: unilateral velaric clicks (Click Number 2), as for a horse.

[14]   This explanation was provided by the informant himself.

10. To chase it off, send it off (for example when caught eating growing corn, or after release from work), to make it gallop round the threshing floor: *šta-ddu!*.

C. DONKEY The donkey is the normal beast of burden for lighter work, and for those who cannot afford a mule.
1. To make it advance: *(r)ⁿa!, rra-y-a!, rra-ddu!* The masculine plural *rrat!* and feminine plurals *rramt!, rramt-a!* are also possible. The same prepalatal velaric click (Click Number 3) that is used to make a mule advance is also used for a donkey.
2. To make it come to the caller: as for a mule.
3. To make it slow down or stop: as for a mule.
4. To make it get up: *rra-nšr!*
5. To make it put itself straight: *rra-sššr!*
6. To make it advance to be tied up: *rra-qqn!*
7. To make it drink: as for a horse or mule.
8. To make it roll: as for a horse or mule.
9. To make it serve a mare: a rapid series of bilabial affricative velaric clicks (Click Number 4), implosion taking place between the pursed lips ("kissing" sounds).

D. CAMEL Only a few individuals possess camels, which are unable to stand the cold of winter at an altitude of 2,000 meters and have to be taken to lower ground.
1. To make it advance: *zaṭṭ!, zaṭṭ-a!, zaṭṭ-ddu!* A masculine plural form *zaṭṭat!* might be used, for example, when attempting to separate two fighting males.
2. To make it come to the caller: *ččay!* (repeated).
3. To make it stop: *u(z)ⁿʒ!*
4. To make it get up: *zaṭṭ-nšr!*
5. To make it put itself straight when blocking the way: *zaṭṭ-sššr!*
6. To make it kneel: *zaṭṭ-ʒn!* (accompanied by blows with a stick on the front of the legs above the knees: *ʒn* is identical with the imperative of the verb meaning "to lie down").
7. To make it change direction: *uzzʒ s-a!* (while striking it with a stick on the ribs of the side opposite to the direction in which it is to go; *s-a* means "towards there").

E. COW Nearly every family has a cow, which is looked after by the women.
1a. To make it advance: *zaw!, zaw-a!, zaw-ddu!* The feminine plural

* zawmt!* can be used when driving a number of cows.

1b. To make a calf advance: *ppɡtt!* or *ppɡšš!*

2a. To make a cow come to one: *ppɡya!* (repeated).

2b. To make a calf come to one: *ppɡza!* (repeated).

3. To make a cow stop: *pp(ɡ)ⁿh!*

4. To make it get up: *zaw-nšr!*

5. To make it get straight: *zaw-sššr!*

6. To make it advance to be tied up: *zaw-qqn!*

7. To make it drink: *afaḍ!* (repeated).

8. To make a bull serve a cow: *ʒʒ!* (repeated).

9. To warn a cow when approaching it: the same series of unilateral velaric clicks (Click Number 2) that is used to calm a horse. (?)[15]

F. SHEEP Sheep are the principal basis of the local economy, providing wool, milk and butter, surplus animals for sale, manure, meat, and skins.

1a. To make one or more sheep advance: *(š)ⁿ!*, *(š)ⁿ-a!*, *(š)ⁿ-ddu!* A feminine plural form *ššimt!* also exists (for example, *ššimt-ddumt! ššimt-ddumt!*, when driving a flock).

  b. To make rams (*izuliyn*) advance: *ččziyy!*, plural *ččziyyat!*

  c. To make young sheep advance: *tturr!* For a flock consisting entirely of young males (*inuguḍn*), the forms *tturrat!*, *tturr-ddut!* can be used, and for a flock of young females, (*tizuliyin, tinuguḍin*) *tturrmt!*

2a. To make sheep come to the caller: *ppɡ(š)ⁿ!* (repeated) or *ppɡššu!* (repeated).

  b. To make a ewe come and get her lamb when separated from it, or come to lick it after she has given birth: *ppɡttšš!* The same call is used to bring a lamb back to its mother when separated from her.

  c. To make a lamb come to the caller: *ttɡš!* (repeated).

3a. To make sheep stay where they are: *d(r)ⁿs!* and the feminine plural *drrsmt!*

  b. To make sheep turn from the direction in which they are going: *a(ʒ)ⁿy!* The corresponding feminine plural form *aʒʒymt!* is also employed.

  c. To direct them in a given direction: *aʒʒy s-a!*

4. To make them get up: *(š)ⁿ-nšr!* Both *šš-nšrmt!* and *ššimt-nšrmt!* were given as feminine plural forms; they might be used, for example, if the owner wanted to cross the room where the sheep were kept at night and they were lying so tightly packed on the floor that he could not avoid walking on them.

---

[15]   Originally described by the informant as a call to make a cow halt, and subsequently altered to this meaning during questioning. It is to be expected that a male informant will show less familiarity with calls used for an animal normally managed by women.

5a. To make them follow behind one: *yiʒɛ!* (repeated).

b. To make a ewe follow him, a shepherd may also imitate the bleating of her lamb. For instance, when a lamb is born and after the mother has licked it, the shepherd puts it inside a fold of his robe in order to carry it. To call the mother to him, or make her follow him, he will call *ppɛttšš!* (repeated) *ŋ(ɛ̆)ⁿ!* (repeated).

6. To make them drink: *ʒɛččiw!* (repeated). Also, the same series of bilabial whistles as are used for the horse, mule, and donkey.

7. To make them lick salt: *w(ts)ⁿ!* Also the same series of retroflex velaric clicks (Click Number 1) as is used to call a horse to one. Also a series of alveolar pulmonic clicks with bilabial friction (Click Number 5) produced by drawing air into the mouth through the pursed lips by means of the lungs and interrupting the flow with a rapid series of tongue taps against the alveolar ridge. Although, strictly speaking, this click is not affricative (the stop and the friction not being homorganic), it produces a similar acoustic impression; it is in fact possible that some friction does occur at the tongue tip but that produced by the lip-rounding is much more audible.

8. To make them dig the ground (to uncover roots to eat in winter): *afṛaḍ!* (repeated).

9. To make the leader sheep come: *tɣištt!* (repeated).

10. To make a ram serve a ewe: *uʔzs! uʔzs! (zs)ⁿ!* or *uʔ(zs)ⁿ!* A shepherd may hold a sheep and make this call in order to trick a ram that he wants to catch into approaching. Small boys also occasionally use it to bring two rams together and make them fight.

G. GOAT Quite large numbers of goats are kept along with the sheep.

1. To make them advance: *ččiw!, ččiw-a!, ččiw-ddu!* A feminine plural form *ččiwmt!* also exists.

2. To make them come to one: *hrri!* (repeated).

To make a kid come to one: *hzi!* (repeated) or *h(zi)ⁿ!*

To make goats come when they are at some distance, a series of "raspberry"-like trills is employed, made by blowing with the lips pressed against the palm of the hand (labio-palmar trill).

3. To make them stop wandering off, stay where they are: *arry!, arry-a!, a(r)ⁿy!, arry s-a!* There is also a feminine plural form *arrymt!*

4. To make them get up: *ččiw-nšr!*

5. To make them follow behind one: *urry!* (repeated). The final *y* is sometimes pronounced so feebly as to be almost inaudible.

6. To make them drink: as for sheep.

7. To make them lick salt: as for sheep.

8.   To make a goat stop doing something it should not be doing (a frequent occurrence with goats): *ttɛaw!* or *ttɛaw-a!* Plural forms, masculine *ttɛawat!* and feminine *ttɛawmt!*, also exist.

H.   DOG   Dogs are used to guard the house or tent against thieves, the sheep against jackals, etc.

1a.   To chase it away: *mšši!, mšši-y-a!, mšši-ddu!* The masculine plural *mššit!* exists, as well as the corresponding feminine, *mššimt!* This latter might be used, for instance, by a husband as an insulting way of saying "Get out!" when throwing his wife and daughter out of the house (*mššimt! ffγmt taddart-inw!*).

   b.   To chase away a puppy: *xišš!*

2.   To make a dog come to one: *kkiz!* (repeated) or *kkssi!* (repeated). Also, a rapid series of dental affricative velaric clicks (Click Number 6), made by withdrawing the tip of the tongue from the inner surface of the upper incisors and alveoli with lips widely spread (the sound which, in English, is usually represented graphically as *tut* and which is used singly to express slight annoyance, repeated in series to indicate mild disapproval).

   A series of whistled notes, having the pitch pattern $/-\searrow$ and said to represent the phrase *a-ddu-d a-d!* ($<$ *a-ddu-d!* 'Come here!', with partial repetition) or *a-ddu-d-a!*, or $/- /-\searrow$ representing *a-ddu-d a-ddu-d-a!*, or $/- /- /$ representing *a-ddu-d a-ddu-d a-ddu-d!*, may also be used to call a dog. These whistled phrases do not, however, appear to differ in any important respect from those used when communicating with another human being by means of a local variety of whistled speech and should therefore perhaps not be taken as specialized animal calls. Nevertheless, it is noteworthy that whistled calls are not addressed to any other domestic animal apart from the dog.

3.   To urge a dog to attack (a jackal, a thief, etc.): *štu!* When setting his dog onto a jackal, for instance, the owner will run ahead calling *štu! štu! (ha-^{t})^n!* '... Here it is! Here it is!' until the dog has seen it; then he will encourage it to attack with the words *štu! štu! asy-t! asy-t!* '... Take it! Take it!'

I.   CAT   Most households have one or more cats, whose function is to keep down rats and mice.

1.   To chase a cat away: *ṣabb!* Masculine and feminine plural forms *ṣabbat!* and *ṣabbmt!* also exist. For instance, one might chase a pair of fighting cats out of the house with *ṣabbat! tsddɛm-aγ!* 'Get out of it! You're deafening us with your noise!'

2.   To make it come to one: *(ps)^n!* or *ps(p$^\phi$s)^n!* Also, *sipsi!* (repeated).

J. DOMESTIC FOWL   The majority of households keep chickens, both for eating and as egg producers. The cock is also important for his role of waking the householder at the crack of dawn, although for this purpose he has now been replaced to some extent by the alarm clock.

1. To chase away: *sarr!* or *sa(r)^n!* The masculine plural form *sarrat!* can be used for a group containing both male and female birds, the feminine plural *sarrmt!* for a group of hens. The calls *hušš!*, *kkušš!*, or *kkšš!* may also be used to scare away hens, although these are general calls that can be used against any species of bird.

2. To make them come to one (for feeding): *kkullu!* (repeated). A call *štti!* (repeated) is apparently used only by the women. Unilateral velaric clicks (Click Number 2), as used for calming a horse, are also used to make hens come to one.

III.   An examination of the above corpus reveals that for every variety of domestic animal there are calls for at least two basic commands, which can be rendered broadly as "Go!" and "Come!" In the case of seven of them, there are also calls for a third command, which can usually be rendered as "Halt!" although especially in the case of the herded animals (sheep and goats), this meaning needs some qualification (it sometimes appears to have rather the meaning "Turn!"). Furthermore, with the partial exception of the mule and the donkey, which have certain calls in common, the basic call or set of calls corresponding to each of these commands is different for each species, so that, in effect, each can be said to have its own individual code. This can be seen more clearly if these basic calls are displayed in Table1 and 2.

Table 1. H-J. Animals which range freely in the neighborhood of the house or the tent

	Dog	Cat	Hen
1.	mšši xišš (Y)	ṣabb	sa(r)^n
2.	kkiz kkssi	(ps)^n ps(p$^\phi$s)^n sipsi	kkullu štti

Note: Clicks not shown; Y = young animal.

For these three animals the calls under (1) mean "Go away!"; those under (2) mean "Come here!"

Table 2. A–G. Animals which are ridden, driven, or herded

	Horse	Mule	Donkey	Camel	Cow	Sheep	Goat
1.	xiyy	ušt	rra	ẓaṭṭ	ẓaw pp8tt (Y) pp8šš (Y)	(š)^n ččẓiyy (M) tturr (Y)	ččiw
2.	ttɛay	ttẓay		ččay	pp8ya pp8za (Y)	pp8(š)^n pp8ššu tt8š (Y)	hrri hzi (Y) h(zi)^n (Y)
3.	(s)^n(š)^n (s)^n-hda	ššt(a)^n (š)^{n}t	u(z)^{n}ʒ		pp(8)^{n}h	d(r)^{n}s a(ʒ)^{n}y	arry a(r)^{n}y

Note: Clicks not shown: Y = young animal, M = male.

When used in isolation, the meanings of these three basic sets of calls are broadly: (1) "Advance!"; (2) "Come here!"; (3) "Halt!" (sometimes "Turn!").

For the animals of the first group (H–J), the two sets of calls meaning "Go away!" and "Come here!" are practically the only ones used.[16] Only the dog has one additional call, *štu!*, to urge it to attack.

In the case of those of the second group (A–G), there exists, in addition to the call meaning "Halt!" and a few special calls of more restricted application, a whole series of secondary calls derived from the basic ones by compounding with verb stems of the normal language. The verb stems regularly attested in the corpus as being used in this way are *ddu* 'go', *bdd* 'halt', *sssr* 'put right', *nsr* 'arise', *qqn* 'be tied', and *ʒn* 'lie down', but the list is not exhaustive.[17] All the theoretically possible combinations do not, of course, occur for obvious extralinguistic reasons (sheep, goats, and camels are not tied up individually in stalls, only camels are made to kneel, etc.).

In these compound formations the verb stem always comes after the basic call and the whole is pronounced without pause, apparently (although this aspect has not been properly investigated) as a single stress unit. There is also a strong tendency in these compounds, although it does not appear to be an absolute rule, for the first element to be reduced to

[16]   That is to say, the only generally accepted calls used by any person to address any member of that animal species. In certain cases, it may well be that individual owners develop more or less personal codes for communicating with the animals in their possession. This aspect has not been investigated; but it should not be forgotten either that livestock is constantly being bought and sold, borrowed, pastured in collective groups by individuals who take it in turn to guard them, etc. and that a basic set of generally accepted calls is a practical necessity.

[17]   For instance, the call *ššimt-nḍwmt!* was given by the informant as being used when making sheep ford a river (*nḍw* 'to cross over').

what might be called its base form (*šta-qqn* and *rra-qqn* as opposed to *ššt(a)^n* and *(r)^{n}a* when in isolation).

Usually only one basic call in each code combines with any particular verb stem, it being Number 1 when the verb is *ddu*, *sssr*, *nšr*, and *qqn*, Number 3 when it is *bdd*. The only exception to this is in the case of the mule, for which the first element may be optionally 1 or 3 when combined with *sssr*, *nšr*, and *qqn;* in the case of *ddu*, apparently both *ušt-ddu* and *šta-ddu* exist, the first meaning "Advance (with me)!" and the second, "Go off (from me)!" In this latter case, if the meaning glosses that we have attached to the basic calls when used in isolation were to be retained, we would get the semantically impossible command "Stop-Go!" It is clear therefore that the same meaning cannot be attached to a basic call when it is being used in isolation and when it is the first element of a compound call.[18] Perhaps in this latter case it acts simply as an indicator of the fact that a command is being given and of the identity of the addressee — a sort of species-specific imperative marker. The semantic side of these calls is not as simple as it might appear to be and requires further investigation.

The verb stems used in these compound calls have the same shape as the unmarked (= singular common) form of the imperative (simple aorist stem with ø suffix). Furthermore, some of these calls may take the masculine and feminine plural suffixes (plural masculine *-at/-t*, plural feminine *-mt/-imt*) of the normal language. In the corpus, these suffixes usually appear only with call Number 1, but there are one or two instances of their occurrence with other simple calls (*arrymt*, *ttɛawat*, *ttɛawmt*), and even an occasional example with a compound call (*šš-nšrmt*, *ššimt-nḍwmt*, *ššimt-nšrmt*). In view of these morphological features and of the undisputed imperative function of the calls, it would seem reasonable to treat them simply as imperatives. Because, however, only some of them are capable of taking the imperative suffixes, and even for those which can take them they are optional, the situation is a graded one and the assimilation to the imperative system of the normal language is only partial.

[18] Similar problems of variation in meaning according to context exist in the case of certain European calls to domestic animals. Compare, for example, English *gee!* 'a word of command to a horse, variously used to bid it turn to the right, go forward, or move faster' (*Shorter Oxford English dictionary* 1965); French *hue!* 'terme dont se servent les charretiers, les cochers, pour faire avancer les chevaux, et pour les faire tourner à droite' (*Petit Larousse* 1948); German *hü!* 'in der fuhrmannssprache, antreibender zuruf...; auch zuruf an das zugvieh, links zu gehen'; *hott! (hotta! hotte!)* 'zuruf an thiere, meist fuhrmannswort:... ermunternder zuruf an zugvieh; häufiger zuruf nach rechts zu gehen...; adverb der richtung...' (Grimm 1887, see *hü, hott*). The suggestion is made by Grimm that these dual meanings may have developed because, when driving with two horses, the call *hott* was directed mainly to the "saddle horse" situated on the right, and *hü* to the horse on the left.

In addition to the calls corresponding to these three basic commands and the secondary ones which result from their combination with various verbal stems of the normal language, there remain a few others of more restricted application. Some of these are for commands given to a single animal species (for example, the call used to bring together a ewe and her lamb when they have become separated); others are for commands given to more than one species but with the same call being used for all of them (the three equines, for example, share calls for "Drink!" and "Roll!" sheep and goats for "Drink!" and "Lick salt!"). With the notable exception of certain of the clicks, however, in no case does a call have one meaning in the code of one species and a different meaning in the code of another species — there are instances of the sharing of calls but none of cross-code homophony.

IV.   On the basis of the nature of the sounds they contain, the calls of the corpus can be divided into two distinct categories: (A) those which are made up of sounds identical with the minimal segmental units of the normal language, supplemented by a very small number of sounds of similar type; (B) those which consist of sounds totally foreign to the articulatory system of the normal language.

A.   Structurally, the calls of the first category do not appear to differ in any significant way from bare stems of the normal language.[19] Practically the whole inventory of sounds of the normal system is represented, the few gaps being best attributed to chance in so small a corpus.[20] The supplementary sounds are seven in number and all clearly result from minor and obvious modifications of or extensions to the articulatory system of the normal language:

1.   *p* (voiceless bilabial plosive) is the normal allophone of /b/ in voiceless clusters and that is certainly its status here in the three calls to make a cat come. In all the other cases of its occurrence (in calls to cows, calves, sheep, and lambs) it forms a homorganic cluster with a following bilabial trill, and there might be grounds for treating the sequence as a single affricative unit were it not for the trill sometimes being prolonged. It

---

[19]   This statement may appear exaggerated when faced with totally vowelless and voiceless calls like *(s)ⁿ(š)ⁿ!*, but parallel formations are not uncommon in the normal language (e.g. *ks!* 'guard!', *kks!* 'remove!', *čč!* or *ttətt!* 'eat!', etc.).

[20]   In particular, all those sounds usually considered characteristic of words borrowed from Arabic (*ṣ*, *z*, *ε*, *h*) are present. The sounds not represented are the affricate *ǧǧ*, the emphatic *ẓ*, three other very rare emphatics *ḷ*, *ṣ̌*, and *ẓ̌*, and the whole set of labio-velarized palatals and uvulars (*kʷ*, *gʷ*, *xʷ*, *γʷ/qqʷ*). Out of all these, the only lacuna to which some special significance might be attributed is that which concerns the labio-velar series, for these are not particularly uncommon in the normal language and are also almost totally unrepresented in the nursery lexicon.

should be noted, however, that *p* does have independent phonemic status in at least one word of nursery language (see Bynon 1968: 116).[21]

2.   *ʙ* (voiced bilabial trill) is also found in two nursery words, although one of these is in fact a borrowed animal call. It should perhaps be interpreted here as a labial counterpart of rolled /r/.

3.   *ʙ̥* (voiceless bilabial trill) is the voiceless counterpart of *ʙ*.

4.   *ʍ* (voiceless labiovelar fricative) is the voiceless counterpart of /w/. In the one call in which it occurs it is produced with pronounced lip-rounding.

5.   *pᶲ* (a *p*-like glide produced with incomplete lip closure, the tongue tip being maintained in position for the articulation of the preceding and following /s/) clearly results from a lax articulation of the *p* in (*ps*)ⁿ.

6.   *ʔ* (glottal stop) is the plosive which corresponds to /h/, a normal member of the system. It is also found in one ideophone (see Bynon 1970: 70).

7.   *i̧* (the vowel sound in the French word *thé*) exists in the normal system as the allophone of /i/ in the environment of an emphatic consonant.

None of the above are particularly startling innovations and all combine easily with the normal speech sounds. It is perhaps noteworthy that five out of the six supplementary consonants are labials and the other is a glottal, as if there were a tendency for additions to the system to take place at the two extremities of the articulatory tract, thus underlining their peripheral character.

B.   None of the sounds found in calls of the second category occur in the normal language; they comprise six different clicks (sounds produced by implosion or an influx of air into the mouth), a bilabial whistle, and what might perhaps be described as a labio-palmar trill. The clicks may be labeled most economically, in terms of the place and manner of influx and the proximal limit of closure, as: (1) retroflex velaric; (2) unilateral velaric; (3) prepalatal velaric; (4) bilabial velaric; (5) alveolar pulmonic; and (6) dental velaric.[22] These sounds are not employed in combination either with each other or with any of the normal or supplementary sounds,[23] so that in every case a call involving one of them consists simply of the sound itself, usually extended by means of reduplication or

---

[21]   Although a bilabial trill would appear to require a plosive attack, this need not necessarily be bilabial; cf. the call *ttʙ̌!* to a lamb.

[22]   For the method of their production, see descriptions in the corpus.

[23]   This statement is strictly true only if the affricative clicks are treated as single sounds. It is, however, possible to think of them as consisting of a sequence of a fricative and a plosive, and being to some extent parallel in structure, with the order plosive + fricative reversed, to calls of the type *(ps)ⁿ!*, *(kkš)ⁿ!*

repetition. Nor do the calls of this type form compounds with stems of the normal language, although they are often used in association with calls of the first type when the meanings so permit (for example, to make a mule advance from rest, a frequent combination is a sharp prepalatal velaric click followed by *ušt!*, both these calls representing the same command).

In view of the limited number of distinctive clicks that are produced, and because these do not combine with other sounds in calls, it is perhaps not surprising that some of them are employed with more than one meaning, depending upon the species of animal being addressed (a situation which, as has already been remarked, does not exist in the case of calls of the first category, where the combinatory possibilities are practically limitless). Thus, Click Number 1 is used to make a horse, mule, or donkey come to one, to make a domestic rabbit come to be fed, and to encourage sheep and goats to lick salt, while Click Number 2 is used both to warn a horse, mule, or cow that it is going to be handled and to make hens come to one.

Whistling appears to occupy a very minor place in the system, although it has been developed to some extent as a means of communication between humans.[24] Finally, the trill produced by blowing with the lips against the palm of the hand stands out as the only example in the corpus of a method of sound production which is more reminiscent of wild than of domestic animal calling.

V.   All these calls are subject to the operation of certain structural and suprasegmental mechanisms, the main effect of which would appear to be a reinforcement of the message. These include punctual (that is, non-extended) realization, the prolongation of one or more segments, reduplication (partial or total), and repetition, these structural features being associated with characteristic patterns of pitch, loudness, rate of delivery, and intonation. There appears to be a large degree of correlation between the structural and suprasegmental mechanisms on the one hand, and, on the other, the patterns which result from the interplay of these and the nature of the message being conveyed. The following analysis is provisional and tentative.

A.   Punctual, or nonextended, realization must be set up as a positive feature because it is opposable within the system to various types of extended realization. It is usually associated with features of loudness,

---

[24]   A brief description of the main characteristics of this apparently rather rudimentary whistled speech of the Ayt Hadiddu will be published in the near future.

initial high pitch, and rapidly falling intonation and correlates in particular with the command "Go!; Go away!" (call Number 1). It also appears to be used for most of the secondary derived commands, except where these mean "Stop!" Examples are: *xiyy!* 'Go!' (horse); *ṣabb!* 'Go away!' (cat); *šta-nšr!* 'Get up!' (mule).

B. Prolongation, for a duration which is unspecified but which is always greater than that which would result from simple gemination, of a particular segment or segments. In the corpus the prolonged segment is in fact always either a sibilant (*s*, *š*), a trill (*r*, *ꞩ*), or the vowel *a*. This feature of prolongation is associated with a wide range of commands — cf., for example, $(r)^n a!$ 'Go!' (donkey), $\check{s}\check{s}t(a)^n!$ 'Stop!' (mule or donkey), $pp\mathring{g}(\check{s})^n!$ 'Come here!' (sheep) — but appears to correlate most frequently with calls meaning "Stop!" in which case it is accompanied by an almost flat but slightly falling intonation pattern. Examples are: $(\check{s})^n!, (\check{s})^n t!, (s)^n(\check{s})^n!, pp\mathring{g}(\check{s})^n!; (r)^n a!, sa(r)^n!, pp(\mathit{8})^n h!, ttu(r)^n!; \check{s}\check{s}t(a)^n!, (s)^n\text{-}hd(a)^n!$

C. Reduplication may be partial or total. The number of repetitions is unspecified but always exceeds five or six. The intonation pattern remains approximately level throughout, although sometimes there is a slight drop on the final group. In the corpus the reduplicated group most commonly consists of a consonant (often a plosive) followed by a sibilant, a pattern which is to some extent echoed in the affricative clicks and even in the reduplicated realization of the bilabial whistle.[25] Reduplication is characteristic of calls of a persuasive rather than an imperative nature, including some meaning "Come here!" Examples of partial reduplication are: $w(ts)^n!, ps(p^\phi s)^n!, u\mathrm{P}(zs)^n!, h(zi)^n!$, and the whistle $(\mathit{P}^-)^n\mathit{P}\searrow!$ Examples of total reduplication are: $(kk\check{s})^n!, (ps)^n!$

D. Repetition differs from total reduplication in that the intonation does not remain level but falls at the end of each repetition of the call, the rate of delivery tends to be slower, and there is often a short silence between calls. Repetition and reduplication are often applied alternately to the same call, for example: *kkiz! kkiz! kkiz! kkiz! kkizkkizkkizkkizkkiz!* or, for the bilabial whistle, $\mathit{P}\searrow\mathit{P}\searrow\mathit{P}\searrow\mathit{P}\searrow\mathit{P}^-\mathit{P}^-\mathit{P}^-\mathit{P}^-\mathit{P}\searrow!$ Repetition correlates very commonly with the command "Come here!"

[25] This close structural connection between calls consisting of a plosive plus fricative and affricative clicks is perhaps most noticeable in the case of the pair $w(ts)^n!$ and Click Number 5, both used to encourage sheep to lick salt, for here the click appears to be no more than the call produced backwards (that is, with inspiration rather than expiration of the air and with friction preceding rather than following the plosion), with lip-rounding maintained throughout.

To summarize, for the three basic commands and with very few exceptions, punctual realization is characteristic of the command "Go!" prolongation of the command "Stop!" and repetition or reduplication of the command "Come here!" In view of their plosive or affricative character, clicks are not capable of prolongation and no click corresponds to the command "Stop!" The prepalatal velaric click (Number 3), used for "Go!" when addressing mules and donkeys, can produce quite a loud, almost whiplike crack, and is used punctually. With this one exception, however, clicks are always reduplicated or repeated to give relatively quiet "persuasive" calls ("Come here!" "Be calm!" "Lick salt!" etc.).

VI.   In addition to these structural and suprasegmental mechanisms, one other way should be mentioned whereby reinforcement of the message is achieved, namely through the extension of commands by means of elements of the normal language. This is not to be confused with the process already described whereby new calls are obtained by compounding basic calls with verb stems of the normal language; in the present instance it is not a question of creating new calls but simply of reinforcing or supplementing the message of existing ones.

An element commonly attached to imperatives in the normal language is the suffix -a (separated by a linking -y- when the imperative ends in a vowel), which is used to reinforce a command in a friendly and positive manner (for example, speaking to a guest at one's table, the command čč! 'Eat!' is unmarked for attitudinal content, whereas čč-a! corresponds to something like "Come on there, eat up! You're starving yourself!"). The corpus contains numerous examples of this intensifying suffix attached to commands to animals (e.g. ẓaw-a!, rra-y-a!, etc.).

More powerful reinforcement is obtained by following an imperative with a-wa (singular masculine), a-ta (singular feminine), a-wi (plural masculine), a-ti (plural feminine), for these expressions imply a degree of annoyance, impatience, and unfriendliness on the part of the speaker toward the person addressed (for example, one might say to a child doing something wrong, r̥ṣṣa! 'Stop it!' the first time but if he persisted, this would be followed the second time by the harsher form r̥ṣṣa-y-a-wa! 'Stop that, you there!'). Expressions of impatience are often used after animal calls when the animal fails to respond satisfactorily to the initial command — e.g. xiya a-wa!, aw a-ta, aw! (cf. Galand-Pernet 1966).

And finally, a command to a domestic animal is commonly followed by a more or less sustained sequence (repetition of the command, pejorative comment, etc.) of normal speech. Thus, for example, to a mule that is going too fast for his comfort, the rider might shout šštaaa! ddu *ss-ttawil! matta twada-nnay?* 'Slow! Go gently! What's that gait?' In such a case the rider is behaving, as far as the outside observer is concerned, exactly as he would if he believed that the animal understood normal human language and as if he intended to convey information to it by this means "for the purpose of influencing its behavior." Whether or not he genuinely believes this, or to what extent such a belief might in fact be justified, or whatever other useful functions such behavior might in fact fulfill, would appear irrelevant from the purely linguistic point of view.

If such supplementation by means of sequences of ordinary speech is part of the normal behavior of a person using animal calls (and the evidence suggests that it is), then these sequences must be taken account of in the description. But, because they do not constitute a closed set, this can only be done by including within the description a very large part of the normal language. We have already seen that even the individual calls can be most economically described in terms of the phonological system of the normal language, with a few minor extensions. From the purely descriptive point of view, therefore, it would seem simplest to treat domestic animal calling as a part of the language, a register specifically reserved for addressing domestic animals and characterized by certain special features and restrictions.

Such a description, however, even though it may account adequately for the caller's utterances, may not be the best from the point of view of man-animal communication. To account for the way in which this actually takes place — WHEN in fact it DOES take place — a description which treats domestic animal calling as operating through a restricted set of discrete acoustic signals (optionally supplemented by some elements of normal language) may prove more effective.

There can be no doubt that it is the individual calls that carry the main burden of the message but, at least as the bearers of intonational and other suprasegmental patterns, the sequences of normal speech which accompany them may also transfer some information, for there is plenty of evidence to suggest that domestic animals do learn to interpret and respond to suprasegmental speech features. The information transferred in this way may, however, be restricted to such things as the attitude of the caller, the urgency of the message, the likely consequences if it is not obeyed, etc. But these are matters rather for experimental investigation by the biologist than for speculation by the linguist or the anthropologist.

We know that communication of a sort DOES take place between man and his domestic animals, although the exact part played in this process by the traditional calls, by accompanying patterns of pitch, intonation, etc., by gesture, and in fact by the whole context of the situation in which the call is uttered remains to be determined. When investigating the communication process, the calls will have to be examined from the viewpoint of an animal which has no background of human language to which to relate them, but rather a system of oppositions of its own. For it, much of the "linguistic" structure of these calls must be mere "channel noise."

Finally, it should be remembered that human speech is not merely a passive vehicle for the transfer of messages but also performs an important expressive function for the speaker himself, and we may suppose that a sentence such as the one above shouted to a mule will afford a very much more effective outlet for the frustration of the rider than a simple monosyllabic animal call, however forcefully delivered.

VII.   Leaving behind the purely descriptive aspect of these calls and of the manner in which they are used, what can be said about them from the diachronic point of view? Here we are severely handicapped by the almost total lack of material for comparison from other areas and periods and by the inadequacy of the few descriptions that do exist.[26] A few tentative observations can, however, be made.

Within the Berber-speaking area, at least some of these calls have a very much wider geographical extension than that of the immediate neighborhood from which our data was obtained. Thus the call *hawa!*, reported as being used in the territory of the Guedmioua (Chleuh, southwest of Marrakesh) "pour faire avancer... des boeufs" (Galand-Pernet 1966; cf. also Schulthess 1912: 19, 23, 60), clearly corresponds to our *zaw-a!*; the Ayt Ouriaghel (Rif) *sehda!* 'cri employé pour faire arrêter un cheval' (Renisio 1932: 130) is our *(s)ⁿ-hda!*; the Ayt Seghrouchchen calls *herrey!* 'cri pour appeler une chèvre' and *atšiu!* 'cri pour éloigner une chèvre' (Destaing 1920: 315) are almost the same as the corresponding Ayt Hadiddu forms *hrri!* and *ččiw!* Other calls, while not identical, are certainly connected — for example, Ayt Seghrouchchen *ddāsseš!* 'cri pour faire arrêter un cheval' (Destaing 1920: 315) and Ayt Hadiddu *(s)ⁿ(š)ⁿ!* or Beni Iznassen and Iboqqoyen *kes-kes!* 'cri employé pour appeler un chien' (Renisio 1932: 130, 342; cf. also Schulthess 1912: 24, 74) and Ayt Hadiddu *kkssi!* (repeated).

[26]   The principal sources for domestic animal calls in Berber are: Destaing (1920: 315, under "Interjections," seventeen calls in the dialect of the Ayt Seghrouchchen); Renisio (1932: 130, 294, 319, 332, 342, 348, 377, 388, under "Interjections," fourteen calls in the Iznassen, Rif. Iboqqoyen, Senhaja de Sraïr, and Ouriaghel dialects); Destaing (1940–1945: 338, Note 3, six calls in the Aksimen dialect); Nicolas (1953: 66, under the title "Langage tenu aux animaux," some twenty calls in Znaga); Galand-Pernet (1966: 18, Note 2, two calls from the Isaffen, five from the Guedmioua). For Arabic, the important work is that by Schulthess (1912), in which a quantity of material from all over the Arabic-speaking world is brought together.

In some cases the geographical distribution of a call includes Arabic-speaking areas of North Africa as well, and may even extend as far as Spain. Thus, Ayt Hadiddu *rra!*, which must be equated with Ayt Segh-rouchchen *ṛṛa!* 'cri pour faire marcher un âne, un mulet' (Destaing 1920: 315), Beni Iznassen and Rif *arra!* (Renisio 1932: 130, 332), and Guedmi-oua *iṛṛa! iṛṛa ttidu!* (Galand-Pernet 1966) with the same meaning, is also found in Moroccan Arabic — *erra!*, *erra-zid!*, this latter corresponding exactly to Ayt Hadiddu *rra-ddu!* (Mercier 1945: 212; 1951: 34; Ferré n.d.: 192; cf. also Schulthess 1912: 66, 67) — and in Spanish — *arre!* (Renisio 1932: 332; Coromines 1954–1957: I, 278). Ayt Hadiddu *sabb!*, to chase away a cat, is also used by the Ayt Seghrouchchen — *ṣĕb!* 'cri pour faire fuire un chat' (Destaing 1920: 315); in the Rif — *eṣṣåb!* 'cri employé pour chasser un chat' (Iznassen, Rif, Senhaja de Sraïr [Renisio 1932: 130, 319]); by the Ayt Sadden — *ṣṣåb, ṣṣåb!* 'exclamation généralement usitée pour chasser un chat' (Laoust 1920: 252); but also in Moroccan Arabic — *ṣebb!* (Mercier 1945: 69; 1951: 192) and in Spanish — *zape!* (Renisio 1932: 319; Coromines 1954–1957: IV, 835). On phonemic grounds this word gives the appearance of being Arabic rather than Berber in origin.[27]

Other calls have obvious Arabic etymologies. Thus the call *zaṭṭ!* to a camel clearly comes from the Maghribi Arabic verb *ḥeṭṭ* (classical Arabic *ḥaṭṭa*) 'to put down, unload a beast of burden, set up camp, etc.' (Mercier 1951: 67; Ferré n.d.: 72; Boris 1958: 118; Wehr 1961: 185–186; Schulthess 1912: 71) and *mšši!*, to chase a dog away, found with the same form and meaning among the Ayt Seghrouchchen — *mšši!* 'pour faire fuire un chien' (Destaing 1920: 315), has an obvious etymology in the Maghribi Arabic verb *mši* 'to go, go away, go off, leave, etc.' (classical Arabic *mašā* 'to go on foot, walk; to go, etc.' [Mercier 1951: 139; Wehr 1961: 910–911]).

Although a comparative study of the various forms which correspond to Ayt Hadiddu *ššt(a)ⁿ!* or *(š)ⁿt!* in the different regions has yet to be made, in its base form *šta* it so closely resembles Latin *stā* (imperative of *stō,stāre* 'to stand') that a Latin origin would appear to be a distinct possibility.[28] It is in fact precisely in the field of agriculture that the greatest number of words of Latin origin have survived in Berber.

In the case of *(ps)ⁿ!* or *ps(pᵠs)ⁿ!*, to make a cat come to one, this is exactly the same call as I myself learned to use as a child in the north of

[27] The emphatic *ṣ* is not one of the original sounds of the Berber phonemic system (see Basset 1952: 6). Perhaps, in view of the cat's well-known dislike of having water poured over it, there might be a connection with Maghribi Arabic *ṣebb* 'to pour (water, rain)'.

[28] For Latin *s* represented by Berber *š*, see numerous examples in Schuchardt (1918) and Colin (1926–1927), and notably Latin *august(us)* → Berber *ɣušt*.

England and which I have subsequently heard used in a number of places on the continent of Europe.[29] The Berber calls noted as *bšš bšš bšš!* (Ayt Seghrouchchen [Destaing 1920: 315]) and *bešbeš!* (Iznassen, Rif [Renisio 1932: 130, 294]) are certainly connected, as must be English *puss!*, Low German *puus!*, Dutch *poes!*, Lithuanian *puž!*, Romanian *pis!*, etc. (Buck 1949: 181–182; cf. also Schulthess 1912: 24, 77 [Egypt]), although the precise nature of the connection is still an open question. A first step towards its solution would have to be a careful study of the different forms taken by the call and their distribution throughout Europe and the Middle East.

A basic problem highlighted by this particular call, although not peculiar to it, is whether or not there may be a natural or biological component in the forms of certain calls to domestic animals. We know this to be the case for wild animal calls of the mimicry type, for these are in fact no more than imitations of naturally occurring cries. The call to make a cat come does not appear to echo any sound made by the animal itself, but that does not rule out the possibility that certain of its acoustic qualities might have some naturally based influence upon its behavior.

The hearing system of the cat is specifically designed for the hunting of small animals, and it would be interesting to know: (a) how the sibilants which this call contains compare acoustically with such noises as the rustling made by small creatures in leaves, the cheeping of young birds, or the squealing of mice; (b) whether a cat's ears are particularly sensitive to sounds in the frequency range characteristic of the sibilant consonants (4,000–10,000 cycles per second, with maximum amplitude around 8,000 cycles per second, for *s*; 3,000–6,000 cycles per second, with maximum amplitude around 4,000 cycles per second, in the case of *š*); (c) whether the cat displays any inherent or acquired reaction to noises of this type (other than to the call itself).

These are questions for the biologist to answer rather than the linguist, but if it were in fact demonstrated that there were a biological component, however small, in such a call, this would have important consequences from the linguist's point of view. Firstly, it would mean that in such a case the relationship between the form of the signal and its meaning would no longer be an entirely arbitrary one, because certain acoustic features present in a call would make it more effective in its function of influencing the animal's behavior than others. This in turn would raise the question of what pressures such greater appropriateness might exert upon the

---

[29] Unfortunately I am obliged to rely here on my memory of haphazard observations, but a colleague from Swabia confirms that in that region of Germany the second form of the call (with glide) is the normal one used for calling a cat.

selection and subsequent evolution of a particular sign — would such a call, for instance, tend to resist the normal patterns of change or of replacement, or be more susceptible to loaning?

Another set of calls for which we must ask the same question is $sa(r)^n!$, used to scare away chickens, and the corresponding calls *huš̌!*, *kkuš̌!*, and *kkš̌!*, for scaring away birds in general. Here again we would ask the biologists to tell us whether or not certain sounds have more inherent likelihood of scaring away birds than others. In other words, do birds react instinctively (or as a naturally acquired habit) by taking flight to the whirr and swish of wings, sounds which could be to some extent echoed in the trill of the first call, the sibilant of the others?[30]

This short examination of the calls from the diachronic point of view would be incomplete without some mention of their importance as a source of lexical innovation. The sector which borrows most freely from domestic animal calls is that of nursery language, and, in the case of our present corpus, no less than nine of the calls have given rise to nursery names for domestic animals. When the command ends in an open syllable, it has often passed over unchanged; otherwise the vowel has been repeated to give a form which complies more closely with the pattern of nursery words. Usually it is the call to make the animal come to one which has been chosen:

1.   *kkullu!* (call to make a chicken come) → *kkullu* 'chicken' in nursery language.
2.   *ttɛay!* (call to make a horse come) → *ttɛaya* 'horse' in nursery language.
3.   *ttzay!* (call to make a mule come) → *ttzaya* 'mule' in nursery language.
4.   *sipsi!* (call to make a cat come)→ *sibsi, sipsi* 'cat' in nursery language.
5.   *ppɤya!* (call to make a cow come) → *ppɤya* 'cow' in nursery language.
6. $h(zi)^n!$ (call to make a goat kid come) → *zizi, hzizi* 'goat' in nursery language.

In two cases, however, the call to make it advance has been used:

7.   *rra!* (call to make donkey advance) → *rrarra* 'donkey' in nursery language.
8.   *ɤaw!* (call to make cow advance) → *ɤawa* 'cow' in nursery language.

And in one instance the call to make it stop has been used:

9. $š̌t(a)^n!$ (call to make a mule or donkey stop) — *štašta* 'mule' in nursery language.[31]

---

[30]   Cf. also English *shoo!*, attested since 1483 (*Shorter Oxford English dictionary*, 1965); French *ch-ch!* and the bilabial trill used in France to scare away birds; classical Arabic *kiš̌* used to chase away a hen.

[31]   Another Ayt Hadiddu nursery word for mule, *š̌aš̌a*, while it does not correspond

VIII.   In conclusion, then, if we compare wild animal calls with domestic animal calls, the former may be said to consist principally of mimicked NATURAL signals and to carry a false message, whereas the latter consist of ARBITRARY signals carrying a true message. Some apparently arbitrary calls (mostly scares) are, however, addressed to wild animals while mimicked calls may occasionally be addressed to domestic animals (for example, the shepherd imitating the bleating of a lamb in order to make a ewe follow him), and the message of a call addressed to a domestic animal may occasionally be false (for example, the ram tricked into approaching by the shepherd making the service-eliciting call). These are, however, the exceptions. There is, further, the possibility (which deserves properly controlled investigation) that certain apparently arbitrary calls, in particular scares to both wild and domestic animals but also certain other domestic animal calls, may contain an acoustic component having an inherently attracting or repelling effect upon the species to which it is addressed.

While wild animal calls are uttered as complete and independent signals, domestic animal calls are very often accompanied by elements of normal language which may go from verb stems and intensifying suffixes to complete sentences. As a result, there seems to be no clearly defined limit between domestic animal calling and normal interhuman speech and it would seem best therefore, for the purpose of description at least, to treat domestic animal calling simply as a register of the language characterized by certain restrictions and additional features. These can be briefly summarized as follows: (1) the addressee is a domestic animal, (2) the message is a command, although sometimes accompanied by comment of a friendly or critical nature, (3) an utterance consists of, or is initiated by, one of a limited set of lexical items peculiar to the register and to the species addressed (domestic animal calls), and (4) certain special suprasegmental and morphological features (prolongation, reduplication, repetition, etc.) may be present.

Looked at in this way, domestic animal calling can be seen to have many points in common with another register, namely that used for addressing very young children (baby talk, nursery language). Both make use of special lexemes taken from a limited set characteristic of the register, often in combination with short simple utterances. These special

---

to any call to a mule presently used in the immediate neighborhood, does seem to have an obvious etymology in *ešša!* 'cri employé pour faire arrêter une bête de somme' (Senhaja de Sraïr [Renisio 1932: 130, 384]; see also Schulthess [1912: 65]). The call must either have been lost in the Ayt Hadiddu area or the nursery word is an interdialect loan.

lexemes precede the utterance in the case of domestic animal calling and lare embedded in it in the case of nursery language. In neither case is it an essential requirement that the utterance as a whole be comprehensible to the addressee, the special lexemes being the main bearers of the message. Just as domestic animal calls are partially integrated into the imperative system of the normal verb, so are nursery words partially integrated into the nominal and verbal systems of the normal interadult language. Such an approach from the direction of normal language may not, however, prove so useful when it comes to trying to understand just how domestic animal calling actually functions as a channel of communication.

No attempt has been made here to deal exhaustively with the diachronic side of the corpus, largely because of the lack of material for comparison from other regions. The present distribution and the historical connections of these calls would, however, certainly repay investigation and might provide information concerning cultural origins, contacts, and substrata, and perhaps even the place of origin and direction of diffusion of particular species of domestic animals. Finally, an investigation of the sociolinguistic aspects of domestic animal calling might produce interesting results, as the following remark, made at the beginning of the century by a Frenchman with rural experience, suggests:

... de même que dans nos villages de la Comté le père et la mère qui, généralement, s'entretiennent en patois, parlent toujours français à leurs enfants; à un chien, à un cheval, on donne des ordres en français; à un chat, à un boeuf, on ne se sert que du patois (Destaing 1905: 95–96).

That a somewhat similar situation may well exist, or have at one time existed, for Berber is suggested by the number of calls apparently of Arabic origin used in addressing certain species, notably the dog.

REFERENCES

ARMSTRONG, E. A.
   1963   *A study of bird song.* London: Oxford University Press.
BASSET, A.
   1952   *La langue berbère.* London: Oxford University Press.
BEACH, D. M.
   1938   *The phonetics of the Hottentot language.* Cambridge: Heffer.
BORIS, G.
   1958   *Lexique du parler arabe des Marazig.* Paris: Klincksieck.
BUCK, C. D.
   1949   *A dictionary of selected synonyms in the principal Indo-European languages: a contribution to the history of ideas.* Chicago: University of Chicago Press.

BYNON, J.
    1968   Berber nursery language. *Transactions of the Philological Society*, 107–161.
    1970   A class of phonaesthetic words in Berber. *African Language Studies* 10:64–80.
COLIN, G. S.
    1926–1927   Etymologies maġribines. *Hespéris* 1926:55–82; 1927:85–102.
COROMINES, J.
    1954–1957   *Diccionario crítico etimológico de la lengua castellana*, four volumes. Bern: Francke.
DESTAING, E.
    1905   "Quelques particularités du dialecte berbère des Beni Sous," in *Actes du XIVème Congrès International des Orientalistes (4ème section)*, 93–99. Algiers.
    1920   *Étude sur le dialecte berbère des Aït Seghrouchen*. Paris: E. Leroux.
    1940–1945   *Textes berbères en parler des Chleuḥs du Sous*. Paris: Geuthner.
FERRÉ, D.
    n.d.   *Lexique marocain-français*. Fédala (Morocco): Editions Nejma.
FRIEDMAN, H.
    1955   *The honeyguides*. Bulletin of the United States National Museum 208:1–292.
    1958   Advances in our knowledge of the honey-guides. *Proceedings of the United States National Museum* 108:309–320.
GALAND-PERNET, P.
    1966   Termes de dépiquage en chleuh: *yahu* «aller au *yahu.*» *Group Linguistique d'Études Chamito-Semitiques* 10:18–25.
GARDNER, R. A., A. T. GARDNER
    1969   Teaching sign language to a chimpanzee. *Science* 165:664–672.
GRIMM, J., W. GRIMM
    1887   *Deutsches Wörterbuch*, iv, 2. Leipzig: S. Hirzel.
LAOUST, E.
    1920   *Mots et choses berbères*. Paris: Challamel.
MERCIER, H.
    1945   *Dictionnaire français-arabe (Méthode moderne d'arabe parlé marocain, iii)*. Rabat: Les Éditions la Porte.
    1951   *Dictionnaire arabe-français (Méthode moderne d'arabe parlé marocain, iv)* Rabat: Les Éditions la Porte.
NICOLAS, F.
    1953   *La langue berbère de Mauritanie*. Mémoires de l'Institut Français d'Afrique Noire 33. Dakar: Institut Français d'Afrique Noire.
Petit Larousse
    1948   *Nouveau Petit Larousse illustré: dictionnaire encyclopédique*. Paris: Larousse.
RENISIO, A.
    1932   *Étude sur les dialectes berbères des Beni Iznassen, du Rif et des Senhaja de Sraïr*. Paris: Leroux.
SCHUCHARDT, H.
    1918   "Die romanischen Lehnwörter im Berberischen," in *Kaiserliche Akademie der Wissenschaften in Wien, Philosophisch-historische Klasse*,

Sitzungsberichte, Band 188, Abhandlung 4:1–82.

SCHULTHESS, F.

1912 "Zurufe an Tiere im Arabischen," in *Abhandlungen der Königlich-Preussischen Akademie der Wissenschaften (Philosopisch-historische Klasse)*, 1–92. Berlin.

SEBEOK, T. A., *editor*

1968 *Animal communication: techniques of study and results of research.* Bloomington: Indiana University Press.

Shorter Oxford English dictionary

1965 *Shorter Oxford English dictionary* (third edition). Oxford: Clarendon Press.

THORPE, W. H.

1961 *Bird song: the biology of vocal communication and expression in birds.* Cambridge: Cambridge University Press.

WEHR, H.

1961 *A dictionary of modern written Arabic.* Wiesbaden: Otto Harrassowitz.

ZEUNER, F. E.

1963 *A history of domesticated animals.* London: Hutchinson.

Infant Vocalization:
Communication Before Speech

MARGARET BULLOWA, JAMES L. FIDELHOLTZ, and
ALLAN R. KESSLER

Understanding the development of communicative skills in infancy is for both practical and theoretical reasons an urgent problem today. We have come to believe that optimal human development depends to a large degree on the development of communication and especially on speech, the vocal component of language. We trace many social, educational, and psychiatric maladaptations to failure in this sphere. It is therefore important that we understand the underlying processes on which each person builds his speech capacity.

We must be clear in distinguishing between communication and language (Jakobson 1969:81, 90). Communication is the more inclusive term. Communication is carried on by means of signs. For humans, we may

... make a distinction between prelinguistic, linguistic, and postlinguistic signs. PRELINGUISTIC SIGNS are those which occur in the child's behavior before it speaks, or which later, even in the adult, are independent of language signs. LINGUISTIC SIGNS are those which occur in a language considered as a system of interpersonal signs restricted in their possibility of combination. POST-LINGUISTIC SIGNS are signs which owe their signification to language but which are not themselves elements of language (Morris 1964:58).

The data base was collected under National Institute of Mental Health research grant M–04300 (1960–1965). Recent work and this paper originate from the laboratory of the Speech Communication Group of the Research Laboratory of Electronics, Massachusetts Institute of Technology, Professor Kenneth N. Stevens, director under grant NB 04332 from the National Institutes of Health. We wish to thank Glenn Aker, T. Berry Brazelton, Judith T. Irvine, Estill Putney, Raymond Stefanski, and Kenneth N. Stevens who read portions of the text and gave us the benefit of their suggestions. We also thank Mrs. Hedy Kodish who typed the manuscript.

The most familiar sign system for human communication is the linguistic one which is basically manifest in speech, a vocal-auditory modality. Some other modalities of human communication are visually perceived body movement, touch, and smell. In infancy, before speech and language have developed, the vocal-auditory channel is already operative. We have every reason to believe that this mode is already adapted to communication, i.e. that it can transmit and receive in a systematic way signals which serve a communicative function.

The dictionary (*Webster's* 1967:367) defines communication as "... the act of imparting, conferring, or delivering from one to another ...." All members of the animal kingdom communicate. In ethology (the study of animal behavior) "... a communicative event occurs when one individual establishes a social relationship with another through the use of a signal [a display]" (Smith 1965:405). It is not our intent to offer rigorous definitions of such terms as communication or social relationship but to employ these concepts in their usual broad meanings.

The human infant communicates about his internal state through signals, which Morris (1964) calls prelinguistic signs. It is this aspect of communication we believe the human infant shares with other animals. In addition, the infant is interacting with adults who are concurrently producing both linguistic and prelinguistic signs to which infants appear to respond. We believe this is the analogue of signal or "display" as used by ethologists (Ficken and Ficken 1966: 644; Wilson 1972: 56). This signaling interaction between infants and adults provides a foundation for socially appropriate communication patterns. For example, for adult conversation, Argyle and Kendon (1967) and Kendon (1970) have described the characteristics of alternation of vocalization, posture, social distance, and eye contact, all prelinguistic aspects of communication. Bateson (1971) has shown that from a few weeks of age, infant-adult vocal interaction has characteristics of similar form. For instance, infant and adult tend to wait for one another to finish vocalizing when face to face, one to two feet apart with intermittent episodes of eye contact. These are the kinds of concepts we will discuss.

Many of the sounds we hear from infants are simply inevitable concomitants of physiological activities. In studying communication among adults, linguists tend to exclude such sounds (coughs, hiccoughs, burps, etc.) from consideration because they are clearly not part of the linguistic code. However, folk psychology often notes the significance of these sounds, and psychiatrists are likely to assign communicative value to them. Given the current state of knowledge of the human infant's entire communicative system, we feel we need to attend, for our study of potential communication, to all the vocal sounds that are produced. We also need to take note of the behavioral responses of caretaking adults, even those produced without awareness. In the study of infant vocal behavior the distinction between relatively automatic physiological sounds and others thought to be prelinguistic signs, such as a "hunger cry," is not always clear-cut. Even in older babies, as linguistic sign-using emerges, it may be that prelinguistic and linguistic signs are not always clearly distinguishable. For example, observers of early language acquisition sometimes report mixed utterances in which babbling sounds unintelligible to adults appear (Bloom 1970:22).

The communicative behavior of human infants is in some ways more reminiscent of animal communication than of adult language. Both human infants and animals can impart information about their own current condition and intention, and neither, so far as we know, can make reference to the distant past or future, or state a proposition (Hockett 1960). Both are essentially creating signals. For both, when we speak of the "meaning" of vocalization, we refer to meaning in a basic biological sense (Smith 1965). Our use of "meaning" belongs to semiotics (Sebeok 1968).

When language provides the capability, people communicate relatively more by speech than by action. Speech can take over the function of direct action for the purpose of communication. "Much of man's life involves linguistic contacts, and many of the activities which appear as motor acts in lower species appear linguistically in man" (Freedman 1967: 182). This process can be seen developing as the infant and then child masters more communicative modes. The child learns to ask for something instead of grabbing or reaching for it. Within the repertoire of communicative behavior, the infant produces proportionately more with his body than the adult. As differentiation (defined from the adult viewpoint) increases in all modes, the balance shifts away from more massive body action toward more subtle use of the body in relation to speech. A number of students of non-verbal communication have shown for adults the intimate tie-in between speech and motion of other parts of the body. Condon and Sander (1974) have recently demonstrated that one- and two-day-old infants respond with synchronous body movement to adult speech in the same manner as adults (see "Non-Verbal Communication" section below).

Even recently scientists and physicians were denying that infants communicate with their caretakers with any specificity beyond the general expression of comfort and discomfort states. It was up to the caretaking adult to guess or discern from the accompanying situation what the infant needed (Spock 1968: 183). More recently, however, some pediatricians and other scientists have been willing to take infants seriously and to investigate the old wives' tale that they can be understood and communicated with. Some, but not all, mothers in our culture seem to be aware of the things we are considering, and so are some child care professionals. We do not know how this knowledge is attained, nor whether it is always available but suppressed by our culture.

We believe the first step toward understanding a social process is to observe and describe it. The way in which it is observed, the sampling technique, the relationship between observer and observed, as well as the theoretical frame of reference, all influence our perception of what is going on and our interpretation of it. By applying observation techniques from several disciplines in this study, we hope to decrease the bias of our perceptions and to expand the range of our interpretations.

We will first describe our data base and discuss its appropriateness to the problem we are investigating. Then we will discuss the relevance of certain disciplines and how we are drawing on them for our research. Finally we will make recommendations for further research, in particular how anthropologists and ethnologists could contribute to this area.

DATA BASE[1]

We are looking at data from the first few months in the lives of five infants from white, non-academic, middle-class families living in the Boston area. The parents had used English exclusively all their lives. Since these infants were born to mothers already enrolled in the Maternal-Infant Health Study[2] at the Boston Lying-In Hospital, we have records of each of the pregnancies in more detail than is usual in clinic records.

---

[1]   This data base has been described previously in Bullowa, Jones, and Bever (1964, reprinted 1970 in *Cognitive development in children: five monographs of the society for research in child development*, 385–391. Chicago, University of Chicago Press; and 1971 in *The acquisition of language*, edited by Ursula Bellugi and Roger Brown, 101–114. Chicago, University of Chicago Press); and in Margaret Bullowa, Lawrence G. Jones, and Audrey Duckert, 1964, "The acquisition of a word," *Language and Speech* 7(2):107–111; and in Margaret Bullowa, 1970, "The start of the language process," in *Actes du Xe congrès international des linguistes, Bucarest, 28 août–2 septembre 1967*, volume three, 191–200, Editions de l'Académie de la République Socialiste de Roumanie.

[2]   The Maternal-Infant Health Study was the name for the local Boston unit of the Longitudinal Study on Perinatal Factors of the (then) National Institute for Nervous Diseases and Blindness. It was a prospective study based on over 50,000 births.

We also have access to the observations of that study group during deliveries, in the neonatal period, and periodically thereafter. We have results of a neurological examination at four months and of EEG's (electroencephalograms) taken in the neonatal period for each infant. We have every reason to consider all of these infants organically intact.

Each of the infants we studied was the mothers' firstborn. This selection was made because in pilot work with the second child of another family we had found the interaction in the household to be too complicated for us to deal with in our initial study.

We usually managed to be present in the delivery room and to tape-record the birth cry. Within an hour of birth the infant was examined using the Brazelton Neonatal Behavioral Assessment Scale (1973) — in the stage to which it had been developed at that time: the early 1960's. This was documented on tape and with 100 feet of black and white sixteen-millimeter silent film showing spontaneous behavior, neurological tests, and important responses in an interactional situation. During the hospital stay two or three more neonatal assessments were done by our "child development team" (see below), and the baby was observed with the mother during two feedings using our "vocal observation" technique.

The vocal observations (illustrated in Plates 1 and 2) consisted of continuous half-hour tape and film recordings taken weekly in the infant's home. The tape utilized two parallel tracks. On one track we recorded from an ElectroVoice 664 microphone (cardioid pattern) aimed in the infant's direction from our apparatus stand several feet away. This inevitably picked up environmental noise as well as human voices. We felt this to be appropriate because this is the sound environment in which the infant has to develop auditory perceptual capacities. M. Bullowa recorded on the other track a running commentary on and description of the ongoing scene. This was done in the presence of the subjects by whispering into a microphone embedded in a "Hushaphone"[3] which effectively kept her voice from being heard in the environment. Whispering was necessary in order to prevent leakage of sound from her throat. The descriptions were free-form with no precoding because we did not know what information would prove relevant.[4] A patterned electronic signal was placed on this descriptive sound track every five

---

[3] "Hushaphone" is the trade name for a device used to shield a telephone mouthpiece so that the speaker's voice does not leak into the environment. We embedded a crystal microphone in one and added urethane foam for greater sound absorption. We found that the whispered voice was so well shielded that we felt no constraint on describing the behavior of subjects in their presence.

[4] When M. Bullowa was contemplating the development of a method of field observation and recording, she wished to devise a way of describing ongoing behavior of

seconds, both in order to segment the data on both tracks for indexing and for synchronization with the film.

A film frame (sixteen-millimeter black and white double X) was taken by a Kodak Ciné Special camera every half-second; thus the half-hour could be recorded on a standard 100-foot reel of film. The film was taken under room lighting to avoid the stimulating effect of flood lighting. Because the pictures were taken as single frames and the film was forced in the developing, most of the pictures are sharp and a great deal of detail can be read from them.

It is possible to synchronize tape and film in the laboratory or to study either separately. Each of the three streams of data can be analyzed separately and related through the segmental indexing system. The field descriptions have been transcribed onto sheets ruled to correspond with the segmentation. The lexical content of adult speech picked up by the open microphone has also been transcribed onto such sheets. Interesting portions of the vocal output of our subjects can be transferred to a special tape accepted by the sound spectrograph[5] and analyzed. Film can be studied one frame at a time, pulsed by hand, or at a selected rate from one to twenty-four frames per second by use of an L-W 224A Flickerless Projector.[6]

The original plan was to follow these infants from birth to thirty months of age. For three of the five this was accomplished, and all were followed for at least seven months so that we have data obtained by this method for the first six months of life for five normal first-born American infants.

Such data gathering lends itself to certain kinds of investigation and precludes others. No experimental intervention would have been compatible with our objective: to record the natural history of language development. In the fieldwork phase we would have wished to be nonparticipant observers, but this was in practice impossible. Rather than behave in a stilted manner, which would have distorted the behavior of

---

infants and children in their own homes and their interaction with their parents. The intention was to describe the observations in free form, but as objectively as possible. As an aid to accomplishing this objective it was decided to do the first longitudinal recording in a family which was monolingual in a language unknown to her. It was expected that the combination of a strange culture and lack of linguistic clues would make her a better observer and it probably did. But she found very soon that she could understand a great deal of what was going on between members of the Chinese family being visited weekly.

[5]   A sample sound spectrogram is shown in Plate 3. It displays energy at various frequencies over time.

[6]   The L–W Flickerless Projector is a modified Kodak Analyst Movie Projector which makes it possible to view film at slow speeds without flicker.

our subjects, we interacted with them during recording when they initiated it. This usually was confined to brief interchanges which are easily identified in the data.

For a first approach to the vocal aspects of communicative development, our once-a-week schedule is probably closely enough spaced to bring out the general outline. We took a second observation each week in one family using tape only and found, on the basis of listening, that the sounds on the second tapes did not yield new kinds of information. When we feel we have a complete inventory of infant vocalization and of behavioral units, it would be worthwhile to make closely spaced prolonged observations[7] with attention focused on communicative behavior, as Wolff (1959) and others have focused on other developmental issues.

In addition, we have records for each infant from "developmental" examinations taken once a month in their own homes.[8] The developmental observers were T. Berry Brazelton, a pediatrician with special research interest in infancy and child development, and Grace C. Young, a developmental psychologist. They interviewed the mothers on developmental and other events since the last visit, observed spontaneous behavior, and used developmental tests and schedules, including Gesell (1940) summaries. Thus this team made a twofold attempt to understand the development of each infant. On the one hand, through free-flowing observation they investigated how the mother and infant interacted with one another and with the observers, and noted how they dealt with being observed. On the other hand, in the structured situation of the Gesell tests they subjected the pair to the stress of a performance situation. They considered not only the success but also the quality of the performance.

---

[7] M. Bullowa has tested the feasibility of prolonged observation by dictating field notes on home observation of an infant into a shielded microphone for twelve hours with one two-hour break during the infant's nap. She experienced almost no voice fatigue from the whispered speech. Four- or five-hour sessions would be practical. The major problem would be transcription time and analysis of the large amount of data which would be generated.

[8] The developmental observations were documented with tapes and 100 feet of silent black and white ciné film. The hand-held camera was a Bolex Rex with Pan Cinor zoom lens. The same audio-visual technician who participated in the "vocal observations" took these developmental recordings. We strove to minimize the number of different people from our study group in contact with the studied families. During the major part of the fieldwork (1961–1964) two undergraduate psychology students from Northeastern University, Edward Basinski and William Weiner, alternated as audio-visual technicians.

RELEVANT DISCIPLINES

Child Development

Child development has roots both in the medical discipline of pediatrics and the academic field of psychology. By a variety of methods the investigators in this field concern themselves with the child as a developing organism. There is a tendency to fragment the field according to focus (cognition, personality, physical growth, etc.), and there is no unified theory. There is always concern with progress from one stage or phase to another in the course of development from neonate (or even from fetus) to adolescent and adult. Two principal modes of study are employed. The same individuals may be followed over time in respect to one or more characteristics. This is known as "longitudinal" study. Our data base belongs to this tradition. The other method is called "cross-sectional." Similar data are gathered from samples of children at different ages, and the succession of ages is expected to yield a developmental sequence. Individual characteristics are averaged out.[9]

The observations of our child development team (pediatrician and psychologist) were partly traditional and partly innovative. The use of Gesell (1940) summaries month by month makes it possible to compare our five children with developmental norms from Gesell and his co-workers based on a large number of intensively studied infants. On the other hand, some of the examination methods used by Dr. Brazelton were among those used in the development of his Neonatal Behavioral Assessment Scale (1973). Our method of vocal field observation and recording, while drawing on many sources, was in its entirety innovative.

Up to now there have been two main trends in the study of infant vocalization as child development. One is based on an attempt to classify spontaneously occurring infant vocal sounds using categories based on adult language with little regard for use or context. The other, while attending to, or rather producing, context, elicits the sounds for study by experimental means, thus insuring that the infant's output is in response to the desired stimulation, such as pain or hunger. The former method applied at a linguistic segmental level has produced disappointing results. This is mainly because the adult categories utilized are not relevant to early infant vocal activity.

As an example of the former method in the tradition of phonetic recording and analysis of spontaneous vocalization, the studies from Irwin's child development laboratory in the 1940's are among the best

[9] What is often not realized or understood in the application of such cross-sectional results is that idiosyncratic but normal developmental sequences are also averaged out.

known. A summary of thirty of Irwin's published papers is contained in the encyclopedic article "Language development in children" by McCarthy (1954: 507–509). The vowels and consonants found among infant sounds were classified phonetically, and relative frequencies over time were studied.

Vocalization by infants has been recognized as part of socialization. Rheingold, et al. found that three-month-old institutionalized infants could be induced to increase their vocal responses when offered social reinforcement (smiling, vocalizing, caressing). They remark

... the speech of the infant, if only in a social situation, can be modified by a response from the environment which is contingent on his vocalizing. Hence, what happens after the infant vocalizes has been shown to be important ... If the results can be extended to life situations, then mothers might be able to increase or decrease the vocal output of their children by the responses they make when the children vocalize (Rheingold, et al. 1959).

Caudill (1972), who made comparative studies of mother-infant inter-action in Tokyo and Washington using fixed schedules for recording, included vocalization, categorized as happy and unhappy, among the behaviors he studied quantitatively. He found American infants at three to four months of age to have a higher level of vocalization, particularly of happy vocalization, than Japanese infants from comparable backgrounds. He discussed the difference in terms of culture-specific styles of child care. This study and Rheingold's both point to the bearing of the infant's environmental context on at least the quantitative aspects of vocal output.

The experimental approach when combined with acoustic analysis has yielded increasingly precise descriptions of the acoustic nature of infant vocal output under given conditions. This method makes it possible to detect significant deviations from normal performance, and this knowledge is applied in medical diagnosis of neonatal pathology. Karelitz (and Fisichelli 1962), a pediatrician working in association with psychologists, was a pioneer in this field. The painstaking studies of a group of Scandinavian pediatricians, linguists, and acoustic engineers (Lind 1965; Wasz-Höckert, et al. 1968) produced a great deal of information not only about what the newborn sounds like but also how the sounds are produced. These studies provide a model for correlated vocal and behavioral investigation.

Ethology

The fields of comparative psychology and ethology treat communication as a facet of animal behavior. Comparative psychology developed in America while ethology originated in Europe with Konrad Lorenz. The ethologist studies behavior by observing members of his target species in their natural habitat and, if necessary, in captivity. In the past he used a notebook and pencil and perhaps a watch to record behavior and behavior sequences as they occurred. He tried to achieve as complete as possible an inventory of the behaviors he observed (ethogram; cf. Eibl-Eibesfeldt 1970: 10) and to improve his precision in defining and recording behavior. He often made sketches to help in the construction of what he had seen. With technological advances he has added photographic (Eibl-Eibesfeldt 1970: 11) and acoustic recording techniques to his repertoire so that he can review sequences at will and free himself from "real time" for the purpose of analysis. When studying a developmental sequence he has to determine an observation schedule which will allow him to catch the stages of development. As in child development studies, the ethologist may choose a "longitudinal" or a "cross-sectional" model, although these terms are not used.

In the study of animal behavior by ethologists, a recognizable unit of communicative behavior is called a "display." This consists of a relatively fixed sequence of movements and is usually directed toward one or more conspecifics. It is considered to have a communicative function (Smith 1965: 405). The primate call shares the message aspect of the display of which it forms a part. Thus the message may be deduced from the call even when the visual aspect of the display cannot be observed for some reason, e.g. dense foliage. Some ethologists believe that the message is always about the state of the vocalizing animal at the time of vocalization (Smith 1965:405). Thus it would correspond with the display to which it belongs. Even an alarm call would not be interpreted in the human terms, "There is a predator," but rather something like, "I'm agitated on account of danger." Nevertheless, a great deal of information is carried in calls and displays. Besides identifying the emitter, the display and call specify whether or not the displaying animal is in an agonistic state vis-à-vis the recipient and what it is likely to do next.

A display may be vocal behavior perceived by audition as well as motor behavior perceived by vision. In the literature on primate behavior the term "call" is used for all vocal behaviors. This is different from the general ethological literature, especially on birds, where calls are distinguished from song, and each is thought of as a display in itself. Because we are considering a primate species, we will stick to primate usage and refer to calls as components of, or associated with, displays.

Smith has arrived at some generalizations about vertebrate displays.

He writes, "Displays do not resemble the words of our languages ... Most display messages make the behavior of the communicator to some degree more predictable to the recipient" (1969: 145). He discusses the difficulties of deducing messages from displays and points out that "... the complete range of uses of a display must usually be known before the message the display carries can be determined ..." (1969: 146). All displays include identification of the sender and "probability of occurrence of each behavioral act specified by a display" (1969: 146), but he notes that "some displays are not graded and indicate only a range of probabilities; a recipient then needs contextual sources as an aid in predicting relative probabilities" (1969: 146). In addition to these two kinds of "modifiers," present in all displays, a number of categories of behavior such as attack, escape, and association are encoded. One type of message, the "bond-limited subset" specifies acts occurring between parents and offspring as well as between mates and within other "bonded groups" (1969: 146). We would expect, if this categorization of message types holds for the "prelinguistic signs" of humans, that most of the messages of early infancy would fall in this category.

A classification of the causation of primate calls (not message types) is given by Andrew (1962). This leads to a list of situation categories. This is an unusual approach in ethology as Andrew himself acknowledges. Andrew says ethology has "tended to relate all components of displays to major drives, such as aggression, fear or sex" (1962: 297). This had led to classifying "... the different calls into such functional categories as 'warning call' or 'threat call'" (1962: 296). Andrew proposes the following method for analyzing the causation of primate calls: "The method followed has been to study the form of calls by means of sound spectrographs, and then to discover in how many situations a particular form of call occurs" (1962: 296). We have been applying this procedure to our study of early infant vocalization as a means of entry into the early phases of the human infant's communicative system.

Andrew's Group 2 category contains situations which lead to relatively low intensity calls and is defined as

An encounter with a social fellow after brief separation from him, under circumstances in which no attack is feared ... Such encounters may be divided into: (a) perception of the fellow at a distance and (b) an encounter with close bodily contact and often mutual grooming. A third situation (c) in this group is that of an infant searching for the nipple (1962: 296).

He describes some human infant vocalizations in this category:

"Human infants will give long grunts or segmented grunts [laughter] at the sight of a known face. It is not known yet in detail what relation these bear to the soft grunts sometimes given when searching for the teat" (1962: 301).

He goes on to state:

All of the calls described above, which are given in true greeting [i.e. which are evoked by the perception of a social fellow after separation irrespective of social rank], could be thought of as calls first evoked during contact with the mother which have been extended progressively to other social fellows (1962: 301).

There are precedents for applying the methods of the ethologists to human developmental problems. Prechtl, a physician trained by Lorenz in ethological methods, has spent years in the observation of neonates and infants. In a paper on crying during the first nine days of life he emphasized that "The infant's cry is a communication signal ..." (Prechtl, Theocell, Gramsberger, and Lind 1969:142) and concludes, "Stochastic analysis of cry patterns in newborn infants may supply data which correlate with development and with neurological findings" (1969: 150). He has paid special attention to neurological function and is responsible for defining states of arousal as basic to all other descriptions of human infant behavior (Prechtl and Beintema 1964). His five-place scale includes "crying" as the state of maximal arousal. The coding of arousal states, once learned, is quite simple. It would be useful for this method to become routine in field observation of infants by anthropologists. Such coding is included in the Brazelton scale.

More recently, especially in Great Britain, zoologists are turning to "ethological" studies of children. Their first publications are based mainly on observations of children in nursery school classes. At least two books appeared in 1972 (Blurton Jones; McGrew). Blurton Jones is now engaged in the study of infants in their own families. In Cambridge, England, an ethologically inspired "longitudinal study of mothers and babies" (Richards and Bernal 1972) is under way which has already produced a paper on crying and maternal response during the first ten days of life (Bernal 1972).

Non-Verbal Communication

In addition to inspiration from the ethological approach to the study of communicative behavior, we have built on the work of a number of investigators in the behavioral context of human speech. This leads into an area sometimes referred to as non-verbal communication. Actually this term implies a degree of separation which fails to do justice to the

integration between speech and the motor behavior in which it is embedded. It is this close integration which makes speech part of a total
communicative act in which the entire motor apparatus participates in
an hierarchically structured way.

This has been studied from both ends of the hierarchy. For example,
Condon and Ogston (1967) have taken a microscopic view and, by
painstaking frame-by-frame analysis of sound film taken at rates up to
forty-eight frames per second, have shown that the speaker moves in
synchrony with his own speech — not just with words and syllables but
with even smaller (segmental in the linguistic sense) components. Condon
and Ogston have also demonstrated that a listener moves in synchrony
with the speech of the person he is attending to (1967: 229). Condon
and Sander (1974) have recently shown that neonates at one day and two
days of age move synchronously with the speech of caretaking adults.
It is this kind of attention to the relation between vocal and non-vocal
behavior that we believe will provide fruitful results in the elucidation of
infant communicative acts.

Working from the "macro" end of the hierarchy, Scheflen (1965) and
Kendon (1972) have delineated larger behavioral frames into which
various levels of discourse fit. People signal the beginning and end of
their discourse by major postural shifts involving joints around the pelvis
(Scheflen 1964: 321). Within these positions the change of topic (para-
graph level) is signaled by a definite but less comprehensive shift in motor
activity.

All the advance in this area depends on very painstaking study of ciné-
film and, recently, of video tape. The phenomena dealt with require
slowing down, repeated viewing, and precise coding. An advance was
made in the management of filmed behavioral data when Birdwhistell's
laboratory developed a method of printing serial numbers from a second
negative ("B roll") on each frame of film to be studied (van Vlack 1966).
Condon (personal communication) has used this method with film and
has adapted it to video by including a chronometer in the background
when he takes video tapes. These methods contribute to the possibility
of rigorous study of recorded visual data.

Ekman and co-workers have developed a computerized method for
handling non-verbal behavioral data coded from video (Ekman, et al.
1969). Frame numbers are assigned by computer as a way of segmenting
and indexing the tapes so that any position on the tape can be uniquely
identified, viewed on command, and its already coded data displayed.
This system facilitates data storage and retrieval and makes comparisons
efficient.

Ethnology

We have thought of our study as falling within the scope of ethnology as well as comparative ethology. Primate ethology suggests seeking the meaning of vocalizations in other motor behaviors with which they are associated and understanding these communicative behaviors by seeing how they function in relation to the behavior of other members of the species; it suggests examining their communicative functions. When we started this study in the early 1960's we had to seek elsewhere, possibly in ethnology, for clues as to how to recognize the organization of behavior based on data recorded serially on film. Film had not been the ethologist's tool. In field ethology, units of behavior have become recognizable through prolonged observation, description, and testing until they can be named and coded directly. Social scientists are not used to segmenting much of human behavior in this way. Certain ritualized actions are easy to recognize. Greetings, for instance, stand out clearly (Kendon and Ferber 1973). But people are so convinced of the freedom and flexibility of their own behavior that they do not find it "natural" to break up the "stream of behavior" into small units.

In general, ethnologists have not used the concept of organizing observed behavior hierarchically.[10] Rather, descriptions dealt with behavior as goal-directed: the completion of an artifact, the performance of a ritual. In relation to communication, the focus was not on communicative process, or on analyzing systems of human interaction, but was directed toward decoding language and other symbolic systems.

We might mention an attempt of an anthropologist to deal with the hierarchical structure of social behavior. In Bock's study (1962) of Micmac society, an attempt was made to apply Pike's "unified theory of behavior" (1967) to ethnological description. We attempted to apply this method to our data but could find no way to get it to accommodate the temporal flow of events at the finer level of detail we were using. We suspect that once the management of the full range of detail in the description of human behavioral data has been developed, probably through computerized data management, it will be possible to link it to some such schema as Bock's for higher orders of social organization.

We have sought a model in anthropological film with little success. We expected that ethnology, a field which has specialized in the observa-

---

[10]   Recently, under the rubric "ethnomethodology," an approach to the segmentation of behavior has come to grips with this problem: e.g. Harold Garfinkel (1967); Harold Garfinkel and Harvey Sacks (1969); and John J. Gumperz and Dell Hymes 1972).

tion of "naturally" occurring human behavior, and which has recently contributed fine film studies of aspects of exotic cultures, would have ready-made techniques to offer for our film analysis. This turned out to be a false hope. Bateson and Mead's *Balinese character* of 1942 seemed to presage good things. Here were studies of child development in cultural context based on closely spaced Leica shots and simultaneously recorded field notes in great detail. It was coming close, but not quite close enough, to the contexts for vocalization we wish to establish. Anthropological film making has taken another direction. It has tended to deal with events at a high level of abstraction, presenting a single supposedly representative sequence for each type of behavior considered. But in order to abstract from the actual "performances" a description which concentrates on only the emic aspects of the behavior, it is necessary to have at least several instances to compare. We also found that indexing of "raw footage" of ethnological film is at a very gross level in the hierarchy of behavior, usually at the level of instrumental activity (Eibl-Eibesfeldt 1970: 412).

An example of a use of anthropological film which approaches the material in a way to bring out characteristics of action is the collection of dance sequences assembled for the "choriometric" part of the Canto-metrics Study (Lomax, Bartenieff, and Paulay 1968). Their "effort-shape" analysis is concerned with qualities of movement rather than with segmentation. In the reported study they use their method to apply uniform coding to films of dance from many cultures.

Byers (1972) is another anthropologist who attends to film analysis in great detail and includes the sound track in his analysis. He has utilized available raw footage taken by others to explore ideas on the border between anthropology and the field of non-verbal communication.

It is quite ironical that anthropology, a field which is consciously and avowedly concerned with "enculturation," has traditionally paid scant attention to infancy, the most important period of enculturation. Notwithstanding considerable lipservice to the subtleties and pervasiveness of the socialization process, anthropologists have all too often confined their attention in this area to the direct teaching of rituals at puberty, the oral tradition of poetry, and other such overt matters, while neglecting until quite recently very detailed studies of the interaction of infants and very young children with adults.[11]

In the field it has been customary for the ethnologist to become a

---

[11]   Until recently the outstanding exception has been the field studies of Margaret Mead.

participant observer in the culture he is investigating. At the opposite extreme, recently Schaeffer (1970), an anthropologist working with Scheflen in a cross-cultural study of normal family interaction in urban United States, studied observations recorded by remote control from a robot video camera. We have chosen an intermediate course, the minimally participant observation described earlier (see "Data Base" section). We feel that this degree of participation with our subjects is appropriate to our purpose. It allows us immediate access to what is going on. The observer speaking into the shielded microphone appears to the subject family to be like someone talking into a telephone. This is tolerated in our culture and discourages social interaction. We recognize that any observation, even with a remotely controlled recorder, cannot help but affect the subjects to some degree. We can, if necessary, identify at least the overt evidence of reactions to us in the data.

Linguistics

Linguistics as applied to language acquisition has little to offer to the study of early infant vocalization. As Crystal (1972: 1) points out, "Research into children's language has been almost exclusively segmental and verbal." In an earlier era in the study of infant vocal sounds, an attempt was made to classify sounds as vowels and consonants and to transcribe the sounds either in orthography or in the International Phonetic Alphabet (see "Child Development" above). This was before the technology for magnetically recording and storing sound had been applied to infants (Lynip 1951). By now it is clear not only from the nature of the sounds, but from the anatomy of the infant vocal tract (Lieberman, et al. 1972; Bosma, Truby, and Lind 1965) that young infants are not capable of producing the full range of adult speech sounds. On the other hand, such terms as cooing, mewing, etc. (as used, for instance, by Gesell 1940) are too subjective to be useful for our purpose.

One of the few linguists who has given serious attention to the "non-segmental" aspects of early infant vocal behavior is Crystal (1970). In his recent review (1972), "Non-segmental phonology in language acquisition," he supplies an exhaustive review and critique of the literature in this sphere. Under non-segmental phonology he subsumes "intonation, stress, rhythm, speed of speaking, and the many effects loosely referred to as 'tone of voice'" (1972: 1). After pointing to the terminological chaos in all aspects of the field, he defines vocalization as "any vocal sound pattern produced by an infant for which there is no evidence of

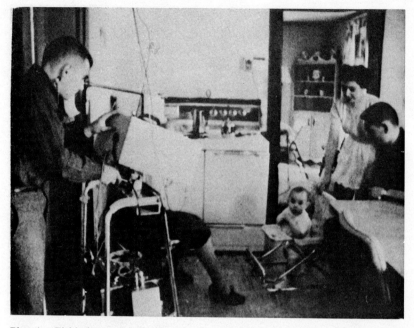

Plate 1.   Field observations method for "vocal observation." Observers: audio-visual technician (behind apparatus stand) and "observer" (partly hidden by camera box) with a subject family in their kitchen

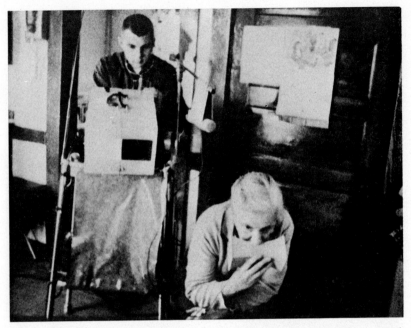

Plate 2. Field observation: as seen by subject family. Technician monitors tape and keeps camera (enclosed in sound insulated box) and microphone (shock-mounted on boom on apparatus stand) direct toward infant by sighting through view finder at right rear corner of box. Observer (seated on camp stool) dictates whispered description of ongoing activity and interaction into Hushaphone-shielded microphone

Plate 3. Five successive film frames from vocal observation when infant was twenty-eight days old. (Picture has been cropped to fit space.) Arrows indicate approximately where frame was taken in relation to sound spectrogram of infant's cry shown below. The sound spectrogram is narrow band (45 Hz filter), and the frequency range is 0–3500 Hz. The diagram under the spectrogram shows on the same time scale the form and the value in Hertz (Hz) of the fundamental frequency of each of the four sounds (Numbers 11–14 given in parentheses on the diagram) in this "vocal passage." The time scale (below) is in seconds. The first picture shows the father, with his crying son on his lap, looking away from the baby's face (his face and eyes and the baby's had been oriented toward one another) toward the kitchzn where his wife is preparing food for the baby. This frame was taken before the beginning of this spectrogram. The baby's facial orientation is toward where his father's was. In the second frame, which coincides with the first sound in the passage, the father's face and gaze have returned to his pre-glance position, but by now the baby has moved his head toward the father as shown by the greater exposure of hair visible. The third frame comes at the beginning of the fourth and last sound of the passage, a long drawn-out wail which shows a rising-falling-rising-falling pitch contour and clear harmonic structure. Father and baby have not yet re-established eye contact. By the fourth frame, midway through the wail, contact has been re-established through slight readjustments by both of them. In the meantime the father's left hand has started the movement (Frame 3) which will enable him to reposition the baby (Frame 5). Frame 5 occurs at or slightly after the termination of vocal sound

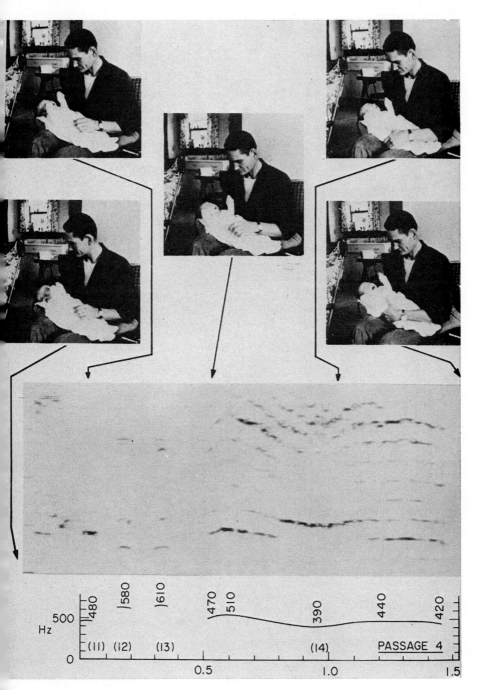

late 3.

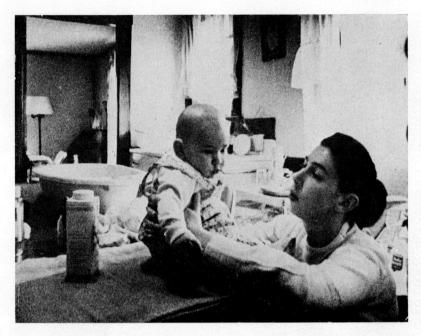

Plate 4. Single film frame (cropped at top) from observation M032: during proto-conversation. Infant is three and one-half months of age. Graininess of blown-up picture does not appear on projection screen

language-specific contrastivity" (i.e. which is not linguistic) and considers the sound patterns "biologically controlled" (1972: 6). For him, intonation "refers to a system of non-segmental linguistic contrastivity which varies primarily in terms of pitch direction and pitch range" (1972: 6). This precludes his using the term intonation in relation to vocalization, and he suggests "melody" to refer to the auditory correlate of fundamental frequency variation in vocalization (1972: 6). He calls for studies to determine the characteristics of infant vocalization and recommends acoustic specification. He also recommends cross-cultural studies to search for points of divergence from early biologically controlled sound patterns which he appears to consider universal.

Lieberman (1967: 41) states that infants: "communicate by means of sound from the moment of birth onward ... The infant cry has a characteristic pattern. The pattern is apparently innately determined and is a characteristic human attribute." He describes the fundamental frequency contour of the infant cry and relates it to his concept of "breath-group" which he has studied by relating acoustic to physiological data (subglottal air pressure) in adults (1967: Chapter 3).

A useful tool for the study of infant sound is the sound spectrograph, an instrument devised for the analysis of adult speech sounds.[12] It produces a permanent record of energy at various frequencies in temporal sequence (see Plate 3 for an example of a spectrogram). Despite the fact that our vocal samples were obtained in a noisy environment, a practiced eye can detect patterns produced vocally by infants, even in the presence of background noise and adult vocalization.

How much can be learned from spectrographic analysis of infant vocalization has been demonstrated by the Scandinavian groups mentioned above in the "Child Development" section (Lind 1965; Wasz-Höckert, et al. 1968). These interdisciplinary workers have focused a great deal of technical skill on the study of the birth cry, pain cry, hunger cry, and "pleasure" cry. The latter three were produced experimentally. Not only have they studied spectrograms and defined acoustic parameters for the cries they have studied, but also they have worked out in detail the relation between phases of sound production and configurations of the vocal tract as shown on serial X-rays, phases of the respiratory cycle, and subglottal pressure changes. They have followed these intensive studies on "normal"

---

[12] The sound spectrograph gives a great deal of information to the linguist and acoustic engineer but is an expensive and specialized instrument found in only a few laboratories. The oscilloscope, a much more universally available instrument, can be used to assist in extracting information about timing, intensity, or pitch, any of which may be useful for special purposes.

cries with comparative studies on sounds produced in certain severe pathological conditions of the newborn (Vuorenkoski, Wasz-Höckert, et al. 1971; Michelsson 1971) and have shown that these can be differentiated by ear (Vuorenkoski, Lind, et al. 1971). They have stopped short of studying the full range of infant vocal communication because this was not their aim. We have found their spectographic work very suggestive and are extending it to spontaneous sounds produced in the course of the infant's ongoing interaction with his caretakers.

INFANT VOCALIZATION

Until recently the neonate was seen by psychologists as a purely reflex animal, responding to most stimulation with random activity except for a few well-defined responses to specific maneuvers such as the Moro [extensor] reflex to jarring the surface on which the supine infant is resting. Intensive study of human neonates in recent years has led to a very different view. The cognitive organization of the newborn has been investigated in many laboratories with findings which show a great deal of sensorimotor organization already functioning. For instance, visually guided reaching for an object in the midline can be demonstrated at seven to fifteen days (Bower 1972). This had not been thought to occur until the fourth month of life. Because the neonate cannot show this performance when lying down, he had not been credited with this capacity. This is only one among many suggestive findings, but gives an idea of the level of capacity available and makes more plausible a view of the young infant as an active participant rather than the passive, simple-reflex-dominated organism we had become used to considering him.

Devereux (1964: 267) describes how, among the Mohave, "... even fetuses about to be born as well as twin infants and nursing babies are believed capable of understanding, and responding to, rational verbal admonition even though they are manifestly incapable of speech." It would be of some interest to determine, in cultures with such different attitudes from ours toward infant understanding, whether infants in fact begin babbling or talking at an earlier age than in Western societies. As far as we know, no one has investigated carefully the actual development of language in babies of Mohave culture or of similar cultures, so it is difficult to do more than speculate about the significance of these Mohave beliefs.

A related result of our studies and others is that babies in fact can communicate (or at least indicate) more things than most adults in our culture expect them to. Therefore it is not unreasonable to expect that in an environment of greater expectation and encouragement an infant's vocal and verbal development might be speeded up relative to that in Western societies, and possibly even some sequential differences might show up. One of our babies, whose parents were especially verbal and tended to include her in family conversations from the time when she was able to sit in a highchair at the dining table, began talking relatively earlier than other babies whose development we followed, and whose parents did not treat them in this way. Our data, however, are only suggestive on such issues. A wide and representative sample would be necessary in order to eliminate the complicating factor of individual differences to which this isolated example could be ascribed.

In another case from our data, one child's father began to understand him to be speaking and responded to him on this basis several weeks sooner than his mother did. We attribute this difference to a difference between the parents in their attitudes toward their son. The father expected his son to exhibit competence in many spheres; the mother, on the other hand, was always skeptical about accomplishment until it was unmistakable. In general, however, we must be careful to distinguish individual differences (in ontogenetic development and in behavior and attitudes of one or both parents) from cultural differences.

Let us look at what the newborn does which may be considered communicative. Traditionally we are most aware of his "telling" us when he is hungry or in pain, both states of strong discomfort. Pain and hunger cries have been the subject of much investigation, including detailed studies of their acoustic characteristics. Less attention has been focused on the communication of comfort and the seeking of social interaction. Sleep has been considered the best evidence of comfort, but in fact a satisfied and comfortable baby, after the first few days of recovery from the vigorous experience of birth (and in our culture very often also recovery from the chemical sedation received via the placenta), shows kinesthetically by snuggling into a warm soft surface that he is comfortable, whereas in discomfort he is likely to arch away.

Non-cry vocalization is usually said to begin around one month of age. But in our data we find from the first days on a large range of sounds produced, often of low intensity. Many of these do not seem to be associated with discomfort. It is likely that much of this has been overlooked because it is so much less prominent than the characteristic sharp, loud discomfort sounds. After identifying the characteristic infant sounds associated with social interaction (Bateson 1971), we were able to recognize a very brief example of this sound on a tape taken at six days and then found that the corresponding film showed typical though fleeting adult-infant social interaction.

The obviously distressed infant's sounds are relatively well known as are those of the socially interacting infant. In view of Andrew's analysis of primate calls (see "Ethology" section), it is doubtful that this represents the full range of what the infant can communicate about vocally.

It is for this reason that we are undertaking a survey of the infant sounds occurring on our tapes. We are trying to establish relationships between categories of infant sound (studied spectrographically) and behavioral and interactive situations. From simultaneously dictated notes and films we are able to reconstruct the context and behavior of which the vocalization formed a part. In other words, we are considering infant vocal sound to be the "call" aspect of "displays," as in some recent primate studies.

While we do not know of any similar approach to the elucidation of human infant vocal sounds, there are models in studies of primate vocalization. One which is particularly pertinent is a study of the vocal development of Japanese rhesus monkey infants, one hand-raised by the investigator, Rumiko Takeda, and the other by its own monkey mother (Takeda 1965, 1966). Takeda found initially six "vocal stocks" and traced their development through differentiation or extinction throughout thirty weeks' observation. She felt that she could identify the vocalizations both by listening and in relation to specific situations, and that she had identified the precursors of the adult monkey vocalizations classified by other Japanese investigators. She relates parts of her classification to sounds described by Hayes (1952) in the hand-rearing of the chimpanzee, Vicki. Takeda alludes in her paper to parallels with human infant vocalization (1966: 113) and in private conversation has said that she felt similar processes were taking place in the subsequent rearing of her own two children. This needs to be verified or disproved by more disinterested observers.

A study is currently in progress on vocal development in chimpanzees (Plooy 1972). He and his wife are working with the colony well studied by Jane van Lawick-Goodall (1968) in the Gombe Preserve in Tanzania. The longer time spans involved in chimpanzee development, compared with monkeys, make it necessary for the Plooys to record from a number of young of known ages. They are aided in their work by the already existing knowledge of the behavioral repertoire of this species, to which they have added previously unobserved items.

In the current state of our knowledge of early communication, one way of judging whether a behavior should be considered communicative is to observe the interpersonal situation in which it occurs and the behavior of all participants in that interaction. One might suppose that in the young infant, discomfort crying is an automatic accompaniment of internal distress, perhaps for the purpose of discharging tension, and only incidentally a signal to caretaking adults. Close observation of instances, however, shows that even in distress an infant can be busy with social interaction. A crying sequence, probably caused by discomfort from an overstuffed belly, is in our data. The twenty-eight-day-old infant was propped extended across his father's lap (see Plate 3). The cries came in a rhythmic series of sobs and wails. The film frames at half-second intervals showed the infant's and father's faces oriented toward one another despite the infant's crying with his eyes closed part of the time. The father turned his head away for one second (first frame). When his gaze returned to his son's face (second frame), the baby had turned his face away, and it took another second for him to turn back and re-establish mutual gaze (fourth frame).

While mutual gaze is certainly not the only situation in which communication between infant and adult occurs, when mutual gaze does occur (Robson 1967) even naive observers "feel" that it signifies communication. It is the earmark of "proto-conversation" as described by Bateson (1971: 171). We can therefore feel reasonably confident that when eye-to-eye contact is mutually sought, the activity accompanying it is tagged for communication. Setting eye contact as a criterion would lead to gross underestimation of communicative activity, but when it is present we feel confident that we have genuine examples of such activity.

Eye-to-eye contact sets a limit on interpersonal orientation and distance. Between adult and infant this distance is approximately one and one-half feet (see Plate 4). Based on what we know about infant vision, this is the distance at which the adult's face is in sharpest focus for the infant. When psychologists test babies with visual test objects, they use this fact in deciding where to place the stimulus.

Because we do not yet have a firmly established behavioral inventory for the human infant and his parents, we have had to devise a model for coding and analyzing behavior from which it is possible to derive such an inventory. At the lowest level in this behavioral hierarchy is the single pulse of sound. Because of the sparseness (two frames per second) of our photographic images, we cannot establish the rest of the behavioral pattern at this level of detail from our data. The work of William Condon (Condon and Ogston 1967: 225–229) on speech-body synchrony assures us that there is such a correlation. Even with our own two-frames-per-second film data we are able to see that the onset of prominences in the

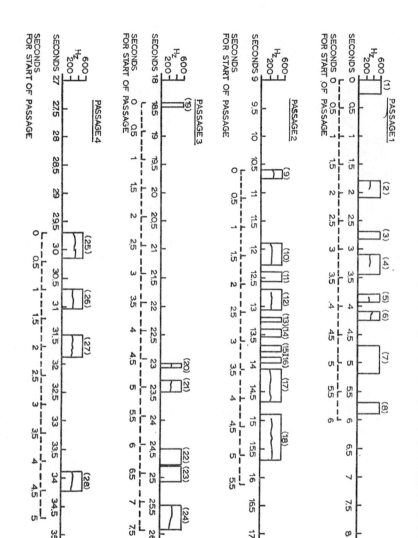

Figure 1.   Diagram showing relative duration and timing of infant sounds during a stretch of "proto-conversation" at three and one-half months of age. Sounds are grouped into "vocal passages." Sound Number 19 could perhaps be considered a separate passage but was arbitrarily assigned to passage Number 3. The width of rectangles shows the duration of sound on the time scale shown on the baseline. The height of the rectangles has significance. Lines drawn within the blocks show the form of the contour of fundamental frequency when harmonic structure is present in the spectogram. Where no pitch line is shown, the sound lacked harmonic structure

infant's vocal output are associated with onset or change in direction of gross movement.[13]

We doubt that single sound pulses will yield specific messages. It is quite likely that similar pulses occur in different higher order elements which are quite dissimilar in total configuration and effect, just as a small number of distinguishable phonetic elements are used in many combinations in adult speech.

We have designated as "passage" a unit of complex behavior which includes both auditory and visual information for the receiver. We view our term "passage" as the ethologist's "display," but always with both kinesic and acoustic components. One of the most difficult tasks is to specify how to recognize a passage. Sometimes this is made easy by an apparent segmentation based on pauses with or without change of "speaker." This was the case with an analyzed sequence of proto-conversation activity between a three-and-one-half-month-old boy and his mother. There were bursts of vocal activity separated by silences longer than any pauses occurring within the bursts. Even though the infant's activity was all of the same general kind, a "natural" segmentation emerged (see Figure 1).

The next higher level of organization is passage context. At this level we attend also to interactant behavior. For the passage just described, the mother and infant were face-to-face, and the mother vocalized between infant vocalizations. These are two of the main characteristics of the passage context which led to classifying this interaction as "proto-conversation" at the next higher level: social context. Because for our present purpose instrumental activities are considered as social contexts, it is possible for two or more to co-occur. A proto-conversation may be going on while the mother is undressing her baby for his bath. Of course still higher levels of hierarchical organization could be specified, but under the conditions of our observation this would serve no useful purpose because the next higher level would always be the context of our visit to the household with two observers and equipment.

CONCLUSION

We believe that it is important to understand human communication at

---

[13]   This statement is based on a frame-by-frame analysis of a continuous two-minute segment of simultaneously recorded tape and film with continuous spectrographic analysis of all the infant vocal sound occurring during this period. We selected this portion for intensive study because the infant was vocalizing almost all the time with considerable variety. In the analysis, the data from each frame of film was lined up with the point on the voiceprint at which it was taken.

its basic level as it exists between the infant and his caretakers in early extra-uterine life. Without this knowledge we cannot hope to solve many practical and theoretical problems. On the practical side, we need this knowledge in order to optimize child-rearing practices for "normal" infants and to design better practices for handicapped ones. We need this knowledge to solve problems in psychiatry and in education. Theoretically we need to understand the communication in this early period in order to gain insight into the processes of language acquisition, of language universals, of socialization, and of enculturation.

The kind of knowledge we need is of a very precise sort. We will need a great deal more of the kind of exacting close examination of the communicative activities in which infants participate, such as those we have been engaged in (but with more dense sampling of the visual component). General impressions will not give us this knowledge. It will require a great deal of help from modern technology (e.g. low cost portable video recording equipment) in recording, analyzing, and compiling at least the audio-visual data (and eventually data involving other sensory modalities such as touch, pressure, and smell). It will require investigation into developmental anatomy, physiology, and especially into rhythmic activity. We know quite a lot about the neonatal situation but very little about how and how fast it changes. Also required will be field recording in many cultures and subcultures to sort out universals from culture-specific elements. We would recommend that field recording on film or video tape be done in such a way as to facilitate close-grained audio-visual analysis. It will take long hours of looking, listening, and acoustic analyzing to define the behavioral units at successive hierarchical levels so that they can be identified and perhaps eventually, if we can learn to specify them with enough precision, be sorted out automatically.

This is an enterprise which should be of interest to anthropologists and ethnologists because it is basic to an understanding of the transmission of culture from generation to generation. Both infants and adults contribute to enculturation through their communicative activities. We propose that it is this basic level of communication shared by infants and adults which makes enculturation possible, including the acquisition of the mother tongue. There are certainly many variants in the details of parent-infant interaction from culture to culture. What all have in common may represent what is basically human and essential to human survival. We hope anthropologists will share in this investigation.

REFERENCES

ANDREW, R. J.
1962 The situations that evoke vocalization in primates. *Annals of the New York Academy of Sciences* 102:296–315.

ARGYLE, MICHAEL, ADAM KENDON
1967 "The experimental analysis of social performance," in *Advances in experimental social psychology*, volume three, 55–93. New York: Academic Press.

BATESON, GREGORY, MARGARET MEAD
1942 *Balinese character: a photographic analysis.* New York: New York Academy of Sciences.

BATESON, M. C.
1971 The interpersonal context of infant vocalization. *Quarterly Progress Report 100* (January 15, 1971):170–176. Research Laboratory of Electronics, Massachusetts Institute of Technology.

BERNAL, JUDY
1972 Crying during the first ten days of life and maternal responses. *Developmental Medicine and Child Neurology* 14:362–372.

BLOOM, LOIS
1970 *Language development: form and function in emerging grammars.* Cambridge, Massachusetts: M.I.T. Press.

BLURTON JONES, N. G., *editor*
1972 *Ethological studies of child behaviour.* London: Cambridge University Press.

BOCK, PHILIP K.
1962 "The social structure of a Canadian Indian reserve." Unpublished doctoral dissertation, Harvard University.

BOSMA, JAMES F., H. M. TRUBY, JOHN LIND
1965 "Cry motions of the newborn infant," in *Newborn infant cry.* Edited by John Lind, 61–92. Uppsala: Almqvist and Wiksells.

BOWER, T. G. R.
1972 Object perception in infants. *Perception* 1:15–30.

BRAZELTON, T. BERRY
1973 *Neonatal behavioral assessment scale.* Clinics in Developmental Medicine 50. Spastics International Medical Publications. London: William Heinemann Medical Books. Philadelphia: J. B. Lippincott.

BULLOWA, MARGARET
1970 "The start of the language process," in *Actes du Xe congrès international des linguistes, Bucarest, 28 août–2 septembre 1967*, volume three, 191–200. Bucharest: Editions de l'Académie de la République Socialiste de Roumanie.

BULLOWA, MARGARET, LAWRENCE GAYLORD JONES, THOMAS G. BEVER
1964 *Development from vocal to verbal behavior in children.* Monographs for the Society for Research in Child Development 29 (1).

BULLOWA, MARGARET, LAWRENCE GAYLORD JONES, AUDREY DUCKERT
1964 The acquisition of a word. *Language and Speech* 7(2): 107–111.

BYERS, PAUL
1972   "From biological rhythm to cultural pattern: a study of minimal units." Unpublished doctoral dissertation, Columbia University.

CAUDILL, WILLIAM
1972   "Tiny dramas: vocal communication between mother and infant in Japanese and American families," in *Mental health research in Asia and the Pacific*, volume two: *Transcultural research in mental health.* Edited by W. P. Lebra. Honolulu: The University Press of Hawaii.

CONDON, WILLIAM S., W. D. OGSTON
1967   A segmentation of behavior. *Journal of Psychiatric Research* 5:221–235.

CONDON, WILLIAM S., LOUIS W. SANDER
1974   Neonate movement is synchronized with adult speech: interactional participation and language acquisition. *Science* 183:99–101.

CRYSTAL, DAVID
1970   "Prosodic systems and language acquisition," in *Prosodic feature analysis*. Edited by P. Leon, 77–90. Montreal: Didier.
1972   "Non-segmental phonology in language acquisition: a review of issues." Preprinted manuscript for the First International Symposium on Child Language Acquisition, Florence, Sept. 1972.

DEVEREUX, GEORGE
1964   "Mohave voice and speech mannerisms," in *Language in culture and society*. Edited by Dell Hymes, 267–271. New York: Harper and Row.

EIBL-EIBESFELDT, IRENÄUS
1970   *Ethology, the biology of behavior*. New York: Holt, Rinehart and Winston.

EKMAN, PAUL, WALLACE V. FRIESSEN, THOMAS G. TAUSSIG
1969   "VID-R and SCAN: tools and methods for the automated analysis of visual records," in *The analysis of communication content*. Edited by George Gerbner, Ole Rittolsti, Klaus Krippendorff, William J. Paisley, and Philip J. Stone, 297–312. New York: Wiley and Sons.

FICKEN, ROBERT W., MILLICENT S. FICKEN
1966   A review of some aspects of avian field ethology. *The Auk* 83:637–661.

FREEDMAN, DANIEL G.
1967   "A biological view of man's social behavior," in *Social behavior from fish to man*. Edited by William Etkin, 152–188. Chicago: University of Chicago Press.

GARFINKEL, HAROLD
1967   *Studies in ethnomethodology*. Englewood Cliffs, N.J.: Prentice-Hall.

GARFINKEL, HAROLD, HARVEY SACKS
1969   "On formal structures of practical actions," in *Theoretical sociology: perspectives and developments*. Edited by John C. McKinney and Edward Tirejakian. New York: Appleton.

GESELL, ARNOLD
1940   "The first years of life," in *The first five years of life: a guide to the study of the preschool child*. By Arnold Gesell, et al., 16–28. New York: Harper and Brothers.

GUMPERZ, JOHN J., DELL HYMES
1972 *Directions in sociolinguistics: the ethnography of communication.* New York: Holt, Rinehart and Winston.

HAYES, C.
1952 *The ape in our house.* New York: Harper and Brothers.

HOCKETT, CHARLES F.
1960 The origin of speech. *Scientific American* 203:88–96.

JAKOBSON, R.
1969 "Linguistics in its relation to other sciences," in *Actes du Xe Congrès international de linguistes,* volume one. Bucharest: Editions de l'Académie de la République Socialiste de Roumanie.

KARELITZ, SAMUEL, VINCENT R. FISICHELLI
1962 The cry thresholds of normal infants and those with brain damage. *Journal of Pediatrics* 61:679–685.

KENDON, ADAM
1970 Movement coordination in social interaction: some examples described. *Acta Psychologica* 32:100–125.
1972 "Some relationships between body motion and speech," in *Studies in dyadic communication.* Edited by A.W. Siegman and B. Pope, 177–210. Elmsford, New York: Pergamon Press.

KENDON, ADAM, ANDREW FERBER
1973 "A description of some human greetings," in *Comparative ecology and behaviour of primates.* Edited by R.P. Michael and J.H. Crook, 591–668. New York and London: Academic Press.

LIEBERMAN, PHILIP
1967 *Intonation, perception, and language.* Cambridge, Massachusetts: M.I.T. Press.

LIEBERMAN, PHILIP, EDMUND S. CRELIN, DENNIS KLATT
1972 Phonetic ability and related anatomy of the newborn and adult human, Neanderthal man, and the chimpanzee. *American Anthropologist* 74:287–307.

LIND, JOHN, *editor*
1965 *Newborn infant cry.* Uppsala: Almqvist and Wiksells.

LOMAX, ALAN, IRMGARD BARTENIEFF, FORRESTINE PAULAY
1968 "The choreometric coding book," in *Folk song style and culture.* Edited by Alan Lomax, 262–273. Washington, D. C.: American Association for the Advancement of Science.

LYNIP, A. W.
1951 The use of magnetic devices in the collection and analyses of the pre-verbal utterances of an infant. *Genetic Psychology Monographs* 44: 221–262.

MC CARTHY, DOROTHEA
1954 "Language development in children," in *Manual of child psychology* (second edition). Edited by Leonard Carmichael, 492–630. New York: John Wiley and Sons.

MC GREW, W. C.
1972 *An ethological study of children's behavior.* New York and London: Academic Press.

MICHELSSON, KATERINA
  1971   Cry analyses of symptomless low birth weight neonates and of asphyxiated newborn infants. *Acta Pediatrica Scandinavica.* Supplement 216.

MORRIS, CHARLES
  1964   *Signification and significance.* Cambridge, Massachusetts: M.I.T. Press.

PIKE, KENNETH L.
  1967   *Language in relation to a unified theory of the structure of human behavior* (second revised edition). The Hague: Mouton.

PLOOY, F. X.
  1972   *Yearly Report May 1971 – May 1972.* Unpublished document. Netherlands Foundation for the Advancement of Tropical Research (WOTRO), grant number w84-66.

PRECHTL, HEINZ, DAVID BEINTEMA
  1964   *The neurological examination of the full term newborn infant.* Clinics in Developmental Medicine 12. London: Spastics International and William Heinemann.

PRECHTL, H. F. R., K. THEOCELL, A. GRAMSBERGER, J. LIND
  1969   A statistical analysis of cry patterns in normal and abnormal newborn infants. *Developmental Medicine and Child Neurology* 11:142–152.

RHEINGOLD, HARRIET L., J. L. GEWIRTZ, HELEN W. ROSS
  1959   Social conditioning of vocalizing in the infant. *Journal of Comparative and Physiological Psychology* 52:68–73.

RICHARDS, M. P. M., JUDITH BERNAL
  1972   "An observational study of mother-infant interaction," in *Ethological studies in child behaviour.* Edited by N. Blurton Jones. London: Cambridge University Press.

ROBSON, KENNETH S.
  1967   The role of eye-to-eye contact in maternal-infant attachment. *Journal of Child Psychology and Psychiatry* 8:13–25.

SCHAEFFER, JOSEPH
  1970   "Videotape in anthropology: the collection and analysis of data." Unpublished doctoral dissertation, Columbia University.

SCHEFLEN, ALBERT E.
  1964   The significance of posture in communication systems. *Psychiatry* 27:316–331.
  1965   *Stream and structure of communicational behavior.* Behavioral Studies Monograph 1, Eastern Pennsylvania Psychiatric Institute. Philadelphia: Commonwealth of Pennsylvania.

SEBEOK, THOMAS A.
  1968   "Goals and limitations of the study of animal communication," in *Animal communication.* Edited by Thomas A. Sebeok, 3–14. Bloomington: Indiana University Press.

SMITH, W. JOHN
  1965   Message, meaning and context in ethology. *The American Naturalist* 99:405–409.
  1969   Messages of vertebrate communication. *Science* 165:145–150.

SPOCK, BENJAMIN
1968   *Baby and child care* (revised edition). New York: Pocket Books.
TAKEDA, RUMIKO
1965   Development of vocal communication in man-raised Japanese monkeys, I: from birth until the sixth week. *Primates* 6:337–380.
1966   Development of vocal communication in man-raised Japanese monkeys, II: from the seventh to the thirtieth week. *Primates* 7:73–116.
VAN LAWICK-GOODALL, JANE
1968   "A preliminary report on expressive movements and communication in the Gombe stream chimpanzees," in *Primates: studies in adaptation and variability*. Edited by Phyllis C. Jay, 313–374. New York: Holt, Rinehart and Winston.
VAN VLACK, JACQUES D.
1966   "Filming psychotherapy from the viewpoint of a research cinematographer," in *Methods of research in psychotherapy*. Edited by Louis A. Gottschalk and Arthur H. Auerbach, 15–24. New York: Appleton-Century-Crofts.
VUORENKOSKI, V., J. LIND, O. WASZ-HÖCKERT, T. J. PARTANEN
1971   Cry score: a method for evaluating the degree of abnormality in the pain cry response of the newborn and young infant. *Speech Transmission Laboratory, Quarterly Progress and Status Report* 1:68–75.
VUORENKOSKI, V., O. WASZ-HÖCKERT, J. LIND, M. KOIVISTO, T. J. PARTANEN
1971   Training the auditory perception of some specific types of the abnormal pain cry in newborn and young infants. *Speech Transmission Laboratory, Quarterly Progress and Status Report* 4:37–48.
WASZ-HÖCKERT, O., J. LIND, V. VUORENKOSKI, T.J. PARTANEN, E. VALAMME
1968   *The infant cry: a spectrographic and auditory analysis.* Clinics in Developmental Medicine 29. London: Spastics International Medical Publications.
Webster's dictionary
1967   *Webster's new twentieth century dictionary of the English language* (second edition). New York: Publisher's Guild.
WILSON, EDWARD O.
1972   Animal communication. *Scientific American* 227:52–60.
WOLFF, PETER H.
1959   Observations on newborn infants. *Psychosomatic Medicine* 21:110–118.

Early Language Learning:
A Sociolinguistic Approach

MICHAEL A. K. HALLIDAY

This paper is about the learning of the mother tongue in the period extending roughly from six to eighteen months. It might equally have been called a SOCIOSEMANTIC approach, because I am considering the learning of the mother tongue as the learning of a system of meanings. The child who is learning language is learning how to "mean"; in this perspective the linguistic system is seen as a SEMANTIC POTENTIAL, or range of possible meanings, together with the means of their REALIZATION, or expression.[1]

The viewpoint that I am taking is a functional one, in the sense that meaning is in turn related to linguistic function — to the functions that language is made to serve in the life of the growing child. There are two reasons for looking at it in this way. The first is that the functional approach is of value in its own right in that it gives us some insight into the reasons why the child takes the steps he does. If we have a functional viewpoint, we can suggest why it is that the child builds up the system in this particular way — for example, why there comes a point where he has, as it were, to move into the adult language, to build certain of its

This paper was prepared during my tenure of a fellowship at the Center for Advanced Study in the Behavioral Sciences, Stanford, California. I should like to record my gratitude for the opportunity thus afforded.
[1] The term SEMANTIC is not to be understood in the restricted sense of "lexico-semantic," i.e. concerned with the meanings of words. It refers to the totality of meaning in language — the "semological stratum" of Lamb's stratification theory (1970) — whether encoded in vocabulary or not. A child cannot learn word meanings unless he also has words, i.e. an organized vocabulary, not necessarily in the phonological shapes of the adult lexicon. But the contention of this paper is that the learning of language is essentially the learning of a semantic system, and that this process is already well underway before the child moves into the lexical mode of its realization.

features, such as structure and vocabulary, into his total potential.

The second reason for looking at the process from a functional point of view is that it also gives us some insight into why the adult language has evolved in the way it has. The human brain would have been capable of constructing a dozen-and-one different types of semiotic system; why is it, then, that language evolved in this particular way as a semiotic system with the particular properties that it has? If we examine this question developmentally, we can see that the adult linguistic system is structured in a way which very closely reflects its functional origins.[2]

There is still relatively little literature on the early period, before eighteen months or so; probably because it is quite difficult during this period to recognize that the process of language learning is taking place at all. This is the period before the child has really started to use the adult language as his model. It might be said, in fact, that the language that is learnt at this stage owes nothing at all to the adult language that the child hears around him.

This would be an oversimplification, since in fact the child MAY use imitations of the adult phonology as part of the resources for expressing his meaning. But, equally, he MAY NOT; and the point is that it does not matter at this stage whether he does or not. Children vary enormously at this age in the extent to which they attempt to construct some kind of imitative phonological system. It is not entirely clear why they vary in this way; presumably, partly because of differences in their innate ability to imitate adult speech sounds and partly because of differences in the environment — how much speech they hear, but also, and perhaps more important, from how many different people, how much from adults and how much from other children, how much is addressed to them, how much their own efforts are reinforced, and so on. And also, no doubt, because of differences in personality, children differ very much in how they respond to other people's reaction to their own efforts, how far they are perfectionists — there are some children who appear simply not to attempt things, at least in public, until they are satisfied with their own performance.

So there may be all sorts of factors contributing to the very noticeable

---

[2]   Similarly the term FUNCTIONAL is not to be understood in the sense of the specific hypothesis that the child interprets the names of objects by reference to the functions of these objects (see Lewis 1957), or that he learns word classes by reference to structural functions, e.g. agent of a transitive verb, which reflect the potentialities of objects in the real world (see Ingram 1971). It refers to the general notion that the child learns language as a system of meanings in functional contexts, these contexts becoming, in turn, the principle of organization of the adult semantic system (as this is recognized in "functional" theories of language; see Halliday 1973).

difference among children at this age, when some of them attempt a great deal of phonetic imitation, others practically none. In both cases there is a source of difficulty for the investigator. If the child does imitate the phonology of the adult language, then one is inclined to use this as the criterion for deciding whether his sounds are linguistic or not, whereas it is really not the relevant point. His own system is a system of meanings, and some or all of these meanings may be expressed through sounds borrowed from the adult language. On the other hand, none of them may be, and in that case the investigator tends not to recognize that there is any language learning taking place at all. In fact there is: there is a great deal of language learning at this stage. The child is already both responding to and producing signals of a linguistic kind.

In the very first instance, he is learning that there is such a thing as language at all, that vocal sounds are functional in character. He is learning that the articulatory resources with which he is endowed can be put to the service of certain functions in his own life. For the child using his voice is doing something; it is a form of action, and one which soon develops its own patterns and its own significant contexts. With what criteria, then, do we decide that the sounds which the child is making do in some sense constitute a linguistic system, if they are not themselves identifiable as sounds drawn from the adult language — or if they MAY NOT be, since it does not matter at this stage whether they ARE or ARE NOT? Here we have a further reason for adopting a functional standpoint. As any parent knows, we can observe at a very early stage, typically perhaps beginning in the period from six to nine months, that the child begins using vocal sounds consistently and systematically, developing some kind of constant relation between sounds and meanings. But these meanings are not something which can be glossed in terms of the adult language, something which we can enter into a dictionary and which corresponds to the meanings of words and phrases and structures in the adult language. They are meanings which we can interpret if we begin with some kind of functional hypothesis, a hypothesis about what it is that the child is doing with his voice, what it is that he is making the speech sounds do for him; in other words, if we recognize that there are certain fundamental goals or purposes that the child achieves through the use of vocal sound. He uses his voice to order people about, to get them to do things for him; he uses it to demand certain objects or services; he uses it to make contact with people, to feel close to them; and so on. All these things are meaningful actions.

I have attempted a fairly intensive study of the language of one particular child beginning at this early stage; and I have compiled a number of descriptions of his language covering the period from nine to eighteen months. It seems odd to refer to these as "grammars" when the one level that is totally absent from the child's linguistic system at this period is that which we know as grammar (it has neither structure nor vocabulary in it), so let me revert to an earlier terminological practice and call them descriptions. I have written a number of descriptions of this child's language which I think are complete. (If they are, then they are the only complete descriptions of any language that I have ever written or am ever likely to write.) It might be of interest to say briefly what form these descriptions take and how they were arrived at.

I made notes of the child's utterances, using the traditional equipment of the fieldworker, well suited to this stage, a notebook and pencil. I listened in, sometimes taking part in the situation and sometimes staying outside it, hiding behind doors and furniture; and I noted down any meaningful expression that I thought I was observing for the first time. Then I also noted down expressions which I considered to be the same as those I had observed before; not every time I heard them, of course, which would be impossible, but at fairly frequent intervals, the point being that at this stage it is not enough to assume that because some item has been observed to occur it is now part of the child's linguistic system.

Language learning at this stage is not a steady advance; like other forms of learning, it has its ups and downs. Elements of the system come and go; they get learned and they get forgotten, or else modified or altered. For example, for a period of something around four months, the child I was working with, Nigel, had a particular sound which he used for commenting on the presence of an airplane flying overhead, and it was a sound which, it is fair to guess, was his imitation of the noise of the airplane. After a while, it simply dropped out of the system; and then later on, after an interval, a gap of about three months, came another word for an airplane which was an imitation of the adult word. I would not, incidentally, regard these two terms as synonymous. The functional meaning of the item which we interpret as "airplane" in the first instance was rather different from the functional meaning of the second one; the semantic system had changed in the interval. Other elements which entered into the system and subsequently disappeared included a number of forms of demand and of response to offers; these are shown in the accompanying tables.

Then, at intervals of six weeks, I interpreted these notes into a description of the system, so that the system was reinterpreted and described afresh each six weeks. This seemed to be the optimum interval. If I had chosen a longer period, then certain significant steps in the development would have been left out, whereas if I had chosen a shorter period I would have been at the mercy of random nonoccurrences, items which simply had not been observed over the period but which should have been recognized as present in the system. So a month and a half seemed to work out the best for the purpose. This practice I began at nine months, because before the age of nine months Nigel had no system at all; and indeed the very first description represents a stage that I would also regard as prelinguistic, because it does not meet the criteria which I set up for recognizing the presence of a linguistic system. That one I have coded as NL-0, NL standing for "Nigel's language"; so we have NL-0 at nine months, NL-1 at 10½ months, NL-2 at 12 months, NL-3 at 13½ months, NL-4 at 15 months, NL-5 at 16½ months, and NL-6 at 18 months.

Now there are certain theoretical considerations which I think have to be built into any study of language development at this early stage. These center around the concepts of what we may call the CONTENT and the EXPRESSION, or the meaning and the sound. The first point is that these are all you have. That is to say, the child's language system at this stage is a two-level system. It consists of a content and an expression, and each element in the system is a simple sign having just these two aspects: it is a content-expression pair. In other words, the system differs from the adult language system in that it has no intermediate level; it has no stratum of grammar (we should say LEXICOGRAMMAR, since this stratum includes vocabulary) intermediate between the meanings and the sounds. So we shall consider the system as made up of a content and an expression, and each element in the system as itself made up of a meaning and a sound.

Second, there are certain features that we need to specify about the content and the expression. As far as the expression is concerned, one point has already been made: the particular expressions are not, or may not be, imitations of the adult language. In principle, at this stage the expression owes nothing to the adult language at all. It is a system of vocal postures including both articulation and intonation. I say POSTURES because I want to stress that, for the notation of the expression system, the International Phonetic Alphabet is not really appropriate; it is too specific. What one requires is something more in the nature of a prosodic notation, which is postural in this sense; it represents postures which are taken up by the articulatory organs, general configurations rather than the specific bundles of contrastive phonetic features which make up the elements of the adult sound system.

By analogy, we can make the same point about the content. In general, we cannot represent the content of the child's system at this stage in terms of the words and structures of the adult language. We cannot match the child's meanings with the elements of the adult semantic system, which are again much too specific. We need in similar fashion a kind of postural notation for the content. What does this mean in fact? It means we need a form of functional representation. The content, in other words, has to be specified in relation to the functions of language.

This point needs to be elaborated in order to explain why we consider that these early vocalizations constitute language. Let us return, first, to the nature of the system itself. It is very clear that we cannot define language at this early stage in terms of either structures or of words. In the first place, there are no structures; each utterance consists of one element only. This is not to imply that an utterance which consists of one element only can never have a structure; there are many items (clause types, phrase types, etc.) of the adult language which do consist of one element, and these are undoubtedly structures, so that the utterances which stand as tokens of these types are themselves structured. But one cannot recognize a one-element structure except by reference to the existence of at least some structures of two or more elements, and these are not present in the child's system. There are no two-element utterances; hence there is no structure, and hence we cannot describe language acquisition at this stage in terms of structure, or in terms of any measure, mean length of utterance for example, which implies the presence of structure.

In the second place, there are no words. The point has already been made that the child's utterances are not imitations of adult words — they are not words in the sense of items deriving their phonological shape from the English lexicon. Neither, however, are they words in the more important sense of vocabulary items with matching definitions. Putting these two facts together, that there is no structure and that there are no words, we can summarize by saying that the language we are describing has no level of FORM; as we said earlier, it does not possess a lexico-grammar, a level of organization consisting of a grammar and a vocabulary.

This would suffice to exclude it from the domain of language, since language is normally defined as a tristratal system, having a semantics, a grammar, and a phonology. In the last resort, of course, it does not matter whether we call the system the child develops at this stage language or not, provided we relate it to the total picture of language development. But in order to bring out the underlying continuity between the child's system and that of the adult we identify those features of the former which show it to be language in the making.

What it has is a set of content-expression pairs, and this enables us to define one criterion for characterizing and for accepting anything as an element in that system, namely, that there should be a constant relation between the content and the expression. Let me give an illustration of this. Whenever, for example, Nigel says *nananana* it always means something like "I want that thing now"; and when he expresses the meaning "I want that thing now" by means of a vocal symbol, he always does so by saying *nananana*. This meaning-sound relation can therefore be part of a language. Let us refer to this requirement of a constant relation between content and expression as the requirement of SYSTEMATICITY.

The other requirement that we can set up on the basis of the child's system is that of FUNCTIONALITY. In order to qualify as part of his language, the child's vocalizations were required to be not only systematic but also functional. This means that the content should be such that it can be interpreted by reference to a prior established set of functions. To continue with the same example, the meaning "I want that thing now" is derivable from one of the functions that we are postulating as the set of original developmental functions from which the child starts, namely the instrumental function, the use of language to satisfy the child's material needs. In other words, there is no system of content as such, in abstraction from the context of situation. There is only content WITH RESPECT; that is, with respect to the functions that language serves in the life of the developing child.

We are not here setting up some arbitrary meanings that are, as it were, floating in the air. We are setting up meanings in terms of certain generalized contexts of language use. The child is learning to be and to do, to act and interact in meaningful ways. He is learning a system of meaningful behavior; in other words, he is learning a semiotic system. Part of his meaningful action is linguistic. But none of it takes place in isolation; it is always within some social context. So the content of an utterance is the meaning that it has with respect to a given function, to one or other of the things that the child is making language do for him. It is a semiotic act which is interpretable by reference to the total range of semiotic options, the total meaning potential that the child has accessible to him at that moment.

The question then is: what are the functions that we recognize as determining the child's semiotic system at this stage, and how do we arrive at them? Here we have, as always, to keep a sense of proportion, and to try and face both ways, shunting between sensible observation on the one hand and imaginative but at the same time goal-directed theory on the other. On the one hand, we can see ourselves, as any parent can see, what the child is doing when he is uttering speech sounds, and what contributions these speech sounds are making to his total activity. We have some reasonably clear impression of function in a context; and we can characterize this very adequately in quite general terms in relation to the context of a situation. In other words, proceeding solely from observation, and using just the amount of common sense the researcher ought to possess if he did not suspend it while on duty, we could reach generalizations such as "this child says *nananana* whenever he wants to get something handed to him." And we could reach this on a purely inductive basis, or as nearly inductive as one ever gets: the educated adult cannot really proceed without imposing some kind of theory as he goes along.

On the other hand, while we could draw some interesting conclusions in this way, there would be a very severe limitation on how far we could go. If we want to understand the nature of the developmental process, and in particular to make the bridge between the language that the child creates for himself at the very first stage and the adult language that he comes out with at the end, then we have to relate the generalizations that we make about these uses of language to some hypothesis about the overall functions of language in the life of social man.

Clearly we will not be able to do this from a purely empirical standpoint, since by the time a child is, say, two and one-half, we will no longer be able to give any kind of significant general account of his uses of language. By this time, like the adult, he already uses language for so many different purposes that if we try to list them we shall simply get an endless catologue; or rather, we shall get a whole series of catalogues with no reason for preferring one over another. We have to find some other more theoretical basis for matching the observations about language use with some theoretical construct of a functional nature. And there are two possible sources for this type of a theory of language functions, one from within language itself and one from outside it.

Let us look at each of these briefly in turn. If we consider first the linguistic system itself, we find that the adult language displays certain features which can only be interpreted in functional terms. These are found, naturally, in the area of meaning: the semantic system of the adult language is very clearly functional in its composition. It reflects the fact that language has evolved in the service of certain particular human needs. But what is really significant is that this functional principle is carried over and built into the grammar, so that the internal organization of the grammatical system is also functional in character. If we consider language as a meaning potential, an open-ended and theoretically infinite range of options in meaning, then we find that these options are grouped into a very small number of sets such that each set of options is subject to strong internal constraints but very weak external constraints. In other words, when the speaker makes selections in the system (which are essentially selections in meaning), a choice that he makes in one set of options has a great deal of effect on the other choices that he makes within the same set, but practically no effect on the choices he makes among the options in the other sets. These sets of options constitute the functional components of the semantic system.

Broadly speaking we can characterize these functional components as follows. First, there are the IDEATIONAL options, those relating to the content of what is said. With this component, the speaker expresses his experience of the phenomena of the external world, and of the internal world of his own consciousness. This is what we might call the OBSERVER function of language, language as a means of talking about the real world. It also includes a subcomponent concerned with the expression of logical relations which are first perceived and interpreted by the child as relations between things.

Second, there is the INTERPERSONAL component of the semantic system, reflecting the function of language as a means whereby the speaker participates in the speech situation. This we may call the INTRUDER function of language. Through the options in this component, the speaker adopts a role, or a set of roles, *vis-à-vis* the participants in the speech situation, and also assigns roles to the other participants, while accepting (or rejecting) those that are assigned to him; he expresses his own judgments, his own attitudes, his own personality, and in so doing exerts certain effects on the hearers. These have been known as the "expressive-conative" functions of language. The options that the speaker takes up in this area of meaning, while they are strongly interrelated among one another, are in large measure independent of the options which he takes up of an ideational kind, those under the first heading.

And then, finally, there is a third semantic function which is in a sense an enabling function, one without which the other two could not be put into effect; this we shall refer to as the TEXTUAL function, the function that language has of creating text. It is through the options in this component that the speaker is enabled to make what he says operational in the context, as distinct from being merely citational, like lists of words in a dictionary, or sentences in a grammar book. The textual function we can regard as being that which breathes life into language; in another metaphor, it provides texture, and without texture there is no text.

We can take account of this functional organization of the semantic system of the adult language in helping us to determine what are likely to be the developmental functions from which the child starts. Somehow, the child moves from the one to the other, from his own system to that of the adult; and our hypothesis must be such as at least to show that it would have been possible for him to make the transition. Ideally, of course, we would like it to be rather stronger, in the sense that it should show some clear motivation why the child should move into the adult language as the means of extending the functional potential that he already has. All this is looking at the question from inside language.

Outside language, we turn to some kind of social theory that accommodates language as an essential element, and in particular one that embodies some notion of functional contexts of language use that are likely to be critical for the child. Here we turn, obviously, to the work of Basil Bernstein (1971), whose theory of social structure and social change embodies a concept of cultural transmission in which he has been able to identify a number of what he calls "critical socializing contexts," types of situation involving the use of language which play a key part in the transmission of culture to the child. Bernstein has identified a certain number of such contexts in what amounts to a sociological theory of linguistic functions. At one point he enumerates four such contexts, which he refers to as the regulative, the instructional, the imaginative or innovative, and the interpersonal. The fact that in Bernstein's work language is the central factor in cultural transmission makes it likely that contexts which Bernstein recognizes as critical for cultural transmission will also be critical in the language learning process.

We can now put together the various strands that make up a pattern in thinking about language in functional terms: in the first place, observations relating to the use of language by a very small child and, in the second place, theoretical considerations about linguistic function, which break down in turn into those which are essentially linguistic in nature, functional theories of language and of the semantic system, and those which are essentially extralinguistic in nature, sociological theories embodying a concept of cultural transmission and processes of socialization.

Taking these factors into account I suggest a set of functions which would serve for the interpretation of the language of a very young child; that is, as an initial hypothesis for some kind of functional or sociolinguistic approach to early language development. The particular set of functions which I suggest is as follows: (1) instrumental, (2) regulatory, (3) interactional, (4) personal, (5) heuristic, and (6) imaginative. Let me comment briefly on each of these in turn.

1.   The INSTRUMENTAL function is the function that language serves of satisfying the child's material needs, of enabling him to obtain the goods and services that he wants. It is the "I want" function of language; and it is likely to include a general expression of desire, some element meaning simply "I want that object there" (present in the context), as well as perhaps other expressions relating to specific desires, responses to questions "Do you want ...?" and so on.

2.   The REGULATORY function is related to this, but it is also distinct. It is the function of language as controlling the behavior of others, something which the child recognizes very easily because language is used on him in this way: language is used to control his own behavior and he soon learns that he can turn the tables and use it to control others. The regulatory is the "Do as I tell you" function of language. The difference between this and the instrumental is that in the instrumental the focus is on the goods or services required and it does not matter who provides them, whereas regulatory utterances are directed towards a particular individual, and it is the behavior of that individual that is to be influenced. Typically therefore this function includes meanings such as, again, a generalized request "Do that," meaning "Do what you have just been doing" (in the context), "Do that again"; as well as various specific demands, particularly in the form of suggestions "Let's do ...," such as "Let's go for a walk," "Let's play this game," "Let's sing a song," and so forth.

3.   The INTERACTIONAL function is what we might gloss as the "Me and you" function of language. This is language used by the child to interact with those around him, particularly his mother and others that are important to him, and it includes meanings such as the generalized greetings "Hello," "Pleased to see you," and also responses to calls "Yes?" as well as more specific forms. For example, the first names of particular individuals that the child learns are typically used with a purely interactional function; and there may be other specific meanings of an interactional kind involving the focusing of attention on particular objects in the environment, some favorite objects of the child which are used as channels for interacting with those around him.[3]

---

[3]   In view of the great variety in young children's use of the *mummy* and *daddy* forms and the continuing discussion around the question whether they are or are not proper names, it should be made clear that in Nigel's system these items functioned unequivocally as proper names: they were used only interactionally (and never, for example, as expression of a demand), and were attached from the start uniquely to specific individuals. The forms themselves had the distinctive phonological shape that Nigel reserved for proper names and no instance was noted of their use in any other context. See Tables 2 to 5.

4.   Fourth, there is the PERSONAL function. This is language used to express the child's own uniqueness; to express his awareness of himself, in contradistinction to his environment, and then to mold that self — ultimately, language used in the development of the personality. This includes, thus, expressions of personal feelings, of participation and withdrawal, of interest, pleasure, disgust, and so forth, and extends later on to more specific intrusion of the child as a personality into the speech situation. We might call this the "Here I come" function of language.

5.   Fifth, once the boundary between the child himself and his environment is beginning to be recognized, then the child can turn toward the exploration of the environment; this is the HEURISTIC function of language, the "Tell me why" function, that which later on develops into the whole range of questioning forms that the young child uses. At this very early stage, in its most elementary form the heuristic use of language is the demand for a name, which is the child's way of categorizing the objects of the physical world; but it soon expands into a variety of more specific meanings.

6.   Finally we have the IMAGINATIVE function, which is the function of language whereby the child creates an environment of his own. As well as moving into, taking over, and exploring the universe which he finds around him, the child also uses language for creating a universe of his own, a world initially of pure sound, but which gradually turns into one of story and make-believe and "let's pretend," and ultimately into the realm of poetry and imaginative writing. This we may call the "Let's pretend" function of language.

Later on there is in fact a seventh to be added to the list; but the initial hypothesis was that this seventh function, although it is the one which is undoubtedly dominant in the adult's use of language, and even more so in the adult's image of what language is, is one which does not emerge in the child until considerably after the others. This is the one that we can call the INFORMATIVE function of language, the "I've got something to tell you" function. Now, the idea that language can be used as a means of communicating information to someone who does not already possess that information is a very sophisticated one which depends on the internalization of a whole complex set of linguistic concepts that the young child does not possess. It is the only purely intrinsic function of language, the only use of language in a function that is definable solely by reference to language. And it is one which is not at all present in the phase of language development which we are considering here. In Nigel's case, for example, it did not begin to appear until a much later stage, at about 22 months. It is useful, however, to note it at this point, particularly because it tends to predominate in adult thinking about language. This, in fact, is one of the reasons why the adult finds it so difficult to interpret the image of language that the very young child has internalized. The young child has a very clear notion of the functions of his own linguistic system. He knows very well what he can do with it. But what he can do with it is not at all the same thing as what the adult does (still less what the adult thinks he does) with his linguistic system.

These, then, are the initial functions with respect to which we identify the content of what the child is learning to say, the meanings that are present in this very early linguistic system. All those utterances which we identify as language can be interpreted in the light of some such set of functions as these. Within each one of these functions, we shall recognize a range of alternatives, a range of options in meaning, that the child has mastered at this particular stage; this is the set of possibilities that is open and accessible to him in this particular function of language.

It is this notion of a range of alternatives, a set of options, that I think provides the real foundation of a functional approach to early language development. Somewhat surprisingly, perhaps, the distinction between what is and what is not part of the system seems very easy to draw at this stage; at least I found it so. It was very rare that there was any doubt as to whether a particular sound was or was not functional in the defined terms, and so was or was not an expression in the language.

This is part of the value of the functional approach: it provides a criterion for identifying what is language and what is not. It should be noted that this criterion excludes all instances which are interpreted as linguistic practice. When the child is practicing speech sounds, or later on words, phrases, structures, or whatever they are, this is not regarded as language in use; it is not an instance of meaning. This is merely tantamount to saying that the learning of a particular system cannot be categorized in terms of the use of that system, and therefore in the present study those utterances which were purely directed towards the learning of the system were omitted from consideration. It happened that Nigel was a child who did very little practice of this kind; some children apparently do a great deal more.

Tables 1 to 6 show the system of options that Nigel had in his language at each of the six-week intervals which I referred to earlier, from $10\frac{1}{2}$ months to 18 months. At 9 months it was possible to identify just two expressions which apparently fulfilled the criteria for being language; they had constant meanings which could be interpreted in terms of these functions, one being interactional, the other personal. These need hardly be regarded as constituting a linguistic system, because in each case there were no alternatives; there was one possible meaning only in this function, and no choice.

The set of options that Nigel has at 10½ months, represented in Table 1, is I think the earliest that we can significantly characterize as a linguistic system. At 10½ months, the child can already use his vocal resources in four out of the six functions that we have identified. In the instrumental function he has one utterance which is a general demand meaning something like "Give me that" and referring always to some object which is clearly specified in the environment.

This contrasts with the specific demand for a favorite object, in this case a toy bird; and it is possible that this represents the one element in the system whose expression is in fact borrowed from the adult language: it may be an imitation of the word *bird*. In the regulatory function he has a generalized request, which is always directed to a specific individual, requiring him or her to do something that is again clearly specified in the context, usually by the fact of its having been done immediately before, so that it is equivalent to "Do that again"; this contrasts with an intensified form of the same meaning which carries with it the additional feature of urgency, which I have attempted to convey by the gloss "Do that right now."

In the interactional function he has a couple of initiating expressions and one response. Of the former, one is a form of greeting, used typically when another person comes newly to his attention, for example someone coming into the room as he wakes up; the utterance directs attention to a particular object, typically a picture, which is then used as the channel for the interaction. The nearest one can get to this in a gloss is something like "How nice to see you, and shall we look at this picture together?" suggesting that the picture becomes the focus of what is in fact a form of interaction taking place through language.

The other is again an intensified form, an impatient greeting unmediated by any joint action, something like "Nice to see you, and why weren't you here before?" In addition there is a response form, used in response to a call or greeting when someone else begins to interact verbally with him. And finally there is a little set of meanings within the personal function, five in all, one of which expresses a state of withdrawal and the others the opposite, a state of participation, involving the expression of some form of pleasure or of interest.

The whole system comprises a set of twelve distinct meanings, and this represents the total semantic potential that the child has at this stage. It is not, of course, his total semiotic potential, if we define "semiotic" as the information system that is embodied in the whole of the child's behavior. But it is his total semantic system — that part of the semiotic that he encodes by means of vocal symbols. It represents what the child can do linguistically, or in other words what he can mean.[4]

We have said that the child's expressions at this stage owe nothing to the adult language. The sounds he makes are not, in general, imitations of the sounds of English words. What then is the origin of these sounds? This is something to which I would certainly not attempt to give any kind of general answer. But in one or two instances it is possible to derive a hint which throws an interesting sidelight on classical theories of the origins of language.

At least one of the expressions in Nigel's earliest linguistic system originates as an imitation by the child of a sound that he heard himself make naturally. In NL-1 the form $ǵ^wɣɪǵ^wɪǵ^wɣɪ$ appears, interpreted as having the meaning of withdrawal, and more specifically "I'm sleepy; I want to go to sleep," within the personal function. Now this sound was originally a sound which the child made as an automatic accompaniment of the process of going to sleep. It corresponds to a vocalization of the noise of sucking, perhaps with thumb or bottle in mouth. There came a point when the child transferred the sound into his linguistic system as the expression of one of the meanings in that system. It is interesting to note that shortly afterwards he once again reinterpreted the same sound, this time in the imaginative function as a form of play: at about $13\frac{1}{2}$ months, Nigel would curl up on the floor and produce this sound in a pretense of going to sleep. There are one or two other sounds in Nigel's early systems that could possibly be traced to similar origins.

But there is no obvious source for the great majority of the child's expressions, which appear simply as spontaneous creations of the glossogenic process. As far as the content of the child's early systems is concerned, the same observation might be made: it is not, in general, derived from the meanings of the adult language. No doubt, however, the adult language does exert an influence on the child's semantic system from a very early stage, since the child's utterances are interpreted by those around him in terms of their own semantic systems.

In other words, whatever the child means the message which gets across is one which makes sense and is translatable into the terms of the adult language. It is in this interpretation that the child's linguistic

---

[4] We use this formulation in preference to "what he knows," considering language development not as the acquisition of knowledge but as the development of a behavior potential. In a sociolinguistic perspective there is no need to postulate a level of cognitive organization between "can do" and "can mean "

efforts are reinforced, and in this way the meanings that the child starts out with gradually come to be adapted to the meanings of the adult language. We have no way at this stage of following through this process in any detail; but it is possible to see in the progression from one stage to the next in Nigel's developing linguistic system how the functional meanings that he expresses gradually become more and more recognizable, as they come to look more and more like the meanings that are encoded in the adult language.

Let us give an example of the way in which the meanings that the child expresses do not correspond exactly to the meanings of the adult language, and the distinctions that the child makes do not correspond to the adult's linguistic distinctions. In NL-3 there is a form *yi yi yi yi* (high level tone) which Nigel used to respond when he was asked whether he wanted a particular object to be given to him, meaning something like "Yes, I want that." There was also a form *a:* (high rise-fall) meaning something like "Yes, I want you to do what you have just offered to do," used in response to questions beginning "Shall I ...?" — for example "Shall I draw the curtains?" or "Do you want me to put some music on?" These two meanings represent options within the instrumental function. The first is a response to the offer of some object, which is either named or referred to, e.g. by *that* (or both); while the second is a response to the offer of a service, one which may also involve the naming of objects but which itself refers to the performance of an action. The two have quite different intonation patterns; the first is high level, which does not occur systematically in adult English, whereas the second one has something very like the rise-fall tone (tone 5) of the adult language, which gives a sense of "Yes, you've got it: THAT's what I'm after." The distinction is expressed in the description as a system of options within the instrumental function, subsystem of the general meaning of RESPONSE; the meaning RESPONSE is in turn contrasted with the meaning of INITIATION, the initiating of a demand by the child himself.

Now any translation of these response items such as *yes, please,* or an explanation such as "positive response to a question," would be quite inadequate as an interpretation of these expressions. At this stage, Nigel cannot respond to questions at all, except those in which the answer serves one of the functions that is in his linguistic system, either an instrumental function or a regulatory function. In other words, he can respond to questions of the type "Do you want?" or "Shall I?" but not to questions seeking information such as "Is there?" or "Have you got?"

It is not until after 18 months that he begins to be able to respond to questions of this kind, and when he does, he does it in a very different way. There is nothing in the child's system that corresponds to the general notion of question and answer. These notions depend on a concept of dialogue, of social roles that are defined by the communication process; this concept the child has not yet mastered, and will not master until he is in the process of transition from his own protolanguage to the adult language.

Let me take another example. In NL-5 Nigel has two requests for joint action of the type expressed in adult language by *let's*; these are "Let's go for a walk" and "Let's draw a picture." The first is expressed by a sound of his own invention, a very slow vibration of the vocal cords; the other first by a sound which is probably an imitation of the word *draw* and later more often as *bow-wow*, meaning etymologically "Let's draw a dog," but now generalized to a sense of "Let's draw a picture." Now these are regulatory in function — they refer to the behavior of a particular individual; and within the regulatory function they are specific, as contrasted with the general expression meaning "Do that." Further, they are requests for joint action of the "Let's" type, as distinct from requests for action on the part of the other person, such as "Come for lunch." So at this stage Nigel has a little system of just two options within the meaning of "Let's"; and we can see here the earliest manifestations of what gradually develops into an important area of the adult grammatical system, namely the system of MOOD.

This is not the place for a detailed commentary on each stage in the child's development. It is hoped that the representations given in NL-1 to NL-5 are reasonably self-explanatory. They show at each stage the child's meaning potential represented as a network of options deriving from the small set of initial functions that were postulated at the start. They show the child's meaning potential developing from an initial point at which he is able to express about twelve distinct meanings to one in which the number of meanings has increased to somewhere around fifty. We have represented these meanings in "systemic" terms; that is to say, as options in the environment of other options. In other words, language is being represented essentially not as structure, but as system. The underlying concept is one of choice: EITHER this MEANING OR that. Structure, the combination of elements one with another (BOTH this CONSTITUENT AND that), is regarded as a mechanism by which meanings are expressed; moreover it is only one of the possible mechanisms, and one which is not yet present in the child's linguistic system at this stage. But this does not prevent us from recognizing that the child has a language.

NL-5 represents the final stage in what we may refer to as Phase I of the child's language development, the phase in which the child is developing a protolanguage of his own. From this point on, he begins the transition into the adult linguistic system. NL-5 is already characterized by the presence of a considerable number of expressions that are taken from the adult language, recognizable words of English; but, more important, it is characterized by the opening up of new functional meanings. The new developments that are taking place can be seen in the sort of exchange that begins to appear in the period around 16½ months. Here is a typical sequence of events.

The child asks [ádᵛdà] "What's that?" The answer is given *That's an egg*. The child imitates *egg* [aₗyi:], repeating the sound a considerable number of times. Shortly afterwards, the child sees the object in question, or a picture of it, and produces the same sound; and after a further interval he begins to use the same sound without the stimulus of the object, but in terms of one of the functions for which he uses language, for example, in the instrumental meaning of "I want an egg." Then, when he starts to engage in dialogue proper, the word turns up in contexts such as the following (near the end of NL-6, at 15½ months), where the function is no longer obviously interpretable in the earlier terms:

MOTHER: Did you tell Daddy what you had for tea?
NIGEL (to mother, excitedly): aᵛì ... ò̤ ... aᵛì ... aᵛì 'egg, ooh! egg, egg!' gɔgˡgɔgʷa 'cockadoodledoo' (= cornflakes, because of picture on packet; also = weathercock on church so, having just returned from walk, continues with inventory of things seen) tìkᵃ 'and sticks!'
MOTHER: You didn't have cornflakes for tea!
NIGEL: lò̤u 'and holes!'
MOTHER: You didn't have sticks and holes for tea!
NIGEL (returning to the subject in hand): dò̤uba 'and toast.'

It might be thought, as I myself thought at first, that the principal incentive for the child to learn the vocabulary of the adult language would be of a pragmatic nature, that he would learn the new words primarily in order to be able to ask for the objects they represented. But NL-6, which shows a very sudden increase in the total number of meanings to something of the order of 200, includes a considerable number of items that it would be very unlikely to find in a pragmatic context: words such as *bubble, star, blood, eyelid,* and *weathercock*. If one comes to examine carefully the utterances that the child makes at this stage and the particular contexts in which they occur, it turns out that the majority of those in which the newly acquired vocabulary items figure are not pragmatic in function at all. They occur, rather, in contexts of observation, recall, and prediction.

First, the child uses the new word to comment on the object as it comes to his attention; for example *stick*, translated as "I see a stick." Second, two or three weeks later, these words come to be used in contexts of recall: not "I see a stick" but "I saw a stick when I was out for a walk." In such instances Nigel often produced long lists of words, for example ("I saw") [kàkàbàbàbàuwàugɔʔ¹gɔʔ¹tìkᵘtìkᵘlɔulɔu] 'I saw *cars, buses, dogs, weathercocks, sticks, and holes,*' likewise *sticks, holes, stones, trains, balls, and buses.* Third, after another short interval again of a week or two, the same items appear in contexts of prediction: "I shall see sticks when I go out for a walk," typically said as he was being dressed to go out.

What is the function of utterances of this kind? Clearly they are not pragmatic in the sense that utterances of an instrumental or regulatory nature can be said to be pragmatic; but equally clearly they are not meaningless. In terms of the child's semiotic potential at this stage, it seems that their function is a learning function; not in the sense that they contribute to the child's learning of language — they are quite distinct from instances where the child is practicing the items in question, instances which we have already rejected from our functional analysis of the system — but in the sense that they contribute to the child's learning about his environment.

The language is being used in a function that we might code as MATHETIC. The origin of this function can be found in the initial set of functions from which we started out. Just as we can regard the PRAGMATIC use of the new words as arising directly from the instrumental and regulatory functions, so we can interpret this MATHETIC function as arising primarily from a combination of two others, the personal and the heuristic. It is possible in fact to trace a direct development from some of the earlier meanings which the child had evolved under these headings: expressions of pleasure and interest on the one hand, and on the other hand the demand for the naming of an object, typically a picture, with which the child was already familiar.

Contexts of this kind, in which from about NL-4 onwards Nigel would begin to combine the personal and the heuristic in a little series of interchanges, a sort of protodialogue, lead gradually and naturally into contexts in which the child is using newly acquired vocabulary for the purpose of categorizing the phenomena of the environment and relating them to his own experience. At this stage, therefore, we can see a process of functional generalization taking place whereby the newly acquired words and structures are put to use either in a context which we are labeling pragmatic, arising from the instrumental and regulatory functions of Phase I, or in a context of the kind that we are calling mathetic, which arises out of the personal and heuristic functions, the interactional function making some contribution to both.[5]

This interpretation is one which we are led to quite naturally from an inspection of the utterances which Nigel was making at this time, utterances such as on the one hand *more meat, mend train, come over there, draw for me*, which are clearly pragmatic in the context, and on the other hand *green car, black cat, tiny red light*, and *bubbles round-and-round*, which are equally clearly not in any sense pragmatic but are representations of what the child observes around him. But it happened that Nigel made the distinction between the pragmatic and mathetic function totally explicit in his own expressions, because from this point on for six months or more, he spoke all pragmatic utterances on a rising tone and all others on a falling tone.

The rising tone meant in effect that some form of response was required, a response either in the form of action or, after a time and increasingly throughout this period, a verbal response. The falling tone meant that no response was required, and the utterance was, as it were, self-sufficient. This particular way of encoding the pragmatic/mathetic dinstinction is of course Nigel's own individual strategy; but it is likely that the opposition itself is the basis of the child's functional system at this stage, since not only is it observable in the child's own use of language but, more significantly, it serves as a transition to the functional organization of the adult language. It is the child's way of incorporating the functions into the linguistic system. In this way he arrives ontogenetically at a linguistic system whose major semantic components are in fact based on a functional opposition, that between the ideational and the interpersonal functions which we referred to earlier.

Essentially the pragmatic function of the child's transitional phase, Phase II, is that which leads into the interpersonal component of the adult system, while the mathetic leads into the ideational component. The child learns at this stage that in any use of language he is essentially being either an OBSERVER or an INTRUDER. He is an observer to the extent that the language is serving as the means whereby he encodes his own experience of the phenomena around him, while himself remaining apart. He is an intruder to the extent that he is using language to participate, as a means of action in the context of situation.

But whereas at the beginning of Phase II, the child can use language in

[5]   Cf. Lewis' opposition (1951) of "manipulative" and "declarative" functions.

only one function at a time, being either observer or intruder but not both, by the end of Phase II he has learned to be both things at once; and this is the essential property of the adult language. In Phase II, which in the case of Nigel begins rather suddenly at stage NL-6 (16½ to 18 months) and continues until roughly the end of his second year, the child is making the transition from his own protolanguage to the adult linguistic system, and this transition involves two fundamental steps.

In the first place, the child has to interpolate a third level in between the content and the expression of his developmental system. The adult language is not a two-level system but a three-level system; it is composed not merely of meanings and sounds, but has another level of coding in between, one which, using folk linguistic terminology, we may refer to as a level of WORDING. In technical terms, in addition to a semantics and a phonology, he has a level of linguistic form, a lexicogrammar.

And the need for the lexicogrammatical level of coding intermediate between meaning and sound arises not merely because of the increased semantic load that the system has to bear, but also because there has to be a means of mapping on to one another meanings deriving from different functional origins. This is achieved by grammatical structure. Grammatical structure is a device which enables the speaker to be both observer and intruder at the same time; it is a form of polyphony in which a number of melodies unfold simultaneously, one semantic "line" from each of the functional components. With a grammar one is free to mean two things at once.[6]

The second of the two fundamental steps that the child takes in embarking on Phase II, the transition to the adult language, is that of learning to engage in dialogue. Dialogue is, for him, a very new concept. Dialogue involves the adoption of roles which are social roles of a new and special kind, namely those which are defined by language itself. We may refer to these as COMMUNICATION ROLES.

A speaker of the adult language, every time he says anything, is adopting a communication role himself, and at the same time is assigning another role, or a role choice, to the addressee, who, in his turn, has the option of accepting or rejecting the role that is assigned to him. In Phase I, the child has no concept of dialogue or of communication roles; but toward the end of this phase he begins to get the idea that language is itself a form of interaction, and he starts to engage in dialogue. Nigel, at the same time as he was beginning to build a grammar and vocabulary,

---

[6] As this stage it becomes possible to interpret the child's semantic development in terms of a lexicosemantic theory such as that of "semantic feature acquisition" proposed by Eve V. Clark (i.p.).

also took the first steps in dialogue, learning to interact linguistically in a limited number of ways. He learned to respond to an information or "Wh-" type question, one in which the respondent is required to fill in a missing item, such as "What are you eating?" He learned to respond to a command, not only obeying the instruction it contained, but verbalizing the process as he did so. He learned to respond to a statement, not only repeating it but continuing the conversation by adding his own contribution. And, finally, he learned to initiate dialogue himself, having first of all only one option under this heading, namely the question "What is that?" He could not at this stage ask any other questions, nor could he respond to questions of the confirmation or "Yes/no" type. But he had clearly internalized the notion that language defines a set of social roles which are to be taken on by the participants in the speech situation; and this is the essential step towards the mastering of the final one in the list of functions that we enumerated at the beginning, namely the informative function.

The use of language to inform is a very late stage in the linguistic development of the child, because it is a function which depends on the recognition that there are functions of language which are solely defined by language itself. All the other functions in the list are extrinsic to language. They are served by and realized through language, but they are not defined by language. They represent the use of language in contexts which exist independently of the linguistic system. But the informative function has no existence independent of language itself. It is an intrinsic function which the child cannot begin to master until he has grasped the principle of dialogue, which means until he has grasped the fundamental nature of the communication process.

Some way on into what we are calling Phase II, Nigel did begin to use language in the informative function; but when he did so he introduced into the system a semantic distinction of his own, another example of a semantic distinction that does not exist in the adult language, between giving information that is already known to the hearer and giving information that is not known. By this stage, Nigel had learned the grammatical distinction of declarative and interrogative; but he used this distinction not to express the difference between statement and question, since as we have already noted he had at this stage no concept of asking "Yes/no" questions, but to make a distinction between the two types of information giving. He used the declarative form to give information that he knew was already possessed by the hearer, to represent experience that had been shared by both; and he used the interrogative form to convey information that he knew the hearer did not possess, to refer to an experience which had not been shared between the two. So, for example, if he was building a tower and the tower fell down, he would say to someone who was present and who was taking part with him *The tower fell down.* But to someone who had not been in the room at the time, and for whom the information was new, he would say *Did the tower fall down?* This is a rather useful semantic distinction, and it seems a pity it should be lost in the adult language.

The important point concerning the two major new developments that define the beginning of Phase II, the learning of grammar and the learning of dialogue, is that they take place at the same time. These are the two essential characteristics of the adult linguistic system that are absent from the protolanguage that the child creates for himself. It is as if up to a certain point the child was working his own way through the history of the human race, creating a language for himself to serve those needs which exist independently of language and which are an essential feature of human life at all times and in all cultures.

Then comes a point when he abandons the phylogenetic trail and, as it were, settles for the language that he hears around him, taking over in one immense stride its two fundamental properties as a system: one, its organization on three levels, with a lexicogrammatical level of wording intermediate between the meaning and the sounding, a level which generates structures which enable him to mean more than one thing at a time; and two, its ability to function as an independent means of human interaction, as a form of social intercourse which generates its own set of roles and role relationships, whose meaning is defined solely by the communication process that language brings about.

These two developments take place more or less simultaneously. They are the crucial features of Phase II, which we have defined as the phase that is transitional between the child's protolanguage and his mastery of the adult linguistic system. By the end of Phase II, the child has effectively mastered the linguistic SYSTEM of the adult language. He will spend the rest of his life learning the language itself.[7]

Let us attempt now to summarize the main points of this presentation. We started with the hypothesis that learning the mother tongue consists in mastering certain basic functions of language and in developing a meaning potential in respect to each. The hypothesis was that these functions, namely, the instrumental, the regulatory, the interactional, the personal, the heuristic, and the imaginative, represented the developmental functions of language, those in respect to which the child first

---

[7] See Halliday (i.p.) for further discussion of Phase II.

created a system of meanings; and that some ability to mean in these functions, or in a majority of them, was a necessary and sufficient condition for the learning of the adult language. It is presumed that these functions are universals of human culture, and it is not unreasonable to think of them as the starting point not only for linguistic ontogeny but also for the evolution of the linguistic system.

Within each function the child develops a set of options, a range of alternatives whose meanings are derived from the function in question. The language which the child develops in this way is a simple content-expression system. It contains no grammar and no vocabulary; that is to say, no level of coding intermediate between the semantics and the phonology. It represents a meaning potential, what the very small child can do with his language, together with the resources for expressing the meanings in question. What the child can do at this stage is not a great deal, but it is significant in terms of his own needs.

In the case of Nigel we find the system expanding from an initial stage, NL-1 at $10\frac{1}{2}$ months, in which he has twelve choices in meaning at his command, to a stage, NL-5 at $16\frac{1}{2}$ months, when the total number of semantic options has reached fifty. This is still, of course, a very slender resource by comparison with what we know as language; but it is worth noting not only that each element in the system is used very frequently — on numerous occasions, not counting repetitions — but also, and more significantly, that some elements are very general in their application.

In each function there tends to be one semantically unmarked term, whose meaning is equivalent to that function in its most general scope; for example, "I want that" represents the generalized meaning of language in the instrumental function, where "that" is clearly indicated by the context. This appears to be the origin of what I have called elsewhere the "GOOD REASON" PRINCIPLE in the adult language, a very general and all-pervasive principle whereby, at very many points in the system, the speaker has an option which is unmarked in the sense that it is the option that he selects unless there is good reason for selecting something else. In many of these functions, the child will have one option which he selects as the expression of a general meaning in the absence of any reason for selecting a more specific option within the same function.

In Phase I the child uses the vocal resources of intonation and articulation. He knows from observing linguistic interaction around him that these resources are used by others in meaningful ways. He cannot, of course, copy the particular sound-meaning correspondences, but he invents a set of his own, using, for example, rise and fall in pitch to express meaning distinctions that exist within his own system. For some time, often perhaps for about 6 or 9 months, the child continues to expand the system that he is creating along these lines by adding new semantic contrasts within the existing range of functions; he goes on inventing his own sounds, but comes increasingly to borrow the expressions from the words of the adult language.

There comes a point, however, at which he moves into a new stage of development, characterized on the one hand by the introduction of a level of vocabulary and structure and on the other hand by the beginning of dialogue. In Nigel's case this stage began at NL-6, at which the number of distinct meanings rose sharply from fifty to something approaching two hundred. But, by the same token, it ceases at this point to be possible to interpret the system as a simple inventory of meanings, so that there is no longer any significance to the figure that is obtained in this way. This is because the child is now entering on a new phase of semantic development.

The fact that he begins to engage in dialogue, taking on different social roles and assigning these roles to others, means that we can no longer make a simple list of the meanings that the child can express. Furthermore, he is developing a semantics that is not only a lexical semantics but also a grammatical semantics, a meaning potential that is organized in sets of options which combine; each choice is by itself very simple, but the combinations form highly complex patterns. The system network that represents the semantics at this stage is no longer a simple taxonomy, as it was before.

The new meanings are incorporated into the child's existing set of functions. There is no discontinuity here in the meanings as there is in the expressions, but rather a continuing development of the potential that is already there. At the same time, however, the very expansion of this potential leads to a development of the child's functional system into a new form: from having been equivalent simply to "uses of language," the functions come to be reinterpreted at a more abstract level, through a gradual process whereby they are eventually built into the heart of the linguistic system.

This happens in two stages: first, by the generalization out of the initial set of developmental functions of a fundamental distinction between language as doing and language as learning — the pragmatic and the mathetic functions, as we called them; and secondly, by the process of abstraction through which this basic functional opposition is extended from the semantic system into the lexicogrammatical system, being the source of the systematic distinction in the adult language between the ideational component (that which expresses the phenomena of the real world) and the interpersonal component (that which expresses the structure of the communication situation). Thus there is a total continuity between the set of functions formulated as part of our initial hypothesis and the functional organization of the linguistic system that has always been recognized in one form or another in functional theories of language.

There is continuity at the same time on another level, in that the initial functions which language serves for the child evolve at the same time into the types of situation, or contexts of language use. The situation type determines for the adult the particular variety or register he uses and the set of semantic configurations (and the forms of their expression) that can be recognized as typically associated with the abstract properties of the context of situation.

We could express this dual continuity another way by saying that, whereas for the very small child in Phase I, the concept of FUNCTION OF LANGUAGE is synonymous with that of USE OF LANGUAGE, for the adult, however, the two are distinct, the former referring to what are now incorporated as components of the linguistic system while the latter refers to the extralinguistic factors determining how the resources of the linguistic system are brought into play. But both FUNCTION and USE develop in a direct line from their origins in the child's first system of meaning potential.

We have interpreted the linguistic system as essentially a system of meanings, with associated forms and expressions as the realization of these meanings. We have interpreted the learning of language as learning how to mean. At the end of Phase II, which in the case of Nigel was at about 22½ to 24 months, the child has learned how to mean, in the sense that he has mastered the adult linguistic system. He has mastered a system that is multifunctional and multistratal.

This system has a massive potential; in fact it is open-ended, in that it can create indefinitely many meanings and indefinitely many sentences and clauses and phrases and words for the expression of these meanings. The child will spend the rest of his life exploring the potential of this system; having learnt how to walk, he can now start going places. Language can now serve him as an effective means of cultural transmission, as a means whereby in the ordinary everyday interaction in which he himself takes part the essential meanings of the culture can be transmitted to him.

The culture is itself a semiotic system, a system of meanings or information that is encoded in the behavior potential of the members, including their verbal potential — that is, their linguistic system. The linguistic system is only one form of the realization of the more general semiotic system which constitutes the culture. But perhaps it is the most important form of realization of it, because it is a prerequisite of most if not all the others. Although there are many aspects of the social semiotic that are not encoded in linguistic forms and expressions, it is likely that most of these draw in some way or other on the system of meanings that constitutes the essence of language.

The child who has learned how to mean has taken the essential step towards the sharing of meanings, which is the distinctive characteristic of social man in his mature state. But in following through any one child's progress we are bound to proceed with caution. Certain of his forward moves no doubt represent universal patterns of human development; others, equally certainly, are his own individual strategy, representing patterns which are no necessary part of the semogenic process. In between these two extremes lies a vast area in which we do not know how much of what we interpret as taking place is to be projected as universal.

The steps in Nigel's progression from protolanguage to adult language have been mapped out and formulated here in terms which would allow them to be considered as part of a more general hypothesis. But a general hypothesis does not consist solely of statements of universals. It is as much a hypothesis about human variation as about human invariance, and is as much concerned with what is more or less likely as with what is certain. In the last resort it is only the end product that we can be sure is in some sense universal; and we still do not know any too much about that.

REFERENCES

BERNSTEIN, BASIL
  1971   *Class, codes and control*, volume one: *Theoretical studies toward a sociology of language*. Primary Socialization, Language and Education Series. London: Routledge and Kegan Paul.
CLARK, EVE V.
  i.p.   "What's in a word? On the child's acquisition of semantics in his first language," in *Cognitive development and the acquisition of language*. Edited by T. E. Moore. New York: Academic Press.
HALLIDAY, M. A. K.
  1973   *Explorations in the functions of language*. Explorations in Language Study Series. London: Edward Arnold.
  i.p.   "Learning how to mean," in *Foundations of language development: a multidisciplinary approach*. Edited by Eric Lenneberg and Elizabeth Lenneberg. UNESCO and International Brain Research Organization.

INGRAM, DAVID
1971   Transitivity in child language. *Language* 47.

LAMB, SYDNEY M.
1970   "Linguistic and cognitive networks," in *Cognition: a multiple view*. Edited by Paul Garvin. New York: Spartan Books.

LEWIS, M.M.
1951   *Infant speech: a study of the beginnings of language* (second edition) International Library of Psychology, Philosophy and Scientific Method. London: Routledge and Kegan Paul. (Originally published 1934.)
1957   *How children learn to speak*. London: Harrap.

SECTION THREE

Language Acquisition

The Role of Social Context in Language Acquisition

TATIANA SLAMA-CAZACU

There is a problem which seemed to have been solved for the most part, but which has suddenly become the object of doubt, controversial discussion, and even sharp polemics. Succinctly stated, extremely simplified and even somewhat misrepresented, the problem is that of the relationship between the biological and social factors in language acquisition. Of course this problem is worth discussing for its intrinsic interest; looking at it here, however, might prove particularly useful because this offers an opportunity to expound facts and ideas which transcend the problem and seem to indicate goals for scientific research in the future.

It is well known that during the last few years some people have again strongly supported the hypothesis (peremptorily set forth and considered to be almost a thesis) that in language acquisition the individual is guided by determinations originating within himself rather than determinations coming from the environment. The Chomskyan formulation of this concept has become well known: a "language acquisition device" (LAD) receives a corpus of utterances (representing various concrete aspects, the components of the system of each language) and comes to construct a grammar, that is, comes to build an individual concrete grammatical system. The child has an "innate predisposition to learn a language" (Chomsky 1959; 1965: 25). It is also well known that the development of this thesis, provided by McNeill, assumes not only the existence of an "inborn capacity for language," but also of inborn aspects of the details of language such as, for instance, "the concept of a sentence" (McNeill 1968a; 1971a: 54, and others).

This thesis shows many "variations on the same theme," encompassing the following points: (a) the primordiality of the biological foundation (see Lenneberg 1967) as against education, the former being a background which evolves as a result of inner means and not through learning; (b) learning is considered to be "creative," i.e. surpassing any mechanically acquired formulas, only if it implies self-development or development by one's own means; (c) one may possibly assume a self-maturation process (one fails to see how it can be made to agree with the social ambient and educative influences, etc.); and (d) ultimately (a logical conclusion, even if not all scholars are willing to admit that this is the final point necessarily derived from the explicit thesis), there is the primordiality of heredity, of fate against education. The keywords or, in linguistic terms, the "lexical field" of such a conception (in its entirety and with logical implications, even if some authors do not resort to all these lexical devices) are: "inborn linguistic ability," "innate ideas," "rationalism" (as opposed to "empiricism"), creativity, (productivity, rule generation), self-development, self-maturation, and primordiality of all innate factors (heredity, fate).

As is known, this conception has given rise to heated controversy either with the view of completing or altering the thesis, or of combating it. Let us mention here — by naming their organizers — only two of the debates that have been conducted at various symposia (and published later on): D. Slobin (Berkeley 1965–1970, see Slobin 1971) and J. Morton (London 1969, see Morton 1971). One may observe that neither of the discussions mentioned (nor the respective publications) has reached a clear-cut conclusion. The problem has remained "open," without solution, at the end of these debates (giving rise to even more perplexity because of the effort to put forth an increased number of pro and con arguments).

The supporters of the nativistic conception are not ready to accept arguments or agree to a compromise. The opponents belong either to the neobehaviorist trend (see, for instance, the paper by Palermo and Staats in Slobin 1971), which is too closely linked to the old psychological mechanistic model to be convincing today when a goodly amount of material has been accumulated regarding creativity, self-formulation of rules, and even awareness while learning a language, or else these opponents are not firm enough, failing also to put forth convincing data.

The debate, as a rule, is conducted at a speculative level, because, on the one hand, there are no convincing facts that may support either position, and on the other hand, the EXISTING facts are presented by both schools as arguments meant to support their theory. The example offered by the discussion of the "regularization" phenomenon (in Slobin 1971) is significant: the same facts are presented as arguments by both schools. In fact, the thesis that present-day nativism (or that the supporters of "self-maturation" or of the primordiality of biological background) peremptorily asserts, even if it fails to be based on convincing facts and also on facts accumulated in a great number, has not met with an equally violent reaction; in any case, the position presented is not efficient enough (one of the best organized and balanced positions among those presented in recent studies is that of Campbell and Wales [1970]).

In addition to the old behavioristic arguments — which are mostly defensive and which ultimately propose the replacement of a *deus ex machina*, LAD, by another *deus ex machina*, Stimulus-Response (S-R) — the reactions sometimes reveal weariness (these disputes being very often otiose, arguing in a vicious circle) or show a character of merry, ironical, puzzled protest as might be caused by farce or nonsense. Such reactions sometimes seem to represent the common sense of public opinion. There are also ideas, synthetic statements, and replies that could be taken as arguments by both theories (as the one by George Miller, for example, which explicitly maintains only that animals cannot acquire language: "the ability to acquire and use a human language does not depend on being intelligent or having a large brain. It depends on being human" [G. Miller 1967: 176]).

The reaction from a Marxist viewpoint was presented in the symposium whose proceedings are included in the volume edited by Morton (1971; see also Leontiev 1971; Leontiev and Leontiev 1959; and A. R. Luria, in the conclusions to the symposium [not published in Morton 1971]; Luria, the well-known Soviet psychologist and neurologist, was chairman at the Congress). The Marxist conception solved the problem long ago, from the philosophical standpoint, in terms of the relationships of the individual to society and biological phenomena to social phenomena, and the answer to any of these questions seems to be clear enough. At least at the symposium mentioned above, the opposition offered to the modern avatars of nativism (and all its corollaries), although representing a definite position regarding the matter, was a riposte less violent than nativism itself (the argumentation also needed to be more strongly backed by facts).

Of course, I cannot presumptuously claim to solve the problem here, by my own means. But I feel it a duty to present my point of view, not yet expressed in print, regarding this problem, almost as a "profession of faith." For this is a key problem of the sciences of man.

The debate per se, such as is conducted by nativism, appears otiose, and the SOLUTION to the dilemma cannot be efficiently sought when making use of the same means used in the discussion carried out within the nativist camp. I therefore think that the SPECULATIVE DISCUSSION proper should be brought to an end, thus allowing all forces and attention to be directed towards the accumulation of FACTS (aiming not at collecting facts designed to back either of the theories, but at manipulating facts in an unbiased manner, in order to study reality such as it is).

Let me discuss some of the arguments pro and con as well as certain facts that were meant so far to support one or the other of the two positions. The definitely opposing position can be set forth in the classical behavioristic terms of mechanical learning according to the S-R model, and we think one could identify classical behaviorism with neobehaviorism. In fact, despite all the mediationist additions, no matter how many "levels" these terms may describe, they are not essentially different from the classical model because they are not capable of explaining the entire complexity of verbal behavior. As Osgood himself says: the "three-stage mediation-integration model," the "souped-up kiddie-car" replacing the "kiddie car," or even the "horse-and-buggy model" is not complex and subtle enough (Osgood 1967: 112–113, 125).

The child does not assimilate everything he hears, he does not link every stimulus to a reaction. He learns selectively, choosing at each stage various words, grammatical structures, etc., according to the abilities of his entire development: he is a "selective echo" (Slama-Cazacu 1957, 1973). The social milieu, represented at first by his parents, remains relatively the same in the course of a child's language evolution. Why is it that at a given time he learns the present tense, then the past tense continuous, and only later on the other tenses and moods? Why does he first single out the meaning of concrete words from the strings heard in the speech of adults? He has practically the same opportunities of hearing various forms and nevertheless he retains (or, in behaviorist terms, he associatively links S to R) only some of them, and, not at random, retains certain forms only, also determined by certain features of his thought (such as the propensity toward the concrete, particular, or present).

1. We have been able to notice the correct use by children aged two to three of certain utterances that seem to operate as syntagms (noun + preposition: *sub pat* 'under the bed'); but the necessity of using one of the components separately, in a new situation, leads to

mistakes ([*Am pus jucăria*] *la su*[*b*] *pat la bancă* 'I put the toy under the bed to the bench'). This shows nonanalytical learning, at the beginning, of certain "syntagmatic blocks" (or units). Later on, the child will be capable of analyzing correctly, but it will be at that stage that he will make mistakes even when using expressions he was previously able to set forth correctly; these mistakes prove that the "syntagmatic block" has been broken, being no longer used mechanically. We have compared this fact with data provided by another experiment of ours. When little children were asked to separate the words of a sentence by counting on "their fingers," they tended to merge into a single whole the noun and the preposition, the noun and the verb, etc. (*Pune pîinea/ pe dulap* 'Put the bread/on the cupboard'). It is only at the age of four or five or even six that they are able to correctly differentiate the components, those which before were linked together in a sentence, or, better said, those of the various initial "syntagmatic blocks."

2.   In verbal-associative experiments carried out with children of different ages, I have been able to observe a definite evolution: the word 'death' (only the English translation of the Romanian stimuli and responses will be given here) brings from three- to four-year-old children such responses as 'grave, earth', etc.; it is only at about the age of six to seven that children supply answers of an abstract type such as 'life'.

3.   All the sounds a child hears around him are the same when he is three or eight months, or three years old. Nevertheless, it is not these sounds, which represent the phonemes of his mother tongue, that are learned at the beginning (and not all of them, simultaneously), although an infant's repertoire of sounds contains many vocal sounds much more "difficult" as regards articulation.

4.   In the Romanian language one may build the oblique cases (genitive, dative) with the article in both a proclitic and an enclitic position: *cartea băiatului* 'the boy's book', *dă pisicii oasele* 'give the bones to the cat' — synthetic form; or, for male given names (and in a popular incorrect form also for nicknames, with the proclitic article or with a preposition: *cartea lu*[*i*] *băiatu* [*l*] 'the book of the boy', *dă oasele la pisică* 'give the bones to the cat' – analytical form. Children choose the second form and generalize it, up to the age of five or six, even when in their milieu both structures are used to the same extent (I must add here a significant fact: this structure was used in archaic Romanian and it may still be found in some Romanian dialects south of the Danube). And what is more, various errors of the "regularization" type (English 'foot', 'foots'; 'go', goed'; Romanian *sunteam* instear

of *eram* 'I was', etc.), as well as lexical creations, etc., prove that the child thinks about language, assuming an active, even a conscious, attitude while acquiring it.

We could provide further facts to demonstrate how hard it is to support the thesis of mechanical learning of the S-R type throughout the process of language acquisition by the child. There are facts which show that language acquisition is an active process, carried out by a *sui generis* selection, and even a creative process.

Does the solution to the alternative initially presented here, therefore, consist of the adoption of a model of language acquisition through self-maturation, or through the inborn character (which is self-determined) of a selection operation in learning, in setting up "rules," etc.? Does society play an important role in the course of development of the child's LANGUAGE, or is it only an ancillary role?

If I were to analyze the McNeill type of arguments meant to support the nativistic thesis (represented by ideas expressed in some of his previous works), I should argue in methodological terms, as follows (and this does not refer only to the studies made by this outstanding author, but also to those pertaining to the same type of orientation).

1.   The conclusions are based on the study of a very small number of languages (English, French, Japanese, sometimes Russian), which cannot justify the generalization (just as one cannot generalize in this way about "linguistic universals" either).

2.   Too few cases have been analyzed (also, the facts borrowed from other authors [cf. McNeill 1971b: 23] do not refer to a wide number of cases, studied longitudinally and comparatively for several languages). It is self-evident that one cannot draw scientific conclusions regarding the relationship of the individual to society by relying on a small number of cases (a comparison in different milieus being absolutely necessary).

3.   Even when examples from other authors are quoted, the facts are insufficient for the argumentation, especially if the respective authors have not studied the same problem and have not created methodological conditions for an adequate comparative study (some of them actually combat the nativistic thesis: Brown, et al. [1968: 46], for instance, from whose work data are taken as arguments by some nativists, state that they have found no grounds to believe that there are innate subcategories, except for the fact that it is very hard to show the categories that are learned).

4.   The investigations and studies of various facts presented by other authors do not exactly cover the problems about which conclusions

are reached. McNeill (1966:36) states that the child acquires language very rapidly, this being a proof of the existence of an inborn language acquisition capacity; but this conclusion is not supported by facts. Whoever has watched this process in a large number of children (I personally have observed more than 600 children) knows that the process is spectacular indeed; the child performs it admirably efficiently, but he has to make efforts (we have recorded the great "pains" — apparent even physically — that four-month-old infants or three-year-old children take to imitate). This effort takes a fairly long period of time, if one considers the ENTIRE verbal system of signs, including the phonetic level, the dynamics of the development of word meaning, and the brushing up of the grammatical structure through style refinement, etc. To what level and pattern (or particular aspect of a pattern) do scholars refer in assessing the "rapidity" of acquisition? Do they also include in this assessment the tribulations, hesitations, and the mixing up of correct and incorrect expressions for the same pattern? (E.g. 'man', 'men', 'mans', ect.; cf. Miller and Ervin-Tripp in Slobin 1971: 33; or 'feet', 'foots', 'footses', 'footiz', etc., in the same child, cf Slobin 1971: 9–10; cf. also our own observations of the Romanian language.) And should one consider two to two-and-one-half years to be an "early age," for certain forms reported by McNeill?

5.   Some other methodological deficiencies also render the theory questionable: we are not always exactly informed at what age certain facts presented as arguments were recorded, we do not know whether it was the first appearance of a certain form or whether there were other previous attempts (correct or wrong) which constitute the "history" of that form. The errors which occur at the beginning, to be replaced later with correct forms, may cause us to wonder why these mistakes were made if there is an infallible linguistic capacity or "competence." On the other hand, some initially correct forms replaced later on with "creative" errors show that in the beginning, as mentioned above, there is somehow a mechanical type of learning.

6.   Finally, no precise definition is offered of the concept of "innateness" (general psychic capacities, biological background, etc.?) and of the details this type of study refers to as concerns language acquisition (only a predisposition to formulate grammatical rules up to the "concept of a sentence," or also for lexical acquisition, for the acquisition of word meanings, etc.?). In the discussion, aspects are put forward pertaining to cognitive structures, thinking mechanisms or operations, levels of logical analysis, "surface structure" phenomena, etc.

I find it personally difficult, or maybe even pointless, to also discuss from a strictly theoretical standpoint the arguments invoked by the generative-transformational proponents of the nativistic thesis. The speculations about the fundamental LAD hypothesis seem to me uselessly tiresome, as I do not know for sure what LAD is, and I do not quite understand how language facts from the social context can "penetrate" into this pattern. I was also unable to find out, in this concept, what the real role of education in foreign-language learning is, how early bilingualism can be explained through this "device," etc. Perhaps some of the supporters of this concept have become aware that they do not fully understand these concepts either, and the most brilliant of them, such as McNeill, have already altered their former exaggerations.

I think it now necessary to discuss succinctly the thesis of social determinism which is assigned a *sui generis* meaning by the school of Bernstein, for instance (see Bernstein 1972 and other works). It is probable that most of the modern supporters of NATIVISM — and first of all Chomsky — are not aware that this concept logically leads to racialism or may offer arguments to support it. Although in the Chomskyan conception "competence" is, like "*la raison*" in Descartes, provided to everyone by his biological background, the same starting point, if one refuses to admit the primordiality of social factors, may generate arguments in two directions. Hence, arguments contrary to the initial intention may be made just because they derive from the thesis of the supremacy of biological heredity.

On the other hand, stressing the importance of a single aspect or fragment of society does not represent a strong argument that is able to combat the nativistic thesis. The social context is an ENSEMBLE, whereas the social class Bernstein and his school are referring to — showing that "the class system" determines the choice of a "restricted" or "elaborated code" — does not provide a powerful argument for combating the nativistic thesis. (Bernstein sometimes says that "the focussing and filtering of the child's experience within the family in a large measure is a microcosm of the macroscopic orderings of society" [1972: 169]). The impact of education as a social factor on language (generally on what in French is meant by *langage*) may not serve the argumentation regarding the importance of social factors, as long as other different contextual levels coexist, which are not taken into consideration but whose influence continues in another direction or even in the opposite direction.

As was said before, the different concepts must be accurately defined in this debate. Among other concepts it is necessary to define those of "society" and "social context" in their relationships with "language"

(and *langage*) and "communication" as a whole. The message is integrated in the course of communication (as well as in the language
acquisition act) in a context which can be analyzed at different levels
(see Figure 1; cf. also Slama-Cazacu 1961a, 1970, 1973): the explicit
context (linguistic and extralinguistic) of the expression properly
speaking and the implicit context (the situational context – momentary
physical ambience, etc., the context created by relations between
partners which is part of the social context, the code acquired from
outside, and the restricted social group — family, class, etc. — the
social-historical moment, the wider community, the "human society" in
its entirety).

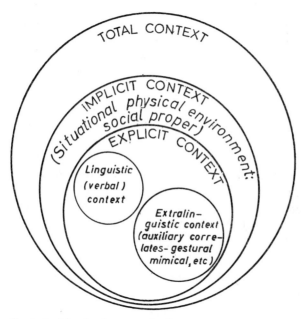

Figure 1.   Contextual levels of communication

Emission and reception of the message are influenced by these
different contextual levels, ultimately by the "total context." The debate
on language acquisition must take account of all these levels.

In tackling the problem that I posed initially, and that was recently
formulated as a "nativism-empiricism" contention, I did not support
any pro or con presumptive theory and endeavored to stick to a
position of theoretical independence, so that I might primarily analyze
real facts.

However, the facts I know directly — from the material I collected in the course of investigations of the Romanian language conducted for many years with over 600 children — and also other similar facts found in the works of various authors do not entitle me either to reject outright the behaviorist thesis or to adhere to such a doctrine of innateness as is advocated by some representatives of generative-transformational linguistics. Truly, there are some facts which testify to the existence of some moments of mechanical learning or imitation, but there are also moments of creativity or productivity, of conscious acquisition, of self-formulation of rules (which, however, in my opinion, fail to be an argument in favor of innateness, as I shall try to demonstrate later).

The following are some facts about language acquisition. The problem has been posed, in regard to the phonetic level, of whether there exists an inborn basis of articulation, a thesis upheld some time ago by van Ginneken (1933). Experiments on white and Negro newborn infants made by Han Piao Chen (see Slama-Cazacu 1966: 172) form one of the objective arguments opposing this thesis. An international cooperative investigation conducted according to a common set of methods (cf. Slama-Cazacu 1966), which is in progress, constitutes the only way of enabling us to get a definite and objective answer to this question (and also to the question relating to the time when the various sounds gradually appear in a LARGE NUMBER OF CHILDREN, within the same language, so that afterwards some "universalia" at this level may be established). Even preliminary observations, however, including recordings of individuals and of "dialogues" between mothers and their infants in the first months of life, have led me to assume that the initial sounds may be considered as "biological sounds": they are probably the same in all children all over the world, occurring prior to any social vocal influence.

Subsequently, the child produces an enormous number of different sounds, sometimes even very intricate sounds, in a phase in which I also noticed the efforts of infants, aged three to four months, to render the sounds produced by grownups (to "imitate" them); this is obviously a prephonemic phase in which, in addition to biological sounds or sounds produced apparently in a completely spontaneous way, genuine prephonemes may be described. Later on, the sounds which are extrinsic to the phonematic system of the language that is to become the child's mother tongue are eliminated and only those which correspond to the phonemes are retained. The intermediate, prephonematic phase seems fascinating; I think that it provides the "key" in the evolution of phonematic systems and is one of the important aspects of the problem we are concerned with here. As the sounds in this phase are "no less difficult" than those which correspond to the phonemes, it is probably not here that the cause lies for the child's failure to select, from the very beginning, the phonematic sounds of the language concerned.

The phonemes appear gradually, after many attempts at approximating them (which we eventually may designate as "imitative" efforts). This gradual assimilation does not plead either for the thesis of innateness (because the articulated sounds of a language do not come forth from the beginning, but rather only clicks, champs, etc.) or for a behaviorist model of learning (because the phonematic sounds do not assert themselves as faithful — as one-to-one — and immediate imitations and are not acquired simultaneously for all the phonemes). The behaviorist model of learning does not help us to understand this "appropriation" of the sounds related in a system and dependent on each other, nor does the term "imitation," which, as a matter of fact, we do not know the meaning of. But the effort of appropriating what is to be found in the social environment, of transcending what exists in one's self in the primary individuality, is obvious. It may be that such an appropriation starts very early, helped by visual-kinesthetic cues. Zazzo (1957) relates that he has noticed the imitation of tongue protrusion as early as the first month. It is likely that an important part in the process of primary acquisition of verbal sounds is the infant's seeing the movements of the lips, which are involved in the act of articulation (particulary of the lips of the mother, who, as a rule, is the first human being whose face the infant sees very closely during nursing, caring, and caressing). The efforts of the investigations should be centered on this phase of active selection, of evolution from the biological sounds and individual "vocal exercises" to the adoption of the sounds produced by people with whom the infant comes into contact.

The manifest awareness concerning the various linguistic units (detected through word-division experiments [see above], through inversions of words containing diphthongs [see Slama-Cazacu 1973: Part 3, Chapter 1], through investigations into lexical or morphological elements, etc.) is also a touchstone for the validity of the theories discussed. We cannot dwell here any longer on this important aspect; we want, however, to mention the impact of the metalanguage schemas and even of the linguistic theories found in the grammar books and textbooks used in schools (consequently, the social influence) in determining this "competence" (in the Chomskyan sense, consequently, what is considered as inborn) of the average speaker, who is an outsider as far as linguistic science is concerned.

The investigations I made disclosed that there are certain dynamics in the course of the child's assimilation of words and their meanings. A certain primary way of learning is noticed which often may be interpreted in terms of S-R, in any case through nonanalyzed "syntagmatic blocks" (see above); the creative acquisition is ulterior (on this level, at least). The question of whether the inborn competence should not have evinced the creative or productive attribute from the very beginning should be raised.

Numerous facts should also be taken into consideration, which indicate the overlapping of phases or downfalls to previous levels, rather than a linear evolution, in the sense either of a growth of automatization or a clear-cut progression of stages, or a continuous productivity. Facts reveal the existence (sometimes simultaneous) in the development of a child's language of both mechanical acquisition and creative acquisition (as a rule, the former coming chronologically first).

A number of facts which appear in the development of child language (and which also appear in foreign-language learning by grown-ups) are quite relevant from this point of view and give weight to the position which may be taken in the controversy in question. On the other hand, these facts prevent us from completely agreeing with the statement of Brown et al. (1968: 60), according to which the very data, irrespective of the processes through which the grammar is acquired, originate from the utterances the children hear around them. There are expressions – and at a given moment their number is quite large — which do not originate *tale quale* from what children hear around them.

Experiments we made with learners of English and Romanian as foreign languages — which led to the creation (see Slama-Cazacu 1972a) of an "acquisition corpus" (the answers to the propounded tests), an "aberrant corpus," and a "hierarchical system of errors" (the frequency of errors being estimated statistically) — as well as data mentioned by other authors point to the existence of a category of errors (of the type 'goed', 'foots', etc., i.e. regularization errors) which frequently appears in children, too, at certain ages (particularly over three years old, i.e. after they have accumulated a store of facts sufficient to enable them to derive some rules spontaneously). There is a general human tendency to integrate the various facts into categories and, as such, to derive a common criterion and to formulate a rule to be applied in any situation which would seem to be consistent with the seemingly efficient criterion. It should be emphasized that in adults such errors do not appear in the first stages of their learning a foreign language, but only after a minimum store has been accumulated. Likewise, such errors appear in children after a phase in which they apparently learned the CORRECT FORM (see above, 'foot', 'feet', 'footses', etc.), which is exactly at the age (two to three years) when the "syntagmatic blocks" are noticed as well.

Facts consequently point both to creative learning, on the basis of inferred rules, and to relatively mechanical learning, with no rigid chronological demarcation line between them: the phases overlap and the PROCEDURES coexist. The forced choice, which generative-transformational linguistics in particular and the psycholinguistics derived from it have imposed, between either a mechanistic (behaviorist) type of learning or no learning at all (an "all or nothing" decision) is not scientifically efficient. In addition, the substitution of the term "acquisition" for "learning" (be it of a behaviorist type or not), arguing that the latter has been used in a certain meaning (cf. Campbell and Wales 1970: 242), while no other clear-cut model of acquisition was formulated, has not proved to be fruitful. When examining such facts, it is also difficult to find the clear pattern of automatization, of univocal development of a self-system, etc., and the always identical process of exclusively mechanical learning.

A flexible approach is required because reality is so complex: both creative learning and also moments, which are necessary, of mechanical learning exist. What is important here from a theoretical and also from a practical point of view is that both procedures occur naturally in the human being, that no arguments exist upholding unilaterally one type of procedure alone, that discussion is likely to drag on endlessly and inefficiently, if unilateral aspects of the same fact (e.g. "regularization") are put forward to support one or the other of the theories (see in this respect the probehaviorist arguments of Palermo and Staats [in Slobin 1971: 60 ff., 131 ff.], and the pronativism of Mc Neill [1971b]; it should be remarked that the subtle and generally correct discussion of McNeill [1971b: 32–33] seeks, at all costs, to be integrated in a theory of innateness, which is farfetched and difficult to defend).

It is not the creativity in learning that may be doubted (neither can it be exclusively resorted to as an argument in favor of nativism), but rather its limits; this is a question that has to be accounted for (cf. also Campbell and Wales 1970: 248).

Finally, in order to approach more directly the problem of the part played by social determinism we shall mention here two more categories of facts. In the nativistic theory, the subject of numerous discussions is furnished by data relating to the acquisition of grammatical structure, the inference of rules, etc., while other language levels (lexical-semantic, phonetic, etc.) and also the dialogue form of language are left aside. Out of all the functions of language, the function of communication is perhaps the most important or, at any rate, an essential one: no discussion on language acquisition should omit it.

This function starts developing at an early stage, particularly in the course of mother-child interaction and subsequently in the interaction between children. It might be argued that it is an inborn function, if we are consistent with the argumentation pattern of nativism. However, it is rather strange that a great psychologist (Piaget) denied the early manifestation of this function, asserting that *"le langage socialisé"* does not manifest itself before the age of seven or eight. As regards my own investigations, I ascertained the existence of genuine dialogue, which had a communicative function, among children as early as age two (Slama-Cazacu 1961b). It is clear that the different results have originated, to a great extent, not only from the different methods used in investigation, but also from the different educational conditions, which did or did not determine the early development of the communicative function. The existence or nonexistence of an inborn drive is theoretically and practically less important than the fact that, under certain conditions, this drive toward communication may not materialize, or that the social environment can cause an early development of the main function of language, i.e. that of communication.

The role of education, which means the purposeful action of social determinism, may sometimes be ascertained by means of experimental educative intervention. I shall quote an example, which also refers to "competence." In some experiments (see Slama-Cazacu 1957), I noticed an evolution in operating with notions of genus ("animal," "bird," etc.) and in a growing support provided at various ages by the respective integrative word. The teaching of a new and rather difficult notion ("plant"), with the simultaneous utilization of the integrative word (in the course of a well-organized experimental lesson, delivered simultaneously to a group of children aged three to seven), produced, even in the three-year-old children, a substantial improvement in the results obtained in the experiments based on the utilization of a verbal integrator. I emphasize that, correctly viewed, this was an attempt to teach *langage* as a total and complex phenomenon.

When facts are better known, many opinions have to be modified. What matters, however, is to specify the CONCEPTS and the METHOD.

It is also necessary to refer here to the following point: to a great extent the solution of the problem discussed depends on the theoretical background included in the concepts of "language behavior" (better named in French *langage*, i.e. the ensemble of psychical processes for encoding-decoding, etc.) and "language" properly speaking (French *langue*, i.e. the code itself). Even language as such (the code, the system of signs) should not be viewed only as an ensemble of forms, and expressions; rather, the mental content included in meanings, rules, "the linguistic awareness," etc. should be involved as well (and this is the very reason why I personally cannot accept a sharp distinction between the Chomskyan "competence" and "performance" and the use of a sharp split, when discussing these constructs, in the unit that exists in reality).

When specialists come to argue about language as an inborn phenomenon, they often forget that meaning and, in general, mental content are at least as important as form itself, and that the child cannot assimilate one aspect (the form) without the other (the content). Moreover, when a discrepancy between form and content seems to appear in the process of mother tongue acquisition by the child, neither of the two aspects has been assimilated: the form cannot exist as a speech unit, efficient in communication or in behavior in general, without a corresponding appropriate content, at least rudimentary, given by a background formed of inner intellectual networks, nor can the content develop without the help of the tools given by the tongue learned from the social milieu. It may be said that, if there is something that is inborn, this cannot but be a very general cognitive structure, a human capacity of thought which permits the assimilation of forms of expression (predication itself, for instance, is not a mere speech phenomenon, but a simultaneous speech and thinking one and, in any case, a mental phenomenon). When an expression is really assimilated, it is because the connected mental content has also developed: otherwise, we have a mechanically reiterated stereotype, which may be fortuitously adequately used in a certain context but wrongly employed in another one.

We reach now, finally, the core and final point of this discussion based on facts. We have seen that the alternative of creativity versus mechanical learning requires a flexible position. A similar position also has to be taken for the alternative of the biological versus the social, the innate versus the acquired.

Sometimes it is asserted that there is an interaction between what is innate and what is learned (Marshall 1970: 239). But what does this mean? What is the inborn basis? It must be acknowledged that a biological basis (in fact the normally developed human brain) is a necessary condition. But it is not a sufficient one (it seems even that in our day this "normal brain" may be "built" through surgical operations and the administration of medicines to the fetus and, subsequently, through rational nutrition), and I even venture to say — and this does not express farfetched optimism — that, if there is a "normal brain," judicious educational intervention can bring about the normal development of language behavior.

In my opinion, a general and normal development is a more important basis for the learning of foreign languages than the existence of some hypothetical and fatefully predetermined "linguistic abilities." A normally developed child may become bilingual without any danger that the bilingualism might trigger an intellectual handicap. A handicap (intellectual, but of an affective origin) may appear, if the attitude of the social group produces emotional stress or if it does not create motivations for the learning of the second language; this is, however, a different problem from that which we are discussing. Let us also refer to another example: the deaf and dumb individual who does not get special education may develop an expressive system of his own, but it is only intensive education which can make him attain a normal intellectual level and sometimes even excel the normal limits.

The human being is biologically "equipped" to learn a code, to have linguistic behavior. But without the integration in society, this equipment atrophies (while within the society it may develop to such an extent as to go beyond the biological limits). The modern controversies over "innateness" and "empiricism" have not tackled the "trite" example of the children brought up in the wilderness by wolves, she-goats, or other nurses who do not belong to the normal human social environment. However, this is a keystone, a thrilling one even, although at first sight it may seem trivial. Brought too late into society (see, for instance, the report of Itard in Malson 1964), they fail to manifest any linguistic competence or any trend to productivity, etc.; as a matter of fact, they have no time to do this, because generally they do not survive and, in any case, do not live long enough to reach the mental age of the normal speech stage. Did the "inborn capacities" wither away, because too long a time had elapsed before they could start working? Or does the matter also involve the transmitting by the "society" of the various tools required for thinking, for eliciting the language-acquisition mechanisms, for creating the motivations to communicate, etc.?

If the biological basis is necessary, it is the social environment which is the prerequisite for development and which perhaps even provides the initial framework that allows the appearance of some cognitive, operational, primary structures (what is apparently sometimes interpreted as "predication," the "inborn concept of a sentence," operation through rules, etc.). Could it not be that integration from the very beginning into society, which lives on the basis of rules, also imparts the tendency to look for structures? Could it not be that the well-known Gardner chimpanzee, Washoe, has reached the noted stage of learning of a code just because she has been intensively "bombarded" with the gadgets of human social life?

From a practical point of view, what really matters is the fact that the social context CAN achieve a great deal, either in a negative or in a positive direction. It can determine NEGATIVELY, because its procedures are not adequate to a positive development; and it can determine POSITIVELY merely because it exists as a positive factor. This again is a simple truth which is often forgotten, just as we forget that it is not "education" by itself, or "school" as an institution, or "language" which is responsible for failure, but the means that are employed, the "methods" or, more correctly speaking, the modality of their application.

It is necessary to notice, however, that social stimulation and its result, social determinism, are not to be conceived as a mere one-sided action (see above, the discussion on society considered as an ensemble). Likewise, we have to emphasize once again that the social influence, in order to be efficient (in general, or for language behavior only), should be exerted on that ensemble which is the human individual, and not on a single compartment or fragment detached from the system. Another idea should be discarded also, namely that the individual contribution in learning, the "productivity" or "creativity," would not be consistent with the idea of strong social determinism. What we need is a genuinely modern psychological science, able to account for the coexistence of the creative aspect of language (we no longer call them "inborn," as Campbell and Wales do [1970: 248]) and for the role of social action.

CONCLUSIONS AND PROSPECTS: What we can especially see from the above analysis is, I think, the necessity of gathering a massive collection of facts instead of engaging in as yet sterile speculation. As we know rather little about human psychic phenomena in general, and about the way in which "acquisition" or "learning" (or whatever term we want to assign to this process) occurs, we cannot think that we have time enough for speculation in a world which wants to be known as it really is and which is waiting for us to discover that reality. I shall succinctly present what I think to be the necessary and scientific actions and procedures for the future:

1.   Investigation of language acquisition based on MANY CASES, so that correct generalizations may be reached.

2.   The study of many cases in VARIOUS SOCIAL CONTEXTS, aiming at the same correct generalizations.

3.   COMPARATIVE investigations, both in the same linguistic community and cross-culturally. We have, for instance, to find out accurately whether an early impact of the society on phonetic development EXISTS; if so, WHEN it begins, HOW it materializes, and WHAT the influence of a certain language, at the phonetic level, consists of.

4.   Investigations covering ALL the languages of the world (or all the types); otherwise, the study will keep on being nonscientific, much the same as the one concerning linguistic universals.

5.   MULTIDISCIPLINARY research (in which, as a matter of fact, it is difficult to specify the particular traits of each of the approaches): psycholinguistic (in a broad sense) combined with sociolinguistic, pedagogical, biological, anthropological, semiotic and other investigations.

6.   OBJECTIVE analyses (tape recordings, sonograph analyses, etc.).

7.   The notation of the ENTIRE ENSEMBLE of expression (verbal and nonverbal components).

8.   The notation of the ENTIRE CONTEXT of expression (situational, personal, social-historical, etc.)

9.   Comparison between mother-tongue acquisition in the child and the adult acquisition of foreign languages, in various social contexts.

10.   Comparison between language acquisition and that of other expression tools, in various social contexts.

11.   Comparison between the acquisition of the systems of signs and the formation of other psychical habits or functions, in various social contexts.

12.   The study of the development of child language as a function of the influence of the social environment (particularly the deliberate educational influence) by means of ample investigations, beginning with the first days of life, in various social contexts.

It would not be too optimistic to assert that such studies will be made, and that they will be carried out under the ideal conditions I have mentioned. Some of these studies have already been started in various places; some I am carrying on myself or have suggested to others who have already initiated them. It may be that the above suggestions will be helpful in launching other studies as well.

It is well worth emphasizing, however, that some of these studies had a strong motivation in the very polemic we have dealt with: they have been brought about by the need either to answer the questions posed by the discussion or to produce new arguments. The latter may be of service — if the facts have been correctly collected — not to the polemic as such or to any of the extreme theories which elicited it but to the progress of science as a whole, and this is above any controversy.

While concluding that at present and particularly in the near future it will be more useful to collect facts than to indulge in absurd speculations, I would also remark that this is far from being an easy task. Fact collecting is much more difficult than speculation, and this "comfort" is not mentioned as being the true reason when it is asserted that facts should be abandoned because they are not necessary any longer, and that the deductive method is nowadays "the optimal device" in detecting the ways to be followed by a science. The task is not easy, because reality in general is exceedingly intricate and the human reality is one of the most complex within this intricacy. From this reality, however, it is IMPOSSIBLE to tear away the social context. The studies which I have outlined above will be useful to the extent to which they are correct, ample, working within the social context, complex by themselves, far-reaching, and included in vast perspectives, and their usefulness will depend upon our ability to consider all possible conclusions and to accept those which accurately reflect reality.

REFERENCES

BERNSTEIN, B.
  1972 "Social class, language and socialization," in *Language and social context*. Edited by P. P. Giglioli, 157–178. Harmondsworth: Penguin Books.
BROWN, R., C. CAZDEN, U. BELLUGI-KLIMA
  1968 "The child's grammar from 1 to 3," in *Minnesota symposia on child psychology*, volume two. Edited by J. Hill, 28–73. Minneapolis: University of Minnesota Press.
CAMPBELL, R., R. WALES
  1970 "The study of language acquisition," in *New horizons in linguistics*. Edited by J. Lyons, 242–260. Harmondsworth: Penguin Books.
CHOMSKY, N.
  1959 A review of B.F. Skinner's *Verbal behavior*. *Language* 35:26–58.
  1965 *Aspects of the theory of syntax*. Cambridge, Mass.: M.I.T. Press.
DIXON, T., D. HORTON, *editors*
  1968 *Verbal behavior and general behavior theory*. Englewood Cliffs, N.J.: Prentice-Hall.

LENNEBERG, E.
    1966   "A biological perspective of language," in *New directions in the study of language*. Edited by E. Lenneberg, 65–88. Cambridge, Mass.: M.I.T. Press.
    1967   *Biological foundations of language*. New York: Wiley.

LEONTIEV, A. A.
    1971   "Social and natural in semiotics," in *Biological and social factors in psycholinguistics*. Edited by J. Morton, 122–130. London: Logos Press.

LEONTIEV, A. N., A. A. LEONTIEV
    1959   The social and the individual in language. *Language and speech* 2(4).

MALSON, L.
    1964   *Les enfants sauvages. Mythe et réalité*, followed by *Mémoire et rapport sur Victor de l'Aveyron* by Jean Itard. Paris: Union Générale d'Editions.

MARSHALL, J.
    1970   "The biology of communication in man and animals," in *New horizons in linguistics*. Edited by J. Lyons, 229–241. Harmondsworth: Penguin Books.

MC NEILL, D.
    1966   The creation of language. *Discovery* 27:34–38.
    1968a   "Empiricist and nativist theories of language: George Berkeley and Samuel Bailey in the 20th century." Paper for the symposium New Perspectives in the Science of Man, Austria 1968; preprint.
    1968b   "On theories of language acquisition," in *Verbal behavior and general behavior theory*. Edited by T. Dixon and D. Horton, 406–420. Englewood Cliffs, N.J.: Prentice-Hall.
    1971a   "Explaining linguistic universals," in *Biological and social factors in psycholinguistics*. Edited by J. Morton, 53–60. London: Logos Press.
    1971b   "The capacity for the ontogenesis of grammar," in *The ontogenesis of grammar: a theoretical symposium*. Edited by D. Slobin, 17–40. New York and London: Academic Press.

MILLER, G.
    1967   "Some preliminaries to psycholinguistics," in *Readings in the psychology of language*. Edited by L. Jakobovits and M. Miron, 172–179. Englewood Cliffs, N.J.: Prentice-Hall.

MILLER, W., S. ERVIN-TRIPP
    1964   "The development of grammar in child language," in *The acquisition of language*. Edited by U. Bellugi and R. Brown, 9–34. Yellow Springs, Ohio: The Antioch Press.

MORTON, J.
    1971   "What could possibly be innate?" in *Biological and social factors in psycholinguistics*. Edited by J. Morton, 82–97. London: Logos Press.

MORTON, J., *editor*
    1971   *Biological and social factors in psycholinguistics*. London: Logos Press.

OSGOOD, C.
1967 "On understanding and creating sentences," in *Readings in the psychology of language*. Edited by L. Jakobovits and M. Miron, 104–127. Englewood Cliffs, N.J.: Prentice-Hall.
SLAMA-CAZACU, T.
1957 *Relaţiile dintre gîndire şi limbaj în ontogeneză* [Relationships between thought and language in ontogenesis]. Bucharest: Ed. Acad. R.P.R.
1961a *Langage et contexte*. The Hague: Mouton. (Originally published 1959 in Romanian by Ed. Ştiinţifică.)
1961b *Dialogul la copii* [Dialogue between children]. Bucharest: Ed. Acad. R.P.R. (To be published in English by Mouton.)
1966 Quelques remarques théoriques et méthodologiques sur le problème de la forme et de la substance dans la genèse du système phonématique. *Cahiers de linguistique théorique et appliquée* 3: 171–179. (Republished in 1967 in *To honor Roman Jakobson, 1857–1965*. The Hague: Mcuton.)
1970 The power and limits of social context of language behaviour. *Cahiers de linguistique théorique et appliquée* 7:31–41.
1972a "The concepts of 'acquisition corpus,' 'aberrant corpus' and 'hierarchical system of errors' in contrastive analysis." Paper presented at the Third International Congress of Applied Linguistics, Copenhagen, August 1972. (Also in *The psycholinguistic approach in the Romanian-English Contrastive Analysis Project*. Bucharest: University Press, 1975.)
1972b " 'Regularization': a universal of the acquisition of language (native tongue and foreign languages) by children and adults." Paper presented at the International Conference on Recent Advances in the Psychology of Learning, Frascati, Italy, September 1972. (To appear in the Proceedings; also published in 1973 in *Invăţarea limbii* [Language acquisition]. Edited by T. Slama-Cazacu. Bucharest: University Press; and in *The Romanian-English Contrastive Analysis Project: reports and studies*, IV. Bucharest: University Press, 1974.)
1973 *Introduction to psycholinguistics*. The Hague: Mouton. (Originally published 1968 in Romanian by Ed. Ştiinţifică.)
SLOBIN, D., *editor*
1971 *The ontogenesis of grammar: a theoretical symposium*. New York and London: Academic Press.
VAN GINNEKEN, J.
1933 "La biologie de la base d'articulation," in *Psychologie du langage*, 266–320. Paris: Alcan.
ZAZZO, R.
1957 Le problème de l'imitation chez le nouveau-né. *Enfance* 2:135–142. 142.

Reading and Stages of Language Acquisition

RAGNHILD SÖDERBERGH

EARLY READING

Recently there has been an increased interest in the abilities and achievements of the very young child. Within the framework of this interest fall experiments in early reading. I mention here only two names: those of Omar K. Moore and Glenn Doman. Both have shown that children about two years of age learn to read with remarkably great ease — Doman by showing words written on big cards, Moore by letting the children play with a "talking typewriter."

The Early Language of Children: Onset of Speech

How is it that children of two can learn to read, when normally they are considered "mature" for this task at a much later age — in England at five and in the Scandinavian countries at seven, to mention only two examples. Linguistic research during the last fifteen years might throw some light on this problem.

Eric H. Lenneberg (1967) has convincingly shown that the onset of speech and of certain linguistic abilities such as babbling, speaking isolated words, producing two-word sentences, etc., are determined by maturational processes. That is why children start to talk at roughly the same age all over the world and have acquired a "basic language" by three to four years of age, regardless of what language is their mother tongue.

Another interesting question is HOW a child acquires his first language.

How is the First Language Acquired?

As early as 1915 the linguist Otto Jespersen in *Børnesprog* drew attention to the CREATIVITY of the child: the child observes the language spoken around him and to him, takes it in and works at it, producing, as it were, his own grammatical rules, which are sometimes "correct," sometimes "wrong" from the point of view of the adult's language. Research in child language, however, has traditionally been the concern of psychologists. Thus the behavioristic theory has for a long time dominated the view of language acquisition: the child learns to talk by IMITATION. When he speaks correctly he is rewarded, when he makes mistakes he is criticized; therefore correct speech will finally prevail.

In the 1960's linguists were beginning to take more interest in language theory: the aim was to construct a universal theory of grammar and in this connection the language of the child was considered a central research topic. Particularly, research workers from the workshop of Chomsky (Brown, Bellugi, Ervin, etc.) sponsored the old view of the creativity of the child: the child listens, makes out his own grammatical model, tries it out on people around him by constructing sentences according to this model, then changes it little by little until finally it converges with the adult model. For a child to learn to speak, the chief requirement seems to be that he is exposed to language, i.e. gets the material necessary to construct his models.

Reading is Learning a Written Language

Now if a child acquires his SPOKEN language if only he is EXPOSED TO IT, why should not the same be true of WRITTEN language? The reason, then, why Doman's and Moore's two- and three-year-old "pupils" learn to read while other children of the same age normally do not, should be that only the former have been exposed to written language.

SOME SWEDISH EXPERIMENTS IN EARLY READING

In 1965 I decided to try out the Doman method on a girl then two years and four months old. By this method the child learns whole words as entities. The experiment showed that the child, as she learned more and more words, made spontaneous attempts at reading the new words presented. When trying to read the new words she broke them down into smaller entities, first morphemes, but at a later stage also graphemes. Finally all by herself she arrived at a complete understanding of the correspondences between sound (phoneme) and letter (grapheme) and was then able to read any new word presented to her, by means of analysis and synthesis. This stage was reached after fourteen months of reading, when the girl was three and a half years old (Söderbergh 1971).

But the way the girl tackled the written material shown to her also tells something about the correspondence between a child's development of spoken language and the way he acquires a written language. To get some more data I interviewed the parents of three more children who have for a longer or shorter time been exposed to the same reading method. All the data obtained have then been compared with a collection of data on Swedish children's language acquisition between the ages of one and a half and three and a half years.[1] (In the discussion below the children in these experiments are referred to as A [main experiment, see Söderbergh 1971], B₁, B₂, and B₃.) This comparison suggests that when teaching two- to three-year-old children to read *one should take care to let the reading material presented roughly follow the stages by which a child normally acquires his spoken language.* What, then, are these normal stages and how is the Doman method related to them?

Swedish Children's Early Language Development

The early language development of Swedish-speaking children is very similar to that of English-speaking children as described by, for example, Louis Bloom, Roger Brown, Ursula Bellugi, Susan Ervin, and Paula Menyuk. After a long period of babbling, where the general traits of intonation are those of the Swedish language, the child starts to talk in ONE-WORD SENTENCES, i.e. he uses one single word that combined with gestures, tone, mimicry, and the total situation in which the word is spoken HAS THE FUNCTION OF A WHOLE SENTENCE.[2] Let us give an example. A girl of one and a half plays with a model car. A wheel is missing. She shows the car to her mother and says *laga* [mend, repair]

[1] At Stockholm University we are conducting a longitudinal study of the language of six children, who are tape-recorded for half an hour every two weeks from when they are one and a half till they are three and a half years old. The immediate concern of this investigation is the emergence of syntax.
[2] The first one-word sentences may appear already when the child is only eight months old.

in a prompting voice. A seven-year-old child in the same situation would have said: "Mummy, please mend this car." But the baby cannot produce sentences longer than one word and thus she chooses the most essential word *laga* [mend]. Her gesture towards her mother corresponds to the seven-year-old child's word "Mummy," the car that the baby presents to her mother corresponds to "this car" and the prompting tone has the same function as the older child's "please." We now assume that Mother is busy doing something else and that Father takes the car. The baby then shouts *Mamma* [Mummy] until her mother pays attention. Then she repeats *laga*, and if the mother should then take another toy the girl would present the car, saying *bil* [car] or *den* [this one]. Only a few weeks later the same girl will be able to express herself more clearly by means of language. Then she will have started to talk in TWO-WORD SENTENCES,[3] and in the situation just described she will say either *Mamma laga* [Mummy mend] or *laga bil* [mend car], *laga den* [mend this one]. Still later she will be able to use three-word sentences, saying *Mamma laga bil* [Mummy mend car] or *Mamma laga den* [Mummy mend this one].

There is no doubt that understanding language comes before the actual use of language. It is also clear that the three utterances *laga*, *laga bil*, and *Mamma laga bil* must be given the same semantic interpretation in the situation given. Thus it is the child's FORMAL GRAMMATICAL CAPACITY that develops. It is generally assumed that the development from one-word sentences toward sentences consisting of three or more words reflects a restriction on the memory of the child which gradually disappears as the child matures. This seems all the more plausible as the development from the one-word sentence on holds true for all children whatever language is their mother tongue.

There is, however, not only a question of NUMBER of words. Still more important is WHAT words are used. The earliest combinations of words are simple constructions containing concrete substantives or verbs denoting things immediately present and visible actions, or deictic words like *där* [there], *den* [this/that one], *titta* [look]. Only gradually are the nouns and verbs given determiners, i.e. adjectives and adverbs turn up. As determiners like *alla, många* [all,many] appear, the morphology of the noun is also developed: plural endings and definite articles are added. As the morphology of the verb develops, the modals appear. By this time the prepositions also begin to turn up.

Thus we see that in Swedish, as in English, the earliest sentences of

---

[3]   The child may talk in two-word sentences when it is fourteen or fifteen months old, although the normal age seems to be around eighteen months.

children contain words with a heavy semantic load, CONTENT WORDS, whereas FUNCTION WORDS, such as modals, prepositions, and articles, turn up at a later stage. To characterize this early speech, Brown and Bellugi use the term "telegraphic speech." One reason for this absence of function words — apart from the already mentioned restriction on memory — seems to be that the child, having great trouble in learning not only the phonology, syntax, and lexicon of language, but also choosing the appropriate words, pronouncing them, and putting them together, concentrates on the most indispensable parts of the sentence and skips what is redundant or predictable from context.

As the child masters his language better and better, he also begins to make sentences containing more than one clause. Relative and temporal clauses are among the earliest.

THE GLENN DOMAN METHOD

A method of presenting reading material to a child with a minimum of instruction is described by Glenn Doman (1964). Words are written on cards, one word on each card. To begin with, the letters should be red and 12.5 centimeters high. The cards are presented to the child at a maximum rate of one a day.

The first word is "mother." When the child says "mother" as soon as you show that card, you go to the next card, which reads "father." When you are sure that the child can discriminate the "mother" card from the "father" card you proceed to nouns denoting parts of the body (hand, nose, ear, etc.). These words are written with red letters 10 centimeters high. Then you go on to what Doman calls the vocabulary of the home: words denoting the child's toys and other personal belongings, words denoting well-known things in the house, etc. The child should be able to see and touch the thing at the same time as the "teacher" pronounces the word and shows the card to him.

The domestic vocabulary also includes some verbs denoting simple actions well known to the child. The teacher may, to begin with, illustrate a verb by performing the action at the same time as he pronounces the corresponding word and shows the card. The domestic vocabulary should be written down in red letters 7.5 centimeters high. All the time, the "teacher" should be careful not to present new words without making sure that the child recognizes the old ones.

Then a book is provided. It should be a very simple and short book, containing not more than 150 different words. The letters should be

7.5 millimeters high. The "teacher" copies the book, rewriting it in black letters 2.5 centimeters high. Then each word is written on a card, in black letters 5 centimeters high. These cards are presented to the child one by one in the same way as before.

When the child knows all the words, the words are put together to form the sentences of the book. The cards are put on the floor side by side, and the child now learns to read sentences, one sentence a day. When the child can read all the sentences of the book in this way he is given the handwritten copy of the book and is taught to read the sentences from this copy: reading left to right and from the top of the page to the bottom of the page.

When the child is well familiar with this handwritten copy, the printed book is presented to him. And now he will be able to read this fluently, in spite of the fact that the letters are only 7.5 millimeters high.

You go on with other books, and now it is not necessary to have an intermediate handwritten copy. All words new to the child are written down on cards and shown to him. When the child knows these words he gets the new book, etc. After the child has read one or two books, you write down the alphabet in small letters and capitals, each letter on one card. You present the cards to the child, telling him the names of the letters like this: about *a* "This is a small 'ei'," about *A* "This is a capital 'ei'," etc.

It should be noted that the child is not taught the sound values of the letters but is just given the conventional names — with the qualifier "small" and "capital" included in the name of the letter. This is obviously done to help the child to discern the letters within the word units.

By presenting the letters you no doubt draw the child's ATTENTION to the code. But as one avoids any kind of sounding and instead obscures what associations there might occur between letter and sound by adding the qualifier "small" and "capital" to the conventional name of the letter, this presentation cannot be said to help the child discover the relations between letters and sounds. Nor, as the letters are presented in their alphabetic order without being grouped according to distinctive features, do you give any hints about the graphematic system; instead, the child is left to make the discoveries totally on his own.

The way of presenting the letters of the alphabet to the child in order to help him to discern the letters within the word units might be compared with what most adults do when they hear that a child who has begun to talk does not master a particular sound: they pronounce the sound separately and ask the child to do the same.

*The Adaptations of the Doman Method Compared with Adaptations
Made in Talking to Children*

As we see, Glenn Doman not only randomly exposes children to
written language, but he also makes definite ADAPTATIONS of the material presented. But that is exactly what happens when a child is exposed to spoken language: the child's family makes adaptations when
talking to the child in order to help him understand.

In Doman's written material the letters are bigger than normal; when
addressing a small child learning to speak you often talk in a distinct
and clear voice. The child is first presented with written nouns and
verbs; in the same way you talk to a baby in very short sentences, repeating or putting heavy stress on particular nouns and verbs that
carry the essential meaning of what you want to say. As was mentioned
above, the first sentences of the baby are one-word sentences, often
consisting of one noun or one verb. The words first presented in the
Doman method are concrete and they are illustrated so as to make sure
the meaning is understood; similarly a child learns to speak in concrete
situations where the things spoken about are present.

But the adaptations made by adults in talking to small children go
far beyond this. Catherine E. Snow (1972) has found that "Mothers'
speech to young children was simpler and more redundant than their
normal speech" and that "experienced mothers were only slightly better
than nonmothers in predicting the speech-style modifications required
by young children." From this Snow infers that "children who are
learning language have available a sample of speech which is simpler,
more redundant and less confusing than normal adult speech." In her
experiment recording mothers talking to two-year-old children, Snow
found that mothers use shorter utterances, fewer subordinate clauses,
and fewer compound verbs. Mean preverb length was also shorter and
selfembedding did not occur. Moreover, 16 percent of the utterances
were simple phrases lacking either verb or noun, which was due to the
frequent repetitions of parts of sentences in order to make the child
understand: "Put the red truck in the box now. The red truck. No, the
red truck. In the box. The red truck in the box." Thus mothers seem
to adapt intuitively to the primitive grammar of the children: shorter
sentences, less complex sentences etc. This simplified speech, according
to Snow, not only adds to the child's comprehension but is also "admirably designed to aid children in learning language."

Not being a linguist but a doctor of medicine, Glenn Doman has not
paid any attention to sentence length or to syntactical complexity in his

reading instruction. After teaching the first fifty words to their children, the parents are left entirely on their own in choosing books. Book-minded parents with a sure linguistic sense no doubt make this choice in a reasonably good way; tentatively they choose what is suitable just as any parent by intuition adapts his spoken language. But if the parents do not have this linguistic insight they may fail altogether in finding the reading material appropriate to the child's linguistic stage. (There are in fact very few books that consistently keep the style needed.) Another less obvious problem is that if you use the Doman method with a very advanced child of three, he might be too clever to take interest in the reading cards, i.e. linguistically he has long passed the stage where the single word will attract his attention.

Let us consider these facts while looking at the experiments in teaching two- to three-year-old Swedish children to read by the Doman method.

WHAT THE EXPERIMENTS TELL ABOUT EARLY READING AND LANGUAGE ACQUISITION

The Function Words

We have mentioned that the early sentences of the child are syntactically simple, consisting of few words and leaving out what is redundant or predictable from context. That means that the so-called function words — modals, prepositions, etc. — are missing during the earliest stages. The child is only gradually mastering these words. As regards the prepositions, they first emerge as murmured sounds, then one single preposition *i* [in] serves as an all-round locative preposition, and finally the other prepositions turn up, locatives first. This development takes several months, starting around two years of age. Thus a child of two being presented to written language containing function words may be supposed to have certain difficulties with them. Such difficulties were observed in Child A (the main experiment). When the girl was going to learn the words of her first book, she was two years and five months. The book chosen had generally very short sentences, but one of the first sentences was unfortunately nine words long and contained five function words: "Vet du vad det är för dag i dag?" When I showed the reading card with the first of these function words to the girl, the word *vad* [what], she said: "När vi läser *tunga* gör vi så här [when we read TONGUE we do like this]" — she puts out her tongue — "*men* vad?

[but WHAT?]." She objected to the function word *vad* as it was not possible to illustrate it — although her own language by that time was advanced enough to contain most of the function words. To have a still smaller child that is linguistically at so primitive a stage that he has not developed the function words try to read and understand a sentence like the one mentioned above seems to me to be a hopeless task.

The reason why the girl had objections to make against *vad*, in spite of the fact that she had already mastered the function words in her own spoken language, is probably that the word was shown to her as a single word written down on a card. Function words very seldom occur alone, either in spoken or written language, and in presenting a child with a single function word you construct a NONLINGUISTIC SITUATION. The fact that function words only occur in combination with, and, as it were, semantically subordinate to, content words makes them less obvious to the speaker. This seems to be true also about adult speakers. In a reading experiment with adults at the beginning of this century Edmund Burke Huey presented isolated words on squares of cardboard. The connective and relational words did not then suggest any imagery to the readers. "Because of this absence of imagery the exposure of these words was regarded with much displeasure, their isolated appearance seeming to be regarded as anomalous," Huey wrote (1908: 154).

The remedy, when the girl failed to read the function words of the book chosen, was to write a book for her, containing short sentences almost completely made up of content words. When choosing new books for her to read I took great care to let them only gradually become syntactically more complex.

Combinations of Words

A crucial point in the child's oral linguistic development seems to be when he leaves the one-word stage and starts to combine two words into sentences. There are great differences among children as to the age when this step is taken. In fact the emergence of the two-word sentence seems to be related not so much to age as to the child's active vocabulary. In the weeks before a child begins to make his first two-word sentences you often notice a remarkable increase in his vocabulary and a very keen interest in learning new words. Jaroslava Pačesová (1968) relates the linguistic development of the child — prosody, phonology, and parts of speech — not to age but to *the number of single words used by the child.* Thus she has made a distinction between the period of the first 50 words, of the first 100 words, and of the first 500 words. From Pačesová's material it is evident that the child enters into the two-word stage during the period of the first 100 words.

The one-word stage may start already at eight to ten months. The increasing interest in learning new words during the end of this period manifests itself in several ways. The child points — often using some deictic word of his own, normally pronounced by Swedish children with the intonation typical of questions — to make clear that he wants to know the word for what he is pointing at.

It seems that the first step of the Doman method — that of showing isolated words denoting persons and things in the child's immediate surroundings — is very well fitted for a child at the end of the one-word stage.

Let us return to the Swedish experiments. Only Child B_1 was shown the first written words when she was still at the one-word stage. Child B_1 was only one year and one month when "reading" her first word. Her parents went on slowly for eight months, all the time only showing single words to the girl. Then they broke off for lack of time. The girl had by that time left the one-word stage, her mean sentence length being two words. Eight months later, when the girl was two years and five months, reading was taken up again. Then the girl was linguistically advanced, using sentences of four to six words, containing function words such as pronouns, modals, prepositions, and adverbs. The parents then almost immediately began combining words into sentences, and the girl was extremely interested. Two months later, when she was two years and seven months old, the girl had already succeeded in breaking the code. The father, who is a linguist, followed the same path as I had done with Child A, beginning with very easy sentences and slowly increasing the syntactic complexity.

Let us now compare Child A and Child B_1. Child B_1 started to read when she was one year and one month and she attained full reading ability when she was two years and seven months. *The total time elapsing from the start to the breaking of the code was eighteen months,* but as there was a break of eight months *the active reading instruction time was only ten months.* A very important fact is that the reading instruction approximately followed the linguistic development of the child: during the first eight months of instruction when the child was mostly at the one-word stage and in the beginning of the two-word stage she was only shown single words. After the break, when the girl had reached an advanced linguistic stage she was shown new words AND sentences of increasing complexity. It is to be noted that she was immensely interested in reading during this second period of instruction.

Child A started reading much later. She was then at about the same linguistic stage as Child B_1 after the break. Child A, however, was shown sentences after only seven weeks of reading. As a matter of fact, she urged the experimenter to show her more and more words during the seven weeks, and her interest markedly increased when going over to reading sentences and books as well as cards. The experimenter was obliged to keep a higher tempo than intended because of the girl's impatience to get on. *The total time elapsing from the start to the breaking of the code was fourteen months for child A* and *the active reading instruction time was thirteen months,* three months more than with Child B_1. For Child A the reading instruction in the beginning lagged behind her linguistic development, but by the time the code was broken this gap had been closed.

A quite different course was followed by Child B_2, who started to read by the Doman method when she was three years old. Child B_2 was at about the same linguistic stage at three years of age as B_1 was at two years and five months: her sentences were normally four to six words long, containing pronouns, modals, certain prepositions, and adverbs. Child B_2 was shown single words during a period of four months; then the parents went on to make simple sentences out of the words. The girl took an immense interest in this reading of sentences. Then the parents suddenly discovered that they had made a great mistake: they had written all the words in CAPITALS, and thus were not able to let the girl begin to read books. Instead, they decided to start from the beginning, teaching the girl the words in small letters. After two months, however, the girl lost interest in reading and the experiment was broken off.

The reason why the reading instruction was not successful in this case seems obvious: already at the start, the reading instruction lagged behind the child's linguistic development. She was, however, said to have a great interest in reading when she arrived as far as reading sentences. But instead of rapidly going on to fill the gap between spoken and written language by letting the child read sentences of increasing complexity, the parents were then obliged to go back to the original stage in order to teach the appropriate written symbols.

The last child observed was B_3. He was three years and two months when he was first confronted with the Doman method. Linguistically, he was then an extremely advanced child. At two he had already been talking in sentences of up to five words or more, and at three he was

using complex sentences consisting of two or more clauses. Even his
morphology was almost complete by that age. Let us just give two
examples of sentences which he used when he was three. *"När vi skulle
åka dit till Lysekil så åkte vi en Götakanal-båt som var jättestor* [When
we were going to Lysekil, we went by a Götakanalboat which was
frightfully big]." *"Om man trycker hårt på den där knappen så kom-
mer det vatten ur den där slangen* [If you press that button very hard
water will run out of that pipe]."

The mother had made quite a lot of reading cards for the boy (fifteen
to twenty). He took them all and put them away when they had been
shown to him, and he did not seem to take any particular interest in
the cards. A few days later, however, he fetched the cards. When his
mother asked him what was written on them, he was first embarrassed,
then he answered, and it was evident that he remembered most of the
words. He did not want to have any new cards, but instead he asked
his mother about the single LETTERS and tried to read them.

This case is not clear enough to give any definite evidence. We see
that the boy, however, had reached a very advanced linguistic stage
and did not take any particular interest in the cards but instead started
to ask about the letters. With Children A and B_2, who also started
rather late, although much earlier than B_3, it was clear that (1) A urged
the experimenter to go on quickly, and (2) B_2 was immensely interested
when arriving at the sentences but lost all interest when going back
again to reading only single cards. Child B_3, then, may have been so
advanced that the method of showing only single cards was not a good
one for him — he was too far from the oral one-word stage. It is very
interesting to notice that he immediately took an interest in the LETTERS
and tried to tackle the problem that way instead: by learning the code
and using it, not by learning words and then finding out about the code.
At this point I want to mention a small case study by Brantberg-Frigyes
(1969), who noticed that her boy, when he was three years and two
months, began to take an interest in written words and LETTERS. By
comparing letters in different words and sounding these letters out to
the boy as soon as he put questions about written words, and by letting
the boy play with biscuits formed as letters, the mother stimulated the
boy to find out about reading. By three and a half he was able to read.
This gives a hint that a child whose interest is caught by the written
word *will notice the letters by three to three and a half*. The best
method of teaching reading might then be tackling the code directly.

As a last and very interesting fact it may be mentioned that Child B_1
began putting questions about letters during her second reading period

(after the break of eight months) and that her father then combined the phonics method and the whole-word method in teaching her. Child B_1 was then two years and six months. Child A began to take an interest in letters after two months of reading whole words. She was then also two years and six months. The method of teaching her was not changed because of this, however, as the central aim of the experiment was to find out how a child could succeed in breaking the code all by itself.

Let us now draw some conclusions from what has here been said about reading and stages of language acquisition. A child can easily learn to read at the same time as he learns to talk. One may successfully use a whole-word method like Glenn Doman's. Only one should take care EITHER (1) to closely follow the oral linguistic development of the child, showing him only concrete nouns and verbs when he is at the one-word stage, two-word sentences when he talks in two-word sentences, etc., OR (2) if the child has reached a more mature linguistic stage when the teaching starts, to follow the normal track of a child's oral linguistic development, only advancing a bit more quickly through the first stages, trying to put the words together in sentences as soon as possible. If the child takes an interest in letters a phonics method might be used here in addition to the whole-word method.

It thus seems evident that in teaching a small child to read one must adapt the reading material to the linguistic development of the child. Our only way to get knowledge about this development is from the evidence of THE SPEECH of the child. The PASSIVE linguistic knowledge of the child — his understanding — usually far precedes his "output." It is therefore possible, as soon as the technical problem of reading is solved and the code has been broken, to give very young children increasingly complex reading material that will finally far surpass their oral linguistic capacity. The written language will then begin to influence the child's spoken language and his way of thinking and reasoning. But that is a topic which goes beyond the scope of this paper.

THE READING MATERIAL AND THE "CULTURAL SETTING" OF THE CHILD

Finally, I want to say a few words about the early reading material and its relation to the "cultural setting" of the child. The evidence here is taken exclusively from Child A.

To invoke and maintain the interest of the child the material must

TELL the child something.[4] Thus one takes care when choosing the first fifty words to write on reading cards to take not only words that are known by the child but words denoting things that are DEAR to the child: his favorite toys, his pillow, his new red shoes, etc. When the child is very young this greatly promotes learning, as to the child the written words ARE the things.

To illustrate this I shall give a few examples from the study of Child A. She sometimes got words with unpleasant associations. These were met with disgust, e.g. *hemskt* [frightful]: "Mother, I get so frightened when it says 'frightful' on a reading card." The first book read by Child A was a home-made one dealing with her cousin Anna and herself and their families. A's interest in the book was highly increased by the fact that it dealt with things familiar to her. One passage told about how Anna was pushing her dolls in a pram. Having read this passage the girl asked one day for the reading card with 'pram' on it. She took this card in her hand, looked up the passage about Anna and the pram in her book and said: "Now Anna is driving her pram and I am driving mine." This shows that when the contents of a book are related to the child's world and knowledge of the world the experiencing of the contents when reading must be very powerful.

Child A's reactions to another passage in her first book show that the child at two and a half was also able to make the distinction between reality and written representation of reality, but that she asked for absolute conformity between the two. The passage said that A's father, who lived in another country, would come and spend the Christmas holidays with her. Now, Father fell ill and was taken to the hospital, so he could not come. The girl did not make any comment on this passage until two months after she had read the book for the first time. Then she suddenly said: "My big book is wrong when it says that Father came on that day — he was in the hospital. I am going to check it. When I become a big girl I am going to write it correctly."

Child A always tried to relate the new words given and the content of the books to her knowledge of reality. When at three years and four months old she got the word *såld* [sold], she made the comment: "Perhaps it is my pram that has been sold; for I did not need it." When, two years and eight months old, she was reading about Babar's marriage she said "Why should he get married? An elephant!" Among the

---

[4] Good reading teachers have, of course, always been aware of this. Here I only want to mention Sylvia Ashton-Warner, who in her works takes the view that the only way to make reading material meaningful and interesting to children is to let them write their own books.

twenty small books she read during the first fourteen months the experiment went on, her favorite ones were two richly illustrated books: *The new house* and *The new road*, the first one very concretely telling about a new big apartment house being built, the second one telling about the construction of a new road — both well-known events to Swedish children during the 1960's. Another book telling how a canary grew as big as an elephant and was greeted outside the Town Hall by the Mayor and the Guard of the town, was met with complete indifference. It was almost impossible to make her read the book. The reason was twofold: first, the Mayor, the Town Hall, the Guard, etc., were altogether outside the range of her experience; second, she did not know that a canary did not normally grow as big as an elephant, so she missed the point entirely.

Just as the syntactical complexity of the reading material may be successively increased even beyond the oral capacity of the child, so the contents of the books may gradually extend beyond the immediate experience of the child. Child A when she was between three and a half and four years old began to read books in which many things and phenomena were unknown to her. In some cases I have seen that her later experience of the thing in real life became much more intense and rich than it would probably have been without this literary anticipation.

Thus she was all in raptures over her first sunset, experienced when she was four years and three months, and the first time she saw cows grazing she shouted in a voice full of joy: "Oh, this must be a PASTURE." The sunsets and pastures of literature had finally come to life. But also from a purely practical point of view it may sometimes be very useful to have read about a thing before you meet it. The child may thus be relieved from the awe of the unknown; he knows beforehand what he may expect to find and how to tackle a new situation.

CONCLUSIONS

Thus we see that during the period of LEARNING to read, the two- to three-year-old child's reading material should be adapted, (1) LINGUISTICALLY to the stages by which a child normally acquires his spoken language and to the learner's actual linguistic capacity, and (2) AS REGARDS CONTENT to the actual experience, "the cultural setting," of the child. When the art of reading is mastered, however, both language and content may successively pass beyond the learner's capacity of spoken language and his immediate experience of life. Reading then at a very early age will become a means of developing the child's linguistic and cognitive capacity and a source of knowledge of world and man that goes far beyond what is afforded by a child's daily environment.

REFERENCES

BRANTBERG-FRIGYES, B.
   1969   *Kan en treåring lära läsa?* [Can a three-year-old learn to read?]. Lund: Gleerups.

BROWN, R., U. BELLUGI
   1963   "Three processes in the child's acquisition of syntax," in *New directions in the study of language*. Edited by E. H. Lenneberg, 131–163. Cambridge, Mass.: M.I.T. Press.

CHALL, J.
   1967   *Learning to read: the great debate.* New York: McGraw-Hill.

DOMAN, G.
   1964   *How to teach your baby to read. New York:* Random House.

HUEY, EDMUND BURKE
   1908   *The psychology and pedagogy of reading.* New York: Macmillan.

JESPERSEN, OTTO
   1923   *Børnesprog, en bog for foraeldre* [The language of children, a book for parents]. Copenhagen: Nordisk. (Second, revised edition of *Nutidssprog hos born og voksne* [Present-day language for children and grown-ups].)

LENNEBERG, E. H.
   1967   *Biological foundations of language.* New York: Wiley.

MC CARTHY, D.
   1954   "Language development in children," in *Manual of child psychology*. Edited by L. Carmichael, 492–630. New York: Wiley.

MENYUK, P.
   1969   *Sentences children use.* Cambridge, Mass.: M.I.T. Press.
   1971   *The acquisition and development of language.* Englewood Cliffs, N.J.: Prentice-Hall.

PAČESOVÁ, J.
   1968   *The development of vocabulary in the child.* Brno: Universita J. E. Purkyně.

SMITH, F., G. A. MILLER, *editors*
   1966   *The genesis of language.* Cambridge, Mass.: M.I.T. Press.

SNOW, CATHERINE E.
   1972   Mothers' speech to children learning language. *Child Development* 43:549–565.

SÖDERBERGH, R.
   1969   Strukturer och normer i barnspråk. *Nordisk tidskrift* 45:67–82.
   1971   *Reading in early childhood: a linguistic study of a Swedish preschool child's gradual acquisition of reading ability.* Stockholm: Almqvist and Wiksell.

WARDHAUGH, R.
   1969   *Reading: a linguistic perspective.* New York: Harcourt Brace Jovanovich.

Competence in English-Language Learning by American Indian Monolinguals and Bilinguals

MARY R. MILLER

Fieldwork not only serves the primary objectives for which research is undertaken; it can also have important secondary consequences. While the researcher is in pursuit of certain limited objectives regarding the language of a specific group, their sociolinguistic setting, or even the more limited aspects of a single language, he also has ample opportunity to assess the theoretical framework within which the work is being done. There is the opportunity to prove the merits and defects of theory and often the occasion for new insights and attempts at empirical verification. This is essentially what happened in the research about to be described.

The study was one of English-language acquisition in monolingual and bilingual Pima children on the Salt River Reservation in Arizona. The objectives of the study were to determine what these children knew about the English language and to further determine how their knowledge compared with that of a similar group of Maryland children. Stated more precisely, was the maturational schedule of the Pima children the same as that of the Maryland children, and was it the same for monolinguals as for bilinguals? The answer to both these questions was no, and it was at this point that a careful reexamination of the theory of competence and performance seemed necessary. Repeated considerations of these terms and their usefulness in fieldwork, and indeed in all such research, did not lead to the rejection of either term. Rather it led to a reaffirmation of their usefulness. PERFORMANCE as a term could not be discarded because it represented the data which had been collected from the children. COMPETENCE likewise could not be discarded because it appeared ultimately useful for the researcher. What was needed in the case of linguistic competence was some slight clarification and realignment of definition.

The matter of linguistic competence and what it implies for the research done with Pima children is the subject of this paper. Such conclusions would have been impossible without the unanswered questions raised by the study of English-language acquisition in Pima children.

Fifty children took the tests given on the Salt River Reservation. Nearly all of them were between the ages of eight and eleven, and the results are limited to a compilation of the data of these age groups. They were identified as monolingual or bilingual by a questionnaire concerning their knowledge and use of Pima and other languages.

The main portion of the test was individually administered and dealt with selected constructions in syntax and selected inflections and derivations in morphology. Children were tested for their ability to produce grammatical structures involving the interrogative, imperative, tag questions, verb particle permutations, reflexives, and passives. They were also tested for their ability to add appropriate endings for plurals, possessives, tenses, and comparatives, as well as for agent, abode diminutive and quality suffixes. This last portion of the test was patterned on that of Jean Berko (1958: 150–177) while the syntax portion was original.

There was no phonological test, although some material of phonological interest was gleaned from other portions of the test. The above tests were closely structured in order to eliminate acceptable but irrelevant data, but there was also a less structured test dealing with sentence-embedding and conjoining. Children from three suburban counties of Maryland were the control group for this research, and this data was used to arbitrarily establish norms of English-language acquisition.

A word of explanation is in order concerning the theoretical orientation of the research. In this paper, knowledge of language has no reference to how well a child reads or writes, nor how well he can explain what he has learned in a formal course in grammar. This knowledge refers rather to the speaker-hearer's knowledge of his language, with such knowledge presumed to consist of a system of rules which he has mastered and which he puts to use in speech. This system is an internalized generative grammar which determines how sentences are to be formed, used, and understood. This theory relies heavily on the supposition that human beings come equipped with large amounts of information concerning the nature of language in general, and only need to hear limited samples of the language at hand. The matter of the right grammar is simplified considerably by assuming the existence of linguistic universals, which may be defined as properties of natural language common to all languages.

Chomsky (1964: 51) emphasizes the basic human equality in the ability to acquire language by stating that "each normal human has developed for himself a thorough competence in his native language." Competence is defined by Chomsky (1965: 4) as the speaker-hearer's knowledge of his language, and is seen as both the cognitive means for acquiring language and the end product of that acquisition. Competence, therefore, is at once the capacity for language, and the product of that capacity. During acquisition it is the capacity; at maturity it is the accomplishment itself. Katz (1964:415) says a viable theory requires that each speaker be able to perform (and hence have competence) much as every other one. Individual differences are considered extralinguistic in origin. The most pertinent portion of the definition of competence for this research is not that it differs from performance, which can be characterized as actual linguistic behavior, or that speakers may possess linguistic knowledge which is not evidenced in performance, but the fact that it is a species-specific capacity supposedly equal among all human beings.

Its place as part of the competence theory was brought into question by the often wide range of performance between Pima children and Maryland children of the same age in as nearly as possible identical circumstances. While Maryland children continued to increase their language prowess performancewise, Pima children tended to show a leveling off or even a decrease in performance as they grew older. The theoretical framework of this research presumes, in addition to such facets of language acquisition as the internalization of grammar, the presence of linguistic universals, and the ideas of competence and performance, that language development is a maturational matter paralleling other forms of maturation in the child.

In this view, language training and social setting are of minor import, with speech onset occurring regularly no matter what the other circumstances, and with children exhibiting equal or nearly equal aptitude for language in all normal circumstances. In addition, puberty is considered the end point for most maturational processes, including language, and language acquisition in the first-language sense terminates at about that time. However, what has not been determined is the maturational schedule for language. No one knows how closely structured the acquisition schedule is, how wide the range of variation may be within the normal classification, and how it may be altered. Presumably intelligence is not a factor.

The difficulty with competence as defined thus far is that it is ephemeral, illusive, and incapable of empirical verification. This is much the same as saying that it is a wonderful idea but what does one do with it.

Performance cannot directly reflect competence since performance is affected by "such grammatically irrelevant conditions as memory limitations, distractions, shifts of attention and interest, and errors (random or characteristic) in applying his knowledge of the language in actual performance." In linguistic performance, "we must consider the interaction of a variety of factors, of which the underlying competence of the speaker-hearer is only one" (Chomsky 1965: 3, 4).

The primary aims of the research were to establish a maturational schedule in the English language for normal middle-class children in the Maryland suburbs and to test and verify the theories utilized in that research by comparing the results with the Pima tests. However, the idea that one might be testing only isolated samples of performance was a disheartening one. The results of the data compilation show that Pima children know almost but not quite as much English as Maryland children do at eight years of age, which was the beginning point for the test compilation, and they definitely know less English than Maryland children at age eleven, which was the end point for the test. It is hypothesized that at some time previous to age eight they are equal in their knowledge of the English language, assuming that they have been exposed to it prior to that time in a regular and consistent fashion. This would not preclude a Pima-speaking home, provided their playmates spoke English.

By age eleven Pima children as a group trail suburban children in language acquisition by two or three years with two exceptions. In interrogative constructions they trailed by only one year, and in negative constructions they trailed only slightly. Noteworthy was the actual decline in the scores of Pima children from age ten on. While Maryland children slowly but surely increased their ability to produce simple grammatical constructions from one year to the next, Pima children not only failed to increase their scores but in some cases actually showed declining scores.

The results of data compilation for monolingual and bilingual Pimas show that Pima-English bilinguals compared very favorably with Pima monolinguals at age eight. This general equality endured until about age ten when monolingual Pima children began to acquire English more rapidly than did their bilingual peers. When the three groups are compared, Maryland children showed the most consistent and greatest progress from age ten onward. They were followed by monolingual Pima children who began to acquire English more slowly after age ten. The third group, the bilingual Pima children, show even more slowing in the rate of acquisition than do Pima monolinguals, and in some cases their scores actually decline from earlier levels of acquisition.

It is clear that many Pima children never reach the performance standards of Maryland children in standard English. This is in spite of the fact that many of them are English monolinguals. The question is whether such differences can be attributed solely to memory limitations, distractions, shifts of attention and interest, and random or characteristic errors in the application of their knowledge to actual language performance. It seems doubtful that this can be the case. The only one of these factors which might bear such responsibility is that of errors, random or characteristic, in applying language knowledge. The fact that monolingual Pima children can produce acceptable passive constructions only 40 percent of the time at age eleven while Maryland children of the same age can do this 80 percent of the time indicates the width of the discrepancy.

Although some grammarians attribute all dialect differences within a language system to low level rules, such rules as those for the passive transformation are far more basic to the language. The same might be said of the relatively simple transformation involving the movement of particles in two-part verbs from a position immediately following the verb to a position immediately following the complement. Yet the percentage of all Pima children, monolingual and bilingual, who could successfully manipulate this simple permutation at eleven was 62 percent, while for Maryland children the figure was 100 percent. Since in terms of this theory language acquisition tapers off or terminates at puberty, when all types of maturation are essentially complete, children of eleven have very little remaining maturational time in which to acquire English or any other language on a first-language basis.

Another factor which bears on the competence-performance relationship is the fact that Pima scores begin to decline or flatten out after about age ten while Maryland scores continue upward. Again we can resort to such explanations as memory limitations, distractions, shifts of interest and attention, and errors, random or systematic, which function in various ways to make performance less than true linguistic competence. In testing both groups, the conditions were made as similar as possible in order not to affect the results in any way. While the actual conditions may have varied in some minor ways which were beyond the control of the researcher, it would seem that the distraction-interference factor[1] for both groups would remain fairly constant, and that there would not be notice-

---

[1] The term distraction-interference is not used here in the sense of linguistic interference from another language, but in the sense in which the flow of electrical current encounters resistance in electrical conductors. Thus performance would equal competence minus the as yet undetermined distraction-interference factor.

ably more distraction-interference factors affecting performance at eleven than at nine or ten.

If Pima children suffer more distraction at eleven than at eight, it follows that a similar reaction might be expected in Maryland children. Yet scores for Pima children of eleven often fell below those of younger Pima children. For example, while 58 percent of all Pima children tested at nine years of age employed – ING by attaching it to the verb base in the proper context, by the age of eleven only 37 percent were doing so. There was no corresponding drop in Maryland children, who performed at 100 percent beginning at age nine and continued to do so at ages ten and eleven. In no case did Maryland children perform at a lower score at age eleven than they did at age ten. Pima children of ten, however, showed a higher score than did Pima children of eleven in interrogatives, and Pima children consistently lowered their score for all variants of the plural suffixes between ages ten and eleven.

Again it seems illogical to attribute this variation to distraction-interference factors affecting performance, while permitting the competence of all children to remain at a magic and unverifiable equivalence. Moreover, if sampling techniques have resulted in unequal populations, it should be sufficient to recall that if competence is the same for all, there is no need for employing scientific sampling. Consequently, any demonstrated evidence for questioning the competence of one group when compared with that of another cannot be attributed to sampling, since competence would be the same for all individuals and groups. While there may be variation in performance in intellectual tasks due to individual differences, this fact contrasts with the performance of speakers with respect to linguistic skill, where no significant individual differences are found (Katz 1964:415).

On the contrary, my suggestion is that the differences in the two populations, and the tapering off and/or actual decline in the performance of the Pima children as contrasted with the steady rise in the scores of the Maryland children, strongly indicates that more than performance is at stake here. Such wide divergence cannot be attributed solely to performance, and the researcher must come to grips sooner or later with the idea of competence. The inevitable conclusion, however reluctantly made, is that competence is not the same for everyone. In attempting to mediate between the grammatical theorists on the one hand whose chief concern is with the ideal speaker-hearer, leaving questions of individual and group deviation on the periphery of concern, and the sociolinguists on the other hand, one of whose concerns is with sociocultural linguistic divergence, it is important to attempt to relate theory to data.

Sociolinguists tend to be as different from one another in orientation as grammatical theorists, and there are a number of views on this subject. However, two important viewpoints regarding language variation which receive substantial support are viewing language divergence as deficient versus viewing it as merely different. The idea of language as deficit is that there is a developmental lag in the language acquisition of the impoverished child. The poor environment of the home results in disadvantage and alienation in school, which in turn results in economic and social disadvantage, and the cycle is repeated endlessly from generation to generation. In this setting language development and all intellectual development lags, and the acceptance of this view implies tacit rejection of equal linguistic competence for all human beings.

The other view is that of difference, which holds that language varies from group to group regardless of the sociocultural and economic situation, and that it tends to vary more in groups which are isolated in some way – geographically, culturally, economically, or racially. This view can be reconciled with competence in one of two ways. Either one can consider that all speakers of a particular social dialect have competence in that dialect, and label it a system apart from standard English, or one can consider all English as being systematic, with low level rules to account for the minor variations which occur in nonstandard dialects.

In the case of the Pima children, the results show what appears to be both difference and deficit. There are phonological differences in the speech of Pima children, with the differences mainly being the neutralization of some stops, fricatives, and vowels. The neutralization of stops appears to result from interference from a quite different system of stops in the Pima language. The neutralization of /b/ and /v/ among fricatives may be due to Spanish interference, although the extent of Spanish influence in the community today remains to be assessed. Vowel neutralization may be due to either Pima or Spanish interference. The consonantal neutralization affects inflectional suffixes in the English of the children, and accounts in part for low scores in the morphology portion of the test. It cannot, however, account for declining scores in the older age groups. Among Pima children, the plural and the possessive, which utilize sibilant fricatives, all show declining scores between the ages of ten and eleven.

The possessive suffix, in which a single variant was tested, declined from 50 percent at age ten to 37 percent at age eleven. The plural/z/ variant declined from 73 percent at age ten to 48 percent at age eleven. The plural /s/ variant declined from 100 percent at age ten to 45 percent at age eleven. The plural /ez/ variant was used by 32 percent of the

Pima children at nine years. At ten its use had declined from 32 percent to 20 percent, and by age eleven it had declined further to 13 percent. In testing for all variants of the plural suffix, it was not uncommon to find the base form left uninflected. This occurred more frequently when the base form terminated in a sibilant, leading to the conclusion that a nonsense word ending in a sibilant was considered already inflected. For example, a nonsense word like NIZ may have been thought to require no plural suffix because of the sibilant ending. On other occasions, the uninflected base terminated in a voiced consonant, which was then devoiced by the Pima child before addition of the plural suffix. For example, a nonsense word like WUG might be pluralized as WUKS.

In vowel sounds, many Pima children had difficulty repeating the same vowel in a single syllable word, although this difficulty was limited to certain vowels. In contrast, no Maryland child ever showed any hesitancy or error in repeating the base form as given. The phonological system of Pima English, therefore, can be said to be a partially separate system, and dialectal in nature. However, the same cannot be said for syntax. There seems to be no justification whatsoever for claiming a separate system for syntax in this community either at the adult level or among the children. While occasional deviations from standard usage occurred at adult level, they appeared to be the minor deviations found among white speakers of English of similar socioeconomic status. Unlike Black English, there is no evidence of restructuring of the verb phrase, and the telltale omission of the third person singular verbal inflection, so prevalent in the Black community, was not noticeable for its omission in this community. Among the Pima children tested, 75 percent of those of eleven used the third person singular verbal inflection. This was also the highest score for any inflection at that age. The sense of this state of affairs seems to be that Pima English has its own dialectal differences in phonology, making it in effect different, but the same system in syntax, making it only deficient.

The inevitable conclusion is that syntax is either more slowly acquired, pushing the end age for syntax acquisition beyond the usual limit, or it is never completely acquired. To the extent that English is not completely acquired, either as a first or second childhood language, then we must conclude that adult competence in this community is not adult competence in the Maryland community. Moreover, it is entirely possible that their life-style does not make the same verbal demands as ours. At the same time it is becoming more and more evident that the idea of competence is in urgent need of redefinition in order to accommodate the most obvious variations in language communities. I propose to make competence significant again for the researcher, and to suggest what can be done to give it viability in the field. To do otherwise is to continue the divergence between theory and practice which is presently the case. On the one hand are the grammatical theorists who concern themselves with the mythical ideal speaker-hearer. On the other hand are those researchers who cannot relate data to theory because of its unassailability and invulnerability.

Under the terms of the proposed redefinition, competence can still be defined as the speaker-hearer's knowledge of his language. It can still be defined as the internalized generative grammar in terms of which the adult speaks and understands his language. The assumption that every speaker of a language, and in more general terms, every human being, has equal competence should be deleted from the definition. There is no reason to assume that innate language capacity is inherently equal for all when humans are so obviously unequal in so many things.

It is more to the point to state that all humans have the capacity for language, but that the range of that capacity varies for a number of reasons. The range of the human capacity for language in normal adults is the range of competence. Ultimately this range can probably be divided into subnormal competence for subnormal individuals, low normal competence for low normal individuals, average competence, and above average competence. The overall ranges for competence in general and for the different levels of competence can be tentatively fixed through investigation, subject to continuing verification and adjustment. Whether linguistic competence will then correlate closely with overall intellectual capacity is presently unknown, but certainly worth investigation.

The reasons for variation in competence would by definition be only those factors which produce significant and lasting effects on the individual. If we assume a certain inheritance of linguistic capacities, i.e. competence, at birth, we still assume variation in the inheritance. In addition, competence may be adversely affected by such devastating and ordinarily prolonged conditions as malnutrition, sociocultural and economic deprivation, severe illness, and psychological conflicts. While such misfortunes are occasionally overcome, it is more likely that the damage will be permanent. To the extent that linguistic capacity is permanently affected, competence is lowered.

The Pima children who were tested in this investigation have suffered from socioeconomic deprivation since birth, and probably from psychological conflicts since school age. It remains to be explained why such deprivations do not affect them until approximately age ten. It may be possible to raise competence beyond its level at birth, but this has yet to

be ascertained. We have no way of knowing at present whether competence is at its optimum at birth, and if continuing optimum conditions
only serve to maintain that optimum, or whether optimum conditions
can actually enhance the inherent level of competence. On the other side
of the coin, however, there is already considerable evidence that poor
conditions lower the level of competence. Sociolinguists have been saying
for some time that language learning is affected by adversity of various
kinds. There is ample evidence to sustain that conclusion.

We have redefined competence as a more or less permanent and un-
changing capacity for language in the child, i.e. competence potential,
which may be lessened nevertheless (also permanently) by certain factors. We also consider competence as the product of language acquisition
in the mature adult, varying due to the factors which have shaped it. The
result or product of acquiring a language may be called acquired competence, and competence losses which occur after maturation should be
considered pathological in nature. We can now distinguish between the
capacity for language acquisition and the product of that acquisition as
competence potential and acquired competence respectively, thus eras-
ing the ambiguity with which the term is often used. However, there
are occasions when the term competence at once applies to both the
process and the product and can be used in those contexts simply as
competence.

We have redefined competence potential as varying with the individual, both at birth and on account of subsequent major childhood occurrences visited upon him. However, acquired competence in no way replaces the concept of performance. Performance is still found in actual
linguistic behavior, and is dependent not only on the underlying competence of the speaker-hearer (child or adult), but also on "such grammatically irrelevant conditions as memory limitations, distractions, shifts
of attention and interest, and errors (random or characteristic) in applying his knowledge of the language in actual performance" (Chomsky
1965:3).

The definition of performance remains the same, but its relationship
to all competence has changed. Performance, as before, is altered by
distraction-interference in the linguistic circuit. The distraction-interference will vary due to circumstances, but probably never will be entirely eliminated. Performance, therefore, is affected by minor and
temporary conditions of various kinds. All competence is characterized
by stability, however, and is altered only by profound and potentially
permanent influences. By careful assessment it should be possible to
determine the average performance of individuals and then to determine

capacities of an individual and his average performance. The average a fairly consistent working relationship between the permanent linguistic distraction-interference which cannot be eliminated in data collection will equal the difference between competence and performance and permit the formulation of a mathematical ratio between performance and competence.

Assuming once again that language maturation terminates with puberty, we now can state that Pima children who are far behind the Maryland norm show a lower linguistic competence, no matter what their performance. This is based on the conclusion that performance fluctuations are of minor nature, and that major variations indicate a lower or lowered competence. There is copious evidence of what we now call lower competence in disadvantaged children. Not only do they have more limited vocabularies, but when compared to middle-class children they also show less complex syntactical usage. While there is no evidence whatsoever to show that disadvantaged children as a group have inherently lower competence at birth, since their early language development more closely parallels middle-class children, there is ample evidence that later language development is slowed and sometimes halted by yet to be ascertained factors. The Pima children as a group undoubtedly reflect a case of lowered competence due to external factors; there is no evidence that their competence was lower in infancy. On the contrary, there is some evidence that at some time previous to age eight competence was equal or nearly equal to that of Maryland children.

The proposed modification of the term competence would reaffirm the distinction between competence and performance while extending the utility of the term competence. It would reconcile the views of those favoring hereditary factors in language acquisition with those favoring environmental factors and would open new avenues of investigation into the relative roles of heredity and environment in competence and possibly produce information on what factors are involved in competence change and to what extent. This in turn could establish more precise mathematical relationships between competence and performance. Such research could provide important information on the relationship of linguistic competence to other intellectual capacities.

In the research which has been described in this paper, and which deals with the English language acquisition of Pima monolinguals and bilinguals, competence would have a new importance. A comparison of the competence of Pima children with that of Maryland children would be possible. It would also be possible to determine the amount of decline in Pima competence, and to probe for the reasons. It would allow for experimentation in the restoration of lost competence as well as in methods of sustaining competence under adverse conditions. It could establish a possible correlation between language competence and school achievement, ultimately explaining the widespread phenomenon of academic failure among Indian children.

REFERENCES

BERKO, JEAN
  1958   The child's learning of English morphology. *Word* 14:150–177.
CHOMSKY, NOAM
  1964   "Current issues in linguistic theory," in *The structure of language.* Edited by Jerry A. Fodor and Jerrold J. Katz, 50–118. Englewood Cliffs: Prentice-Hall.
  1965   *Aspects of the theory of syntax.* Cambridge: M.I.T. Press.
KATZ, JERROLD J.
  1964   "Semi-sentences," in *The structure of language.* Edited by Jerry A. Fodor and Jerrold J. Katz, 400–416. Englewood Cliffs: Prentice-Hall.

Linguistic Universals in Anthropological Studies of Bilingualism

CAROLYN KESSLER

When an anthropologist, linguist, or casual observer moves into a bilingual speech community, he is generally struck by the ease with which the bilingual speaker shifts between his linguistic codes. For the anthropologist, the study of such a language contact situation holds clues to the social structure of the group; for the linguist, such a study invites examination of a theory of language, its acquisition, variation, and change. Any serious investigation of bilingualism, whether from the anthropological or linguistic viewpoint, must take note of the strict limits to the range of variations in natural language. Those limits reflect underlying sames common to all languages. These sames are the linguistic universals that make it possible for an individual to have access to more than one linguistic code as he carries out his daily activities.

The questions at the root of anthropology are basically the same as those at the root of linguistics: how does one account for the apparent similarities and differences of various communities of men around the world and of what do similarities consist? Modern linguistic theory gives the basis for examining language similarities in terms of linguistic universals, differences in terms of language-specific characteristics. Similarities between languages, or universals, consist of primitives in all components of language — semantic, syntactic, phonological — and rules allowing for their combination into larger language units. Such language universals are found in the deep or underlying structure. A series of transformational rules operates on the underlying structures to generate or realize the surface manifestations. Surface structures are the linearly ordered, pronounceable structures actually used in language communication.

To clarify terms, those proposed by Weinreich (1967: 1) will be used as starting points. Languages are in a contact situation if they are used alternately by the same person. Persons alternately using two languages are defined as bilingual. Gumperz (1971: 313) further elaborates:

Bilingualism is primarily a linguistic term referring to the fact that linguists have discovered significant alternations in phonology, morphology, and syntax in studying the verbal behavior of a particular population. While bilingual phenomena have certain linguistic features in common, these features may have quite different social significance.

We intend here to examine the linguistic features of bilingual phenomena, not their social meaning. From the linguistic standpoint, instances of deviation from the norms of either language resulting from language contact are defined as interferences. Interference is sometimes loosely referred to as mixing, a process which may or may not involve a conscious shift from one language to another within the same discourse. For those instances in which the speaker is conscious of the shift, the term code-switching is frequently used. Diebold (1962: 56) defines it as "the successive alternate use of two different language codes within the same discourse; it implies that the speaker is conscious of the switch." Because it is difficult in a field situation to distinguish between conscious or unconscious shifting, we will use the terms code-switching and mixing synonymously in the discussion of such phenomena. This is not to deny the significant distinction between the kinds of interference noted by Weinreich (1967: 3–6) which involve either structural or extralinguistic factors. (Although the latter list is a lengthy one, many of these factors can be summarized under sociocultural considerations.) Nor is it to deny the interplay between linguistic and sociocultural factors. It is not the purpose here, however, to examine in detail the correlation between the purely linguistic and extralinguistic factors that enter into the bilingual situation. Rather, the focus is on the biogenetically determined constraints that enter into bilingualism. These involve the presence of linguistic universals running through language in general.

The following are some of the questions asked: How is it that one speaker can shift from one language to another? How is it that within a single discourse, or within a single sentence, he may shift from one language to another? How is it that a very young child growing up in a bilingual environment acquires, with fluency, both linguistic codes concurrently as his first language?

Given the complexity of the situations, the answers must be sought in elements present in the individual by virtue of his biological endowments. These are species-specific capacities, interlocking the universal, or supracultural, features of language with man's physiology. As Lenneberg (1967: 375) states: "The outer form of languages may vary with relatively great freedom, whereas the underlying type remains constant." For the child acquiring language, his latent language structure unfolds in a process which transforms the deep or universal organizing principles of language into realized structures. The bilingual, then, whether child or adult, has this set of organizing principles which for him can be actualized in more than one surface realization. He can, therefore, move from a single deep structure, made up of those principles universal to language, to multiple surface realizations. This is, in fact, a model which accounts not only for a bilingual realization of an underlying structure but also for dialectal or stylistic variations within a single language. In summarizing the theory, Lenneberg states:

The actualization of latent structure to realized structure is to give the underlying cognitively determined type a concrete form. . . . This formulation might be regarded as the biological counterpart of what grammarians have for centuries called UNIVERSAL and PARTICULAR grammar. Latent structure is responsible for the general type of all features of universal grammar; realized structure is responsible both for the peculiarities of any given statement as well as those aspects that are unique to the grammar of a given natural language (1967: 376; original emphasis).

The notion of universal is hardly a new one to anthropological or ethnographic descriptions of human cultures. As Greenberg (1969) notes, positing the existence of universals involves the assertion of the basic comparability of all cultures. No matter how simple their technology, all human groups possess coherently structured institutions which include functional equivalents of all the basic categories of the most technologically advanced societies. It is in this view that one finds the convergence of approaches to their object of study by anthropologists, ethnographers, and linguists. Greenberg (1969: 476) goes on to point out:

Linguistic universals . . . tend to form coherent groups instead of being isolated statements. The basis of this cohesiveness is that a whole set of them will point to the same hierarchy among linguistic features; that is, they will provide evidence of a panhuman system of preferences.

The literature on bilingual communities is extensive and well documented with examples of social domains prescribing the respective languages. Representative of some of the work which gives linguistic insights into bilingualism as it functions in social groups is that of Gumperz (1967) reporting on Hindi-Punjabi and Kannada-Marathi code-switching commonly found in India. It is significant for understanding the relationship between linguistic universals and language-specific realizations to consider the observation made by Gumperz that to be bilingual in either Hindi-Punjabi or Kannada-Marathi, a speaker internalizes two sets of terms for the same object and grammatical relationship. In other words, the two languages within each set must be utilizing the same realization rules relating underlying or deep structures with surface manifestations.

The following schematic representation illustrates the relationship between deep structure (DS) and surface structure (SS).

$$DS\text{—shared rules} \to \begin{bmatrix} \text{language-specific rules} \to \text{SS of Language A} \\ \text{language-specific rules} \to \text{SS of Language B} \end{bmatrix}$$

Deep structure finds its source in the set of elements and relations shared by all languages. Among the rules leading to surface realizations are those common to all languages as well as those shared by a specific language family or group of languages.

Depending on the linguistic distance between the languages in a bilingual situation, one may be able to analyze a corpus in terms of an entirely shared set of grammatical categories and rules. Differences may rest primarily on the set of lexical items realizing the underlying relationships. This is the situation with Marathi and Kannada, for example. On the other hand, the set of language-specific rules may be extensive as in the Finnish-Swedish bilingual situation of Finland, a situation involving two unrelated languages. In the deep to surface contrasts between the languages of a bilingual community, any number of combinations is possible. Haugen (1967) notes, for example, that Danish and Norwegian share many lexical items, but differ markedly in the phonological component. Swedish and Norwegian share most of the rules of phonology, but differ in lexical items. Swedish and Danish are different in both respects — lexical and phonological.

A not uncommon phenomenon in a bilingual community is that of language mixing. Hatch (1972) gives extensive data for this in discussing the acquisition of a second language by young children. Gumperz (1971: 134) gives an example of mixing within a single discourse:

Estos . . . melos halle . . . estos Pall Malls *me los . . . me los hallaron.* [These . . . I found . . . these Pall Malls I . . . they were found for me.] No, I mean . . . that's all the cigarettes . . . that's all. They're the ones I buy.

For an example of Spanish-English mixing within a single sentence Lance (Gumperz 1971: 132) cites the following:

Se me hace que [it seems that] I have to respect her *porque 'ta* [because she is] . . .

Te digo que este dedo [I tell you that this finger] has been bothering me so much.

To reconcile data from bilingual speakers who clearly use one language rather than another in certain role domains and yet at other times mix their respective codes, a schematic representation using a decision-making flow chart is presented. Figure 1 attempts to relate the linguistic correlates of bilingualism in terms of deep structure meaning-bearing propositions with surface manifestations in respective languages. Using a Spanish-English bilingual situation, a series of propositions are connected in a single discourse. The propositions themselves may stand in an independent relation to one another or may be conjoined through application of the necessary mechanisms.

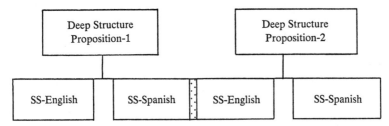

Figure 1.   Bilingual deep to surface structures for a discourse series of propositions

For simplification, only two propositions are considered as comprising the discourse. Decision is here understood as either a conscious or unconscious selection. The overlap area between Spanish and English, in connecting the two propositions, defines language mixing. It is also to be understood that four possibilities for surface realizations may derive from the two deep structures involving proposition-1 and proposition-2.
1.   English-1 followed by English-2.
2.   Spanish-1 followed by Spanish-2.
3.   English-1 followed by Spanish-2.
4.   Spanish-1 followed by English-2.
The fact that a single deep structure can have surface manifestations in more than one language points to elements shared by both languages — elements and rules universal to human language. The first sentence in the data given by Lance illustrates the fourth possibility: *"se me hace que* [it seems that] I have to respect her . . ."
Viewed in terms of constituent structure this model may be diagramed in more detail, as given in Figure 2.

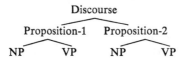

Figure 2.   Constituent structure of discourse

Consideration of lower-level constituents increases the number of decisions leading to surface realizations and, consequently, increases the likelihood of language mixing. Examining a single proposition, Figure 3 illustrates the decisions required in realizing structures only as far as the noun phrase (NP) and verb phrase (VP) constituent level.

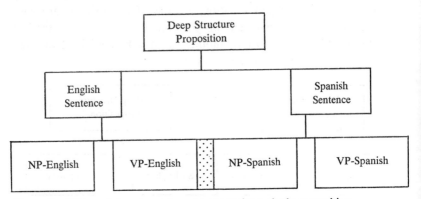

Figure 3. Bilingual deep to surface structures for a single proposition

Within this model the mathematical possibilities for surface manifestations in two languages for respective noun phrase and verb phrase constituents of the proposition are four:
1. NP-English followed by VP-English.
2. NP-Spanish followed by VP-Spanish.
3. NP-English followed by VP-Spanish.
4. NP-Spanish followed by VP-English.
Illustrating the last possibility is the second sentence of the language mixing data given by Lance: "... *este dedo* [this finger] has been bothering me so much."

Further subdivision of constituent structure introduces additional possibilities of mixing. Given the constituents of VP as verb and noun phrase, one may predict mixing of the type produced in data from a young Italian-English bilingual child: "*I don't want fagioli* [beans]." One can easily assume his choice was not determined by role domains, but rather by a type of linguistic constraint that mixes the two languages within the verb phrase construction.

Although biogenetically related decision making involves brain mechanisms not yet understood, one does find evidence that the linguistic constraints in such decisions depend upon universal as well as language-specific characteristics. Data taken from young children acquiring two languages concurrently give evidence that the linguistic codes available to a bilingual individual derive from a single grammatical core reflecting language universals. Consideration will be given to the acquisition of surface realizations for two syntactic primes — names and verboids — by a group of twelve six- to eight-year-old children, bilingual in Italian and English. Following the model of analysis proposed by Di Pietro (1971a), names and verboids are realized on the surface as nouns and verbs by application of the series of rules that take into account both language-universal and language-specific rules. Within this model, linguistically less complex structures should be those acquired first. Complexity is defined here in terms of the number and kinds of rules required to move from deep to surface structures. This results in a sequential ordering within a particular language, with the less complex acquired first, and a sequential ordering across languages.

Names and verboids are marked by restrictions imposed by each language. Although Italian and English draw on the semantic features of number and tense, inflected surface forms in both languages result from shared and language-specific semantic projection rules. Rules of this type are those in which semantic features such as tense and number interact with syntax to form the surface realization. Grammatical similarities are apparent in the shared primes, deep-structure feature markings, and some of the rules leading to surface realizations. The similarities are, in part, manifestations of the set of language universals.

To test the extent of acquisition for noun and verb inflections in Italian and English, Berko-type morphological generalization tests were administered to each child individually. These tests presented a series of nonsense items, based on the phonological and syllable patterning of the respective languages, to elicit plural formation for the nouns and tense marking for the verbs. Tenses were limited to present, past, and future.

The following transformation or T-rules summarize the realization of noun plurals:

Rule (1) N[+ plural]

    N[+ plural] $\rightarrow$ noun + suffixed plural marker

This rule is shared by Italian and English. A further rule, however, applies only to Italian.

Rule (2) N[+ syntactic gender]

$$N\begin{bmatrix} + \text{ plural} \\ \pm \text{ masculine} \end{bmatrix} \rightarrow \text{noun} + \text{suffixed plural/gender marker}$$

The acquisition of plural inflection for Italian is a linguistically more complex process. Consequently, one may predict that it will be acquired later than the corresponding English inflection by the bilingual child. The following schematic representation illustrates the deep to surface relationship for Italian and English plural realizations.

$$\text{DS—Rule (1)} \rightarrow \left[\begin{array}{l} \text{English SS} \\ \text{Rule (2)} \rightarrow \text{Italian SS} \end{array} \right.$$

Mixing is observed in the frequent pluralization of Italian-form nonsense items with English surface markers. An example was the common pluralization of *un botro* as *due botros*.

Table 1 summarizes the percentage of responses, either marking the plural according to the rules of the language, or mixing the rules across languages. Each of the twelve children was given five test items to give a total of sixty responses in both Italian and English.

Table 1.   Acquisition of plural marking in bilingual children, age 6 to 8 (in percent)

	Plural marked	Plural mixing
Italian	25	13
English	67	0

For testing the acquisition of tense markings, an adaptation of the Berko tests was designed to elicit nonsense forms marked for present, past, and future tenses. In order to focus solely on tense markings, person and number were kept constant by testing only third person singular forms. In a very general way, Rule (3) outlines the type of realization tested.

Rule (3) V[+ tense]

   V[+ tense] → verb marked for present/past/future

Closer examination of each tense points up language contrasts. Since the children were all speakers of southern Italian dialects, no overt marking of the future was present. This is in line with the dialect rules which do not observe the overt marking of the standard language but rather substitute present for future. Past tense in Italian is complicated by obligatory rules differentiating aspects of past action. In addition to these complications, Italian has an elaborate inflectional system that builds verb paradigms marking person, number, and tense. Person-number distinctions are minimal in English. Consequently, one may view the latter as less complex linguistically. The future, however, involves a fairly complex phrasal construction in English, giving rise to the prediction that it should be acquired after present and past tense rules.

Cognitively, too, children probably acquire the concept of futurity after that of present and past. This, of course, would make acquisition of the future tense a late one.

The set of realization rules for English and Italian differs, then, in kind and complexity, with English the less complex. The relationship between deep and surface structures again shows the progression from that which is universal to the language-specific forms.

$$\text{DS—Rule (3)} \rightarrow \left[\begin{array}{l} \text{English realization rules} \rightarrow \text{SS} \\ \text{Italian realization rules} \rightarrow \text{SS} \end{array} \right.$$

In terms of percentage of correct responses for the total of forty-eight responses in each language, Table 2 illustrates the progression of tense acquisition in the two languages. Only one case of mixing occurred — marking the Italian past with the English suffix. The nonsense form *bisare* was given in the past as English *bisted* rather than Italian *ha bisato*.

Table 2. Acquisition of tense marking in bilingual children, age 6 to 8 (in percent)

	Present marked	Past marked	Future marked
English	100	65	50
Italian	100	13	0

Examination of the data substantiates universals proposed by Slobin (1971) which are particularly applicable to the acquisition of rules for inflection. The first rule (Slobin 1971: 362) states:

The following stages of linguistic marking of a semantic notion are typically observed: (1) no marking, (2) appropriate marking in limited cases, (3) over-generalization of marking, (4) full adult system.

This rule and the following support the theory that a grammar is constructed from a loosely structured universal semantic base and that the progression is from universal to language-specific in the realization of deep structures. The second rule (Slobin 1971: 363) states explicitly that universals precede particulars in language acquisition:

Rules applicable to larger classes are developed before rules relating to their subdivisions, and general rules are learned before rules for special cases.

In summary, the questions posed here regarding bilingual first language acquisition, codeshifting, and interference are not separate ones. Rather, they are tightly interrelated, striking at some of the root questions involving language similarities and differences. The position taken here in attempting to account for observed phenomena in bilingual communities while reconciling these phenomena with linguistic theory is that the bilingual individual does not encode his two languages separately. Rules shared by his two languages are, in fact, the same rules, allowing for language-specific lexical insertions. Elements and their features common to two languages comprise a single entity. These shared components of a grammar — semantic, syntactic, or phonological — reflect the underlying set of sames or language universals. Analysis of the linearly ordered stream of speech involves examination of the complex set of interrelationships between language universals and language-specific variants. Similarities and differences between languages occur in all components of a grammar.

Anthropologists and linguists alike will undoubtedly agree that verbal behavior is a function of social and linguistic factors, among others. "Linguistic" is here equated with psycholinguistic to incorporate the biogenetic constraints on language and man's predisposition for language acquisition. The model for language analysis of a bilingual community that incorporates the notions of linguistic universals and language similarities, language-specific realizations, and language differences gives a theoretical basis for a unified theory of code-switching, interference, language acquisition, and, beyond that, for any aspect of the total linguistic repertoire of an individual or of a community. Bilingualism in its broadest sense, as Swain (1971) points out, is not unrelated to monolingualism. Both are realizations of a single phenomenon. Language, dialect, and register alternations are all realizations of that single phenomenon which embraces the universal and particular. Utilizing a model of language that interlocks universals and particulars, anthropologists investigating verbal behavior may find some of the answers to their own questions about similarities and differences. The proposal made here is that differences are best understood, perhaps only understood, when similarities are first identified. Fieldworkers in bilingual situations may find themselves standing much more clearly, as Di Pietro (1971b) phrases it, "at the interface between language and man's total being" by first searching out those basic underlying themes which are universal to man and his linguistic codes.

REFERENCES

BERKO, JEAN
  1958   The child's learning of English morphology. *Word* 14:150–177.
CHOMSKY, NOAM
  1965   *Aspects of the theory of syntax*. Cambridge, Mass.: M.I.T. Press.

1968   *Language and mind.* New York: Harcourt Brace Jovanovich.

DIEBOLD, A. RICHARD
1962   Code-switching in Greek-English bilingual speech. *Monograph Series on Languages and Linguistics* 15:53–69.

DI PIETRO, ROBERT J.
1971a *Language structures in contrast.* Rowley, Mass.: Newbury House.
1971b "Contrastive analysis and linguistic creativity." Paper presented at the Pacific Conference on Contrastive Linguistics and Linguistic Universals, Honolulu, Hawaii.

FISHMAN, JOSHUA A., *editor*
1968   *Readings in the sociology of language.* The Hague: Mouton.

GREENBERG, JOSEPH H.
1969   Language universals: a research frontier. *Science* 166:473–478.

GREENBERG, JOSEPH H., *editor*
1966   *Universals of language.* Cambridge, Mass.: M.I.T. Press.

GUMPERZ, JOHN J.
1967   On the linguistic markers of bilingual communication. *Journal of Social Issues* 22:48–57.
1971   *Language in social groups.* Stanford: Stanford University Press.

HATCH, E. R.
1972   "Studies in second language acquisition." Paper presented at the Third International Congress of Applied Linguistics, Copenhagen, Denmark.

HAUGEN, EINAR
1967   "Semicommunication: the language gap in Scandinavia," in *Explorations in sociolinguistics.* Edited by S. Lieberson, 152–169. Bloomington: Indiana University Research Center for the Language Sciences.

HYMES, DELL
1971   Bilingual education: linguistic vs. sociolinguistic bases. *Monograph Series on Languages and Linguistics* 23:69–76.

HYMES, DELL, *editor*
1964   *Language in culture and society.* New York: Harper and Row.

KESSLER, CAROLYN
1971   *The acquisition of syntax in bilingual children.* Washington, D.C.: Georgetown University Press.

LENNEBERG, E. H.
1967   *Biological foundations of language.* New York: Wiley.

LENNEBERG, E. H., *editor*
1964   *New directions in the study of language.* Cambridge, Mass.: M.I.T. Press.

MAC NAMARA JOHN
1967   The bilingual's linguistic performance — a psychological overview. *Journal of Social Issues* 22:58–77.

SLOBIN, DAN I.
1971   "Developmental psycholinguistics," in *A survey of linguistic science.* Edited by W. O. Dingwall, 299–400. College Park: University of Maryland.

SWAIN, MERRILL
   1971   "Monolingualism, bilingualism, and code acquisition," in *Proceedings of the Conference on Child Language, Chicago, Illinois*, 209–224. Quebec: International Centre for Research on Bilingualism.
WEINREICH, URIEL
   1967   *Languages in contact*. The Hague: Mouton.

Implications of Language Contact for Bilingual Language Acquisition

ELS OKSAAR

By bilingual language acquisition (BLA) I understand the process of achieving a linguistic and communicative competence through an environment in which two languages are available to accompany the child's development from the start. He has not only to acquire rules of grammar and rules of semantics but also rules of usage in order to build up the ability to interact socially by generating and interpreting speech acts. In this process of communicative development of the child, the languages come into contact with each other, resulting in a certain amount of linguistic and sociolinguistic interference.[1]

Although research in bilingual language acquisition is far less well developed than its monolingual counterpart, the existing results (with certain exceptions) show the amount of interference to be quite extreme. Consequently, the initial stage of BLA has been characterized as a "mixed-speech" or "mixed-code" stage, followed by a process of differentiation between languages (Leopold 1939–1949; see also Imedadze 1966; Murrell 1966). On the other hand, the efficacy of Grammont's formula (1902) — one person, one language — has shown, as we know from Ronjat's research (1913), that parallel development from the beginning with only isolated instances of interference is possible.

The initial stage of BLA has not yet been analyzed systematically enough in various language contacts to justify generalizations such as "mixed speech." The metalanguage of "mixing" is far from being exact enough to make scientific comparisons possible. Nor do we know much about the process of differentiation, partly because of a lack of compa-

---

[1] For types of interference cf. Hymes (1971: 18–19).

rable conditions under which languages are being acquired: the data rarely afford thorough information about the context of situations. What we actually do know is that a 100 percent differentiation on all levels of language will hardly be met with in the case of adult bilinguals. We must also be aware of the fact that contact of languages will have implications for the linguistic repertoire of the child even during the process of differentiation.[2]

Recent research on unilingual child-language acquisition has concentrated on WHAT the child learns (Menyuk 1969, Bloom 1970). Critics have pointed out that very little can be achieved by this approach, if it is not going to be applied in connection with the question of HOW a child learns.[3] BLA research has to combine these questions in order to answer one of its crucial issues: to determine which strategies are built up to use both languages as an effective means of communication, and thus match the items of languages to the appropriate "items" of situations. Under these functional aspects, the question of interferences appears in a different context. They have to be judged functionally, with respect to the role they may have in the linguistic process in which the child manages the claims of the situation.

The main strategy followed by children learning more than one language, in progression toward the mastery of their communicative competence, is CODE SWITCHING, i.e. the alternate use of two languages with or without interferences on various levels of language — phonological, semantic, lexical and grammatical.

My purpose here is to discuss the dynamics of code switching — a neglected branch within the field of bilingualism — on the basis of longitudinal studies in a bilingual Estonian (L_1) and Swedish (L_2) environment in Sweden. The last decade in child-language research has presented numerous studies in Indo-European languages, especially in English. Cross-language studies, however, usually lack non-Indo-European data. For many topical psycholinguistic questions such as universal aspects of language acquisition, etc., observations about children learning two languages simultaneously, especially when they are not related, promises some information.

Here arises the important question of whether there is any evidence in bilingual children's emerging competence to answer the question raised by Pike (1967: 583). "To what extent does the bilingual act as

---

[2]   Further cases are analyzed by Schmidt-Mackey (1971: 85–118).
[3]   Cf. Schlesinger (1972): " . . . the study of what is learned at a given stage cannot be separated from the study of how it is learned, without degeneration into data-gathering devoid of theoretical interest." See also Oksaar (1970: 112).

if he were using a hypersystem of language, in which the two languages that he speaks somehow fuse into a larger system?" We need many systematic studies in BLA in order to answer this question. The research I have done, some results of which are discussed below, seems to confirm the hypothesis that the totality of the bilingual child's linguistic behavior can be viewed as a manifestation of an overall code.

I shall present a model of emerging Swedish-Estonian bilingualism from the two to four year age group, focusing on the rules of code switching. In order to understand how these rules function, we have to perceive not only the order of acquisition of linguistic units and the internal structure of interferences in different types of lexical items, but also the interplay of inter- and intralinguistic factors as the source of code switching, and we must pay attention to the triggering effects.

A few words about the data collection. The main data are derived from my son Sven, born December 9, 1963, in Stockholm. In the family both Estonian and Swedish were spoken, but his parents spoke only Estonian with him. Up to his tenth month he heard mainly Estonian. From this time on, he heard both languages equally (as the domestic help was Swedish unilingual), and after the twenty-sixth month he heard more Swedish than Estonian for five days a week. When the boy became two years old, recordings were regularly made several times a week in various situations: (1) when the child was alone, playing or before falling asleep (monologue situation), and (2) together with other children or adults (dialogue situation). Every recording also included a thorough description of the situation. At certain times of the day and with the child engaged in the same activities, recordings were made every second week on three successive days in order to get continous recordings. This test was followed by a control group with the same bilingual background.

PHONETICS AND PHONEMICS

First, some general considerations concerning the order of acquisition of linguistic units. The material shows that the Estonian quantity system is acquired before the children have fully mastered the system of segmental sounds. In Estonian, both vowels and consonants (except *v*) have three distinctive degrees of length: short, long, and overlong. These three degrees build phonemically distinct quantities, as will be seen from the following examples. Vowels: short, *sada* 'hundred'; long, *saada* 'send' (imperative); and overlong, *saada* 'to get'. Consonants: short, *lina* 'linen'; long, *linna* 'of the town' (genitive); and overlong, *linna* 'into the town' (illative).

At the age of twenty-five to twenty-seven months this system had already been mastered, before all the segmental sounds (including those phonetically not so complex) were acquired. After twenty-eight months, mastery of this system was apparently so fully acquired that the child reacted against false use by adults in various tests. Up to this age, fluctuation occurred between the long and overlong quantities but never between the short quantity and the others.

It might be interesting to notice that the Estonian case will not fit into Jakobson's law (1969: 76) of the successive acquisition of the phonemic system: "Gegensätze, welche in den Sprachen der Welt verhältnismäßig selten vorkommen, gehören zu den spätesten Erwerbungen des Kindes [Those distinctions which occur relatively seldom in the languages of the world are among the latest acquired by the child]." Before I give an explanation of what I think is the reason for this behavior, I want to say a few words about the child's mastery of the Swedish segmental and suprasegmental system. The toneme distinction in Swedish (accent 1 and accent 2), differentiating words like *stegen* [ste:gen] with accent 1 "the ladder', and *stegen* [*ste:gen] with accent 2 'the steps', however, is not mastered at an early stage, the order being reversed: the segmental system is acquired first. The case is the same with unilingual Swedish children.

How can this be explained? Provided that, concentrating our investigation of child language on certain parts of language, we will not neglect the totality of speech behavior, the answer is not difficult to find; for example, when the acquisition of the phonemic system will not be followed apart from the semantic-communicative one. The Estonian quantity distinctions are, from the beginning, very important for the child to learn, because they cover the whole form system and very frequent lexical items. The child hears them constantly in his surroundings, whereas the Swedish distinctions cover words that are less frequent or forms (like compounds) that are acquired at a later stage.

The stability of the Estonian quantity rules manifests itself when interferences occur. When Swedish lexical items are supplied with Estonian morphemes as in *hälsama* (Swedish *hälsa* 'greet', infinitive; Estonian *ma*, the infinitive morpheme), the Swedish phoneme sequence will usually follow the rule of Estonian quantity (thirty months): *Nenne taha minna ema hälsama* (overlong quantity) 'Nenne wants to go to visit mother'.

It is worth noting that the pronunciation, from the very beginning, resembled that of a unilingual child in both languages, though after Sven's twenty-sixth month he heard more Swedish and his unilingual playmate's pronunciation and simplification of the initial consonants could have influenced him. Both children had their own patterns as to this simplification. The Swedish *traktor* was consequently given by Sven as [śaktu], by the Swedish girl of the same age as [takku].

MORPHOLOGY AND SYNTAX

We also find parallel developments in the morphology and syntax of both languages. No case is observed in which inflectional morphemes interfere in either language. Estonian has fourteen cases; in the Swedish system cases play no role. There is a base form and a genitive with the structure: base $\gamma + -s$.

In another article (Oksaar 1970: 108–136), I have described Sven's emerging grammar of Estonian, in which the case morphemes appeared before the verbal morphemes and in which the child developed a simpler flection system than is applied in adult grammar, although making use of twelve cases at an age of about three years. In Estonian the genitive and partitive singular constitute the base for cases and postpositions. The child consequently used the nominative as a base (thirty-four months): *Sõrm on sinu käsi pääl* 'The finger is on your hand'.

Compared with the normal form *käel*, a genitive, as a base, he is avoiding the morphophonematic change, establishing an economic simplification of the rule. The question arises whether the simpler Swedish system could have interfered. This, however, is rather unlikely, as no case of interference from the inflectional morphemes is known.

The Structure of Interferences

On the level of the lexeme two types of interferences can be noticed: mixed forms — contaminations — that were used (1) in both language situations, and (2) in only one:

1. *slöö* 'beat' from Swedish *slå* and Estonian *löö*, imperative. The form was used during several months up to the age of thirty-two months in both languages, also with person markers, correctly chosen for both languages. After this the word was replaced by *slå* and *löö*.

2. *kats* 'cat' from Swedish *katt* and Estonian *kass*. The form was used between nineteen and twenty-one months only in an Estonian context.

The interference of quantity was discussed above. On the sentence and discourse level, the interferences and code switching cannot be explained satisfactorily when isolated from the situation. Why do we sometimes have a Swedish form like [nü:pade] as the past form of *nypa* in an Estonian sentence, and other times have an Estonian integrated transfer form like [nü:pasin]? Although there are many cases where an answer would be a mere speculation, careful observation of the speech events in which a form occurs may in a variety of cases lead to an explanation.

Sentences which could be classified linguistically as "mixed" must be analyzed in their broadest context. A purely linguistic analysis would not suffice to explain the choice of items and the syntagmatic amalgamation of the forms.

From the outset, the first mixed stretches of speech were the result of intralinguistic factors: the child had heard the words only in one language. They referred to activities carried out by the Swedish domestic help: *moppa* 'to mop', *damma* 'to dust', and *städa* 'to tidy up'. They were integrated into Estonian morphology (from twenty-eight months on) when speaking to Estonians about activities in his home. However, when the topic referred to Swedish playmates and their atmosphere, the Swedish forms dominated in Estonian sentences.

A typical situation: the child (thirty-five months) comes home with a scratch on his face. The mother asks in Estonian who did it and the child gives the name of his Swedish friend. When the mother then asks what he did to her, he replies: *Mina knuffa ja* [nü: pade] 'I pushed and pinched'. The words *knuffa* 'push' (infinitive) and *nypade* 'pinched' (imperfect), are Swedish forms, pronounced with Swedish intonation.

When playing at home, the same verbs are used with Estonian morphemes of person, *nypa* also with the Estonian overlong quantity (thirty-five months): *Mina* [nü: pan] *sind* 'I pinch you'. In this frame, lexical interferences followed the principle of simplicity. In cases where the Estonian word could have been chosen, e.g. *näpistama* 'to pinch' or *näpistan* 'I pinch', the chosen Swedish one was shorter.

There are cases in which only the topic influenced the choice of code. The boy got to know the names of most cars in the Swedish language. When the mother asked him in Estonian what the sliding roof was, pointing at it, he (forty-one months) invented a new designation in Swedish: *takut ruta* [tá:kú:trú:ta], literally 'ceiling-out-pane' (the Swedish word is *soltak*), explaining (inexactly) *kabriole*. This word was used in both languages by the family.

Estonian words and forms seldom appeared in his Swedish sentences.

If they did, they followed the rules of place and person, according to the Estonian. Swedish was usually spoken to unilinguals and the child seems to have learned that he was not understood when using Estonian items.

A special group of switched sentences constituted cases in which items of the other language were quotations. However, they were not identified through pauses or other markers. They stress how important it is to have registered the whole situation with all its details. In a typical case, the child (twenty-nine months) to his mother: *Svenni ei måste minna magama*. 'Svenni has not to go to bed'. The Swedish *måste* 'have to' is a quotation from the sentence said to him shortly before by a Swede: *Svenni måste gå och lägga sig*. As a quotation *Svenni* is also marked; he was called and called himself *Nenne*.

Code switching was also used in several cases between twenty-eight and thirty-four months in an appellative function, strengthening the arguments uttered in Estonian. When the child asked for something and the parents did not react immediately, the request was repeated in Swedish, with paralinguistic support.

I shall now give a few more typical examples of code switching. The Swedish forms are given in a broad transcription.

1. Situation: before going to the Swedish friend, speaking with his mother in Estonian (twenty-seven months). Topic: cold outside. Pause. Packing his toys he switches to Swedish: *Biil oo buss ee mee*. 'Car and bus are with me'. The association with the place he is going to seems to activate the same sentence he hears as a question when he is leaving the Swedish family.

2. Father accompanies him to the family (thirty-two months). Leave-taking is in Estonian. Playmate opens the door. The child switches to Swedish: *Kofferten inte mee, biilen inte mee*. 'The bag is not with me, the car is not with me'. The Swedish forms follow the Swedish grammar. The switch was the result of the place and person.

How strong the influence is of place and persons involved is shown in the following situation. Usually, the father took the child home from the Swedish family (thirty-five months). When the mother did it, she was addressed in Swedish in the presence of the Swedish family. Thus: *Mamma Els! vaa ee pappa? Pappa inte hemma!* 'Mother Els! Where is father? Father is not at home!' Alone with his mother on the stairs outside he switches into Estonian: *Kahekesi lääme*. 'We two are going'.

It is noteworthy here that the question is both asked and answered by the child himself in Swedish — conditioned by the place (and the Swedish persons). A new PERSON did not call forth a switch. (The mother was never addressed at home in Swedish and as *Mamma,* but always by the equivalent Estonian word *Ema.)* Alone with her, however, away from the PLACE, the return switch into Estonian followed immediately. There are numerous cases in my material similar to this one, including the speech of other Estonian-Swedish children.

3.   Special conditions seem to operate in dialogues when the topic acts as a triggering effect. Situation: Sven wants to hear the record of the Swedish song *"Mors lilla olle."* He addresses his mother in Estonian: *Ema, pane murš lilla ulle! Ema, šjunga murš lilla ulle!* (twenty-nine months).

The Swedish *sjunga* 'sing' is used in the infinitive instead of the imperative *sjung.* The Estonian form *laula* was known and used at that time; the topic seems to have called forth this switch. As he was alone with his mother, the Estonian address *Ema* 'Mother' was used.

Already, these cases bear evidence of the fact that the child, through his linguistic activity, tries to develop an instrument as rational as possible to match items of his linguistic repertoire to the requirements of the situations. Paralinguistic features and kinesics play an important role, although an analysis of them cannot be given here.

It must be stressed, however, that this process provides much evidence that the contact of languages, which makes the code switching function in a way that correlates positively with the needs of the situation, also creates awareness of the structure and lexicon of the two languages. This is apparent when the child corrects himself. To the Estonian question about where he was (forty months), he answered: *Mina olen siin kneenade pääl* [short pause] . . . *põlvede pääl.* 'I am here on my knees'. The Swedish form *knäna* 'the knees' (nominative plural definite form) that was connected with the Estonian genitive plural morpheme is replaced by the Estonian equivalent to 'knee' in the genitive plural form. Estonian has no difference between definite and indefinite substantives; the substitution was carried through without interferences.

Also the child's monologues give clear evidence of the frame in which both languages were used and of the strategy of code switching. For example (thirty-three months): before falling asleep, alone in his room: *Ema, Isa, siia magama jää. See on nende säng . . . Tant Ulla kom hiit ja ee vaaken.* 'Mother, Father, here fall asleep. That is their bed . . . Aunt Ulla, come here, I am awake.' The Swedish *säng* (Estonian *voodi)* 'bed' seems to be the trigger word that calls forth a switch — conceptually and in the choice of language. Ulla was part of the Swedish milieu of the child.

The following monologue (thirty-two months) from a situation before falling asleep contains several switches and gives evidence of the fact that the child, reflecting his social contacts of the day, chooses the linguistic possibilities according to the former. In the following text, " . . . " marks a short pause; " ′ " shows very strong stress; Swedish passages are italicized.

Ema, kas sa oled siin kõrval? . . . Mina magan Isa . . . *du kiiver till mei. Ja kiive(r) till dei, ja kiiver till déi.* Sinul on nuga. *Dom ee soo glaada. Anna oo jaa* . . . Ema, miná mágán, emá. *Anna oo jaa haar duu i dansen. Ja kiiver till dei, ja kiiver till Faabu, till Tant Ulla,* Tädi Mai Liisu. Ei ole kodus. Autoga sõita. Lähe vaatama.

(Mother, are you here next [room]? I am sleeping, Father . . . you are writing to me. I am writing to you, I am writing to you. You have a knife. They are so glad. Anna and me . . . Mother, I am sleeping, Mother. Anna and me have you in the dance. I am writing to you, I am writing to Uncle, to Aunt Ulla, Aunt Mai's Liisu. Is not at home. Drive with the car. Go and look.)

An analysis of the linguistic forms of the type Swedish [ki:vər] instead of [skri:vər] and Estonian *lähe* instead of *mine* will be found in Oksaar (1970: 114–130). Here we shall focus on code switching. Though some of the switches were marked by a pause, as a rule they occurred on sentence level without markers. (The text somehow mirrors his leaps of thought.) All Swedish sentences refer to activities Sven had noticed and experienced in the Swedish family during the day, such as letter writing and being read to from a book. The last switch into Estonian is due to the trigger word *Liisu*, the name of his Estonian cousin. Also in this monologue, place and person seem to be the most important variables among the conditioning factors of code switching.

CONCLUSION

The structure and motivation of code switching I have analyzed seem to justify the following model of the developing competence of the child (Figure 1). When the two languages he is hearing are L_1 and L_2, his repertoire is L_3.

L_3 contains elements and rules from L_1 and L_2 as well as elements and rules typical only for L_3. They were activated according to the requirements of the situation. In certain speech events L_1 parts are dominant, in others those from L_2, and in still others the autonomous parts of L_3. The contact of languages gives the child an opportunity to choose the linguistic medium of expression. It gives the child also the chance to create what is most appropriate for him to master in his speech acts.

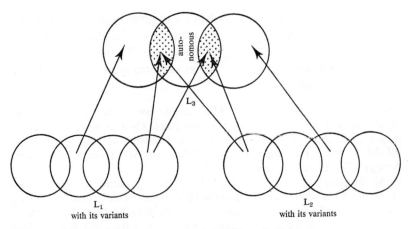

Figure 1.   The developing competence of the bilingual child

Characterizing the first stage as mixed, this point will be missed. It is more precise to speak of an overall code. The emerging grammars of unilingual children include rules and elements that do not exist in the adult's code. The repertoire of children learning more than one language simultaneously also contains rules and elements that cannot be found in either one of them.

Code switching reveals that language contact operates on at least two levels: it creates awareness of two languages, which makes it possible to use the "right" sequences in "right" situations. However, it also seems to develop awareness for rationality in performance: interferences can occur on one occasion and not on another, where they could equally be possible. The L_3 model shows how this contact creates an overall code (for an adult model, see Oksaar 1972), but much further research is necessary to find out how children arrive at a systematization of their languages within this supersystem. As Schmidt-Mackey (1971: 111) wrote:

How the children arrived at a systematization of their three languages is still something of a mystery, although a few theorists of the subjects have suggested tantalizing explanations.

REFERENCES

BLOOM, L. M.
   1970   *Language development: form and function in emerging grammars.*
          Cambridge, Mass.: M.I.T. Press.

GRAMMONT, M.
  1902   *Observation sur le langage des enfants.* Paris: Mélanges Meillet.
HYMES, D.
  1971   "Competence and performance in linguistic theory," in *Language acquisition.* Edited by R. Huxley and R. Ingram, 3–28. London, New York: Academic Press.
IMEDADZE, N.V.
  1966   *Language acquisition in a bilingual child.* Translated by D. J. Slobin. Berkeley: University of California Press.
JAKOBSON, R.
  1969   *Kindersprache, Aphasie und allgemeine Lautgesetze.* Uppsala, Frankfurt/Main: Suhrkamp. (Originally published 1941.)
LEOPOLD, W. F.
  1939–1949   *Speech development of a bilingual child,* four volumes. Evanston, Ill.: Northwestern University Press.
MENYUK, P.
  1969   *Sentences children use.* Cambridge, Mass.: M.I.T. Press.
MURRELL, M.
  1966   Language acquisition in a trilingual environment: notes from a case study. *Studia Linguistica* 20:9–34.
OKSAAR, E.
  1970   Zum Spracherwerb des Kindes in zweisprachiger Umgebung. *Folia Linguistica* 4:330–358.
  1972   "Spoken Estonian in Sweden and the USA: an analysis of bilingual behavior," in *Studies for Einar Haugen.* Edited by Evelyn Firchow, et al. The Hague: Mouton.
PIKE, K.
  1967   *Language in relation to a unified theory of the structure of human behavior.* The Hague: Mouton.
RONJAT, J.
  1913   *Le développement du langage, observé chez un enfant bilingue.* Paris: Champion.
SCHLESINGER, J. M.
  1972   "Acquisition of grammar — what and how should we investigate?" Mimeographed manuscript.
SCHMIDT-MACKEY, J.
  1971   "Language strategies of the bilingual family," in *Conference on child language.* Preprints, 85–118. Chicago, Quebec: Les Presses de l'Université Laval.

Studies in Language Switching and Mixing

EVELYN HATCH

Almost everyone who has grown up in a bilingual community has an emotional attachment to the topic of language mixing and switching; we all find the language behavior of our families interesting. Perhaps that explains our reactions to teachers in the Southwest who often describe their students as: "They can't speak English and they can't speak Spanish either. They just mix everything up. They take one word from here and another from there and think it makes sense. You know, they don't speak any language at all." The capacity of bilinguals to switch rapidly and fluently from one language to another in the middle of a conversation or in the middle of a sentence is, of course, not valued by everyone. Some deny that mixing exists at all. One of my professors once assured me that children are able to switch from one language to another with ease on social cue but that they do NOT mix languages. This gave me two choices in describing the language behavior of my family: either we didn't really do what I thought we did OR we were all alingual. Once I started looking at the literature — and it is a vast literature — I found a third choice. "The ideal bilingual switches from one language to the other according to appropriate changes in the speech situation but not in an unchanged speech situation and certainly not within a single sentence" (Weinreich 1963: 73). So the problem might be that we were not "ideal" types.

All this is exaggeration, of course, but not too far afield from the attitude of many educators toward language mixing. Recent studies of language mixing raise doubts as to the validity of describing mixers as victims of language interference. But what is there to be said about the system of language mixing? What triggers switching and is there any way to predict where and when mixing will occur? As Labov (i.p.) says, it cannot really be that the systems are just mixed together like fruit salad. In this paper I will try to bring together what a number of writers have had to say about these questions and show you some of the data from these studies as well as my own.

While it might be best to start by drawing a distinction between switching and mixing, there really is no sharp distinction to be drawn; rather it is a continuum. This has led some writers to use "switching" for both. I think the difference, if there really is one, will become clear once the data have been presented.

Instead, I will begin with a distinction which Oksaar (1972, see also this volume) used in classifying her data on Swedish-Estonian code switching: external and internal switching. The first — external — has to do with all the social factors which influence switching. The second — internal — concerns language factors, fluency of the speaker, and his ability to use various emotive devices.

EXTERNAL SWITCHING

Ferguson in his study of diglossia (1959) pointed out that in multi-lingual communities each language is assigned a role or function and language choice is then determined by social factors. Different languages may be used for school vs. home, ceremonial vs. family, business vs. private talk. Blom and Gumperz (1972) and Susan Ervin-Tripp (1964, 1967) have cited setting, interlocutor, and topic as the major variables for external switching.

There are many examples of language switching due to these variables. Barber, in his study of a trilingual community (1973), showed that setting was important for language choice: Yaqui was used at ceremonial meetings, English and Spanish were used at the store, and all three were used at work. Uyekubo, in her study of Japanese-English bilinguals (1972), showed frequent switching to accommodate the interlocutor. When monolinguals entered a conversation, the language was switched, and when they left, the language again switched. The children in her study also practiced language courtesy, speaking with their grandmother in Japanese even though she understood English.

But switching to the speech of the interlocutor is not always predictable. Psychological factors are also involved. Rayfield (1970), in his study of the Yiddish-English bilingual community in Santa Monica, shows a monolingual trying to force a language switch without success:

(A and C are bilinguals; B is a monolingual Yiddish speaker.)
A: Lieberman said she'd come, but we won't wait.
B: Lomir anfangen, darling, lomir anfangen. [Let's begin.]
C: Yes, let's begin.
(The conversation continues entirely in English in spite of B.)

And despite repeated prompting in Japanese by Ms. E. Uyekubo, Ken refused to respond in Japanese in the following passage:

E: Kore nani? [What's this?]
K: Hydrant. I have another one of those, I think.
E: Kore dare? Dare deshoo? Shitteru? Ken, shitteru? [Who's this? I wonder who it is? Do you know? Ken, do you know?]
K: Aah, he's he aah hurt the mother. From beginning to beginning ... in the beginning, the mother they trade, they buried it. That's what happened.
E: Ken, kore yomenai no? [Ken, can't you read this?]
K: I can't read ... a little words. ...
E: Chotto yon'de choodai. [Read a little for me.]
K: I can't read that dood.

But when his sister appeared on the scene and E began to talk to her, jealousy sparked a quick switch to Japanese.

I also have this exchange between two of my more obstinate neighbors both of whom speak fluent French but refuse to use it, using their first languages instead even though neither speaks the first language of the other:

A: Hamdella ʕal salama. [Welcome back.]
B: Thanks.
A: Wahashtena. [We missed you.]
B: We were on vacation. To San Francisco.
A: San Francisco. Izzay? BilʔArabiyya? [How? By car?]
B: No, we flew up.

An even better example would have to be shown on videotape. At the last meeting of our sign class, a visitor appeared. Using finger-spelling, she roundly castigated our teacher for teaching us "a street-language"-like sign. (American Sign does not follow English syntax while finger spelling is simply, or not so simply, spelling out English with the hands.) The argument was heated, to say the least, without either deaf person ever changing to the other's system. Obviously, there are many reasons for not switching to the language of the interlocutor. Only an interaction of many factors can account for such instances as this supper-table dialogue collected by Barber where the mother and wife consistently speak Yaqui and the man speaks Spanish in return:

Man: Tienen leche, no? [They have milk in them, don't they?]
Wife: Hewi. [Yes.]
Mother: Munim waata? [You want some beans?]
Man: Sí. [Yes.]

Topic can also trigger language switching. Talk about food is usually in Danish in my family, as in this exchange:

M: Nu . . . skal vi have kaffe. [Now . . . we'll have coffee.]
E: Tak [thanks], I just want to finish this letter first.
D: (Entering with 2½-year-old Kaj) Hey, ma, where's the hedge clippers?
K: Where Tante E?
M: They're right where you left them last.
E: Here, Kaj. Kom så . . . op, op, op. [Come . . . up, up, up.] Vil du ikke have kaffe, D? [Won't you have coffee, D?]
D: Ja, tak. [Yes, thanks.] (Kaj echoes the "Ja, tak.")
E: Er du tørstig, lille Kaj? [Are you thirsty, little Kaj?]
M: Gaaog vask din — (interrupted by D)
D: (Opening fridge) I don't know where I put them. What's this! Æblekage [applecake]?

Repeated cueing in English at the dinner table can, however, force a switch to English.

Some subjects switch fairly consistently by topic: others do not. In her study, Uyekubo found that her subjects talked about personal topics (children, illnesses, fears, etc.) in Japanese and used English for non-personal topics (academic, processional, political etc.). And, in discussing personal topics, if the values expressed were not typically Japanese, subjects switched to English. For example, when talking about their dissatisfaction with life or about Women's Lib, bilingual women switched to English.

In other cases, it is very difficult to know what it is that cues switching. Of course that does not stop us from guessing. Rayfield gives an example of a woman, complimented on her stole, saying, "Is warm. Is wool. Dos hot meyn shvester gemakht [my sister made it] a long, long time ago." Or, when recounting his life, another subject said ". . . affected di leber, liver cirrhosis, zey trinkn a quart of whiskey in one day. Yes, the schnapps affected di leber, di leber is an arsenal fun blood, the liver supplies blood. . . ." Rayfield suggests the first speaker's mention of family calls for a switch to Yiddish and, in the second, perhaps the speaker identifies physiology with English and liver problems with Yiddish. But it's not really all that clear.

In order to account for such rapid mixing one has to turn to Oksaar's second category: internal switching. This includes the fluency of the speaker in each language as well as his ability to use a set of rhetorical devices to establish tone, and the structure of the languages themselves.

INTERNAL SWITCHING

Language Structure

From the structure of language, can we predict where a switch will occur or where mixing will take place? Obviously it is easier, in the sense that syntax does not have to be adapted, to switch at major boundaries — sentence boundaries, major clause breaks, or at the beginning of phrases. Most switching does follow this pattern.

Single word replacement should also occur frequently if it can be achieved without forcing syntactic changes. A few generalizations have also been made about which words occur most frequently in single word replacement. Lance, in his study of Spanish-English bilinguals (1969) has suggested that words for which no ready equivalent exists are very frequently mixed:

DL: Sabes componer *flats*? [Do you know how to fix flat tires?]
DL: Y luego la *meringue* la hago con ... los *egg whites*. [And then the meringue is made with egg whites.]
AU: Kore *Betty Crocker*. [This is Betty Crocker.]
AU: That's what really disgusted me at the *omiai* [meeting of prospective bride and groom].
AU: He's one of the top three *buchoos* [a kind of manager].
EH: Vil du ... *pickles*? [Will you ... pickles?]

Holm, Holm, and Spolsky (1973), studying the speech of young Navajo children, found that, despite the long-standing notion that Navajos do not mix languages and borrow very few words from English, the children did mix and frequently used English vocabulary items while speaking Navajo. Some of the words the children definitely knew and used in Navajo as well; others, such as *pickle, math,* and *raccoon,* had no equivalent in Navajo.

However, even inserting one word can force changes elsewhere in the sentence and morphological integration, as Oksaar showed in her Swedish-Estonian study, is a common phenomenon. In the Navajo study, for example, enclitics were frequently attached to English words: *shi*little sister, *shi*pant [*shi* = my], dormitory*goo* [towards], school*di* [at], book*ish* [Is it a book?], record player*yee* [the late, or no longer working, record player].

In Japanese there is a set of verbs which are constructed from a noun + *suru* [to do]: *benkyoo* [studying] + *suru* = to study; *ryokoo* [travels] + *suru* = to travel. When English verbs were mixed as single words into Japanese, they always followed this pattern. They were always followed by an inflected form of *suru: Tada moo* memorize suru *bakkai dakara. Soo yo, yubi ga koo yuri furi ni* touch shite.

Similarly when an English adjective was inserted into a Japanese sentence, the *na* marker was placed between it and the Japanese noun: intellectual na *benkyoo*, cool na *nominomo*. When both adjective and noun were English, the *na* was omitted: *Anoo*, Japanese company *wa yasumanai yo*.

It has been suggested that this kind of syntactic modification is necessary only when mixing dissimilar languages like Navajo and English or Japanese and English. But, in fact, this does not seem to be the case. It would be interesting to know what kinds of psychological processes make it possible or even necessary for a Spanish speaker to give gender marking to English nouns as if they were the Spanish equivalent that has been replaced. Cornejo (1973) in his study of five-year-old bilinguals found that they used the Spanish article system with English nouns. And they marked the English noun as though it were its Spanish equivalent:

> una bike [una bicicleta]
> el dress [el vestido]
> las dishes [las vasijas — Texan Spanish]
> al shopping center [al centro]

The structure of the languages can, then, give us some information about where switching is most likely to occur but, again, not exact information.

Language Fluency

Certainly language fluency and language development also play a role in explaining internal mixing. In studies of children learning two languages simultaneously, mixing usually does appear. Imedadze (1960), describing the language of a child learning Russian and Georgian simultaneously pointed out that "until the 20th month the child would utter translation equivalents together in one sentence (if she knew both words), spoke mixed sentences, and would not adapt her communication to the language of her interlocutor. Her morphology was productive in both languages, making for word creations of mixed origins." By the age of two she had separated the languages. Yet, even then, once she had established a set for one language, she had difficulty changing language quickly to that of a new interlocutor.

In Leopold's classic study (1939–1949) of his daughter Hildegard, mixing of German and English in the early stages of language development is also reported. She, too, was able to separate the two languages in response to the language of the interlocutor by age two. In contrast, Ronjat (1913) shows little mixing of French and German by his son. According to Ronjat, when a word was borrowed from one language to the other, it was clearly isolated as being a borrowed word.

Studies of sequential acquisition of a second language also vary in the presence and amount of mixing. Paul, the four-year-old Taiwanese child studied by Huang (1971), did not mix languages and switched consistently by setting and interlocutor: English at the playschool and Cantonese everywhere else.

The five-year-old children observed by Cathcart (1972) yield very different data. These children, all Anglos, attended school where the traditional curriculum was taught in Spanish although no special Spanish language lessons were given. The children quickly learned to respond to Spanish commands from their teacher: *Niñas, aquí.* (The girls all get in line.) *Las más calladitas van primero en casa* (Everyone sits very quietly.) Then they began to answer their teacher's Spanish with English much as the Arabic-English exchange of my neighbors: *No has terminado? Not yet. Dónde está su yo-yo? She don't have one. Tienes calor? No, I don't got my undershirt.* Finally, they began inserting Spanish, particularly nouns, into English sentences as a sort of relexicalization process: I got a quarter for *leche. Tres* more *días* and we're going to the zoo. I'm a *avión.* It's a *verde* paper. This later changed to true mixing where word order of each language was maintained: I have a *bicicleta roja.* Actually, the mixing that occurred was little different from that of adult learners who throw in a *sí, pero . . .* or a *más o menos* while speaking English to Spanish-English bilinguals in order to establish an identity, a common bond in communication.

At first glance, Cathcart's data seems similar to mixing data from a nearby school collected by Adams (1973). These children, however, were proficient bilinguals. They used both mixing and switching but not when they spoke to the teacher, only in peer conversations: *Cada uno? I'm gonna do two. Hey, no. Es para la cocina. Get out! Shoo! Está upside down.* The difference between the two groups is quite clear. In the Cathcart study, children mix languages as a way to make communication possible with their teacher. They insert Spanish vocabulary items into English sentences as they learn them. They are not fluent in the two languages. In the second case, the children use mixing as their peer language. For them, it is not a case of deficiency in either language.

Lance and Uyekubo both have stunning examples that show the children in their studies are quite capable of saying whatever they wish in either of their two languages but prefer to combine them for more effective communication with their peers:

C: Cuéntame del juego.
R: Mmm . . . primero they were leading diez pa' nada.
C: ¿Diez a nada? ¡Isssh! ¿Y luego?
R: Then there was our team to bat and we made . . . 'cimos dos carreras. And then ellos fueron a batear. Hicieron una and then nosotros 'cimos cinco. Después 'ciron six, 'ciron cinco.
S: Siete.
R: And then they made dos and then it was our time to bat and we made . . .
C: ¿Cuántas?
R: Ah . . . five or six. And then they beat us by five runs.

If you look at R's speech, you see that he used *carreras* as well as *runs*, *batear* as well as *bat*, and later in the passage he uses *ganaron* as well as *beat*. He uses numbers in both languages. Vocabulary impoverishment or lack of fluency in either language cannot account for such mixing.

Why do children and adults who are quite capable of using each language separately prefer to mix them? I think most mixers will give the same reason that I have. For me, it sounds better. I can say what I want to say with more feeling and more meaning. It's a "better" way of expressing affection, of creating or strengthening family and community bonds. It adds color to the speech and makes for better storytelling.

This sounds very subjective so we have created a more academic term to cover these reasons. It's called tone. This is the person's ability to use a set of rhetorical devices for emotive purposes.

Tone

A number of rhetorical devices appear over and over again in the studies. Emphasis and color can be obtained by using a number of them in a variety of ways. Different people use different devices but it is their skill in using these devices which determines whether or not they can establish tone by mixing and switching. A number of these have been identified by Rayfield, Uyekubo, and Lance. Some of the categories are overlapping and some of them may not be clear from my examples. Once you abstract a mixed sentence from a dialogue or monologue it lacks the tone that you are trying to show has been established by the device.

1. *Repetition of Statement in Two Languages for Emphasis*

RR: She has a dream, ir ken es kulen, you can imagine. [You can imagine]

RR: The water leaked from all sides. He made it worse. Di vaser gest fan ale zeytn.

AU: Kono mae doo natta? What happened to this last time?

AU: Nakanai no, nakanai no. Nobody cry.

DL: But what I usually buy are those thick ones, las más gruesas.

DL: It's real easy. 'Tá bien easy.

EH: Så skal vi spise. Time to eat.

EH: Maleesh, maleesh, cherie, never mind, never mind.

2. *Contrasts Heightened by Switch at Contrast Point*

RR: I wouldn't take my dog to him, aza klug er zey [however clever he may be].

RR: A telephone committee doesn't have to be 1 or 2, es kon zeyn finf oder zeks. [it can be 5 or 6].

AU: Dakara ma futari hataraiteru kar but X says that if I don't want to, I don't have to. [That's why both of us are working. . . .]

AU: Kango fu ga iru yo 'cause I've had enough of good medicine, man. [I need a nurse you know. . . .]

DL: Boy, you get to hurtin so bad you can't hardly even 'cer masa pa' tortillas. [. . . can't make the tortillas.]

3. *To Emphasize the Unexpected*

RR: The kitchen is finf dolar. (Unexpectedly cheap.)

EH: And there in the doorway was . . . en stor mand. (Telling a ghost story.)

AU: Un, Rodan ga tabeta. Oooh, another Rodan! Two Rodans! How do you like that! [Yeah, Rodan ate it up. . . .]

4. *For Parenthetical Remarks*

RR: Tuesday is a busy day — leysn-kreyze, arbeterring [reading circle, workmen's circle] — better another day.

AU: Oichi-ni, oichi-ni, that's the way A walks, oichi-ni, oichi-ni, where's she going? [one-two, one-two. . . .]

5. To Include the Listener by Tags Which Are Emphasized

In Japanese, *ne* and *deshoo* are something like *right?* or *you follow? Yo* is also used at the end of sentences for extra emphasis:

AU: He's unhappy, *ne*, that's the point *ne*.
AU: I guess *ne* that she had a hard life so that she can't believe people *yo*.
AU: Actually they don't have a dining room *deshoo?*
AU: Atashi suki da yo, *you know*. [I like it. . . .]
DL: It's about the same, ¿*no?*
DL: Pero como, *you know* . . . la Estela.

6. To Emphasize Quotations

AU: "Oh no, D, do you think a monkey can fly?" *to ettara ne.*
AU: *She said*, "Asobi ni ikare nai."
DL: *Dice*, "Ay." *Dice*, "You're gonna hit it." *He says*, "I'm a reckless driver." *Le dijo*, "I don't think."
RR: *I asked her*, "Vus veynt ir?"
RR: *I said*, "Leyele, what are you doing?" *She says*, "Ikh darf. . . ."
AH: "Spank you," *ńii łeh.* (he usually says)
AH: "Get in line," *shi'di'mih* [someone says to me].

7. Use of Proverbs in Another Language

RR: "Ven an alte yidene khevet, vert a yunge veyb." I have a wonderful husband and I'm very happy. ["When an old Jewess marries she becomes a young woman."]
EH: Sure I know you will, "bokra fra mish-mish." ["Tomorrow when the apricots bloom" (meaning never.)]
EH: I don't know what to do "el raba wala at ʕel ʕesh." [Better cut my neck than cut off my bread]

8. For Affection, Good-humored Teasing and Swearing

EH: Er du faerdig, *you slow-poke*, saa kører vi. [Are you ready . . . then we'll drive off.]
RR: A couple of *shnorers* [beggars].
AU: A: Yuki is a nut. B: Soo kana. Taberare soo demo nai kedo nee. [Really? She doesn't look very edible.] A: Yuki is a pig! (Rest of conversation in Japanese.)

I want to quote one extended example because it combines not only the use of switching for teasing and swearing but incorporates many of the other rhetorical devices we have discussed. This is a recording made by Ms. Uyekubo during a mah jong game. Much of the discussion about the game itself is in Japanese but the interplay between the players involves frequent mixing and switching to obtain a humorous tone that I think is exceptional.

E: So, do you want something to drink? A beer?

S11: No, thanks. Beer mottai nai yo. Mizu de ii yo. [Beer is too good for them. Water is good enough.]

S9:   No, this is, this means money.

S11: Maketeru kara nominigeyoo to omotte. [Since he's losing, he thinks he can profit by running off with drinking.]

S8:   Miro kore! [Look at this!] God damn it!

S10: What happened? (exaggerated) What happened? Huh, K?

S8:   God damn it!

S11: How're you doing, K?

S10: Are you allright, K?

S9:   God damn it! (This is not K)

S10: Nakanai no, nakanai no. Nobody cry . . . Jaa kore wa . . . nobody's going to cry. [Don't cry, don't cry. Nobody cry . . . then this one. Nobody's. . . .] Come on.

S11: Wait a minute.

S10: What's the matter with you?

S11: Well, excuse me. Tsugoo ga warui yo. [It's inconvenient.]

S10: Nan'da yoo, tsugoo ga warui te. Yameta no? You stinker. [What do you mean by inconvenient? Have you quit? You stinker.]

S11: What are you talking about?

S8:   Shut up. (S8 has just entered the house.)

S10: Omae kuru no osokatta yo. [You're late.]

E: Do you take your coffee black?

S10: He doesn't drink coffee.

E: How about a pie?

S9:   No, he doesn't eat.

S10: He doesn't eat.

S8:   I just ate. . . .

S9:   Whao! This is the first time he refused.

S10: Whao! What happened? Are you allright?

S9:   Are you pregnant or something?

S8:   Shut up, man.

S11: This is the first time he refused.

S8:   Agatchau ha nai ka moo . . . [Hey, you going to go up . . .] (Referring to the game.)

S10: It must be terrible, ne?

Looking at this example, we can see instances of external switching. Language switches when a new interlocutor arrives, when the topic changes from food (English) to the game (Japanese). In the internal category, most of the switches are at sentence or clause boundaries. Finally, a variety of rhetorical devices is used to obtain the tone of the conversation: switching for teasing, for swearing, for tags, repetition of statements in both languages, and so on. The speakers are fluent bilinguals and they have full command of a wide variety of rhetorical devices to establish the kind of tone they want, a tone of comradeship.

Looking at such examples, it is easy to understand Oksaar's claim that language mixers really have three languages, two languages to be used with monolinguals, and a third mixed language to be used among themselves. Ferguson has criticized this notion rather strongly saying that it is always clear which language is the dominant language in such mixed speech. Not knowing the languages that well and not really knowing the situation in Texas where claims of a third language have also been made for language mixers, it is difficult for me to tell. But certainly we would have to agree that teachers are wrong if they think that mixers of this fluency "speak no language at all."

But the questions we began with are unanswered. Can we predict when and where switching and mixing will occur? After the fact, we can look at almost any passage and say the person switched here and mixed here for such and such a reason, but how much prediction could we make before the fact? Very little, I suspect. As Mario Pei was reportedly fond of saying, "You can't tell which way the cat will jump." Maybe that's all there is to be said. We can tell you where the cat went and why afterwards but how could we predict a passage like this final one from Labov's study of Puerto Rican speech in New York:

Por eso cada, you know it's nothing to be proud of, porque yo no estoy proud of it, as a matter of fact I hate it, pero viene viernes y sabado yo estoy, tu me ve hacia mí, sola with a, aquí solita, a veces que Frankie me deja, you know a stick or something, y yo aquí solita, queces Judy no sabe y yo estoy aquí viendo television, but I rather, y cuando estoy con gente yo me ... borracha porque me siento más, happy, más free, you know, pero si yo estoy con mucha gente yo no estoy, you know, high, more or less, I couldn't get along with anybody.

REFERENCES

ADAMS, MARILYN
   1973   "Strategies used by elementary school children in the acquisition of English as a second language." Unpublished master's thesis, University of California at Los Angeles.
BARBER, C. G.
   1973   "Trilingualism in an Arizona Yaqui village," in Bilingualism in the Southwest. Edited by P. R. Turner. Tucson, Arizona: University of Arizona Press.
BLOM, J., J. GUMPERZ
   1972   "Social meaning in linguistic structure: code-switching in Nor-

way," in *Directions in sociolinguistics*. Edited by J. Gumperz and D. Hymes. New York: Holt, Rinehart and Winston.

CATHCART, RUTH
1972 "Second language acquisition strategies of two groups of kindergarten children immersed in a second language." Unpublished master's thesis, University of California at Los Angeles.

CORNEJO, R. J.
1973 "The acquisition of lexicon in the speech of bilingual children," in *Bilingualism in the Southwest*. Edited by P. R. Turner. Tucson, Arizona: University of Arizona Press.

ERVIN-TRIPP, SUSAN
1964 "An analysis of the interaction of language, topic, and listener," in *The ethnography of communication*. Edited by J. Gumperz and D. Hymes. New York: Holt, Rinehart and Winston.
1967 An Issei learns English. *Journal of Social Issues* 23:78–90.

FERGUSON, C.
1959 Diglossia. *Word* 15:325–340.

GUMPERZ, J., E. HERNANDEZ
1972 "Cognitive aspects of bilingual communication," in *Language use and social change*. Edited by W. H. Whiteley. London: Oxford University Press.

HOLM, AGNES, W. HOLM, B. SPOLSKY
1973 "English loan words in the speech of young Navajo children," in *Bilingualism in the Southwest*. Edited by P. R. Turner. Tucson, Arizona: University of Arizona Press.

HUANG, J.
1971 A Chinese child's acquisition of English syntax." Unpublished master's thesis, University of California at Los Angeles.

IMEDADZE, N.
1960 On the psychological nature of early bilingualism. *Voprosy Psikhol.* 1:60–68. (Abstract by D. I. Slobin in *Genesis of language*. Edited by F. Smith and G. Miller, 367–368. Cambridge, Mass.: M.I.T. Press.)

LABOV, W.
i.p. The place of linguistic research in American society. *Linguistics* 70, Center for Applied Linguistics.

LANCE, D. L.
1969 "A brief study of Spanish-English bilingualism: final report." Research project ORR-Liberal Arts-15504, Texas A&M University.

LEOPOLD, W. F.
1939–1949 *Speech development of a bilingual child: a linguist's record.* Evanston, Ill.: Northwestern University Press.

OKSAAR, ELS
1972 "On code switching: an analysis of bilingual norms." Paper given at the Third International Congress of Applied Linguistics, Copenhagen.

RAYFIELD, J. R.
1970 *The languages of a bilingual community*. The Hague: Mouton.

RONJAT, J.
1913   *Le développement du langage observé chez un enfant bilingue.*
Paris: Champion.

UYEKUBO, AIKO
1972   "Language switching of Japanese-English bilinguals." Unpublished
master's thesis, University of California at Los Angeles.

VILDOMEC, V.
1963   *Multilingualism.* Leiden: A. W. Sijthoff.

WEINREICH, U.
1963   *Languages in contact: findings and problems.* The Hague: Mouton.

Mixing and Sequencing

Nonverbal Components in Message Sequence: "Mixed Syntax"

TATIANA SLAMA-CAZACU

If social human reality — even in its most "modern" forms — is analyzed, one fact stands out conspiciously, even without any statistical investigations: oral communication is the most frequently occurring activity, both in everyday life and professional work.[1] Nevertheless, it is that very reality that we ignore almost entirely. Linguistic theories as well as most works on lexicography, grammar, and even stylistics (and, paradoxically, even works on phonetics, and phonology in particular) are based on TEXTS, i.e. on the investigation of languages in their written form.[2]

1. The study of language in its oral form evinces various facts, which, if gathered and interpreted in a generalizing synthesis, might lead to the conclusion that grammars, lexicographical works, etc. that are based on the investigation of written language reveal a unilateral image of language. The study of spoken language — and in this case research concerning DIALOGUE is most necessary — shows peculiarities which might alter, for instance, the present outlook on grammar. For example, a "contextual syntax" is revealed, created by linked replies (i.e. the sequence of utterances by two participants in a dialogue) that make up grammatical units in cases where traditional grammar speaks of isolated

---

[1] The latter situation was analyzed by the author in *Comunicarea în procesul muncii* (1964).
[2] There are exceptions, of course. Yet, unfortunately, one cannot say that the direct investigation of language in its oral form has been the focus of attention so far or that it constitutes the single objective of many systematic studies, handled with an adequate methodology.

sentences (sometimes considered as "elliptical" sentences).[3]

We shall venture here to call attention particularly to an important aspect that could be revealed by the investigation of language in its actualized form, in communication: namely, to the utilization of visual means, in the predominantly verbal message, as a complement and even as a substitute for verbal expression.

2.   Unlike written communication, oral communication implies special relationships between emitter and receiver. This is a result either of its usually being carried on in dialogue form (therefore being exchange of related replies) or of the interference of acoustic (therefore auditory) components, which influence emission or reception. Or, it may derive from the fact that, as a rule (with the exception of telephone conversations and radio monologues), both partners are present in a COMMON SITUATION where they can SEE each other:

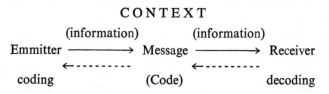

C O N T E X T

In any situation in which oral communication is performed, at least one of the above conditions appears and influences expression. Here we shall deal only with the aspect we find most natural, that is, oral communication in dialogue form, with both partners being present. This PRESENCE has some implications pertaining to the field of the concrete and of direct psychological determinations: space continuity and temporal nearness of the partners, their physical relation to the situation they are in — objects, persons, etc.; the possibility of offering direct cues; the possibility of perceiving the message through several channels (visual as well as auditory) with determinism thereby implied; the appeal to the receiver's direct participation (hence a joint interest and even an empathy, with a stylistic function), etc. In this case, therefore, communication preferably takes place in a situation common to the emitter and the receiver, within the limits outlined by the intersection of the *I-you-here-now* axes.[4] Hence, some specific aspects of the communication

---

[3]   Meillet (1921: 610) pointed out that certain sentences should not be considered elliptical because there exist one-member sentences as well, and not only two-member sentences.

[4]   Bühler (1934: 127) spoke on the *"hier-jetzt-ich* System"; cf. also Benveniste (1966: 252 ff.), who speaks about "this system of internal references whose key is *I*." We consider it necessary to add to Bühler's and others' systems the *you* com-

are: the crystallization in speech of the direct contact between speaker and hearer, the reference to the situation, the appeal to everything existing around the participants — including the physical person of the emitter or of the receiver, who are thus not only "actors" of the communication, but also "objects," instruments of the communication, utilized in emission or in reception.

Reception is a total act that generally refers to context; within oral communication, reception finds many more contextual supports in the surrounding situation itself. On the other hand, the emitter knows this device resorted to by the receiver, and he makes use of situational correlates[5] as either economical or redundant instruments. Within this framework, the receiver's utilization of mimicry or gesture (as expressive means in themselves or only as tools serving to establish a relation with the situation, for example, pointing to something, for indication generally) is natural and very frequent.

What we mean here is not only the parallel utilization of two codes — a verbal and a mimic-gestural one — ALTERNATING in separate, independent units in the course of communication or OVERLAPPING simultaneously or synchronically, bringing in a stylistic "addition" or some actual information, but also their CONCOMITANT but consecutive utilization in the sentence (we are using the term concomitant to designate the "joint" presence in the same sentence of various codes, although the sequence, characteristic of sentence syntax, is also implied). Verbal expression means proper can even be replaced during oral discourse by FACIAL MIMICRY (facial expression) and GESTURE CUES which are therefore INSERTED INTO SPEECH, thus becoming an integral part of the latter.

Within oral communication, the context provides means other than those of written communication. Those linguistic harpoons that link the present utterance to the previous one by special words — the ANAPHORIC words (*this, that, here, there, which,* etc.) — become deictic (*this,* plus "the gesture indicating the respective person") in the case of oral communication *praesentibus partibus.* During the communication, the deictic word may even be dropped (*Give me that over there!* may become *Give [me]!* [with a gesture indicating the object]), the gesture alone, in that case, representing the meaning; the visual reference point (*repère*) becomes the unique element for the completion of the sentence

---

ponent, which is essential for communication, namely for the emitter-receiver relation (see also, more recently, Kuryłowicz 1972): the speaker's orientation is based on the *hic* (*ego*), *nunc* coordinates (Kuryłowicz 1972: 174).

[5]   See Slama-Cazacu (1961: 42 ff.; 1964; 1973), etc.

meaning. There appears what we have elsewhere called *indicatio ad oculos* (see Slama-Cazacu 1970).

What happens, from a linguistic viewpoint, in such a case, when the facial mimicry or gestural element is not parallel or juxtaposed to speech but is INSERTED into the sequence of the verbal discourse, being linked in succession to the verbal element? The mimic or gestural element (which we shall here briefly call a "mimem" [Pottier 1967: 15]) becomes the indicator or describing device of an object, person, or fact, expressing by itself the meaning that a word might have expressed; thus, the visual reference point *(repère)* is INTEGRATED into the verbal message, becoming a component of the sentence. The interlocutor is satisfied and does not protest against it because he understands the message; the fact looks banal to him. Empirically known, in general, the device was mentioned mainly theoretically, and rather casually and vaguely, by K. Bühler,[6] under the name of *demonstratio ad oculos* (Bühler 1934: 80).[7]

3. The problem is worthy of thorough study, by an investigation of concrete languages comparatively and in relation to various social contexts. An adequate method should also be employed, which should distinguish between this device and ellipses, or anaphoric and deictic words.

[6]   We are referring here to the device of *indicatio ad oculos* proper and not to the various brief remarks concerning the role of facial mimicry and gesture in communication (as a parallel auxiliary or as a total substitute for speech as a whole), either under the aspect of the mimic-buccal components of articulation (see, for example, Paget 1930; Mikuś 1935), or as a completely separate system (e.g. in various social groups, etc.), or as a parallel, and therefore redundant, auxiliary of speech (see, more recently, Pottier's very useful analysis [1967: 15]); cf. also Davitz's insights (1964: 201) concerning the great importance of nonverbal stimuli "for the understanding of the expressed message." The abundant utilization of gesture in communication is also mentioned by folklorists (for example, by Romanian fairy tale tellers, c.f. Bîrlea 1966: 103); the profusion of gestures and facial mimicry in meridional societies, like that of Naples, is also empirically known. In social psychology as well (see, for example, the *Journal of Personality and Social Psychology*), the role of facial mimicry and even gaze in establishing "social contact" has been considerably dwelt upon; more recently, some of these specialists have focused their attention generally on "nonverbal communication": see, especially, Argyle (1975) and the references given there; compare, even more recently, the initiative taken by Mary Ritchie-Key (University of California at Irvine) on world-scale information or kinesics, or some of the studies considered as referring to "semiotic phenomena" (e.g. Cicourel and Boese 1972), etc. It is obvious, however, that none of these studies or notes refers to the phenomenon dealt with in the present paper.
[7]   We are adopting another term because we consider it more adequate for the facts we are referring to and, on the other hand, we wish to avoid the rhetorical associations called forth by *demonstratio*.

First of all, it is necessary to record entire conversations, in the live dynamics of real contexts, and to consider precisely all the components of the speech act and of the entire situation. By utilizing what the author calls a "dynamic-contextual method,"[8] we can very often notice that messages that are apparently elliptical from a linguistic-verbal point of view are actually completed by a gesture, for instance, or that a seemingly redundant gesture is strictly motivated functionally, for completing a sentence. Frequently, a profusion of deictic words that have in fact no real function (an abundance of *this's, that's,* etc.), can also be noticed because the actual meaning is provided by the accompanying gesture. In many cases the deictic word could be omitted (it might also be preserved as a verbal automatism); the real function belongs to the facial mimicry and gestural elements, and therefore the form of expression could actually be considered an INDICATIO AD OCULOS.

4.   At the present stage, we venture to predict that this device — fundamental in oral communication — is a universal of human communication. The following examples refer to the Romanian language; they were recorded in everyday life on the one hand, and, on the other, during a special investigation concerning communication during the work process in various fields of activity (Slama-Cazacu 1964).

We shall mention here only a few facts, recorded during an investigation which is far from being concluded, in order to support with concrete examples the ideas presented above and especially to incite further investigation, for other languages as well, of some aspects we consider of definite interest and importance, which might not yet be obvious enough.

The facts recorded belong to both the lexical and the grammatical field. Facial expression and gestural elements may consist of movements of the head, of the hand, facial mimicry proper (indication by gaze, etc.), postural attitude, movement towards an object, etc. Mimems, can replace either words or sentences. On the other hand, in verbal discourse, the analysis can distinguish morphological substitutions or those having a syntactic function.

Kinesic elements can replace nouns, verbs, adjectives, and adverbs. An example[9] of noun replacement is: "GIVE![10] [gesture: 'the book']."

---

[8]   See Slama-Cazacu 1973: Part I, Chapter 4 (Psycholinguistic methodology); Part II, Chapter 3 (Psycholinguistics and the application of the dynamic-contextual method in dialectology), etc.
[9]   The examples will be given in translation; the original Romanian form will be given in the footnotes.
[10]   Romanian *Dă!*

Verb replacements include: "I'VE TOLD YOU. LIKE THAT![11] [action of 'rolling']" (this takes place in an electrotechnical plant as a setter shows a worker how to roll a coil); and, during the shooting of a film, a film director, talking about the Number Five spotlight placed on a balustraded platform, tells the electrician: "FIVE BALCONY![12] [gesture as if switching on the light: 'switch it on!']"; and "ALL READY![13] [specific gesture meaning 'Hush! Keep silent!']." Adjective and verb substitutes are: "Was it good? — IT WAS[14] [gesture: 'excellent']" (this occurs during a dialogue at table); and "Why are you late? — I'VE REPAIRED SOMETHING[15] [gesture toward the window: 'outside']"; and, on a building site, "STRIKE IT[16] (the nail) [gesture: 'upwards']."

The analysis can be made at the syntactic level as well, when the subject, the predicate, and often the complements are replaced by gestures. Facial mimicry and gestural elements can also replace a clause within a sentence which would otherwise seem elliptical. For example, on a building site, while assembling a prefabricated wall: "HEY, LOOK THERE![17] [head motions to the wall, and questioning mimicry: 'Is it well fixed?']." Or: "[head motions to the window: 'Just look!'] IT'S RAINING AGAIN!"[18] Or: "PLEASE![19] [motions to a chair: 'Have a seat on this chair!']."

There are cases in which the sentence is completed and the meaning is thus better clarified by gestures and linked motions representing very complex incidents (which would require long verbal explanations if expressed in words). For instance, a television director explains to the cameraman during a rehearsal: "The cameras will be put like this: for the choir and folk music, Two (= camera Number Two) HERE [goes to the place where the cameraman will stay], and Four HERE [goes to another place]. For the dances, camera Two comes THIS WAY [goes quite far on the film set], and camera Four THIS WAY [points at, and then goes to, the respective place]."[20]

Interesting aspects can be also noticed in connection with the order of the elements. In many of the examples mentioned, the gesture appeared at the end of the discourse because we had to cut down the fragments of speech; but mimems can be introduced in various positions

11   Romanian *Ţi-am spus. Aşa!*
12   Romanian *Cinci balcon.*
13   Romanian *Gata!*
14   Romanian *A fost bun? — A fost.*
15   Romanian *De ce-ai întîrziat? — Am reparat ceva.*
16   Romanian *Dă-i!*
17   Romanian *Ia, vezi aici!*
18   Romanian *Iar plouă!*
19   Romanian *Poftim!*
20   Romanian *Aici . . . aici . . . p-aici . . . pe-aici.*

— at the end, at the beginning, or in the middle of the discourse. For instance: "[head movement indicating 'a beautiful woman' who is walking in the street] WELL, WHAT ABOUT THAT?";[21] or a dialogue between fishermen in a boat: "HAVE A LOOK [gesture: 'there', where the net has caught the boat], THERE'S SOMETHING WRONG!"[22] Detailed investigations, resorting to statistics as well, might show the favorite gestural positions and their consequences for optimal understanding of the message.

5. In laboratory investigations concerning the role of "mixed syntax" in experimental conditions (started in collaboration with Elena Negro, from the University of Turin, Italy, who had a fellowship for studies in psycholinguistics at the Laboratory of Psycholinguistics of the University of Bucharest), we have found that more often than not gestures are rarely entirely and clearly outlined. Sometimes there are only sketches of a gesture, or hasty facial mimicry, or only indications given to the partner by gaze during the communication (even without turning the head to the object or to the partner; these two components of the "indication by gaze" can sometimes be missing, under special conditions, and are revealed only during the above-mentioned analytical research).

The role of gaze in communication — from this viewpoint, i.e. as an intentional cue, an indication relating to an object, etc. and not as mere "eye contact" (whose role in establishing intergroup relations is mainly discussed in social psychology) — is much greater than we have indicated so far. For example, in our research, one of the subject's tasks was to turn right side up two or three cups which were laid bottom upwards on a table. When the experimenter — looking down — gives only the order *"Turn!"* [23] the subject does not know what he is supposed to do. If the INITIATING-DESCRIPTIVE gesture of "turning (the cup)" is added, but the experimenter keeps looking down, some subjects consider the situation still ambiguous and ask what it is all about. The INDICATING gesture (towards the cup), however, facilitates to a far greater extent the understanding of the indication and the performing of the action (here the gesture has the role of introducing the direct object [grammatical *complément direct*], represented here by the concrete object [the cup], which stands for the word "[Turn] THE CUP!"). When the experimenter looks at the object while saying "TURN!" the situation might seem ambiguous if the subject does not notice the direction of the gaze (depending on his position as regards the experimenter); but the

---

[21] Romanian *Ce zici?*
[22] Romanian *Ia vezi, . . . că ţine!*
[23] Romanian *Intoarce!*

situation gets quite clear when there is a slight pause between the verbal order *"Turn!"* and the change of the experimenter's gaze from another direction towards the cup, particularly when the gaze is also accompanied by a slight INDICATIVE HEAD MOVEMENT to the cup (this very movement is by itself indicative of the action).[24]

Consequently, during the communication, the emitter's behavior has many nuances, which are adapted to various situations; he chooses the most adequate cues and resorts to a "lexical" and "morphologic" choice of mimems very well suited to the situation. The receiver is, in his turn, attentive to the various cues — some very detailed ones — given to him during the messages; these are decoded on the basis of long practice in communication, since early childhood.

In our further research, we intend to specify the details regarding both the "form" of the mimems as such and the relation between them and the position of the partners in the space of the communication, their place in relation to the objects, the latters' peculiarities, etc.

6. We should add that in most cases an INTENTIONAL utilization of the facial mimicry and gestural component is implied (as being a language behavior element and not an emotional, involuntary expression). The problem also arises here of the receiver's adaptation to this way of communication: if one gesture is missed, the message may become inefficient. It is this very efficiency of the messages — that is, the habit of resorting to mimems — which shows their general and essential character in oral communication.

These messages certainly have a verbal-oral predominance (depending also on the conditions in which the communication is taking place), but the ensembles in which they can be noticed during oral communication actually have a syntax with mixed elements (which we might call a MIXED SYNTAX): the verbal elements (with their intrinsic components of

---

[24] It depends, of course, on the positions of the partners in relation to each other (face-to-face, side-by-side, etc.). (See also Moscovici and Plon 1966; Moscovici and Malrieu 1966.) We think, however, that the respective experiments might have rendered the situations artificial or that, at any rate, they do not represent typical models of communication (the subjects, pupils in a school ambience, might have been influenced by the routine of talking in a "school-like" way in class — without being noticed by the teacher, sitting side-by-side, for example). We mention that we are not concerned here either with the role of gesture as the ONLY indicator (other visual cues can also have an important part to play), or with gestures as clear-cut, well-defined expressions (there are frequent cases when a mere sketching of a gesture, the beginning of some facial mimicry, etc. — which can be noticed by speaking partners, though easily overlooked by the researcher during the experiment — are sufficient in communication).

buccal articulatory kinesics and the intentionally utilized facial expressions and gestural elements. The reception of oral communication is therefore made both in an auditory way — the channel of verbal means — and in a visual way — the channel by which the elements of mimic and gesture codes are received. As far as expression is concerned, the entire message is achieved, from a peripheral viewpoint, simultaneously or with slight contrapuntal overlapping, both verbally and kinesically, and its reception is equally bivalent. Yet, it is likely that the mental elaboration of the message, as far as the emitter is concerned, as well as the synthesis of the elements at the moment of decoding, is achieved at a single level (marked by a verbal preponderance, at least from the semantic point of view).[25] This brings about the fusion in the receiver's informational INPUT of the temporal elements, dissociated during the circulation of the message.

If we refer to the plane of the outside observer, to that of linguistic analysis (which may also be applied to a problem of metalanguage), we may notice that the codes in the oral communication *praesentibus partibus* are combined to such an extent that, especially in situations like the ones mentioned above, it is still difficult to separate the code of verbal signs from the code of kinesic signs (gestures and facial mimicry). In such cases, these codes, which actually do combine in the subjects' consciousness, also achieve a linguistic synthesis, on the grammatical metalanguage plane, in one single code, structured *sui generis* and comprising verbal and facial mimicry-gestural elements mutually modified and fused in LINGUISTICALLY analyzable units.

7.   Further development along the lines of this pilot study will probably lead to theoretical conclusions which may help to modify the still predominating image of the fundamental features and components of the grammatical model of a language, and to verify the hypothesis concerning the necessity of discussing and analyzing any natural language from the viewpoint of "mixed syntax" as well. On the other hand, in the realm of practical application (in language learning and teaching, in determining the parameters of the optimal communication in various

---

[25] Experiments carried on, in collaboration, in certain variants, regarding the comparative perception of verbal stimuli (VS) and nonverbal stimuli (NS) have shown that not only the verbal but also the motor reaction time (RT) is much smaller for VS (words) than for NS (the drawings corresponding to the objects represented by those words). The human being is accustomed to decoding mentally any percept in the verbal system by inwardly giving the "name" of the object: hence, we see the lengthening of RT in the case of NS because a double decoding intervenes (a simple perceptual one, of the drawing, and a verbal one on the mental plane); cf. Slama-Cazacu (1967).

work situations, within various social relations, etc.) the importance of knowing the real aspects of oral communication should also be underlined. We are certainly aware that the laboratory experiments we have initiated must be corroborated and completed by an extensive, concrete study of the spoken-oral form of various languages — of Romanian, as far as we are concerned, and, at the same time, the various languages of the world — a study which can only be accomplished through the joint efforts of a vast team of researchers.

REFERENCES

ARGYLE, M.
  1975 The syntax of bodily communication. *International Journal of Psycholinguistics* 3.
BENVENISTE, E.
  1966 *La nature des pronoms: problèmes de linguistique générale.* Paris: Gallimard.
BÎRLEA, D., editor
  1966 *Antologie de proză populară epică* [Anthology of epic popular prose]. Bucharest: Editura pentru literatură.
BÜHLER, K.
  1934 *Sprachtheorie.* Jena: Fischer.
CICOUREL, A., BOESE, R.
  1972 The acquisition of manual sign language and generative semantics. *Semiotica* 5:225–256.
DAVITZ, J.
  1964 "Summary and speculations," in *The communication of emotional meaning.* Edited by J. Davitz. New York: Academic Press.
KURYŁOWICZ, J.
  1972 The role of deictic elements in linguistic evolution. *Semiotica* 5: 174–183.
MEILLET, A.
  1921 Remarques sur la théorie de la phrase. *Journal de psychologie* 18:609–616.
MIKUŚ, F.
  1935 Faits phono-optiques et leur part à l'audition. *Journal de psychologie* 2:215–219.
MOSCOVICI, S., D. MALRIEU
  1966 Les situations-colloques, II: Organisation des canaux de communication et de la structure syntaxique. *Bulletin de psychologie* 21:520–530.
MOSCOVICI, S., M. PLON
  1966 Les situations-colloques: observations théoriques et expérimentales. *Bulletin de psychologie* 19:702–722.
PAGET, R.
  1930 *Human speech.* London: Kegan, French, Trubner.

POTTIER, B.
1967 *Présentation de la linguistique. Fondements d'une théorie.* Paris: Klincksieck.
SLAMA-CAZACU, T.
1961 *Langage et contexte.* The Hague: Mouton.
1964 *Comunicarea în procesul muncii* [Communication in work activity]. Bucharest: Ed. Ştiinţifică.
1967 The use of the motor reaction time for the comparison of verbal and non-verbal stimuli, and verbalization in perception. *Revue Roumaine des sciences sociales — Psychologie* 1:81–88.
1970 "L'étude du roumain parlé: un aspect négligé — l'"indicatio ad oculos'," in *Proceedings of the Twelfth International Congress of Romance Linguistics and Philology*, volume one, 591–599. Bucharest.
1973 *Introduction to psycholinguistics.* The Hague: Mouton. (Romanian edition 1968.)

Linguistic and Kinesic Correlations in Code Switching

WALBURGA VON RAFFLER ENGEL

Linguists are gradually returning to join anthropologists and psychologists in the common attempt to analyze the communicative behavior of man.

My research follows within the traditional lines of Boas and Sapir on the relationship between language and culture, both as a social phenomenon and how this relationship affects man's image of himself and his view of the world.

Because of the scarcity of funds my surveys are limited to a small number of subjects, of both sexes, children and adults.

The focus of the research is on minority-majority interaction, minority being understood in respect to the dominant culture or language. The minority group may or may not be numerically inferior. Thus in Montreal, for example, the status of French as a minority language is rapidly passing to that of a majority language due to changes in political power and attitudes. In Montreal the majority of the population has always been speaking French and no drastic change has occurred to alter that pattern during the last decades.

The relationship of language and culture is based on a variety of factors and their multiple interactions. The only thing we know for sure is that this relationship is in no way a one-to-one correspondence. Co-occurence obtains in many instances but a matching relationship seems to result only from cumulative effects. My work in language acquisition leads me to believe that language and culture are two distinct aspects of the psychological and the sociological make-up of man and his behavior. There is a reciprocal influence between language and culture.

The original issue focused on by Boas comprised language, culture, and race. The present-day concept of ethnicity would add a fourth dimension. To investigate the relationship between language, culture, ethnicity, and race, I am in the process of conducting a survey among French-Canadians, but for the moment I have to limit my discussion to language and culture. My conclusions will be adjusted when the new data are in and a fuller picture emerges.

I have tried to approach the relationship of language and culture with some empirical research. The results point to the separation of language and culture and to some aspects of language behavior being more influenced by culture than others. The impact of language on culture, which loomed large in some previous research of mine, in these instances was minimal.

I have chosen the conversational mode. Among linguists it is more common to study monologues. The dialogue is infinitely more frequent in natural language and should provide us with some insight on what language is and how it relates to culture.

Before the speech act can be analyzed, several specific instances of the latter must be described with full coverage of all the factors that go into it, inclusive of the linguistic aspects but not exclusive of any (or all) others.

Language can certainly be analyzed as a self-contained system. Such an analysis, however, does not explain the speech act. To understand the latter, one cannot isolate the verbal aspect from the situation and the context in which the language was produced (Gumperz and Hymes 1964). The situation is frequently accidental while the context is usually purposive.

In our final analysis, the major difficulty consists in correlating the linguistic and the kinesic factors and we have as yet no secure guidelines for accomplishing this. Before we can extrapolate the universals of human communicative behavior, it seems to me that we should view each speech act within the culture, the social system, the situational and contextual setting, the personalities (age, sex, and other), and the interpersonal relationship in which it happens.

It does not seem to me that we are yet ready for a comprehensive theory to be tested against further occurrences. We are probably still largely in the stage of data collecting, if not of pilot studies.

In several sub-areas of the speech act we already have some workable theories and it may not be too long before we will be able to formulate an all-inclusive theory. By theory I mean a loose and open-ended theory, essentially a working hypothesis that is constantly checked against the new data and improved as work progresses all the while the heuristics are being refined.

In the speech act taken as a whole, as happens in the meaning of the sentence compared to the words that make up a sentence, the total of all the features which make up the communicative event does not equal their sum. The totality of its features modifies each speech act and adds to it the multiple relationships of the subfeatures among themselves. The subfeatures can act as single entities and also as entities formed by certain groupings of the latter.

These relationships are extremely complex. Just as social dialects differ in the developmental sequence of language acquisition and the subsequent frequency of certain linguistic patterns (von Raffler Engel 1964; Parisi, et al. 1971), it is likely that differences in the system of kinesics influence the development and frequency of occurrence of certain gestures. It is not impossible that those differences have implications for the process of verbalization.

Besides the more observable overt features mentioned earlier in this paper, a description of the speech act must report the meaning of its message. As a firm believer in a complicated, but nevertheless workable, relationship of co-occurrence between form and meaning, I am convinced that different surface structures correspond to different thought processes (von Raffler Engel 1972a). It is likely that the generative concept of "competence" will eventually turn out to be a myth like the Freudian symptom substitution (Baer 1971).

In comparing the communicative behavior of groups of different languages and/or cultures, the researcher can take the behavior of one group as the basic one, either because he assumes that this is standard for the language or culture in question or because he has decided upon certain universals. Rather than matching the other group against the group which he has selected as standard or measuring it against some universal concept of speech behavior, a researcher could consider both groups on an equal footing and proceed by abstracting some common concept from the behavior of the two groups.

I attempted this latter approach in an analysis prepared with the cooperation of a student of mine (von Raffler Engel and Sigelman 1971). We analyzed a series of freely told stories which I had previously collected from black and white fourth graders. Among others, we isolated the concept of "bringing a character to life." The white children achieved this goal by giving each character a personal name while the black children let their characters speak in dialogue. In the same vein, we looked for the presence or absence of a formal beginning of each story. Seventy-six percent of the black children and 42 percent of the white children started their stories with "Once upon a time." We then refined our analysis and found that a full 75 percent of the white children used the word "once" in some way or another in their introductory remarks. The difference between black and white children with respect to story beginnings was therefore minimal.

The two studies in verbal and kinesic code switching on which I am reporting in this paper followed these same lines of evaluation. Essentially, my procedure is based on an adaptation of Hockett's concept of deep structure (Hockett 1958).

It is difficult to formulate Hockett's concept with great precision. For the time being, such formalization is pointless as our knowledge of deep structure in language is still limited. Our knowledge of deep structure in kinesics is even less extensive. The relationship between language and kinesics, in a certain sense, has been investigated more on the level of structural relationship than on the surface level.

When we know so little about the verbal and kinesic interaction within one language and one culture, it may appear premature to start working on bilingual and bidialectal situations. On the other hand, the researcher can readily identify and isolate the variable of language or dialect change. It is sometimes less easy to document the moment of switching within some of the other variables, such as, for example, a change of subject domain.

The basic problems in language or dialect switching may tentatively be listed as follows:
1.   Does code switching in the language necessarily accompany kinesic code switching, and *vice versa*?
2.   Is kinesic code switching synchronous, or are there delays? If so, which modality precedes the other?
3.   Are (1) and (2) universal or are there linguistic and cultural differences? If so, are these differences inherent in the system of the kinesics or of the language? Are these differences due to cultural, social, attitudinal, or interpersonal factors?
4.   How do kinesic interferences correlate with linguistic interferences?
5.   Can kinesic and linguistic interferences be traced to the same causes?
6.   How does the development of language and kinesics correlate? Leaving second language acquisition completely out of the picture, are there differences between the dominant and the secondary language and/or culture in bilinguals?

7. Is it possible to have dominance in one linguistic code and at the same time in the kinesic code that usually belongs to the secondary language?

8. Is it possible to have linguistic interference without kinesic interference, or *vice versa*?

9. Are there kinesic pidgins that accompany full languages, or *vice versa*? Under such conditions, will the pidgins creolize or revert to the full system that is generally associated with the accompanying language or kinesics, as the case may be?

10. Is the subject and person division of linguistic bilingualism equally valid for kinesic bilingualism? In any case, does the same division apply to both language and gesture within the individual?

11. Are there societal kinesic systems comparable to the well documented societal bilingual languages?

12. In a bilingual community, can one group keep its language and its kinesics, while the other group keeps its language but has fully adopted the other kinesic system?

I surveyed two situations. One was bidialectal, involving black and white speakers of American English (von Raffler Engel 1972b, 1972c). The other was bilingual (von Raffler Engel 1972d, 1972e).

The bidialectal survey was carried out in a welfare office of the central South. Videotape equipment was installed in the room where the social worker interviews her clients as well as in the adjacent waiting room.

After several days of recording without the subjects being aware of it, I evaluated the resulting videotapes and prepared the log. To start the analysis, I isolated one welfare client whose picture and voice came through clearly in both interview and waiting rooms. I then had photographic prints made from selected frames of the video to match the corresponding sections of the audio tape. The latter were transferred to a tape recorder and from there transcribed on strips of paper to be attached to each photograph.

The examination of the photographs with their matching discourse transcripts, comparing the facial expression and the speech patterns of the subjects on videotape in the formal interview situation and in the unstructured waiting room setting, revealed the following:

1.a. In the waiting room, speech tempo in both substandard English and black English was faster (more syllables per second) and the phonation ratio was lower (longer pauses between utterances). The facial expression was more varied and proxemics was closer.

b. During the interview, speech tempo was slower and phonation ratio higher. This greater regularity of verbal expression was accompanied by a more composed face.

2.a.   When changing register, the adult black subjects appeared first to adjust their total composure and speak only after that. This was essentially the same for adult whites except that their paralinguistic behavior, as well as their dialect, did not differ so extensively with change of communicative situation.

As I had expected from my previous informal observations of the lower classes in the South, the greatest divergence between blacks and whites was manifest in the unstructured situation.

b.   Of considerable sociolinguistic interest is the fact that the younger generation among black adults — and among these the females in particular — showed much less kinesic variation in code switching than older blacks.

The bilingual situation involved the comparison of the communicative behavior of Francophone and Anglophone children in the first two elementary grades at the demonstration school of the University of Ottawa Child Study Center.

A videotape recording device was installed in the testing room, a small spot reserved for us in each school. The microphone was firmly taped to the table around which the children were to be seated because children tend to play with such devices. Two small chairs were placed on each side of the table facing each other diagonally for best channeling their voices into the speaker. The television camera and earphones for silent audio monitoring were placed in an adjacent spot, out of the children's sight.

I then entered the testing room with one child to tell him a story he was to retell to another child with whom he was also to comment on the story. This procedure was adopted because, without a firm seating arrangement and a definite commitment to talk about a preestablished subject matter, children of grade school age will not necessarily talk to each other. They play, fight, or inspect the room, moving all around. If the tester asks the children to speak without structuring their theme, they may stare at each other or burst out in giggles, not knowing what to say.

I narrated an identical story to all children, in French and English respectively. Upon completion of the story, I left the room. The child to whom the story was to be retold entered the room to take my chair. The same procedure was repeated for each new set of children. I alternated the combination of children by Francophone-to-Anglophone and Anglophone-to-Francophone groupings.

The evaluation of the videotapes showed that:

1.a.   French children signal their readiness for a friendly chat by leaning forward toward each other, while English children convey the same message by leaning back on the chair and extending their feet in a relaxed manner.

b.   Francophone children underscore what they say with paralinguistic (Bolinger 1968) gestures on the word level. They do this particularly with qualifiers, adjectives, and adverbs.

Anglophone children act out whole situations. They employ what could be termed discourse paralinguistics.

The difference in paralinguistic behavior between the two ethnic groups is striking; the gestures of Francophones are strictly language-related while Anglophone children act out a theme which they also describe verbally at the same time. Their gestures are discourse-related rather than word related.

2.a.   When Francophone children speak either French or English to Anglophones they tend to modify their customary kinesics. They lean forward, but only slightly, and they make far less frequent use of para-linguistic gestures. When they do employ these gestures, they expand their hands less vividly.

b.   When Anglophone children speak English to Francophones, their kinesics do not differ from when they speak to Anglophones.

When speaking French either to another Anglophone — as would be the case in practicing for their school work — or to a Francophone, these children make an effort at copying some kinetic features of the Francophone population. The features copied appear at random but are consistently exaggerated.

I have not observed this behavior in adult Anglophones. The latter generally keep their kinesics identical whether they are speaking French or English. This is more likely due to a difference in the social attitude of the present generation than to a difference inherent in the two age groups.

3.a.   To conclude, bilingual Canadian children seem to have one full kinesic system and two languages. But the two ethnic groups differ radically.

b.   In code switching, the Anglophone children maintain their own customary kinetic system, but sometimes intersperse it with exaggerated Francophone kinesics. Over-correctness is particularly evident when the children are not completely fluent in the French language.

The Francophone children do not correlate kinesics with language code switching. They correlate kinesics with ethnic group switching.

When speaking either French or English with an Anglophone, they will employ a reduced version of their own customary kinesics. When speaking English to Francophones (this instance is more frequent than outsiders would presume), they seem more relaxed when not altering their native kinesics. My data are only scanty and this issue is still in a working stage.

The sociolinguistic implications of the different cuts of relationship between language and culture among Canada's two ethnic groups are profound and merit further investigation.

In the two studies on which I have briefly reported above, it is apparent that "units of communication" (von Raffler Engel 1972b) involving both speech and body motion can be clearly isolated and that the duration of each such unit exceeds that of the spoken message. Thus, the spoken message forms the inner core of the communication unit. Code switching involves both language and kinesics; but the two modalities are not treated in parallel fashion.

The black minority in the United States mastered two languages and two kinesic systems. The Francophone population in Canada has two languages and two types of their own kinesics, the full system and a reduced version of the same.

In both instances, the majority essentially employs only one form of kinesics. Condon (1964) and Kendon (1972) have observed that an interactional synchrony obtains in the rhythm of speech and body movements between two partners in conversation. From the behavior of the subjects it appears that the minority generally adjusts to the rhythm of the majority when interlocutory contact is established.

Kinesics seems more closely associated with culture than with language. This was most clearly evidenced by motion pictures taken by a student of mine in an independent project designed by her to supplement the videotapes in the black and white comparison (French 1973). The work shows that in an experimental situation, children speaking black English demonstrate a somewhat more highly coded system of kinesic expression. Their kinesic messages were decoded more successfully by other children speaking black English, bidialectical black undergraduates and adults, and adult and undergraduate standard English speakers than were messages encoded by standard English speakers of the same age. A complete switch of the two modalities of language and kinesics appears indicative of extreme caution by the minority.

My studies support the division of gestures proposed by Condon (1964) into speech-preparatory and speech-accompanying movements. They also support Kendon (1972) who suggests that these speech-preparatory movements serve to regulate the interchange between interlocutors and that these speech-preparatory movements differ according to the function of the following speech unit in relation to the others in the discourse. Speech-preparatory positioning varied markedly in in-group and out-group situations. In conclusion, my observation of covert videotaping gave evidence for kinesic use in dialect speakers. A change in kinesic style appeared as an integral part of register switching in response to change in social situation. Such changes in register occurred only after the shift in kinesic behaviors. Culture preceded language.

What I have so far reported is incomplete, but hopefully suggests the need for further research in the triple relationship of language, kinesics, and culture. In the realm of culture certain aspects of behavior are due to ethnic differences while others are due to social stratification. The combination of these two forces is not uniform and varies greatly depending on the country in which they occur. In addition, all age groups do not react in the same manner, and men and women may be affected in different ways. More research is needed to explore the ways in which complexities of culture patterns interact with various patterns of language and nonverbal behavior.

REFERENCES

BAER, DONALD M.
   1971 Let's take another look at punishment. *Psychology Today* (October): 34.
BOLINGER, DWIGHT D.
   1968 *Aspects of language.* New York: Harcourt, Brace and World.
CONDON, W. S.
   1964 "Process in communication." Unpublished manuscript, Western Psychiatric Institute and Clinic, Pittsburgh, Pennsylvania.
FRENCH, PATRICE L.
   1973 "White bias in black language studies." Paper presented at the ninth meeting of the Southeastern Conference on Linguistics, Charlotte, West Virginia.
GUMPERZ, JOHN J.
   1971 *Language in social groups.* Essays selected by Anwar S. Dil. Stanford: Stanford University Press.
GUMPERZ, JOHN J., DELL HYMES, *editors*
   1964 The ethnography of communication. *American Anthropologist* 66: 137–153.
HOCKETT, CHARLES F.
   1958 *A course in modern linguistics.* New York: Macmillan.

KENDON, ADAM

1972   "Some relationships between body motion and communication," in *Studies in dyadic communication*. Edited by F. Seigman, 177–210. Elmsford, New York: Pergamon Press.

PARISI, DOMENICO, PAOLA BARBERI, VALERIA SAVONA PIZZINO

1971   *Ruolo della madre nello sviluppo cognitivo del bambino: differenze di classe sociale*. Rome, Italy: Consiglo Nazionale delle Ricorche, Istituto di Psicologia.

VON RAFFLER ENGEL, WALBURGA

1964   *Il prelinguaggio infantile*. Brescia, Paideia.

1972a   Some phono-stylistic features of black English. *Phonetica* 25(1):53–64.

1972b   "Language in context: situationally conditioned style change in black speakers," in *Proceedings of the Eleventh International Congress of Linguists, University of Bologna*.

1972c   "Sociolinguistic research techniques: some new developments," in *Readings in applied educational sociolinguistics*. Edited by Glen Gilbert. (Selected papers from the Workshop on Research Problems in Areal Linguistics, University of Texas at El Paso.)

1972d   *Linguistique appliquée et apprentissage des langues: la place de la psychologie*. Proceedings of the Troisième Colloque Canadien de Linguistique Appliquée. University of Quebec, Montreal.

1972e   "The use of videotape in dialectology." Paper presented at the International Conference on Methods in Dialectology, University of Prince Edward Island.

VON RAFFLER ENGEL, WALBURGA, CAROL K. SIGELMAN

1971   Rhythm, narration, description in the speech of black and white school children. *Language Sciences* 18:9–14.

Language, Paralanguage, and Body Motion in the Structure of Conversation

STARKEY D. DUNCAN, JR.

This paper reports findings from a program of research on the structure of face-to-face interaction (Goffman 1963) in dyadic conversataions. The research was designed to discover and document some of the building blocks or components of conversations, and the rules or relationships specifying how these components are properly combined. In a sense, the goal has been a "grammar" of conversations.

In searching for interaction structure, our research strategy may be compared to that of linguists seeking basic phonological, syntactic, and semantic elements in a given language and seeking rules for the respective uses of these elements. There are, however, three important differences between traditional linguistic research and the research to be reported here.

1. *Broad Inclusiveness of Behaviors Considered*   Every effort was made to minimize *a priori* judgments as to the communicational role of the many different behaviors exhibited by persons in interaction. No assumptions were made regarding which of these behaviors might be more "central" than the others or which might serve to "modify" the others. The

This study was supported in part by Grants MH-16,210 and MH-17,756 from the National Institute of Mental Health and by Grant GS-3033 from the Division of Social Sciences of the National Science Foundation. Susan Beekman, Mark Cary, Diane Martin, George Niederehe, Ray O'Cain, Thomas Shanks, Cathy Stepanek, and Andrew Szasz contributed to the transcriptions and data analysis. I am indebted to Dick Jenney, Wayne Anderson, and the client, who generously consented to serve as participants in this study. Portions of this paper are based on findings reported in Duncan (1972, 1973).

relative contributions to face-to-face interaction of language, paralanguage (Trager 1958), and body motion, as well as of specific behaviors within each of these modalities, was taken as one of the important questions being considered. Consonant with Hymes (1967), the position was taken that the question of what is communicative should be regarded as problematic, the object of investigation. Accordingly, careful transcriptions were made of a wide range of behaviors within paralanguage and body motion, as well as within language (including intonation), and these transcribed behaviors were jointly considered in the analysis.

2. *Focus on Interaction* It was the structure or organization of the interaction that was primarily being sought rather than the structure exemplified in the behaviors of any single communicator. Using data gathered from videotapes of dyadic conversations, the research focused on the effects of one participant's actions upon the actions of the other, and the manner in which the two participants coordinated their respective behaviors in the interaction (Scheflen 1968). This relative emphasis appears to be a sharp departure from traditional linguistic concerns. As Jaffe and Feldstein (1970: 2–3) have pointed out: "The serious study of dialogue patterns makes one poignantly aware that the largest unit dealt with in contemporary linguistics is at most the monologue …." They quote Jakobson (1964) to the effect that pure monologue is extremely rare in nature, entirely absent in many societies, and, where present, exists in highly specialized forms, such as prayer or ceremonial speeches. This research attempted to place both speech and other modes of communication in their natural interactive context.

3. *Nature of Organization Not Modeled on Language* The object of the research being the organization of conversations, it was not appropriate to assume *a priori* the nature of the organization being sought. In particular, care was taken not to attempt any one-to-one mapping of interaction phenomena onto grammatical forms of English, the language used in the interviews studied. Certain minimal assumptions were made, however: (a) the elements of the organization were taken to be discrete and (b) the structure of the organization was assumed to be hierarchical. Relationships obtaining between discrete elements of the organization were described in terms of discrete functions (Klir 1969) in order to preserve the greatest possible generality of formulation.

SPEAKING TURNS

In the case of this research, interaction structure in dyadic conversations was approached through phenomena related to the taking of speaking turns. The results to be described below suggest that these phenomena play an important part in, among other things, the integrating of the respective actions of co-participants in dyads by providing orderly, conventional means (a) for smoothly exchanging the speaking turn, thereby avoiding excessive simultaneous talking, and (b) for marking important segmental units, not only in the stream of communication of one participant but also in the interaction itself.

While there has not been extensive discussion of speaking turns in the literature, the phenomenon has not gone unnoticed by investigators. Goffman (1967: 33–34) commented on integrating mechanisms in general and on speaking turns in particular: "In any society, whenever the physical possibility of spoken interaction arises, it seems that a system of practices, conventions, and procedural rules comes into play which functions as a means of guiding and organizing the flow of messages."

Kendon (1967) dealt in detail with the role of gaze direction in the exchange of speaking turns. Scheflen (1968) discussed turn-taking as one of a number of communication mechanisms in face-to-face interaction which serve the function of integrating the performances of the participants in a variety of ways. Schegloff (1968: 1076) proposed the "basic rule for conversations: ONE PARTY AT A TIME" (original emphasis), and discussed some implications of this rule. Yngve (1970: 568) has commented that the orderly taking of speaking turns "is nearly the most obvious aspect of conversation."

Jaffe and Feldstein (1970: 6) studied temporal patterns of speech and silence in dyadic conversations. Their findings suggested to them "... further interactional rules that govern the matching of speech rates of the participants, the prohibition of interruption, and the requirement for properly timed signals that acknowledge understanding and confirm the continued attention of the listener." They quote Sullivan (1947), who observed careful taking of speaking turns in conversation between chronic mental hospital patients, and Miller (1963), who suggested that turn-taking is a language universal.

Leighton, Stollak, and Ferguson (1971) found more interrupting and simultaneous talking in the interaction of families waiting for psychotherapy than in the interaction of "normal" families.

The term "turn-taking" has been independently suggested by Yngve (1970) and in a personal communication from Goffman, June 5, 1970.

SOURCE OF DATA

Method of Collection

INTERVIEWS   The results to be reported were based on meticulous transcriptions of speech and body motion behavior during the first nineteen minutes of two dyadic conversations, as recorded on videotape.

The first conversation was a preliminary interview held at the Counseling and Psychotherapy Research Center at the University of Chicago. This preliminary interview is part of the routine intake procedure at the Counseling and Psychotherapy Research Center, and the client was a regular applicant for therapy. A preliminary interview was chosen for intensive transcription of communication behaviors, because within a rather compressed period of time a wide variety of types of interaction may be encountered — from simple information giving, such as address, etc., to the more emotionally laden discussion of the client's reasons for applying for therapy. At the same time, there is a strong intrinsic motivation for the interview, namely an application for therapy, thereby avoiding the more artificial experimental situation in which unacquainted subjects are brought together and asked to discuss anything which might be of mutual interest.

The client was in her early twenties, working as a secretary, and had not completed college. The therapist-interviewer was a forty-year-old male, an experienced therapist, who had been doing preliminary interviews for many years.

The second conversation was between the therapist who participated in the first conversation, and a second male therapist, also forty years old. The two therapists were good friends and had known each other for about ten years. Their interaction was relaxed and lively. The topic in this case was another client whom the first therapist had seen in a preliminary interview, and whom the second therapist had at that time seen in therapy for two interviews.

The preliminary interview will be designated as Conversation 1, and the second, peer interaction, will be designated as Conversation 2. The client will be designated as Participant A; the preliminary interviewer, B; and the second therapist, C. Thus, the participants in Conversation 1 were A and B; and the participants in Conversation 2 were B and C.

VIDEOTAPING   To videotape the interactions, the camera was placed so that both participants in each interaction were fully visible from head to foot on the tape at all time. No zoom techniques or other special focusing effects were used. A single camera was set up in full view of the participants. The camera and tape were left running prior to the participants' entry into the room and were not touched again until after the interview.

TRANSCRIPTION   For this study, the principal requirements for the transcription were those of maximum breadth and of continuity (no breaks or interruptions). Maximum breadth is desirable in analysis because it is not yet known which behavioral cues are the primary mediators of any given communication function. And continuity of transcription permits the complete analysis of sequences of events — the basic concern of this study.

Elements of Behavior

PHONEMES

1.   *Segmental Phonemes*   Transcription of segmental phonemes, which describe the way syllables are pronounced within the framework of the English sound system, followed the scheme developed by Trager and Smith (1957). The segmental phonemes were the least important components of the study.

2.   *Suprasegmental Phonemes*   The suprasegmental phonemes are commonly referred to as intonation. They include the phenomena of stress, pitch, and juncture. The Trager/Smith scheme for transcribing suprasegmental phonemes was used, with minor modifications identical to those described in previous studies by this writer (Duncan and Rosenthal 1968; Duncan, Rosenberg, and Finkelstein 1969).

PARALANGUAGE   Paralanguage refers to the wide variety of vocal behaviors which occur in speech but which are not part of the sound system of language, as traditionally conceived. Comprehensive catalogs of paralinguistic behaviors have been compiled by Trager (1958), Crystal and Quirk (1964), and Crystal (1969). Any one speaker will probably use only a small fraction of the total behaviors available. The following list, which uses Trager's (1958) terminology, includes only those behaviors which play a part in the turn system: (a) intensity (overloud — oversoft); (b) pitch height (overhigh — overlow); and (c) extent (drawl — clipping of individual syllables). The terms in parentheses define the anchor point for each behavioral continuum. A wide variety of paralinguistic behaviors was actually encountered in the two dyads and included in the transcriptions.

BODY MOTION   In contrast to paralanguage, there was for body motion no available transcription system which could be readily applied to our videotapes. This situation led to a transcribing method based on the behaviors actually found in each interview. The transcription system for the first interview was created by first making an inventory of the movements used by the two participants, and then assigning either arbitrary or descriptive labels to these movements. This system was then applied to the second interview, after expanding it to include new movements observed in the second interview.

While there is no pretense that the resulting transcription system is able to encompass all movements occurring in this culture, every attempt was made to include all movements observed in the dyads under study. The transcription was in this sense comprehensive. Included were: (a) head gestures and movements (nodding, turning, pointing, shaking, etc.) and direction of head orientation; (b) shoulder movements (e.g. shrugs); (c) facial expressions, such as could be clearly seen; (d) hand gestures and movements of all sorts (each hand transcribed independently); (e) foot movements (each foot transcribed independently); (f) leg movements; (g) posture and posture shifts; and (h) use of artifacts, such as pipe, facial tissue, papers, and clip board.

COORDINATION OF BODY MOTION AND SPEECH TRANSCRIPTIONS   Speech syllables were used to locate all transcribed events. Thus, the movements of both participants in an interview were located with respect to the syllables emitted by the participant who happened to be speaking at the time, or to the pause between two syllables.

THE SPEAKING-TURN SYSTEM

The speaking-turn system consists of the following elements: (a) two sets of postulated states, the respective sets representing adjacent levels within a single hierarchy, and (b) a set of hypothesized signals which aid participants in conversations in the coordination of action with respect to the states, among other things. There are several sets of rules applying to various aspects of the system. These rules will be described in conjunction with the aspects to which they apply.

Turn-System States

PARTICIPANT STATES   Two mutually exclusive discrete states are posited for each participant in a dyadic conversation: speaker and auditor. A SPEAKER is a participant who claims the speaking turn at any given moment. An AUDITOR (Kendon 1967) is a participant who does not claim the speaking turn at any given moment.

INTERACTION STATES The next higher hierarchical level in the system — that of interaction state — may be obtained by jointly considering the respective states of each participant at any given moment. Following logically from the two participant states, there are four possible interaction states within the context of the system.

1. *Speaker — Auditor* One participant claims the speaking turn; no such claim is made by the other participant. In this interaction state the speaker continues his turn uninterrupted by the auditor.

2. *Auditor — Speaker* This interaction state is identical to the one above, except that the participants have exchanged the speaking turn. The participant who had previously been the speaker has now switched to the auditor state; and vice versa. When this exchange is accomplished without passing through the interaction state of simultaneous turns (below), a smooth exchange of the speaking turn is said to have occurred.

In the proposed turn system, the display of a turn signal by the speaker marks points in the interaction at which the auditor may appropriately switch to the speaker state, claiming the turn.

3. *Speaker — Speaker (Simultaneous Turns)* Both participants simultaneously assume the speaker state, claiming the speaking turn. This interaction state represents a breakdown of the turn system for the duration of the state. No attempt is made in the proposed turn system to explain the manner of resolution of such a state, that is, which of the participants will continue claiming the speaking turn and which one will relinquish his claim, reverting to the auditor state. Meltzer, Morris, and Hayes (1971: 401) report some interesting findings on one mode of resolution, based on techniques of "social psychophysics."

"Simultaneous turns" is used here instead of the more usual term "simultaneous talking." Within the turn system there may be instances of simultaneous talking not considered to be simultaneous turns. As will be described below, the auditor responding in the back channel (Yngve 1970), such as "m-hm" or a head nod, does not constitute a claim for the turn. An auditor back-channel response, when it overlaps with the speaker's verbalizing, would therefore be a case of simultaneous talking by the two participants, but not of simultaneous turns. Jaffe and Feldstein (1970) have shown that simultaneous talking in a dyad tends to be quite brief in duration, the mean duration being less than .5 seconds.

Simultaneous turns may be caused by a violation of the system on the part of either participant. The previous speaker may fail to relinquish his turn after displaying a turn signal and after the auditor's subsequent claim of the turn. Or the previous auditor may suddenly interrupt by claiming the turn in the absence of the speaker's turn signal.

4. *Auditor — Auditor* The previous speaker may display a turn signal and cease talking, thereby apparently relinquishing his turn, and the previous auditor may fail to claim the turn. The result would obviously be silence for the duration of that state. Experience suggests that this fourth logical possibility of the two participant states does occur in conversations, but because it was not observed in our corpus, it will not be considered further in this discussion.

Signals in the Turn System

A set of discrete signals provides a means by which participants may coordinate (a) the switching of their respective states (i.e. the smooth exchange of the speaking turn) and (b) other actions related to turns.

In this section the appropriate display of, and response to, the signals will be discussed. In the next section the display of each signal will be defined, and the behavioral composition of each signal will be described.

For the speaker, there are three signals: (a) a turn signal, (b) a gesticulation signal, and (c) a within-turn signal. For the auditor, there are two signals: (a) a back-channel signal and (b) a speaker-state signal.

SPEAKER TURN SIGNAL   The auditor may claim the turn when the speaker displays a turn signal. In proper operation of the system, if the auditor so claims the turn in response to the signal, the speaker is obliged to relinquish immediately his claim to the turn. When the speaker is not displaying the turn signal, however, auditor claims of the turn are inappropriate, leading to simultaneous turns.

The turn signal is permissive, not coercive. The auditor is not obliged to claim the speaking turn in response to the display of the signal by the speaker. The auditor may alternatively communicate in the back channel, or remain silent.

SPEAKER GESTICULATION SIGNAL   This signal by the speaker serves to negate any turn signal concurrently being displayed. The display of the gesticulation signal virtually eliminates claims to the turn by the auditor. Because of the effectiveness of the signal, it was impossible to evaluate from the data whether or not auditor claims of the turn, during display of the gesticulation signal by the speaker, tended to result in simultaneous turns. The gesticulation signal does not similarly affect the auditor's responding in the back channel.

SPEAKER WITHIN-TURN SIGNAL   This signal was used by the speaker, apparently to mark the end of units of his discourse on a hierarchical level immediately lower than that of the speaking turn. Appropriate auditor response to these units would be a back channel communication. Once again, this signal was permissive, not coercive. The auditor was not obliged to respond in the back channel upon every display of the signal.

AUDITOR BACK-CHANNEL SIGNAL   The auditor's communicating in the back channel does not constitute a turn or claim of a turn. The back channel provides a means by which the auditor can give useful feedback to the speaker during the course of his turn. Auditor back channels not infrequently overlap with the speaker's verbalization. These occurrences are considered instances of simultaneous talking, permissible within the system, as contrasted to simultaneous turns, which are not permissible.

Auditor back channels are systematically related to the speaker's within-turn signal, in a manner described below. Auditor back channels may also be used in response to turn signals, in lieu of the auditor's taking the speaking turn. But the pattern of auditor back-channel response to turn signals is quite different from (a) auditor back-channel response to within-turn signals and (b) auditor turn-claiming response to turn signals.

SPEAKER-STATE SIGNAL   This signal marks a participant's shift from the auditor to the speaker state. The signal is characteristically found at the beginnings of turns, but not at instances of auditor back channels. In addition, it is possible that this signal is further used within turns to mark the beginnings of within-turn units. At this writing, however, analyses of this possibility have not been completed.

The proposed turn-system states and signals are shown in their hierarchical arrangement in Figure 1. Elements of the system combine to form higher-level elements, according to the discrete functions (Klir 1969) indicated in italics. These discrete functions represent many of the "rules" operating in the turn system.

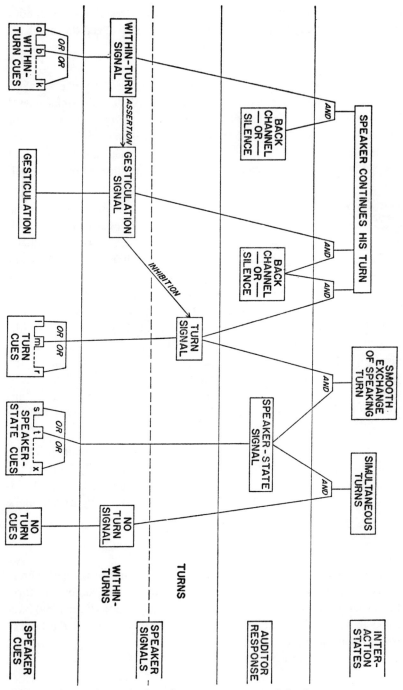

Figure 1.   Proposed organization of turn-system states and signals

Display and Behavioral Composition of the Signals

Each signal in the turn system is composed of a set of behavioral cues. Like the signals themselves, the cues are considered to be discrete.

DEFINITION OF SIGNAL DISPLAY   With the exception of the gesticulation signal, more than one cue was identified for every signal in the system. The display of a signal was in all cases defined as the display of at least one of its constituent cues.

For those signals having multiple cues, two or more of its cues were frequently conjointly displayed, their onset being either simultaneous or in tight sequences. The display of such larger numbers of signal cues or of particular combinations of these cues was not taken to alter the fact that the signal in question was being displayed. In several cases, however, the conjoint display of two or more cues was found to have interesting effects on the actions of the *vis-à-vis*, as will be described below.

EXHAUSTIVENESS OF CUE LISTS   Although pains were taken in the analysis to document as carefully as possible the participation of each of the cues in its respective signal, no claim is made that these cues necessarily represent an exhaustive inventory. Further, undetected cues may be present in the conversations subjected to analysis, as well as in other conversations in this culture. A more complete list might be obtained through a dialect survey which included behaviors in paralanguage and body motion, in addition to those in language.

SPEAKER TURN SIGNAL   The turn signal was defined as the speaker's display of at least one of a set of six discrete cues.
1. *Intonation*   The use of any pitch level — terminal juncture combination other than 2 2/ at the end of a phonemic clause. (These terms and notations follow those of Trager and Smith (1957).) Thus, the cue is defined as being displayed in a clause having some rising or falling properties either in the terminal juncture or in the pitch level on the final syllable. Clauses having such a rising or falling quality will be referred to as "intonation-marked clauses" in the discussion below.
2. *Drawl*   Paralinguistic drawl on the final syllable or on the stressed syllable of an intonation-marked clause.
3. *Termination of Gesticulation*   The termination of any hand gesticulation (Kendon 1967) used during a speaking turn or the relaxation of a tensed hand position (e.g. a fist) during a turn.
To account for the gesticulations observed in the two interviews, it

seems sufficient to define gesticulations as those hand movements generally away from the body which commonly accompany, and which appear to bear a direct relationship to, speech.

Specifically excluded from the definition of gesticulation are self-adapters and object-adapters (Ekman and Friesen 1969). Self-adapters involving the hands are movements in which the hand comes in contact with one's own body, often with the appearance of grooming. Examples observed in our conversations would be: rubbing the chin, scratching the cheek, smoothing the hair, brushing off the pants leg, and picking lint (real or imaginary) from the socks. Highly similar behaviors, termed "self-manipulatory gestures," were also studied by Rosenfeld (1966). Examples of movements considered to be object-adapters in our conversations would be maintaining one's pipe, rubbing the arm of the chair, adjusting paper on a clipboard, and taking a facial tissue.

4. *Sociocentric Sequence*   The utterance of one of several stereotyped expressions, typically following a more substantive statement. Examples are "but uh," "or something," and "you know." The term "sociocentric sequence" was coined by Bernstein (1962), who commented on these expressions in another context. These expressions do not add substantive information to the speech content that they follow. Instances in which the auditor proceeded to take his speaking turn during the completion of a sociocentric sequence are not considered to be a state of simultaneous turns in the conversation. Rather, such an act is considered to be an instance of permissible simultaneous talking.

5. *Pitch/Loudness*   A drop in paralinguistic pitch and/or loudness in conjunction with a sociocentric sequence, as compared to the level of these behaviors at the end of the immediately preceding phonemic clause. When such paralinguistic drops were transcribed for phonemic clauses not involving a sociocentric sequence, this cue was not considered to have been displayed.

6. *Syntax*   The completion of a grammatical clause, involving a subject-predicate combination.

SPEAKER GESTICULATION SIGNAL   This signal was considered to be displayed when one or both of the speaker's hands were engaged in gesticulation, as defined above. Self- and object-adapters do not operate as gesticulation signals. Cessation of the gesticulation signal constitutes a speaker turn cue (Number 3 above). It should be noted that much speech is not accompanied by gesticulation and therefore neither the gesticulation signal nor its coordinate turn cue would be applicable for that speech. This is the only signal in the turn system characterized by a single cue.

SPEAKER WITHIN-TURN SIGNAL   A within-turn signal is defined as the speaker's display of at least one of a set of two discrete cues.

1.   *Shift of Head Direction Toward the Auditor*   The speaker's turning his head towards the auditor, from a previously "away" position. While this behavior is intuitively regarded as a change in gaze direction, difficulties with reliability in transcribing gaze direction (von Cranach 1971) have forced the use of the more reliable head direction behavior.

2.   *Syntax*   The completion of a grammatical clause, defined exactly as for the turn cue (Number 6 above).

BACK-CHANNEL SIGNAL   A back-channel signal might be displayed by either speaker or auditor. In this paper data will be presented with regard primarily to auditor back channels. The definition of the signal is the same regardless of who displays it. The signal is defined as the display of at least one of a set of five discrete cues.

1.   *M-hm*   This expression is used to stand for a group of readily identi-fied, verbalized signals. Included in the group are such expressions as "m-hm," "yeah," "right," and the like and Kendon's (1967) examples of "yes quite," "surely," "I see," and "that's true." Most of the "m-hm" sig-nals may be used singly or in repeated groups, as in "yeah, yeah."

2.   *Sentence Completions*   Not infrequently in our materials an auditor would complete a sentence that a speaker had begun. In such a case he would not continue beyond the brief completion; the original speaker would continue with his turn as if uninterrupted. Sentence completions have been independently reported by Yngve (1970). Example: C (second therapist, above): "... eventually, it will come down to more concrete issues ..."; B (first therapist): "As she gets more comfortable"; C: "and I felt that ...."

3.   *Request for Clarification*   Contrasting with sentence completions are brief requests for clarification. Such requests were usually accomplished in a few words or in a phrase. Example: C: "... somehow they're better able to cope with it." B: "You mean these anxieties, concern with it?"

4.   *Brief Restatement*   This back-channel signal is similar to the sentence completion, except that it restates in a few words an immediately preced-ing thought expressed by the speaker. Example: C: "... having to pick up the pieces"; B: "the broken dishes, yeah"; C: "but then a very ...."

5.   *Head Nods and Shakes*   Head nods and shakes may be used alone or in company with the verbalized back-channel signals. Head nods may vary in duration from a single nod to a rather protracted, continuous series of nods.

On the basis of modality used, we may distinguish the vocal back-channel cues (Numbers 1–4 above) from the visual back-channel cue (Number 5).

It may be useful to mention other terms which have been used to refer to various subsets of the cues described above. Fries (1952), in a study based on recorded telephone conversations, used the term "conventional signals of attention to continuous discourse." Kendon (1967: 44), in a study of British subjects in conversations, found a general class of "accompaniment signals" which were divided into two subclasses: (a) an "attention signal proper in which p appears to do no more than signal to q that he is attending and following what is being said ..." and (b) a "'point-granting' or 'assenting' signal. This most often takes the lexical form of 'yes quite' or 'surely' or 'I see' ...." Dittmann and Llewellyn (1967, 1968) used the term "listener response."

The term used in this paper was suggested by Yngve (1970: 568), who discussed the "back channel, over which the person who has the turn receives short messages such as 'yes' and 'uh-huh' without relinquishing the turn."

SPEAKER-STATE SIGNAL   The speaker-state signal is defined as the display of at least one of a set of four discrete cues.

1. *Shift Away in Head Direction*   Turning of the head from pointing directly toward the *vis-à-vis* to an "away" position. This cue is the exact opposite of the within-turn cue (Number 1).

2. *Initiation of a Gesticulation*   Beginning a gesticulation as defined above. The distinction of gesticulation from self- and object-adapters was maintained. Adapters were excluded from the definition of this cue.

3. *Audible Inhalation*   A sharp, audible intake of breath. Even when an inhalation was visually observable on the videotape, it had additionally to be audible in a distinct and unambiguous manner.

4. *Paralinguistic Overloudness*   The transcription of at least one degree of overloud intensity (Trager 1958) for the speech syllables in question. Transcriptions of paralinguistic overhigh pitch were not considered to be elements of this cue.

RESULTS

The turn-system signals and rules were designed as an initial account of some of the conventions used by participants in face-to-face dyadic conversations. It is reasonable to expect that these conventions would introduce clear-cut regularities in some of the actions of these participants, thereby aiding them in the solution of certain problems of coordination in conversations, such as the avoidance of excessive simultaneous turns.

It follows that the turn system should be capable of accounting for a significant number of instances of smooth exchange of speaking turns, simultaneous turns, and other relevant turn phenomena. The data analyses presented in this section are relevant to the evaluation of the turn system's descriptive adequacy for the transcribed conversations.

Unit of Analysis

In order to subdivide the interviews for purposes of analysis, a unit was chosen which in size lay between the phonemic clause and the speaking turn. Each cue display and each instance of smooth exchange of turns or of simultaneous turns occurring in the transcriptions was located with respect to these units. As with the signals in the turn system, the unit was defined in terms of the display of at least one of a number of behaviors in syntax, intonation, paralanguage, and body motion.

Specifically, boundaries of the units were defined as being: (a) at the ends of phonemic clauses, which (b) additionally were marked by the display of one or more of the turn cues described above and/or by the display of one or more of the following cues:

1. *Unfilled Pause*   An appreciable unfilled (silent) pause following the phonemic clause.
2. *Head Direction*   Turning of the speaker's head toward the auditor. This cue is identical to the within-turn cue described above.
3. *Paralinguistic Pitch and/or Loudness*   A drop in paralinguistic pitch and/or loudness in conjunction with a phonemic clause, either across the entire clause, or across its final syllable or syllables.
4. *Foot Flexion*   (For participant A (client) only.) A relaxation of the foot from a marked dorsal flexion. Throughout the conversation this participant's legs were stretched out in front of her and were crossed at the ankle. From time to time one or both feet would be flexed dorsally, such that they assumed a nearly perpendicular angle to the floor. Their returning to their original position, as the result of relaxing the flexion, was the cue.

As may be seen in Table 1, there were a total of 885 of these units in the two interviews subjected to analysis.

The definition of this unit, a necessary procedural antecedent to analysis, was formulated in a predominantly intuitive manner at an early stage in the research. The unit will be replaced by a more analytically derived unit, when such a replacement is possible. Further studies are underway, directed towards that end.

Turn and Gesticulation Signals

The research issue for the speaker's turn and gesticulation signals was the extent of their success in accounting for instances of smooth exchanges of the speaking turn, simultaneous talking, and auditor's attempts to take the speaking turn. Under the turn-system rules, the occurrence of simultaneous turns should be associated primarily with the auditor's claiming the turn when the turn signal is not being displayed by the speaker (that is, no turn cues displayed at that moment). The speaker's display of the gesticulation signal should sharply reduce the auditor's claiming the turn in response to yielding cues.

Table 1. Auditor turn claims and resulting simultaneous turns as a function of number of speaker turn cues displayed and the display of the gesticulation signal

Speaker turn cue display		Auditor turn claim			Simultaneous turns resulting from auditor claim		
	(A)	(B)	(C)		(D)	(E)	
N conjointly displayed	Frequency of display	N	P^a	SD^c	N	P^b	SD^c
		No gesticulation signal displayed					
0	52	5	0.10	0.04	5	1.00	0.00
1	123	12	0.10	0.03	2	0.17	0.11
2	146	25	0.17	0.03	2	0.08	0.05
3	89	29	0.33	0.05	2	0.07	0.05
4	47	15	0.32	0.07	0	0.00	0.00
5	9	4	0.44	0.17	0	0.00	0.00
6	2	1	0.50	0.35	0	0.00	0.00
Σ	468	91			11		
		Gesticulation signal displayed					
0	56	7	0.13	0.04	7	1.00	0.00
1	109	0	0.00	0.00			
2	138	0	0.00	0.00			
3	105	2	0.02	0.01	1	0.50	0.35
4	6	0	0.00	0.00			
5	3	0	0.00	0.00			
Σ	417	9			8		

[a]   Column B/column A.
[b]   Column D/column B.
[c]   Standard error of the proportion ($\sqrt{PQ/N}$).

Table 1 presents the data, summed over the two transcribed conversations, on which the analyses of these and related phenomena were based. Percentages of auditor turn claims in response to a given number of cues were obtained by dividing the number of claims by the number of displays of those cues. Percentages of simultaneous turns were calculated by dividing the number of simultaneous turns by the number of auditor claims.

TURN SIGNAL   Inspection of Table 1 indicates that the cues, signals, and rules for the proposed turn system were capable of accounting for every smooth exchange of the speaking turn in our corpus. That is, every smooth exchange of the turn followed an auditor turn claim in response to a speaker turn signal.

Every auditor turn claim when no speaker turn signal was being displayed resulted in the state of simultaneous turns. That is, there was at least a momentary dispute over the turn whenever the auditor claimed the turn in the absence of a speaker turn signal. (For purposes of data analysis, simultaneous turns were considered to have occurred when a perceptible overlap of both participant's speech resulted from an auditor turn claim.)

The statistical relationship between the display of a turn signal (or its absence), and the occurrence of simultaneous turns resulting from a turn claim by the auditor may be obtained by applying chi-square to Table 2, a 2×2 contingency table derived from Table 1. The resulting $X^2 = 52.31$, corrected for continuity; $df = 1$. When $df = 1$, a X^2 of 10.83 has an associated probability of 0.001.

Table 2. Smooth exchange of the speaking turn and simultaneous turns resulting from auditor's claiming the turn when the speaker turn signal is displayed and when it is not ($N = 100$).

	Smooth exchange of turn	Simultaneous turns
Turn signal not displayed	0	12
Turn signal displayed	81	7

It was observed that, when no gesticulation was being displayed, a strong positive relationship existed between (a) the number of turn cues displayed by the speaker and (b) the probability of a turn claim by the auditor. The correlations between these two variables was 0.96, $df = 4$. (This correlation included the data points represented by the display of 0 through 5 turn cues. The point for 6 cues was omitted from the analysis because it was represented by only two displays, thereby permitting only

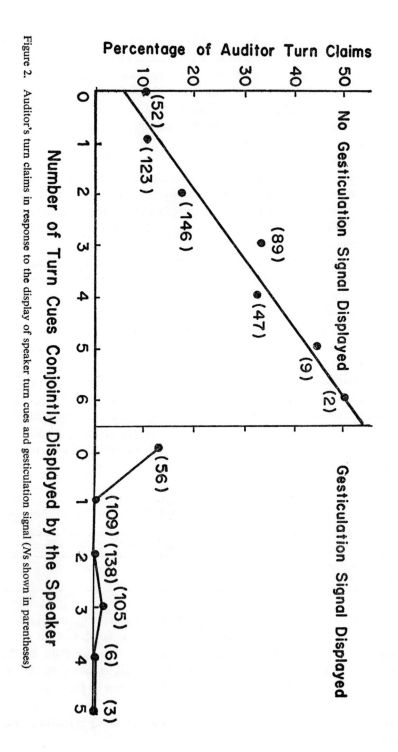

Figure 2.   Auditor's turn claims in response to the display of speaker turn cues and gesticulation signal (*N*s shown in parentheses)

an unreliable estimate of the point.) This correlation included all turn claims by the auditor, both those resulting in smooth exchanges of turns, and those resulting in simultaneous turns. The data points for this phenomenon and their associated regression line are shown in the left half of Figure 2.

When turn claims resulting in simultaneous turns were removed from the analysis, so that only instances of the proper operation of the turn system were considered, the correlation between number of turn cues displayed and percentage of auditor turn-claiming response to that display was 0.987.

ALTERNATIVE TREATMENTS OF TURN CUES   With regard to the conjoint display of cues to form signals, questions may be raised concerning (a) the possibility that certain conjoint displays may carry special significance as signals and (b) the possibility that certain cues should be weighted more heavily than others in the signaling process. These questions were carefully perused in the data analysis.

With regard to the display of cues, it is true that there is variation among the cues in their relative frequency of display. This appears to be in part a matter of personal style among individuals. However, there does not appear to be a similar favoring of certain specific conjoint displays, apart from the favoring of certain cues. This was verified by estimating the frequency of each specific conjoint display on the basis of the combined frequencies of its constituent cues. This basis of estimation was found to provide a close approximation of the obtained frequencies of the respective conjoint displays.

With regard to the special weighting of cues to account for auditor response, it may suffice to reiterate that the results on auditor response were obtained by simply adding the number of cues in any given conjoint display, without regard to the specific cues which made up the display, each cue being given the weight of one. No single cue was present in every conjoint display responded to. While there are many different rules available for combining a given number of stimuli, either discrete or continuous, the combination rule applied to this system was the simplest possible one.

GESTICULATION SIGNAL   The results on auditor turn claims were sharply different when the speaker was displaying a gesticulation signal along with his turn cues. Data on auditor claims in the presence of a gesticulation signal are presented in the lower half of Table 1 and in the right half of Figure 2. With the exception of the display of zero turn cues by the speaker, the curve for auditor turn claims is virtually flat at 0 percent, with no increase of turn claims as the number of turn cues increases.

Speaker Within-Turn Signals and Auditor Back-Channel Signals

Auditor back-channel signals were found to be related to speaker within-turn signals in much the same way that auditor claims were related to speaker turn signals. In the analyses presented below, only those auditor back channels were considered which occurred at, or immediately after, the boundaries of analytic units. Also, those units which were followed by the alternative speaker action — claiming the turn — were not considered.

Table 3 summarizes the data and results on auditor back-channel response to speaker within-turn cues. Of the auditor back channels analyzed, 86.9 percent followed the display of a speaker within-turn signal. Chi-square applied to a 2×2 contingency table for these data, constructed on the same basis as that shown in Table 2, yielded a value of 27.73, once again where $df = 1$, and $p(0.001) = 10.83$. The correlation between the number of within-turn cues displayed and percentage of auditor back-channel response was 0.988. It should be remembered that this correlation was based on only three data points, although there were a large number of observations for each point.

Unlike auditor turn claims, auditor back-channel signals were unaffected by the speaker's display of the gesticulation signal. Considering all auditor back channels occurring in the transcriptions, 52.5 percent were displayed concurrently with the speaker gesticulation signal.

Table 3.   Auditor back-channel response following speaker's display of within-turn cues

N cues displayed	Frequency of display	N	P	Percent of back channels following cues display	X^2	Correlation
0	285	14	0.049			
1	326	44	0.134	86.9	27.73	0.988
2	174	49	0.281			

Speaker-State Signal

It was proposed that the speaker-state signal was used, among other things, to differentiate turn beginnings from auditor back-channel signals. Rates of display of the speaker-state signal with turn beginnings and with auditor back channels are shown in Table 4, along with related statistics.

Table 4. Display of speaker-state signal in conjunction with turn beginnings and with auditor back channels

Signal	Turn beginnings			Back channels			X^{2a}
	N	Frequency of signal display	P	N	Frequency of signal display	P	
	Conversation 2: exploratory analysis						
Head shift and gesticulation	22	21	0.95	85	12	0.14	50.46
Full signal	22	21	0.95	85	16	0.19	42.04
	Conversation 1: validation						
Head shift and gesticulation	59	39	0.66	32	1	0.03	30.89
Full signal	59	44	0.75	32	3	0.09	32.76
Total	81	65	0.80	117	19	0.16	

[a] $df = 1$; $p(0.001) = 10.83$

In contrast to the other signals discussed above, the speaker-state signal was formulated on the basis of analyzing the transcription of Conversation 2 and then applying this formulation to Conversation 1 as a partial validation. Data from each conversation are presented separately in Table 4. For purposes of analysis a speaker-state cue was considered to be displayed when it was transcribed as occurring within an area extending from one unit of analysis prior to the initiation of a turn beginning or of an auditor back channel through to the first substantive word of that turn beginning or back channel. "Substantive" was taken merely to exclude phrases such as "well, uh," which are sometimes found at the beginnings of turns, as well as at other points in speech. Because turn beginnings must be vocalized, only vocalized auditor back channels were included in the analysis. Instances of simultaneous turns were not included in the analysis, because it was desired to consider only those instances of turn beginnings in which the turn system was apparently operating in its proper manner.

Taken as a whole, the speaker-state signal appears to mark a high proportion of turn beginnings, and to be displayed infrequently with auditor back channels. The chi-squares applied to the operation of the full signal in each of the two conversations yielded values comparable to those reported above for other signals in the turn system. The two-cue subset which includes the body motion cues — head shifting and gesticulation — appears to operate almost as effectively as the full, four-cue set.

The relatively positive exploratory findings on the two paralinguistic cues — overloudness and inhalation — were not replicated in the validation conversation. Data on these cues were included in this report because (a) they were significantly active in the exploratory analysis; (b) unknown circumstances in the validation conversation may have decreased the rate of their use; (c) the inhalation cue perfectly discriminated turn beginnings from back channels in both conversations — its increased use might have greatly increased its statistical significance; (d) the overloudness cue finds some support in the related findings of Meltzer, Morris, and Hayes (1971); and (e) these paralinguistic cues might be found to be more effective in other conversations, such as those in which gesticulations are used less extensively than in the two transcribed conversations. Thus, their inclusion in this report may be of some use to other investigators.

Unlike findings for the speaker turn and within-turn cues, no special effects on the response of the *vis-à-vis* have been observed for the conjoint display of two or more speaker-state cues.

DISCUSSION

The results presented above suggest that there are highly structured aspects of dyadic, face-to-face interaction. This structure provides the participants with the means by which to coordinate their respective actions with regard to speaking turns and other phenomena.

In dealing with strong regularities in interaction behaviors introduced by social conventions, it might be said that the object of research is a "grammar of interaction." However, because of the strong linguistic connotation of "grammar" it might be simpler and less potentially confusing simply to speak of social conventions applying to interactions.

Organization of the Signals in the Turn System

Several aspects of the composition and organization of signals within the turn system have already been emphasized: (a) cues for these signals were sought in a wide variety of interaction behaviors, (b) the signals and their constituent cues were treated as discrete entities, and (c) the display of a single cue was considered sufficient to constitute a display of its respective signal. Three other aspects of the formulation and analysis of these signals have particular relevance to the underlying organization of the system. (It will be recalled that the organization of all signals, in terms of their respective cues, was handled in an identical manner, with the gesticulation signal representing a limiting case in that it was composed of a single cue.)

DESCRIPTION OF CUES   The cues were described in terms of general properties of behaviors. In the speaker turn signal, for example, it was not a specific intonation pattern that served as a cue but simply any deviation from the 2 2/ pattern; not a specific gesticulation but rather cessation of any gesture or relaxation of a tensed hand position; not a specific paralinguistic pattern but a drop from the preceding pattern in pitch and/or loudness; and so on. In this manner the cues were able to encompass a wide variety of individual communicational styles, while still functioning as clearly discriminable, discrete events.

WEIGHTING OF CUES   In analyzing the effects of the display of clusters of cues for any given signal, each cue in the cluster was simply assigned the weight of one and these weights were added to obtain the sum for that display. Considering the strength of the relationship between (a) sums for each display and (b) the probability of an appropriate auditor response found for both the speaker turn and the speaker within-turn signals, it seems unlikely that an alternative weighting procedure would yield superior results for these data.

One implication of this weighting procedure is that no special cueing preference is accorded to cues occurring in one of the behavior areas (paralanguage, body motion, and language) over cues occurring in the others. There appears to be more democracy in the operation of these signals than might be expected from the discussions often found in the literature. For example, we do not find within these signals behaviors in body motion serving to modify or to qualify behaviors in syntax or in content.

An identical weighting procedure appeared to be operating in a somewhat different aspect of face-to-face interaction: the unprogrammed communication of an experimenter's expectations to his subject (Duncan and Rosenthal 1968; Duncan, Rosenberg, and Finkelstein 1969). In this case the proposed cues were in intonation and paralanguage.

DISTINCTIVE CUE CLUSTERS   In consideration of the distinctive feature analysis model for language (Jakobson, Fant, and Halle 1952), a concerted data analysis was directed toward the possibility that the signals were composed of unique combinations of cues, as contrasted to being composed of indiscriminate aggregates of cues (including any single cue). This effort, described above in the RESULTS section, failed to produce positive results. No unique combination of cues and no single cue indispensable to the cue clusters could be found in displays prior to auditor responses. In general, the process of summing over equally weighted cues contrasts sharply with the distinctive-feature analysis model and represents a considerably simpler principle of organization.

In view of the considerations discussed in this section, it would appear that the organization of the turn system varies in certain important respects from that of the language used by the interactants: American English.

Units of Interaction

Discussion up to this point has centered on the organization of signals displayed by a single participant. Jointly considering the respective actions of both participants leads directly to the issue of the organization of interaction, the ultimate goal of this research.

As the turn system is presently formulated, a speaker has a means by which he can segment his utterances on two hierarchical levels. The lower level is segmented by the within-turn signal; and the higher level is segmented by the turn signal. There appears to be a range of appropriate auditor responses to each of these speaker signals. To the within-turn signal, the auditor may appropriately respond with either silence or a back channel. To a turn signal unaccompanied by a gesticulation signal, he may appropriately respond with silence, a back channel, or a speaker-state signal, thereby claiming the turn. To a turn signal accompanied by a gesticulation signal, the auditor may appropriately respond with either silence or a back channel.

Data presented above on auditor's turn-claiming responses to speaker's turn signals clearly indicated that a turn-signal display did not automatically result in an auditor claim of the turn. At best, the probability of such a claim appears to be about 0.50. Comparable data were presented for auditor back-channel responses to speaker within-turn signals. Thus, it appears that the auditor retains considerable discretion over both the type and placement of his responses.

These findings, taken together, suggest the operation of two distinct, but interlocking, types of units: (a) units within individual messages, marked by the speaker and (b) units of interaction.

Units within individual messages are marked by only one interactant. In this sense they are comparable to traditional linguistic units on a given level. In the case of the turn-system, the units differ from traditional linguistic units, of course, in that the turn-system units use behaviors from paralanguage and body motion as markers.

Units of interaction cannot be marked by only one participant. These units must be marked by the appropriate, coordinated action of both participants (in the case of dyads).

Interaction units on a hierarchical level immediately below that of turns appear to be marked by a three-stage, sequential process: (a) the speaker displays a within-turn or a turn signal; (b) the auditor responds in the back channel; and (c) the speaker continues with his turn.

Interaction units on the level of the turn require a similar three-stage, sequential process: (a) the speaker displays a turn signal; (b) the auditor shifts to the speaker state, displaying a speaker-state signal; and (c) the previous speaker shifts to the auditor state, relinquishing his turn.

At each stage of these action sequences (after the original signal display by the speaker), each participant ratifies, as it were, the actions of the other. Following the initial signal display by the speaker, each participant has several real options available to him. Each of these options has important implications for the immediately ensuing course of the interaction. Distinctive patterns of option choice by each participant over the course of the interaction may have important implications for the character of that interaction.

Interaction units, created through the coordinated action of both participants in a dyadic interaction, appear to have the potential of constituting a basic building block in the structure of interaction.

Research Method

Developing appropriate methodological concepts and techniques was a central problem at the onset of this research. In time, an approach was evolved that drew variously from linguistics, psychology, and systems theory. The fine-grained transcriptions of behaviors in language, paralanguage, and body motion, and the initial emphasis on discrete units and hierarchical structure were derived from linguistics, as expanded by the work of McQuown, Bateson, Hockett, Birdwhistell, and others in "The natural history of an interview" (McQuown 1971). The use of discrete functions to represent the relations between discrete units was suggested in systems theory (Klir 1969). Finally, statistical techniques typically used in psychology were applied in evaluating the proposed signals and rules.

In general, for dyadic interactions it does not appear difficult to formulate criteria in terms of which a proposed convention can be evaluated statistically. For the turn system, criteria were derived directly from hypothesized regularities introduced by the convention in question into the behavior of participants. These regularities are reflected in nonrandom distributions (a) in specific behaviors of the *vis-à-vis* and (b) in resulting interaction states.

However, in applying statistical methods to conventional phenomena, it seems reasonable to expect significance levels considerably higher than those typically encountered in psychological research, assuming that the convention in question is operating effectively in the interaction. Research results that are just at, for example, the 0.001 level of significance might well be interpreted as indicating that the convention has not yet been adequately described or that, in the contexts from which the data were gathered, the convention in question was not reliably applicable.

Further Research on Interaction Structure

The initial stage of this research, before the turn signals had been formulated, was necessarily laborious, in that fine-grained transcriptions were required for as wide a variety of behaviors as possible. Further research may proceed at a more rapid pace, as hypotheses are formed regarding the behavioral composition of the signals. In Scheflen's (1966: 277) words, the signals then become "RECOGNIZABLE AT A GLANCE AND RECORDABLE WITH A STROKE" (original emphasis). Work is currently under way to transcribe the turn-system signals (and certain other, interesting behaviors) in a series of further videotaped dyadic conversations, with the aim of validating and potentially extending the findings reported here.

The findings reported above were directed at documenting the operation of signals that serve to mark various phenomena in conversations. There is no claim, however, that the lists of cues described as comprising the signals are necessarily complete. Other undetected cues may be present in the conversations studied, as well as in other conversations in the culture of the interactants. These possibilities will be considered in further research, both on the initial two conversations and on new transcriptions.

Research is continuing on the notion of interaction units as structural elements of conversations. The distribution of a number of different phenomena with regard to interaction units is being examined.

Initial analyses suggest that the speaker-state signal, beyond marking the beginnings of turns, may also be used throughout the speaking turn to mark the beginnings of within-turn units. If this suggestion proves correct, means will have been established whereby speakers may mark both the beginning and the ending of units. This possibility is being pursued.

The question arises concerning the auditor's initiation of interaction units. He might do this, either through a back channel in the absence of a speaker within-turn or turn signal or through a speaker-state signal in the absence of a speaker turn signal. (Auditor initiatives of this sort may account for some of the speaker-state signals found in association with auditor back channels.) Attention is being paid to the interactional consequences of such auditor initiatives. Table 1 indicates, however, that an auditor initiation of a turn in the absence of a speaker turn signal leads invariably (in our data) to simultaneous turns.

REFERENCES

BERNSTEIN, B.
    1962 Social class, linguistic codes, and grammatical elements. *Language and Speech* 5:221–240.
CRYSTAL, D.
    1969 *Prosodic systems and intonation in English.* Cambridge: Cambridge University Press.
CRYSTAL, D., R. QUIRK
    1964 *Systems of prosodic and paralinguistic features in English.* The Hague: Mouton.
DITTMANN, A. T., L. G. LLEWELLYN
    1967 The phonemic clause as a unit of speech decoding. *Journal of Personality and Social Psychology* 6:341–349.
    1968 Relationship between vocalizations and head nods as listener responses. *Journal of Personality and Social Psychology* 9:79–84.
DUNCAN, S. D., JR.
    1972 Some signals and rules for taking speaking turns in conversations. *Journal of Personality and Social Psychology* 23:283–292.
    1973 Toward a grammar for dyadic conversations. *Semiotica* 9:29–46.
DUNCAN, S. D., JR., M. J. ROSENBERG, J. FINKELSTEIN
    1969 The paralanguage of experimenter bias. *Sociometry* 32:207–219.
DUNCAN, S. D., JR., R. ROSENTHAL
    1968 Vocal emphasis in experimenters' instruction reading as unintended determinant of subjects' reponses. *Language and Speech* 11:20–26.
EKMAN, P., W. V. FRIESEN
    1969 The repertoire of nonverbal behavior: categories, origins, usage, and coding. *Semiotica* 1:49–98.
FRIES, C. C.
    1952 *The structure of English.* New York: Harcourt, Brace.
GOFFMAN, E.
    1963 *Behavior in public places.* New York: Free Press.
    1967 *Interaction ritual.* Garden City: Anchor.
HYMES, D.
    1967 "The anthropology of communication," in *Human communication theory.* Edited by F. E. X. Dance. New York: Holt, Rinehart and Winston.
JAFFE, J., S. FELDSTEIN
    1970 *Rhythms of dialogue.* New York: Academic Press.

JAKOBSON, R.
  1964   "Discussion of Factors and forms of aphasia' by A. R. Luria," in
          Ciba foundation symposium on disorders of language. Edited by A. V.S.
          de Reuck and M. O'Connor. Boston: Little, Brown.
JAKOBSON, R., C. G. M. FANT, M. HALLE
  1952   *Preliminaries to speech analysis: the distinctive features and their
          correlates.* Cambridge: MIT Press.
KENDON, A.
  1967   Some functions of gaze-direction in social interaction. *Acta Psycho-
          logica* 26–63.
KLIR, G. J.
  1969   *An approach to general systems theory.* New York: Van Nostrand
          Reinhold.
LEIGHTON, L. A., G. E. STOLLACK, R. L. FERGUSON
  1971   Patterns of communication in normal and clinic families. *Journal of
          Consulting and Clinical Psychology* 36:252–256.
MC QUOWN, N. A., *editor*
  1971   "The natural history of an interview." Microfilm Collection of
          Manuscripts on Cultural Anthropology, Fifteenth Series, The Univer-
          sity of Chicago Joseph Regenstein Library, Department of Photo-
          duplication, Chicago.
MELTZER, L., W. N. MORRIS, D. P. HAYES
  1971   Interruption outcomes and vocal amplitude: explorations in social
          psychophysics. *Journal of Personality and Social Psychology* 18:392–
          402.
MILLER, G. A.
  1963   Review of J. H. Greenberg (editor), *Universals of language. Con-
          temporary Psychology* 8:417–418.
ROSENFELD, H. M.
  1966   Instrumental affiliative functions of facial and gestural expressions.
          Journal of Personality and Social Psychology 4:65–72.
SCHEFLEN, A. E.
  1966   "Natural history method in psychotherapy: communicational
          research," in *Methods of research in psychotherapy*. Edited by L. A.
          Gottschalk and A. H. Auerbach. New York: Appleton-Century-
          Crofts.
  1968   Human communication: behavioral programs and their integration
          in interaction. *Behavioral Science* 13:44–55.
SCHEGLOFF, E. A.
  1968   Sequencing in conversational openings. *American Anthropologist* 70:
          1075–1095.
SULLIVAN, H. S.
  1947   *Conceptions of modern psychiatry.* New York: Norton.
TRAGER, G. L.
  1958   Paralanguage: a first approximation. *Studies in Linguistics* 13:1–12.
TRAGER, G. L., H. L. SMITH, JR.
  1957   *An outline of English structure.* Washington, D.C.: American Council
          of Learned Societies.

VON CRANACH, M.

    1971   "The role of orienting behavior in human interaction," in *The use of space by animals and men.* Edited by A. H. Esser. New York: Plenum.

YNGVE, V. H.

    1970   "On getting a word in edgewise," in *Papers from the sixth regional meeting of the Chicago Linguistic Society.* Chicago: Chicago Linguistic Society.

A Study of Interaction Markers in Conversational Spanish

ANA MARÍA MARTIRENA

1. The purpose of this study is to present an analysis of some forms characteristic of one type of discourse — informal conversation. The units analyzed and their combinations are not all limited to this type of discourse. They are included here because of their interactive significance in conversation.

When transcribing a conversation in which we have taken part, we find that, in addition to the utterances or parts of utterances which convey some information or message, we are putting down words or sequences of words we did not hear or we did not pay any attention to during the conversation. Furthermore, if we were asked to summarize or retell the content of the conversation, we would not include these "interaction markers." We may inquire, then, why they occur so frequently in conversation.

There are other characteristics of the utterances in a conversation which do not seem to attract our attention either. We refer to the change of the stream of speech from one person to the other (the exchange of the roles speaker/hearer); the use of certain forms of address; inflections in verbs (high frequency of first person singular and of second person singular or plural, depending on the number of hearers a speaker is addressing himself to); frequent use of pronouns, in agreement with the verb forms; pauses made by a speaker, or unusually long pauses between two utterances; hesitation signals; breathing phenomena, etc. If we were going to interpret all these features, we would readily find explanations such as "He spoke too much about himself" (over-frequent use of the first person singular pronoun); or "There were a number of us" (second person plural); or "We often did not know what to reply" (pauses between utterances by different speakers); or "He was hesitant or insecure" (hesitation phenomena); or "He must have run to get there on time" (breathing difficulties), etc.

On the other hand, we may wonder why a speaker uses the expression "you know" a number of times, or why he prefaces some of his statements with some equivalent of "well" or the like. Expressions such as "you know," "well," "see what I mean," "say," "I don't know," we shall call Interaction Markers [IMs]; they are the main object of our study.

It would seem that we must analyze a substantial portion of a conversation before we attempt to explain why a speaker uses any IMs. To start with, we cannot safely take the utterance in which it appeared and try to determine its meaning from that utterance alone. Being precisely an "interaction" marker, it will be somehow connected to what has happened before, to what is going to happen, and to the people who communicate about the happenings. The danger for the linguist at this point is to step out of his field and try to discover or assign "meanings" which are not directly observable from the material he has collected.

Yet, if we look at conversation as a language situation, we shall agree that people communicate because they have something to communicate, and want someone else to hear about it. We shall also agree that, whatever their intentions may be (concealing something, lying, etc.), they want their messages to get across as effectively as possible. We also know how difficult it is to concentrate on something which is exposed to us for a very short time, and which will be followed by equally transitory events — as is the case with spoken language. Besides, when we are speaking to someone, we want to know what our listener's reactions are to our message (or we want to tell the speaker about them, if the roles are reversed). When engaged in a conversation, we do not behave in the same way as if we were recording the same message for the person who is now the listener. We know that the person listening to the recording could play it back as often as he wanted if he thought he had missed a point; thus we do not need to signal to him when a turning-point in our speech will come. And, since we are not interested in getting his immediate response to our message, we do not elicit it. Even so, the listener may nod or in some way react to the recorded speech.

2.   It is difficult to find any literature on this topic in linguistic publications. The problem analyzed here seems to be considered non-

linguistic by linguists, or as Mahl and Schulze (1964:54) put it, "extra-linguistic."

Before going into the details of the psychological investigations in this area, Mahl and Schulze make a characterization of speech behavior. Under the heading of Interruptions of Continuity they group three kinds of phenomena: Non-Fluencies (speech errors, such as the interchange of words, syllables and sounds; omissions; stutters; hesitation signals, etc.); Silent Pauses (hesitation pauses, breathing pauses, etc.); and Intrusions or Intruding Speech Mannerisms, the name which they give to the features of speech we study here.

Their review of the literature on the three topics shows the existence of much more research done on the first two than on the third one. They discuss the aims and methods of two groups of scientists working in this area — the psychologists and the linguist-anthropologists.

Interest in personality seems to have motivated some psychologists to investigate the use of Intrusions in speech behavior. Sanford (1942) lists some Intrusions in his statistical study of samples of oral speech from two subjects, but he does not seem to regard them as very important categories in determining the linguistic style of his two subjects (he lists them under Miscellaneous categories). They form only 3 of the 234 categories he lists: Phrases of Internal Reference (such as "as I said," "the foregoing"), Parenthetical Formulas or Tag Phrases ("so to speak," "as it were"), and Run-On Phrases ("and so on"). The minor importance they have in his data reflects the kinds of material he is working with: descriptions, comments on pictures, stories. Although they are directed to a listener, they do not share all the characteristics of spontaneous talk. Besides, though the speaker is unaware that his speech is being recorded, the attitude of the other participant is not that of an individual in an uncontrolled conversation (i.e. the aim of the experimenter is to get a sample of the subject's speech, not of his own), and the amount of talk is far from being equally distributed between the two of them.

Mannerisms of Speech are considered by another psychologist, Feldman (1948:356–360), as habits, the analysis of which "often reveals the deepest motives of the normal and neurotic personality." She analyzes the speech habits of some of her patients and finds that they use these locutions "as a kind of crutch, as an aid in overcoming a momentary paralysis or difficulty in speaking." When dealing with "do you know what I did yesterday?" she states the motives the patient may have as he asks that question, since it is obvious that a literal interpretation would be erroneous: (i) to arouse the analyst's interest; (ii) to prepare the listener and make the impact of the story weaker; (iii) to gain time; (iv) to fill the gap caused by the silence of the analyst. Feldman's material is conversational (the patient's communicative behavior is influenced by the analyst's, whereas this was not the case in Sanford's experiment), but she is interested in each mannerism individually, as it reflects the impression of past events on the personality of the patient. She makes two important points about these characteristics of conversation: speakers are usually unaware of using them, and they cannot discard them for more than a few moments.

A thorough analysis of the communicative behavior of two people during a psychiatric interview is made by Pittenger, Hockett and Daneby (1960). They study the linguistic and paralinguistic phenomena in the speech of patient and therapist, and their psychological states as inferred from their linguistic and paralinguistic signals. Then they try to determine the correlations between the linguist's specification of the signals and the psychiatrist's specification of the states. In connection with the phenomena we are studying, the authors say that many of the actions and perceptions involved in communicative behavior have become automatic, performed precisely and appropriately, but also effortlessly and without awareness. Some of the shared conventions in communicative behavior (and behavior in general) are much more subtle than others because they are learned, acted, responded to and taught almost entirely without awareness; and if we examine apparent complexities or anomalies in speaking behavior, we may at a certain point discover a pattern in their occurrence.

Two of the difficulties faced when analyzing the data are reflected in the studies mentioned in this section: are IMs accidental, idiosyncratic, individual characteristics of speech (*parole*), or are they shared by a speech community (*langue*)? How are the units of analysis to be discovered: by purely formal or semantic criteria, or by both?

Having dealt with the first question, we shall discuss the different criteria which have been used for determining the unit of analysis.

Two psychologists, Soskin and John (1963), in their double aim to determine the role of talk in an individual's adjustment to his social environment and the character of this talk, identify two units. When trying to determine the amount of talking of each of the subjects, they define a "unit of speech" as the time interval during which a speaker is judged to be talking; when analyzing what is being communicated (the content of their talk) they use an "idea-unit," because they find that in spoken language sentences are usually reduced to phrases, to units larger than a word but smaller than a sentence. This second classification they find suitable to make a distinction between the relational and informational functions of talk. Yet, it has not been possible to apply it to the corpus used here, since each sentence or information-conveying unit can be included in more than one of the authors' categories (e.g. is "Rivero no sirve para nada" a *metrone* [valuative statement], a *signone* [expression of the psychological state of the speaker], or a *structone* [report of a fact, analysis, clarification]?). The authors include a transcribed portion of one of the dialogues, but they do not indicate how the "idea-units" are identified.

A second analysis of conversation reflects a completely different approach: the analysis excludes any reference to meaning. Although he is not interested in measuring talking time, Fries (1952) uses the same criterion as Soskin and John for defining the unit of speech or utterance unit. Furthermore, Fries adopts formal criteria when classifying these utterance units: (i) the distribution of the utterance in the conversation (whether it began the conversation or occurred after the conversation had started); and (ii) the form of the response which follows the utterance ("action," "oral response," or "oral signal of attention").

As regards (ii) he says "We have assumed that if the responses of the different groups are uniformly different, there must be characteristic formal differences that mark each group and produce the differing responses. We assume that it is possible to discover and describe these differences in form" (Fries 1952:51).

As responses to one kind of utterance he includes signals of continued attention given in some inconspicuous but conventional way. He says that these oral reactions on the hearer's part do not interfere with the continuous flow of the utterances of the speaker. They simply serve to give something of the hearer's reaction and to signal the fact that he is listening attentively to the speaker. Examples are: "Fine," "I see," "Good," etc.

3. Signalling attention is only one of the functions of the system of interaction in conversation which we attempt to analyze here.

We propose to identify the markers of this system in a number of conversations, describe their interactive function, their position in the utterance, their grammatical form, and the correspondence between their lexical meaning and their function. We shall attempt to describe the relationship between the function of IMs and their other characteristics.

The linguistic markers of this system have been identified by considering their role in the transmission of information. They do not alter the message, but rather add something to it that indicates a dynamic relationship between the speaker and his audience.

IMs are usually marked off by pitch (lower than the rest of the utterance, almost like parenthetical remarks if they occur medially in an utterance), by a terminal juncture, by an increase in speed, or by a combination of these. Some linguistic forms have been identified as IMs primarily because their occurrence in conversation is very frequent (e.g. "y," "pero," "es decir"). In other, more elaborate, forms of discourse the speaker is not likely to use expressions like "creo," "bueno," as often as he does in spontaneous talk.

Where an IM is NOT marked off by pitch or contour, it is considered to be one only if the information in the utterance remains unchanged after its deletion. We regard "vos sabés que" in "Vos sabés que yo durante los veranos . . ." as an IM; on the other hand, "sabés" in "Sabés qué es malo, no sólo que los estudiantes . . ." is not analyzed as an IM because its deletion would turn information "given" into information "asked for" ("sabés qué es malo": "I am going to tell you what is wrong," whereas "qué es malo": I am asking "what is wrong?").

We have also found hesitation signals (e.g. "eh . . .") in the utterances which, however, we differentiate from IMs by considering them empty of interactive significance; they are mere accidents of speech. Some IMs may be regarded as being hesitation signals as well (see Section 3.1, class I.a.), but they are included in this study because they also tell us what the speaker is hesitant about (HOW to say something, or WHAT to say).

The corpus we have used consists of four conversations (350 utterances) among speakers of Rioplatense Spanish. The subjects were graduate students at Cornell University. They were all aware that their speech was being recorded for some purpose or other, but they did not know what the aim of the analysis was. Three of them were females and two were males; their ages ranged from twenty-four to thirty. Colloquial Spanish was used throughout. It is perhaps worth noting that the second person pronoun "vos" and the corresponding verb inflections are used, as is customary among peers of the same age in Rioplatense.

In the conversations analyzed there are usually two participants (a third one appears in one of them, but her contribution is not important); this might indicate that "Dialog Markers" could be a better name for the features of speech analyzed here. Yet, this alternative might suggest that the signals occur only when the roles speaker/hearer are distributed between two people, which is not true.

The participants' speech is segmented into utterances according to the definition given by Fries (1952:23). An utterance is thus considered any stretch of speech by one person before which there is silence on his part and after which there is also silence on his part, i.e. a chunk of talk marked off by a shift of speaker. In some cases, B's spontaneous reaction (usually a single, short word) does not interrupt A's speech; nor does A pause deliberately to listen to B's reaction. In such cases, A's utterance is not considered as being interrupted, even though B's interruption is counted as an utterance. If, on the other hand, A pauses (deliberately or not) to get B's reaction, A's speech is considered as consisting of two separate utterances.

3.1 On the assumption that the ways in which interaction is signalled in conversation are culturally determined, shared by a speech community, and that a member of that speech community is to some extent qualified to make inferences about the function of those signals in the speech of other members of the community, these phenomena are classified according to the function or interactive significance they have in the conversations analyzed.

Classification on a strictly formal basis has proved almost impossible, considering the variety and diversity of the immediate linguistic contexts in which these signals appear. Trying to determine the meaning of these signals in relation to the speaker's intended meaning for the utterance or sentence has been found to be even less practicable.

Thus, a tentative classification has been made, the function of an IM being determined mainly from the linguistic context which immediately precedes or follows it, and from the conversation situation as a whole.

The following IMs are used in the conversations analyzed and will be discussed in greater detail below:

I.a. "cómo se dice," "vamos a decir," "cómo te voy a decir," "mm."
  b. "qué sé yo," "no sé."
  c. "es decir," "por ejemplo," "digamos."
II.   "bueno," "ah."
III. "y."
IV.a. "sabés."
  b. "viste," "decí."
  c. "lo que pasa es," "la verdad es."
  d. "creo," "te juro," "te digo," "me parece."
V.   "no," "pero."
VI.   "ahá," "claro," "sí," "no," "mh," "ah."

VII.a.   "mirá," "che," "te das cuenta."
   b.   "así que," "¿no?", "¿sí?", "¿eh?"

A reduced corpus imposes some limitations on the available data. The resulting analysis is therefore undoubtedly not exhaustive, and we would expect that a more extensive corpus would reveal a larger number of IMs, as well as more diversified functions for any given IM. But the proportions of IMs discovered here to their total inventory cannot be calculated or even guessed at.

In the following groupings, we will analyze the situations in which a speaker seems to use an IM.

I.   — when he is searching for an adequate idea or expression.

a.   The speaker is looking for the best way to say something, and generally finds the desired expression and uses it after the IM.

> CÓMO SE DICE
>
> CÓMO TE VOY A DECIR
>
> VAMOS A DECIR
>
> MM

Examples:

". . . y ese dinero va para un . . . CÓMO SE DICE . . . ayuda para los estudiantes que no tienen dinero para estudiar."

". . . si en todas las carreras es importante, en la mía también porque tenés que tener un . . . CÓMO TE VOY A DECIR . . . un feeling por las cosas."

". . . se han acostumbrado a vivir en una ciudad grande y vienen a este . . . VAMOS A DECIR pueblito."

(E asks a question) "MM . . . creo que sí."

b.   The speaker does not find the right idea to complete his message, or he really does not know what to say, as the literal interpretation indicates. The following statement(s) usually reassure the listener that the speaker does NOT know what to say.

> QUE SE YO
>
> NO SE

Examples:

"Y a mí me fastidia. QUÉ SÉ YO. Me pone muy nerviosa."

"Ese es el problema, que la gente / eh . . . NO SÉ, o no tiene demasiado orgullo o dignidad /"[1]

---

[1]   Some conventions used in the transcriptions:
   /   an interrupted statement. It may be followed by silence, by a repetition or rephrasing, by a change of topic, or by an utterance by another speaker.
   / / an unusually long pause.
  . . . hesitation or incomplete statement.

c.   The speaker pauses deliberately to illustrate, restate, or enlarge an idea, and he says he is about to do so.

ES DECIR

POR EJEMPLO

DIGAMOS

Examples:

"¿Qué pensás de la situación política, ES DECIR de / qué pensás del actual gobierno argentino?"

"Sí, yo creo que sí. Es decir, creo que POR EJEMPLO / qué sé yo / la clase intelectual puede interpretar de otra forma una serie de cosas."

"Durante el verano es cuando más nos vemos. DIGAMOS, cuando están de vacaciones."

If we consider subgroup c. above as anticipating the kind of information that immediately follows, then we might want to place it under IV. below.

II.   — when he has found the right idea or expression, has made a decision or choice, or has accepted a situation.

AH

BUENO

Examples:

"Ahá. / / Y . . . / / BUENO, mirá, yo en general nunca tuve mucha opinión . . ."

"¿Qué me vas a preguntar? // BUENO, vos preguntame, está bien."

"Y . . . AH, y me decía . . ."

III.   —- when he wants to indicate some continuity of a (general or specific) topic in his speech.

Y

Examples:

E— "Y mientras tanto te vas haciendo a la idea de /"

C– "Te vas haciendo / Y además das el master y después el examen A es el examen . . ."

A different IM ("no") indicates the opposite attitude; it is grouped under V. below.

"Y" is more clearly classified as an IM when it is followed by a pause as in the first and third examples in II. above.

IV.   — when he is anticipating the character of the information, as:

a.   It is directed to the listener. Although the form of this IM makes it look like a question, its force is that of a command: "The following information is for you. GET IT."

SABÉS

Example:
"SABÉS, también compró uno sencillo porque si lleva uno complicado, mis padres . . ."
b.   It is shared with the listener. The speaker assumes or knows that the listener also has the information, but he wants to refer to it anyway. He also wants to mention that it might have been recognized ("viste") or indeed might be so phrased ("decí") by the listener.

VISTE
DECÍ

Examples:
"VISTE como en Argentina, esa . . . 'Siempre hay gente así' "
". . . pero vos ves a los estudiantes acá, a los que . . . DECÍ que hace dos años que están . . ."
"Qué ignorantes, porque como / claro, DECÍ que nosotros somos un pobre país que está ahí abajo . . ."
c.   It is a fact. The speaker realizes or wants to emphasize that he is not making any personal comments or revealing anything he alone knew. In a more formal style, the expression "el hecho es" is used for this same purpose.

LO QUE PASA ES
LA VERDAD ES

Examples:
"Bueno, LO QUE PASA ES que no me voy a vivir a Chile."
"LA VERDAD ES *que* no tengo más tantos discos de Gardel como tenía antes, ¿eh?"
   Subgroup a. is sometimes combined with subgroup c. as in:
"Sí, pero SABÉS (a.) LO QUE PASA (c.) es conseguir que la universidad se organice, pero ¿con qué gente?"
d.   It is subjective, personal — the opposite of c. The speaker is revealing some of his thoughts or opinions, and at the same time may be giving an impression of insecurity, uncertainty.

(YO) CREO
(YO) TE DIGO
TE JURO
ME PARECE

Examples:
"El principal problema / CREO / de la Argentina es / se acostumbra a ser irresponsables . . ."

(¿Te parece?) "Sí, creo que sí. Es decir, CREO que por ejemplo / qué sé yo / . . ."

"TE JURO que en mí la comparación no existe, que yo . . ."

"Bueno, YO TE DIGO que a veces tengo que pedir que me expliquen qué es lo que pasa . . ."

"Depende CREO un poco del tipo de visa que tengas, pero eh generalmente PARECE que hay problemas en la entrada de todo artefacto eléctrico."

V. — when the following statement reflects a contradiction, an objection, an unfavorable statement, or when the speaker wants to change the topic of the conversation.

NO

PERO

Examples:

(E— ¿Quién era? ¿Cómo era?) C– "NO, te voy a preguntar a vos, mejor."

"NO, a mí me fastidió mucho en la universidad la forma en que . . ."

". . . y me decía PERO, ¿vos sabés los años que hace que estoy estudiando?"

In some cases "pero" might be said to be just an adversative conjunction, the first of the two clauses it relates being absent. However, it is included here because it shares with "no" the functions mentioned in V. above.

VI. — when he wants to show his attention to and understanding of the other person's speech, or his agreement (or disagreement) with it or with his own previous speech.

AHA, AH, MH

CLARO

SÍ, NO

a. Reacting to his interlocutor's speech.

Examples:

(G— "Así que estuviste más o menos dos meses en Argentina / durante el actual gobierno.") E— "AHÁ."

(E— "¿Sabés cuáles son fáciles de entender? Las quo tenemos nosotros, las que traducen.") N— "CLARO, SÍ."

(N— ". . . pasar por Chile, dejar mis cosas allí / ") E— "MH."

(E— "Creo que . . .") G– "Oh, NO, NO."

b. Reacting to his own speech.

Examples:

"... yo este semestre he entregado / NO, el primer semestre / he entregado ..."

"Eso era antes. SÍ, antes en mi universidad también."

VII.   — when he asks for the other person's
a.   Agreement, understanding, attention.

> MIRA, MIRE
> TE DAS CUENTA
> CHE, INTERLOCUTOR'S NAME
> ¿SÍ? ¿NO? ¿EH?

Examples:

"... y decía 'no, MIRE señor, yo no doy el examen.' "

"Bueno, MIRÁ, yo en general nunca tuve mucha opinión ..."

"Es solamente una cuestión de principios, ¿TE DAS CUENTA?"

"CHE, ¿este hombre no canta Malena?"

"La verdad es que no tengo más tantos discos de Gardel como tenía antes, ¿/EH, CUQUI?"

"Yo no sabría /no sabía qué hacer, ¿NO?"

b.   confirmation that he has the right idea, or repetition of information.

> ASÍ QUE
> ¿SÍ? ¿EH? ¿NO?

Examples:

(G— "¿Cuánto tiempo hace que estás aquí en este país?" E— "El mismo tiempo que vos.") G— "ASÍ QUE viniste en agosto del '66." (E— "Sí, en agosto del '66.")

(G— "Casualmente creo que van a venir este mes mis padres.") E— "¿SÍ?" (G— "sí")

(E— "A ver. Cantá, cantá.") H– "¿EH?" (E— "Cantá.")

(C— "It doesn't have a cover.") H— "¿NO?"

3.2   Although the observed occurrence of IMs in a somewhat patterned system seems to be the most important outcome of this study, certain other features of IMs deserve our attention.

Table 1 reflects an analysis of:

A.   the position of IMs in the utterances in which they are identified.
B.   the number of functions (see Section 3.1) each IM has in the corpus.
C.   the correspondence between the lexical meaning and the function in the conversation.
D.   their grammatical form.

A.   Some IMs, or classes of IMs, almost always occur in the same position in an utterance (e.g. "no" as a Class V. IM in initial position). Others can be shifted around without significant change in their function (e.g. "sabés"); and others are restricted to a single position (e.g. Class VI.a., reacting to someone else's speech).

In Table 1, the occurrence of IMs in initial, medial or final position in utterances is counted.

B.   In some cases the same IM appears to have more than one function. In this section of the table we summarize what has been pointed out in Section 3.1 when dealing with the specific functions of IMs.

C.   The function of an IM has sometimes been found to coincide with its lexical meaning; in other cases, an extension or a shift in meaning has been noticed.

The following conventions are used in the table:

=   when the function and the lexical meaning coincide.

+   when the function reflects some of the lexical meaning.

≠   when the function differs from the lexical meaning.

D.   IMs seem to fall into three main form classes: sentences, fragments and sentence modifiers. An IM is considered to be a sentence if it includes a finite clause (e.g. "cómo te voy a decir"). The IMs considered as fragments subdivide into five form-classes: interjections (Int), such as "ah," "che," "ahá"; minor-sentence forms (MS), like "sí" and "no"; adjectives (Adj), as "claro," "bueno"; prepositional phrases (PP), such as "por ejemplo"; and conjunctions (Conj), like "y," "pero." In the group of sentence modifiers, the IMs are verbal constructions which are followed by a pause (e.g. "Vos SABÉS, cuando yo estaba en el secundario ..."), or by "que" plus the sentence they modify (e.g. "Vos SABÉS QUE yo durante los veranos ..."). In other words, the finite verb which they contain is not taken as the main verb of the sentence.

Table 1 illustrates some characteristics of IMs. There is a strong correlation between position in an utterance and function in Classes VI.a. (initially in utterances), VI.b. (medially), and IV. (medially). There is also a very close correspondence between function and grammatical form in Class IV. (all the IMs in this class are sentence modifiers). The more easily identified IMs share some features: they are fragments (Classes II., VI., and VII.), and some of them have a fixed position in utterances (VI., VII.).

4.   On the assumption that the same message can be transmitted in more than one form of discourse, we conducted a rewrite test in which the following changes were introduced into a monolog: (1) a second

Table 1.   Analysis of interaction markers

| Interactive Function | A Position in utterance | | | B | C | D Grammatical form | | |
	Init.	Med.	Fin.	Add. funcs.	Func./lex. m.	Sent.	Fragm.	S. M
I.a. mm	×	—	—	—	=	—	Int	—
vamos a decir	—	×	—	IV.d.	=	×	—	—
cómo se dice	—	×	—	IV.d.	=	×	—	—
cómo te voy a decir	—	×	—	IV.d.	=	×	—	—
b. no sé	—	×	×	IV.d.	=	×	—	—
qué sé yo	×	×	×	IV.d.	=	×	—	—
c. es decir	×	×	×	—	=	—	—	×
por ejemplo	—	×	—	—	=	—	PP	—
II. ah	×	—	—	VI.a., b.	=	—	Int	—
bueno	×	×	—	—	≠	—	Adj*	—
III. y	×	×	×	—	=	—	Conj	—
IV.a. sabés	—	×	—	—	+	—	—	×
b. viste	—	×	—	—	=	—	—	×
decí	—	×	—	—	=	—	—	×
c. la verdad es	—	×	—	—	=	—	—	×
lo que pasa es	—	×	—	—	=	—	—	×
d. creo	—	×	—	—	=	—	—	×
te juro	—	×	—	—	+	—	—	×
te digo	—	×	—	—	+	—	—	×
parece	—	×	—	—	=	—	—	×
V. no	×	—	—	VI., VII.	+	—	MS	—
pero	×	×	×	—	+	—	Conj	—
VI.a., b. ahá	a. ×	—	—	—	=	—	Int	—
mh	×	—	—	—	=	—	Int	—
ah	×	—	—	II.	=	—	Int	—
sí	×	b. ×	—	VII.	=	—	MS	—
no	×	×	—	V., VII.	=	—	MS	—
claro	×	—	—	—	+	—	Adj	—
VII.a. che	×	×	—	—	=	—	Int	—
¿eh?	—	×	—	—	=	—	Int	—
¿no?	—	×	—	V., VI.	=	—	MS	—
mirá	—	×	—	—	+	×	—	—
b. ¿sí?	—	—	—**	—	+	—	MS	—
¿no?	—	—	—	V., VI.	+	—	MS	—
¿eh?	—	—	×	—	=	—	Int	—
así que	×	—	—	—	≠	—	Conj	—

*   The IMs "bueno" (II.) and "pero" (V.) also occur in minor-sentence form in cases when t are the only item in the utterance.
**   IMs "¿sí?", "¿no?" and "¿eh?" occur as only manifestations of an utterance with func VII.b.; "¿eh?" has also been found after major sentences that have this function.

participant was added; (2) the speech of the original text was fragmented to fit the requirements of distribution between two participants; (3) IMs and other characteristics of spontaneous talk (hesitations, rephrasings) were introduced for both speakers.

A — BUENO, sería muy difícil definir qué es el argentino /
B — ¿Te parece?
A — De igual manera que sería difícil definir, POR EJEMPLO, el color rojo, el sabor del café, o . . . QUÉ SÉ YO . . . el tono épico de la poesía, o . . . /
B — MH.
A — Pero entiendo que los argentinos sabemos, o . . . BUENO, mejor dicho sentimos, en qué consiste ser argentino, Y . . . eso es mucho más importante,
B — AHÁ.
(A) CREO, que el hecho de formular o no una definición, ¿NO?
B — BUENO, LA VERDAD ES que nunca pensé en definirlo . . .
A — CLARO, sentimos sin necesidad de definirlo que un argentino difiere del español /
B — ¿Del español solamente?
A — BUENO, del colombiano, del chileno . . . que difiere muy poco del uruguayo,
B —   MH.
(A)   y creo que eso debe bastarnos, ¿NO? Porque, en general, uno no procede en la vida . . . CÓMO TE VOY A DECIR . . . por definiciones, sino por intuiciones inmediatas.
B — SÍ, PERO /
A — Y creo que sentimos el sabor argentino no solamente / VAMOS A DECIR en la poesía gauchesca o en las novelas de Gutiérrez o de Güiraldes, donde
B —   MH.
(A)   se ha buscado ese tono, sino aún en poetas que no se proponen ser ar—
B —   SÍ
(A)   gentinos. ES DECIR, que no son profesionalmente o incesantemente argentinos.
B — PERO, SABÉS LO QUE PASA, hay muchos que piensan que lo único que vale la pena describir es lo típico.
A — MM . . . TE DIGO, no sé si el argentino típico existe, es decir, no sé si hay un . . . CÓMO SE DICE . . . arquetipo del argentino. Además, estar
B —   AHÁ.
(A)   identificado con un país es un poco de trampa, ME PARECE.
B — NO, yo estaba pensando en los personajes de tangos, VISTE, esos que para algunos representan al porteño.
A — NO, el compadrito creo que ya no existe . . . AH, y otra cosa, el culto del gaucho. Y DECÍ que en el Uruguay es aún más intenso que entre nosotros los argentinos.
B — ¿SÍ?
A — Sí, por supuesto. Lo sé por la experiencia de un tío mío, el escritor uruguayo Lafinur /
B — ASÍ QUE Lafinur es tío tuyo.
A — Sí, hermano de mi madre.

The opposite procedure was applied to one of the conversations analyzed for this study: (1) the speech of only one participant was used; (2) separate utterances were turned into the speech of a person in a monolog (verb forms, pronouns, etc., were adjusted to this different form of discourse); (3) IMs and other features of conversational style were deleted.

Yo quería hablar de la situación de Argentina. Yo pienso que la única solución de por lo menos tratar de resolver el problema que había en la universidad era intervenirla desde afuera, porque la universidad por sí misma no era capaz de corregirse.

Yo siempre estuve fuera de cualquier tipo de organización política dentro de la universidad; todo lo que ha sido desde el punto de vista de organización, sin considerar política.

En la Universidad de La Plata había muchas organizaciones estudiantiles, pero no tanto como en Buenos Aires. En La Plata es un poquito más tranquilo, pero asimismo había algunas organizaciones de estudiantes que se dedicaban más a los problemas políticos del país que a la organización de la universidad en sí.

Some interesting details, not only about IMs but also about the form of discourse in which they appear, have been revealed by this test. The hypothesis was that, along with other conversational features, IMs could turn a piece of some other kind of discourse into a conversation, and vice versa.

A monolog has been used for the first part of the test. A previous, unsuccessful attempt with a history text suggested that a nonconversational topic and choice of lexical items could result in a ridiculous form of discourse if IMs were introduced. Even though the monolog is much closer to a conversation, the speaker's careful diction does not seem to tolerate some items as IMs (such as "che").

In the attempt to introduce as many different IMs as possible, we found evidence of another aspect of their occurrence: a speaker does not use all the available IMs for each function, but chooses a few of them (e.g. for the function I.a., the same speaker will not use all four of the IMs listed in Section 3.1).

In addition to IMs, other conversational features have been introduced, such as hesitations, interruptions, repetitions, rephrasings, incomplete statements, etc.

It was difficult to find a continuous topic in a conversation. The few paragraphs in the second part of the test were extracted from almost two pages of a conversation.

Another difficulty met in this second part is mentioned in other sections too — in some cases it was not easy to decide whether a word or construction was an IM, and therefore to be deleted, or whether it had an additional role in discourse.

Of the features introduced or deleted in this test, only IMs and those features providing redundant information seem to have some interactive significance. In conversation, we repeat ourselves very often because we know we do not have our listener's total attention, and because we do not expect him to remember everything we tell him after having heard it only once. Features such as hesitations, incomplete statements, etc., help to make the conversation more like a real one only because spontaneous speech is not smooth, as it is often represented when it is written down.

5.   It was while we were analyzing conversations for a different purpose that the occurrence of IMs first attracted our attention. After looking for linguistic analyses of this characteristic of spontaneous talk, we found that only smooth speech had been the object of study of linguists. On the other hand, psychologists have shown considerable interest in the phenomenon.

We observed these linguistic forms in a number of conversations and attempted to determine their interactive function. The task was not easy because IMs do not constitute a formal or syntactic category in the language, or a privative function of any item or construction. Other formal aspects of IMs have also been analyzed.

A rewrite test has been carried out in order to discover to what extent IMs could serve to turn a different form of discourse into a conversation, and vice versa.

A single instance of the occurrence of IMs might be enough to show their interactive importance. When quoting (more or less freely) another person's speech or our own speech from a previous conversation, we generally introduce IMs. In this case the IM does not have any interactive function in the present, but it tells us something about the past conversation situation. On the other hand, if we are reporting — not quoting — something from a previous conversation, we would not use IMs.

Our own experience gives us some information about the use of IMs. If once a conversation is over we ask the participants to tell us about the messages conveyed and the IMs used, we are likely to learn that he does not remember anything except the messages (unless he happens to be a linguist or a very careful observer of other people's speech habits). And if we ask a speaker when or how he started using a certain IM, his first reaction will probably be to say that he does not know.

Later he may remember having heard it very often from a friend or from a speaker on the radio.

These two ordinary experiences reflect important characteristics of IMs: they are automatically used and reacted to, having been transmitted and learnt without awareness.

REFERENCES

FELDMAN, S. S.
1948   Mannerisms of speech. *Psychoanalytic Quarterly* 17:356–367.
FRIES, C. C.
1952   *The structure of English.* New York: Harcourt and Brace.
MAHL, G. F., G. SCHULZE
1964   "Psychological research in the extralinguistic area," in *Approaches to semioticcs.* Edited by T. Sebeok, et al., 51–125. The Hague: Mouton.
PITTENGER, R. E., C. HOCKETT, J. J. DANEBY
1960   *The first five minutes.* Ithaca: Martineau.
SANFORD, F. H.
1942   Speech and personality: a comparative case study. *Character and Personality* 10:169–198.
SOSKIN, W. F., V. P. JOHN
1963   "The study of spontaneous talk," in *The stream of behavior.* Edited by Roger G. Baker. New York: Appleton-Century Crofts.

Components of Interaction in the Negotiation of a Definition of the Situation

DON HANDELMAN

At the core of anthropological and sociological analyses of face-to-face interaction is the problem of how to delineate the definition of the situation, the common ground upon which participants base their coordinated activities, and in terms of which they gauge the extent to which interpersonal communication develops a desired form in interaction. If the observer's approach to social interaction is "interpretive" then ". . . definitions of situations. . . are not explicitly or implicitly assumed to be settled once and for all by literal application of a preexisting culturally established system of symbols" (Wilson 1970: 701). Instead, "The social act . . . is a continuous process of defining the situation, with each definition evolving, in large part, out of antecedent definitions. In effect, the act becomes a continuous series of contingencies" (Rose 1962: 321). The evolving of a common or congruent definition of the situation is then a process of negotiation between participants which takes ". . . the form of a series of offers and responses that continue until an offer (a definition of the situation) is reached that is acceptable to both parties" (Scheff 1968: 12).

While there tends to be an implicit assumption in much interactionist research that the definition of a given situation does indeed exist and can be labeled, McHugh (1968: 60) pointedly states that the "definition of the situation is often invoked but seldom specified." My contention is that in much informal social interaction there need not be a clear-cut definition of the situation which the observer can infer; but that the emergence of a common basis for interaction can be examined through a textual criticism of sequences of interaction. I am not suggesting that a congruent definition of the situation does not develop in informal interaction, but that this process is problematic in itself and cannot be taken for granted by the observer. Instead of assuming that there is a congruent definition of the situation shared by participants, or trying to specify this common definition as the basis of interaction, we would do better to try and identify components of interaction which lead actors to be more or less open to interacting with one another and prepared to search for a congruent definition of the situation.

In this paper I will consider how one sequence of interaction might be broken down into organizational and thematic components, and how an examination of such components can provide clues to one instance of negotiating the definition of the situation. Since my aim is to identify some properties of interaction through which participants attempt to develop a congruent definition of the situation I have deliberately chosen a sequence which suggests an instance of sporadic, disjointed interaction in which a congruent definition of the situation cannot easily be assumed by the reader.

COMPONENTS OF INTERACTION

If interaction is to occur, the following minimal components must be present: (a) an openness of persons present to focused activity (Goffman 1963: 131ff.; Schegloff 1968: 1088–1089); (b) a topic of interaction; and (c) the allocation and activation of speaker-hearer roles in conversational activity (Speier 1972: 401) or doer-observer roles in nonverbal interaction. Configurations of the extent of participant openness, the treatment of topics of interaction by participants, and forms of role allocation constitute different kinds of interaction "frames." Such frames signify the extent to which participants are moving toward or away from developing a common ground of interaction, but they do not necessarily signify that there is a congruent definition of the situation shared by participants nor what this is.

The idea of "frame" has been used to distinguish forms of expressive behavior like play (Bateson 1972) and joking activity (Handelman and Kapferer 1972) which, if it is to occur successfully, requires participants to accept and clearly denote acceptance of a congruent definition of the situation that is often in marked contrast to antecedent definitions. However, much routine interaction does not contain messages as clear-cut as that of "this is play." So the boundaries of interaction frames, as I have delineated them, may contain messages which overlap these boundaries or may contain multiple messages. In such cases I have opted for describing a frame in terms of its dominant message to interaction. A frame, then, describes the state of interpersonal contacts between participants during a particular segment of interaction, and the capacity such a state of contact has for developing a common basis of interaction for the participants. A sequence of frames is integrated through time by the thematic development of the content of interaction as participants offer and respond to topics of discourse which can come to form the basis of a congruent definition of the situation.

THE SOCIAL SETTING OF INTERACTION

The interaction to be considered occurred in an "absorption center" in Israel. Absorption centers offer new immigrants certain services during their first months in the country. These services include lodging and board, intensive Hebrew language courses, orientation programs and recreational facilities. The absorption center in which the interaction occurred contains a lobby, an open area approximately sixty feet long by twenty-five feet wide bounded by the building entrance, a reception desk, a television room, and hallways leading to living quarters and a reading room. The lobby contains four round tables with three easy chairs placed around each table. This particular center has tended to receive new immigrants from English-speaking countries and from Russia.

Cavan has noted that:

Associated with ... conventional settings, is a standardized pattern of behavior, routinely expected within the setting, treated as fitting and proper for the time and place, and persistently independent of the changing populace. These standing behavior patterns associated with the conventional setting of everyday life are the taken-for-granted, common-sense features of social organization" (Cavan 1966: 3; see also Hymes 1967: 21).

The lobby of the absorption center is a public social setting open to any persons living in the center or their visitors during the day or evening. Within the setting, taken-for-granted patterns of behavior include conversation, waiting for others to appear, and occupying oneself in other ways without attracting undue attention, viz. without one's presence, activities, or sentiments being questioned. However, only persons by themselves who actually turned out to be waiting for someone gave the appearance of being "unoccupied" during the time they spent in the lobby. Persons by themselves who turned out not to be waiting for some-one (or more accurately who were not met by someone) gave the ap-pearance of being occupied in reading, writing, studying, or examining various features of the social setting. When such unaccompanied per-sons made contact with one another in the lobby they did not necessar-ily begin to interact in terms of a congruent definition of the situation beyond the implications of the general rules of the setting which suggest that strangers, or persons who have had only rudimentary contacts with one another, may attempt to make or further their acquaintance there.

THE SEQUENCE OF INTERACTION[1]

The sequence occurs on a Friday evening, the eve of the Sabbath. At approximately 7:25 P.M. a man wearing a sport shirt and slacks enters the empty lobby. He is a new immigrant from the United States, aged fifty, and a widower. During the following twenty-five minutes he ap-pears to absorb himself in examining various lobby fixtures — a bulle-tin board, displays of posters, the front door, hallways, and window blinds. During this period seven persons pass through the lobby. Six pay him no attention. One teen-age girl addresses him but he does not acknowledge her utterance, and she too passes through. The man then sits at a table, and some two minutes later a woman wearing a pants suit enters the lobby. Like the man she is a new immigrant who is living in the absorption center. She is from the United States, aged fifty but appears younger, and is divorced. The woman approaches the table at which the man is seated and sits down diagonally across from him. The elements of the sequence, classified by frame, follow.

I. INTERCHANGE:
1. Woman: "How long have you been here?"
2. Man looks at woman: "Three months . . . but I'm thinking of go-ing back."
3. Woman: "Why?"
4. Man: "It's not quite what I expected."
5. They both sit. The man leans toward the woman.
6. Man: "No . . . it's just not what I expected."

II. PERSON-INCLUSION:
7. Man and woman look away from each other. A party of four peo-

[1] The sequence was transcribed by Paulette Karmiol and reported in her paper, "Evenings in the Lobby of an Absorption Center," Tel-Aviv University, June 1972. A copy of this term paper is in the author's possession.

ple enter the lobby and sit at a nearby table. They both stare at the party of four. The man is grimacing. The woman is smiling. The four are conversing.

8.   Man and woman look at one another and slowly smile.
9.   Woman looks at her watch.
10.   Man and woman stare off in different directions.
11.   Man looks at woman. She catches his glance, gives him a little smile, and then looks down into her lap.
12.   Woman looks up and both stare into space. The man sits upright. The woman shuffles her feet.
13.   The nearby foursome are discussing a dead puppy found in the recreation room of the absorption center.

III.   PERSON-EXCLUSION:
14.   Woman turns toward the foursome and briefly converses with them, commenting upon the dead puppy.

IV.   NARRATIVE:
15.   Woman turns back to man and describes the incident of the dead puppy.
16.   Man nods at what she is relating to him. He is sitting stiffly upright, a grimace on his face, and his hands clasped tightly in his lap.
17.   The woman ends her description with "... and it was so awful!" Woman laughs.

V.   PERSON-INCLUSION:
18   Woman laughs again. Man grimaces.
19.   Woman gives man a series of little smiles. She is wearing sandals. She begins to clean her toes with a fingernail. Man gives her a number of quick glances while she is cleaning her toes. She finishes. Man and woman continue to sit, staring around the lobby.

VI.   TOPIC-REJECTION:
20.   Man looks at woman. Man: "What are your plans?"
21.   Woman: "I don't know. I've been here four months ... I should have brought a car here."
22.   Man and woman look away from one another.

VII.   PERSON-EXCLUSION:
23.   A dog enters the lobby. The man looks at the dog. The dog moves over to the man.

24.   Man begins to pet dog. Woman first watches, then looks away.

VIII.   PERSON-EXCLUSION:
25.   Woman looks at man. Woman: "Dogs are terrible!"
26.   Man immediately ceases to pet dog.
27.   Man looks at dog. Man resumes petting dog.
28.   Woman glances at man a few times. She then rests her head in her hand, elbow on thigh, and looks at the floor.
29.   Man has stopped petting dog. He is again sitting stiffly upright, hands clapsed in lap, legs together. Woman is looking at her sandals. She is now slouched with legs spread apart.

IX.   TOPIC-CONFUSION:
30.   Woman: "Dinner wasn't too good . . ."
31.   Man: "But I know I heard you have to pay a twenty-five per-cent tax on cars after the first year."
32.   Woman nods, stares straight ahead. Her hands are now folded in her lap and her legs are close together.

X.   PERSON-EXCLUSION:
33.   Man and woman sit, look away from one another, and look around the lobby, empty now except for the receptionist.

XI.   TOPIC-REJECTION:
34.   Man looks at woman. Man: "You know Israel is a capitalist country?"
35.   Woman utters a short laugh and looks at her watch.

XII.   PERSON-INCLUSION:
36.   Man and woman sit and look around the lobby. Woman moves about in her chair, stares at a wall, stares at the floor, smiles at the man. Man smiles at the woman.

XIII.   TOPIC-SUBSTITUTION:
37.   Man: "It's nice out."
38.   Woman: "Mmmm." She clears her throat.
39.   Woman scratches her neck. Woman: "It takes ten days to get to Australia by ship, did you know that?"
40.   Man: "Oh . . . really?"
41.   They smile at one another quickly, look away, and look around the lobby.

XIV. TOPIC-REJECTION:

42. Man stands, walks over to a corner table, picks up a book, opens and closes it, and then carries it back to the woman who is still seated. He stands next to her with the book open.

43. Man: "It's hard to read Hebrew without the vowels."

44. Woman nods.

45. Man returns the book to the corner table, and then walks around the lobby. He lights a cigarette and returns to the woman, sits down, and leans toward her.

46. Man: "How's your Hebrew?"

47. Woman looks down, looks around the lobby, grimaces. Man grimaces and looks at the front door.

XV. TOPIC-REJECTION:

48. Woman catches man's eye and smiles to him. Woman: "It's really nice here in the lobby."

49. Man: "Mmmm."

50. Woman stretches, spreads her legs, and looks at them. Woman: "It's nice here on Friday nights."

51. Man: "Mmmm."

XVI. PERSON-EXCLUSION:

52. Man leans back in his chair and looks at the ceiling. Woman is sitting upright, hands in lap, legs close together. First she, and then both, look around the lobby.

XVII. TOPIC-REJECTION:

53. Woman glances sideways at man. Woman: "Seems to be a lot of Russians coming lately."

54. Man nods and looks back at the ceiling.

55. Woman looks at her watch, around the lobby, and back at the man.

56. Woman says in an annoyed tone: "This dog keeps wandering around in here." Man does not react.

57. Woman: "Look at that girl!" She stares at the receptionist and laughs. Man does not react. Woman looks at the floor.

58. Woman: "Dogs have a better life than people." Man does not react. Woman utters a short laugh and looks around the lobby.

XVIII. PERSON-EXCLUSION:

59. Both are looking at the floor. Woman's legs are together, hands

folded in lap. Man pets dog and woman looks away. Man continues to pet dog.

60.   Man leans back and crosses his legs at the knees. He lights a ciga-rette. Woman is biting her lips and appears to be looking at man's shoes.

XIX.   TOPIC-SUBSTITUTION:

61.   Man looks at woman. Man: "They really have strange postal hours here."

62.   Woman nods.

63.   Both look around the lobby.

64.   Woman: "The *ulpan* [intensive Hebrew course] is really bad here, isn't it?"

65.   Man nods.

66.   Woman: "And apartments. . . really expensive here."

67.   Man nods.

68.   Both look at the floor.

69.   Woman: "It's really clean in here."

70.   Man: "Well . . . you bet it's cleaner than New York."

XX.   PERSON-EXCLUSION:

71.   Both look away from one another, at the floor, and around the lob-by. Man taps one foot. Woman shuffles her feet.

XXI.   INTERCHANGE:

72.   Woman looks at man. Woman: "How's your Hebrew?"

73.   Man shrugs: "Not too good."

74.   Woman: "It's different to be an *oleh* [new immigrant] than a tourist, isn't it?"

75.   Man nods.

76.   Both look at the floor.

77.   Woman: "Do you like dogs?"

78.   Man "Uhuh . . . I had a dog."

XXII.   PERSON-INCLUSION:

79.   Man and woman continue to sit. They look around the lobby. They exchange smiles. Man is slouched in his chair. Woman's legs are somewhat spread apart.

XXIII.   TOPIC-SUBSTITUTION:

80.   Woman: "Did you know that Sophie [a young immigrant living in

the absorption center] got engaged?"
81.   Man nods.
82.   Woman: I was in *Yaffo* [Jaffa] yesterday."
83.   Man: "I've been there too."
84.   Woman: "There aren't . . . many older single people in Beit Brodetsky [the absorption center]."
85.   Man nods.

XXIV.   PERSON-EXCLUSION:
86.   They continue to sit and look about. The dog approaches the man. Man pets dog. Woman looks away.

XXV.   INTERCHANGE:
87.   Woman: "The *seder* [Passover ritual meal] was very nice."
88.   Man: "Yeah . . . but the food wasn't too good."
89.   Woman: "Did you know that Joel Hirsch and Sam Weinflash [two residents of the absorption center] are going into business?"
90.   Man: "I don't know who they are . . . but if they're temporary residents they can't work."
91.   Woman: "That's not true . . . but anyway, they can't check on you."
92.   Man: "Yes, they can. They look at your passport."
93.   Woman: "But with all the bureaucracy here they'd never find out."

XXVI.   PERSON-INCLUSION:
94.   They resume looking at the floor and around the lobby. They smile at one another. Man's legs are crossed at the ankles. Woman's legs are somewhat spread apart.

XXVII.   TOPIC-REJECTION:
95.   Woman: "You know, the funniest thing happened where I work . . .They thought I was two different people. You see, sometimes I use my maiden name and sometimes I use the name I had when I was married."
96.   Man: "Mmmm . . . Well, I don't have any problems with name mixups."
97.   Woman utters short laugh.

XXVIII.   PERSON-EXCLUSION:
98.   They both look at the floor, at their hands, and around the lobby.

99.   Man stands up. Man: "Well ... it's getting late ... I guess I'll go up."
100.   Woman nods but does not otherwise respond. Man leaves the lobby in the direction of the living quarters. Woman also leaves after a few moments, in the direction of the reading room.

FORMS OF INTERACTION FRAMES

The frames which operate in this sequence have differential capacities to further the development of a congruent definition of the situation. In some frames the woman is more open to focused interaction while in others it is the man who is more available. At times the man is prepared to interact on the basis of a particular topic of discourse, while in other frames it is the woman who is prepared to interact on the basis of that topic. In certain frames the hearer becomes a speaker, thus extending and elaborating the consequentiality of what was heard (see Speier 1972: 409), while in other frames the hearer acknowledges that role, and the role of potential "next speaker," in only the most limited way, or completely fails to accept the role of hearer as allocated by the speaker.

I will now briefly discuss each kind of frame which appears in the sequence. These frames are: (a) person-exclusion, (b) person-inclusion, (c) topic-rejection, (d) topic-confusion, (e) topic-substitution, (f) narrative, and (g) interchange.

Person-Exclusion

One or both participants exclude the other. This is accomplished by beginning interaction with others, as the woman does in frame III, or through becoming involved in an activity which excludes the other participant, as the man does in frame VII, or by terminating contacts through gaze or smiles, as in frame VIII.

In person-exclusion frames there is no mutual openness to interaction, no topic of interaction, and no allocation of speaker-hearer or doer-observer roles. In this sequence such frames are predominantly silent, and have the least capacity to develop a congruent definition of the situation in terms of which participants can continue to interact. Nevertheless, such frames may accomplish important work by demonstrating that participants are not committed to focused interaction with one another until some common basis for interaction is established. In frame III the woman is, among other things, indicating to the man that she may be open to other, competing, offers of interaction. In frame VII the man indicates to the woman that he is prepared to be attentive to the dog rather than to her. Person-exclusion frames may also function as recesses during which participants can review their evaluations of the others present.

Person-Inclusion

In such frames persons indicate to one another that they are open to further interaction. In this sequence such frames are mainly silent, and openness to further interaction is quite limited since no topic of discourse is introduced and so no allocation of speaker-hearer roles occurs. However doer-observer roles are allocated and coordinated. This kind of frame is a minimal invitation to focused interaction, but it has a very limited capacity to further the development of a congruent definition of the situation since the negotiable properties of utterances and role allocations are mainly absent. For example, in frame II the participants exchange smiles and glances. In frame V the woman first gives the man a series of smiles and then performs what seems to be a quite intimate activity — she cleans her toes with a fingernail while the man watches.[2] The man seems to respond since in frame VI, for the first time in the sequence, the man interrogates the woman. In frame XXII the participants exchange smiles and their respective postures seem to be more open to one another than in other frames (viz. frames XVI and XVIII). The man is slouched in his chair while the woman's legs are somewhat spread apart. Then, in frame XXIII, the woman introduces the comparatively intimate topic (in the context of this interaction) of marital status. Again, in frame XXVI they exchange smiles, the woman's posture seems open, and in frame XXVII she introduces the topic of marital status.

I am not suggesting that there is a necessary connection between person-inclusion frames and subsequent attempts to offer topics which may serve as the basis for negotiations of a common ground of interaction, but I do suggest that the person-inclusion frame can prepare

---

[2]   If these actions of the woman had not been prefaced by her smiles to the man they might be more indicative of her contempt for the man, viz. performing such private actions before the man without visible embarassment. But in the context of the sequence her actions seem more indicative of an intimate invitation.

participants for such negotiations. Nevertheless there is no direct connection between the invitations proffered in such frames and topics introduced subsequently, and therefore negotiations about these topics of discourse can proceed quite independently of the invitation.

Topic-Rejection

Such frames begin with one participant including the other in focused activity through an utterance which introduces a topic of discourse. However all participants are not mutually open to focused activity around this topic. By introducing a topic of discourse one person self-allocates the role of speaker and allocates to the other the role of hearer. However the person addressed either does not acknowledge the topic as one on which to interact or does not in turn accept the role of "next speaker" (Speier 1972: 409), and so is not prepared to negotiate the terms of the topic. But in comparison with person-exclusion and person-inclusion frames there is a process of negotiation in topic-rejection frames, for by refusing to respond to a topic raised by the speaker the hearer is rejecting or questioning the acceptability of that topic of discourse and so indicates that if interaction is to continue a more suitable topic will have to be introduced. Because neither the speaker nor the hearer quickly substitute another topic the capacity of such frames to develop a congruent definition of the situation among participants is quite limited. Furthermore, in this sequence neither participant has either the power or responsibility to insist on a particular topic of discourse after topic rejection has occurred.

Topic-Confusion

In such frames participants are open to interaction, but the allocation of speaker-hearer roles is uncoordinated as each participant attempts to self-allocate the role of speaker without responding to the unrelated utterance of the other. So, in frame IX the woman begins to speak about dinner as the man begins to speak of imported cars. Confusion in the order of speaking connected to the sequential introduction of unrelated topics limits the capacity of the frame in developing the potential of a congruent definition of the situation. Nevertheless, in comparison to person-exclusion, person-inclusion, and topic-rejection frames, topic-confusion frames do indicate the apparent preparedness of participants to talk to one another at a given point in interaction, and so indicate that they are prepared to search for an acceptable topic of discourse.

Topic-Substitution

Negotiation in interaction begins to acquire more replete dimensions in topic-substitution frames where participants are mutually open to focused activity and coordinate the allocation of speaker-hearer roles in sequence. However, participants are unable to agree upon an acceptable topic of discourse. Still, unlike activity within a topic-rejection frame, verbal activity within a topic-substitution frame does not halt with the limitation or rejection of a topic, for another topic is substituted in place of the topic previously rejected within the frame. Thus, participants more actively search for an acceptable topic of discourse upon which to base their interaction. For example, in frame XIX the man introduces the topic of postal hours which receives only a limited response from the woman who then introduces the topic of *ulpan* which receives only a limited response from the man. The woman then switches to the topic of apartments, again receiving only a limited response from the man, and then to the topic of the cleanliness of the setting. The man responds verbally to this last topic, but with a change of venue to which the woman, in turn, does not respond. This active search for a relevant topic of discourse is also found in frame XXIII.

In topic-substitution frames the search for an acceptable topic of discourse begins to take on the fuller dimensions of a process of offer and response in negotiating a basis for interaction. While this search is largely unsuccessful, participants are apparently prepared to attempt to negotiate a congruent definition of the situation.

Narrative

In such frames persons are open to interaction but the topic of focused activity is controlled by the speaker while the participant allocated the role of hearer signals continued attention to the utterances of the speaker. While this permits the speaker to elaborate a definition of the situation this offer remains untested since the hearer can signal continued attention through simple movements and gestures without signifying agreement with the speaker's evaluation of the topic introduced. Narrative frames offer the speaker an opportunity to elaborate a topic which can

subsequently serve as a basis on which to negotiate a congruent definition of the situation; but such frames contain little negotiation about the
acceptability of topics.

Interchange

Of all frames delineated the interchange frame has the greatest potential capacity to develop a negotiated common basis for subsequent interaction. The interchange frame contains one or more exchanges of
utterances about a topic or theme of discourse. Such a state of talk requires that persons be mutually open to focused activity, that a topic
of discourse be introduced, and that there be a clear allocation, and
alternation, of speaker-hearer roles. In such frames exchange of information about topic or theme provides participants with the opportunity to evaluate more clearly whether their respective positions are in-
congruent or not. Thus responses of hearers are coordinated with
topics or themes introduced by speakers, and talk is about the same
subject of discourse. Again, I am not suggesting that such frames do
lead to the negotiation of a congruent definition of the situation, but only that such frames should have the greatest capacity to contribute to
such a development.

For example, in frame I the woman learns that the man is considering returning to his country of origin. She then learns that he is dissatisfied with something in Israel. Through repetition the man stresses this
topic and finds the woman unprepared to pursue it. The participants
discover that a particular theme, which I term "problems of new immigrants," is unacceptable to the woman at that point. In frame XXI the
woman, through a short exchange, confirms that the man finds his position as a new immigrant difficult. Then in frame XXV the participants
manage their lengthiest exchange of the whole sequence in which aspects of the problems of new immigrants are clarified. By this time the
woman is more prepared to talk on this theme and, while the participants discover they hold different evaluations of the theme, they come
closest to defining their positions on this theme through a state of talk.

Frames as configurations of interpersonal presence, topics of interaction,
and role allocation vary in their capacities to provide conditions within which negotiating a congruent definition of the situation can proceed.
So person-exclusion, person-inclusion, topic-rejection, and topic-
confusion frames have no or only limited capacities to clarify the

basis of a definition of the situation, while topic-substitution, narrative, and interchange frames contain greater interpersonal resources to be negotiated and evaluated by participants. That definitional congruency never does develop in the sequence, except in the most general sense of whether a state of talk exists or not, is irrelevant. Of greater significance are the organizational variations which the interaction develops and passes through with their varying capacities to further the development of a common basis for interaction among participants.

THE SEQUENCE AS AN ORGANIZATION OF INTERACTION FRAMES

A cursory reading of the sequence indicates that interaction proceeds spasmodically and this impression is borne out by the frequency with which different forms of frame occur. Fourteen of the twenty-eight frames in the sequence are either of the person-exclusion or person-inclusion kind in which no topic is introduced through utterances and no allocation of speaker-hearer roles occurs. A further six frames take the topic-rejection form and one the topic-confusion form. Then twenty-one of the twenty-eight frames have little capacity for negotiating conditions for a congruent definition of the situation. In contrast, one frame takes the narrative form, three take the topic-substitution form, and three take the interchange form.[3]

Moreover, the sequential emergence of frames does not indicate any striking shift in the frequency with which particular frame forms begin to appear. Such a dramatic shift would indicate that participants were more actively searching for a common ground on which to interact, or the opposite of this. Instead, no one frame form dominates the sequence. The pattern of frame emergence indicates a comparatively high proportion of attempts to initiate discourse by one or the other of the participants (mainly by the woman), but a comparatively low proportion of coordinated exchanges of utterances. In between attempts to initiate discourse there are lengthy pauses and, in fact, person-exclusion and person-inclusion forms occur in virtually every other frame in the sequence.

[3] Work in progress indicates that this pattern of frame distribution differs markedly from frame distributions in sequences of interaction between, for example, customs officials and clients where higher incidences of topic-substitution and interchange frames are found. In such sequences participants may hold quite disparate goals, but they are concerned to resolve their interactions in particular ways. Such resolution is most easily accomplished if a common basis of interaction develops, and so a congruent definition of the situation is more likely to emerge.

However, a closer examination of frame occurrence indicates an interesting development. Frames I-XVIII are dominated by configurations of interaction which have little capacity for negotiation. Of these first eighteen frames, fifteen (83 percent) take the form of person-exclusion, person-inclusion, topic-rejection, and topic-confusion, while only three take the form of topic-substitution, narrative, and interchange. Then, in frames XIX-XXV there is evidence of a shift. Of these seven frames only three (43 percent) take the form of person-exclusion and person-inclusion, while four take the form of topic-substitution and interchange. Thus it appears that in this latter phase the participants make a more sustained and coordinated series of attempts to find a common basis for their interaction. A further indication of this are the first appearances of quite explicit oral markers of agreement and disagreement which enable the hearer to more definitively evaluate the position of the speaker. So in frame XXI the man says: "Uhuh. . ."; and in frame XXV he states: "Yeah. . ." Later in frame XXV the woman states: "That's not true . . ."; and the man states: "Yes, they can . . ." In other frames explicit markers of agreement or disagreement are not produced; or such markers are quite ambiguous.

Thus even interaction which appears spasmodic and largely uncoordinated can be shown to contain thrusts toward congruency as participants attempt to negotiate a common ground for their focused activity. Such trends are further delineated through an examination of the content of utterances introduced by participants.

THE SEQUENCE AS AN ORGANIZATION OF THEMES OF DISCOURSE

Most utterances produced in the sequence introduce topics of discourse which can be negotiated and which can become a common ground for subsequent talk. These topics cohere around a number of major themes which I will term: (a) problems of new immigrants, (b) physical mobility, (c) social setting, (d) personal status, and (e) dogs.

I suggest that when a speaker introduces a topic this indicates the speaker's preparedness to interact on that topic regardless of the way in which the topic is evaluated. The hearer can refrain from acknowledging the topic, viz. by a negative response indicating that the hearer is not prepared to interact on the topic at that time; or the hearer may give a "limited" response to the topic introduced by the speaker, acknowledging its introduction (e.g. by a nod of the head) but leaving it to the speaker to elaborate on the topic or drop it; or the hearer may respond directly and "expand" on the topic raised by the speaker.

In terms of searching for a basis upon which to develop a congruent definition of the situation it is unimportant whether or not the hearer agrees with the speaker's evaluation of the topic, but only whether the hearer is prepared to talk about that topic. If a hearer is unprepared to acknowledge a topic it has little capacity to become the basis of a negotiated definition of the situation. Such a pattern of offer-response will be designated as (–) indicating that the hearer is closed to the topic at that time. If the hearer does respond to the topic introduced, but in an ambiguous and noncommittal way, the pattern of offer-response will have only "limited" capacity to become the basis of a negotiated definition of the situation, and will be designated as (?). If the hearer responds and exchanges information on the topic, his response will be considered "expanded," and this pattern of offer-response will be designated as (+). This latter pattern will have the greatest capacity to develop a common basis for interaction.

Problems of New Immigrants

This theme is introduced in the following frames:[4] I:2 (+); VI:21 (–); IX:31 (?); XI:34 (?); XIV:43 (?); 46 (–); XVII:53 (?); XIX:61 (?), 64 (?), 66 (?); XXI:72 (+), 74 (?); and XXV:90 (+). In frame I the man raises his unspecified dissatisfaction with Israel, but the woman does not pursue this, and the man does not elaborate. In frame VI the woman introduces the theme again, but links it to the theme of mobility which could open the way to more intimate discourse (viz. the woman lacks mobility in a public setting on a Friday evening); and the man does not respond. In frame IX the man pursues the topic of "car" as a straightforward problem of new immigrants, but the frame takes the topic-confusion form. In frame XI the man introduces a topic which concerns him as a new immigrant, but the woman's response is limited. In frame XIV the man introduces the new-immigrant theme again. The woman's response is first limited and then negative. In frame XVII it is the woman who introduces an aspect of problems of new immigrants, and it is the man's response which is limited.

Through frames I-XVIII the man introduces this theme on five occasions and the woman on two. The theme is apparently of interest to the

---

[4] The form of notation used is: frame number, colon, number of segment within the frame, pattern of offer-response.

man, but one which receives little response from the woman. Moreover, in the context of the sequence, it is a theme with little personal content which could further more intimate contacts between the participants. At first appearance the man seems to be limiting his contacts with the woman to impersonal topics.

However, in frames XIX-XXV the woman introduces this theme five times and the man once. In frame XIX the woman appears to try to approach topics which the man might be more prepared to talk about. Here she adopts a critical stance toward aspects of Israeli life which the new immigrant must face, an evaluation she was not prepared to express in frame I. Yet the man's response is only limited. In frame XXI the woman reintroduces a topic which she had previously rejected, and the man's response is expanded. She then restates the problematics of being a new immigrant and receives only a limited response. Subsequently, in frame XXV the participants engage in their most expanded interchange in which they express explicit opinions.

There is a high proportion of limited responses associated with the new-immigrant theme and a low proportion of expanded responses. Yet the participants are in the process of developing more open positions on the theme which in frames XXI and XXV become part of interchange frames. In view of how the sequence ends these developments are abortive, but the woman has begun to accept topics which the man has evinced some interest in and which she previously showed no overt interest in pursuing. She has also begun to evaluate the content of these topics more impersonally in the manner seemingly preferred by the man.

Physical Mobility

The theme of physical mobility, of movement outside or from the social setting is introduced in the following frames: VI:21 (–); XIII:37 (?), 39 (?); and XXIII:82 (+). Without attempting to infer the motivation of the woman in initiating interaction, the theme of physical mobility appears to raise topics related to the woman's overall interests in the sequence. In frame VI:21 the woman may be replying to the man in terms of "problems of new immigrants," but her implied lack of mobility may also be an invitation to him to provide mobility, viz. to remove her from a highly visible public setting to one with more secluded or intimate possibilities. Note that in frame VI: 20 the man's utterance is sufficiently ambiguous to be a probe about the woman's plans as a new immigrant, her plans for the evening, or her plans for him. Frame VI:

21 is the first utterance which could imply future contact for the participants, and the man rejects this.

However in frame XIII:37 it is the man who positively evaluates the "outside," but receives only a limited response. The woman reintroduces the theme in frame XIII:39 but without referents of potential intimacy connected to their presence in the setting, and she then receives only a limited response.

But in frame XXIII:82 the woman reintroduces the theme, without referents of potential intimacy, and the man responds to this "safe" topic in an expanded way. While the theme of physical mobility does not play a major role in the development of the sequence it does point up negotiations between participants as they discover the parameters of discourse which both are more prepared to countenance.

Social Setting

Topics related to the social setting of the absorption center are introduced in the following frames: IX:30 (–); XV:48 (?), 50 (?); XIX:69 (+); XXIII:84 (?) and XXV:87 (+). On all of these occasions the theme is introduced by the woman. Here again there is a trend toward a pattern of more expanded offer-response interactions, and the participants somewhat clarify topics which could form the basis for more expanded talk.

In frame IX the woman's reference to "dinner" in the setting is lost in the context of a topic-confusion frame. When the topic of food in the setting is reintroduced in frame XXV the man gives an expanded response. In frame XV the woman reintroduces the social-setting theme but with potentially more intimate referents. The man's response is limited. When the woman next introduces the theme with impersonal referents, in frame XIX, the man gives an expanded response. In frame XXIII the woman reintroduces the theme with potentially intimate referents and the man's response is limited. But in frame XXV her impersonal reference to the social setting evokes an expanded response from the man.

Like negotiations over "physical mobility," negotiations over references to the social setting indicate that the man is more prepared to expand talk on topics which have no intimate referents in the context of the sequence, while the woman attempts to introduce such topics, but is also prepared to switch to more impersonal topics.

Personal Status

The theme of personal status is introduced by the woman in the following frames: XIII:80 (?), 84 (?); and XXVII:95 (+). Late in the sequence
the woman introduces topics related to changes in marital status, and so
indirectly to the personal statuses of the participants. Such topics could
clearly have the potential to lead to more intimate subjects of discourse.
In frame XXIII the man's responses are quite limited. In frame XXVII,
after the lengthiest interchange of the sequence centered on problems of
new immigrants (an impersonal theme of interest to the man), the woman specifies her own personal status, and hence her availability. She
receives an expanded response which indicates that the man is unprepared to talk about such personal topics. Negotiations over "personal
status" result in a definitive rejection of the woman's attempts to develop a more intimate common ground for interaction, and reasserts the
man's preference for more impersonal topics.

Dogs

The theme of dogs is introduced in the following frames: IV (?); VII:
23 (–); VIII:25 (–); XVII:56 (–), 58 (–); XVIII:59 (–); XXI:77
(+); and XXIV:86 (–). This theme, which develops from the incidental
presence in the setting of a dog, comes to represent the incongruity
between the woman's attempts to negotiate a definition of the situation
with more intimate content and the man's attempts (although fewer in
number) to base negotiations on more impersonal themes.

   In frame IV the woman narrates the discovery of the dead puppy. The
man's response is limited. By frame VII the woman has introduced
the topic of physical mobility and received a negative response when a
dog appears in the lobby. The dog approaches the man (as did the
woman). The man pets the dog and the woman looks away. The man is
more open and responsive to the dog than he has been to the attempts
of the woman to interact. We might say that the man behaves as if he
"likes" the presence of the dog while he has been comparatively indif-
ferent to the presence of the woman.

   In frame VIII the woman repudiates the man's ongoing connection
to the dog by specifying her dislike of dogs. The woman may be inti-
mating here that the man will have to choose between focusing
on the dog to the exclusion of the woman or paying attention to the
woman rather than to the dog. The man responds by ceasing to pet the

dog, but he speedily resumes this activity. The man may be indicating that contrary to the wishes or sentiments of the woman he will continue to respond to the dog. He may also be indicating that he prefers to be responsive to the dog rather than to the woman. I suggest that it is over the dog that the participants establish the incongruency of their respective orientations to interactions in the lobby. I am not suggesting that this is consciously deliberated but that dogs acquire this representation.

By the time references to dogs reappear, in frame XVII, other themes have been more fully introduced into the interaction. The man has offered "problems of new immigrants" (frames IX, XI and XIV) with limited response; and he has offered a more intimate opening in terms of "physical mobility" (frame XIII). For her part the woman has attempted to stress the potentially intimate nature of the social setting (frame XV), with only limited response.

After a period without physical contact between the man and the dog the woman draws attention to the animal by stating, in frame XVII: "This dog keeps wandering around in here." The activity which has been proceeding in a desultory, inconclusive, manner has been their interaction. It has been "wandering" without their being able to clearly negotiate a theme which could become the basis for more coherent activity. The woman appears to be stating that the incongruency in their interaction continues to "wander" in the setting, unresolved, and impeding their contact. Moreover, she is the one who most actively attempts to alter this impasse.

In frame XVII, after failing to elict responses from the man, the woman states: "Dogs have a better life than people." The man has responded to the dog. The woman is a "person." The man has been less responsive to the woman than to the dog. Then the woman may be stating that, within the sequence, the dog is "better" off, or perhaps preferred to the woman. The man then begins to pet the dog once more (frame XVIII), speedily bearing out the woman's statement. As he has, virtually throughout the sequence, the man indicates that his responsiveness to the woman, if any, will be limited to impersonal topics. After attempts to approach the position of the man in terms of "problems of new immigrants" the woman seeks confirmation of the man's responsiveness to the dog by asking (frame XXI): "Do you like dogs?"; and the man confirms his positive affect for the dog, and by contrast the lack of such sentiments for the woman.

It is through the development of the theme of "dogs" that the woman receives the clearest intimation of the dimensions of the incongruity between the positions of the participants toward their interaction. In contrast to other themes considered the woman makes the least effort to approach the position of the man, and instead she uses "dogs" to express her dissatisfaction with the progress of the interaction, and to confirm the affective gulf existing between them in terms of negotiating a basis for a congruent definition of the situation. For the woman "dogs" becomes a symbol of the man's impersonal stance toward her in the sequence.

CONCLUSIONS

An examination of frames and themes shows the sequence not simply as an instance of desultory unsuccessful interaction, but as an instance of interaction in which negotiations between participants do not result in a basis of discourse upon which a congruent definition of the situation can be further negotiated. An analysis of both frames and themes enables the investigator to link the specific content of interaction to the organizational forms through which content is expressed, and to use both content and form to chart the degree of success participants have in finding a common ground for interaction.

For example, frames XIX-XXV have a greater capacity to sustain the search for a common basis of interaction; and it is within these frames that participants search most actively for common ground. The topics introduced in this phase center mainly around "problems of new immigrants" or around more impersonal aspects of "physical mobility" and "social setting." There is sufficient evidence to suggest that the phase of frames XIX-XXV is the apex of the participants' search for a common basis of discourse, and that the kinds of frames and kinds of topics occurring during this phase are the products of negotiations which have occurred earlier in the sequence, as the woman discovers which themes are more acceptable to the man and learns that the man is virtually unprepared to compromise on the thematic content of interaction.

I am not suggesting that the theme controls the form of frame which develops. Rather, topics are an integral component of the frame, and the frame operates as the medium through which topics, and so themes, are given expression. Thus the form a frame develops is dependent on the treatment given a topic, but in turn the extent to which this topic is permitted expression is a function of the form the frame develops.

Note that throughout the analysis it is unnecessary to specify what definitions of the situation the participants hold to. By indicating the pattern of offer-response between them, and concomitantly whether they are expanding or limiting their interaction, it is possible to generally avoid the problem of inferring the motivations of participants while recognizing that their negotiations do acquire some measure of directionality and coherence.

I would also note that this kind of analysis should be quite applicable to comparative research into the negotiating of definitions of the situation where variables like the nature of the social setting, time limits on interaction, and the overt statuses and goals of participants will affect the incidence with which frame forms occur, and will consequently affect the extent to which participants accomplish a congruent definition of the situation.

REFERENCES

BATESON, G.
  1972 "A theory of play and fantasy," in *Steps to an ecology of mind.* Edited by G. Bateson, 177–193. New York: Ballantine.
CAVAN, S.
  1966 *Liquor license.* Chicago: Aldine.
GOFFMAN, E.
  1963 *Behavior in public places.* New York: Free Press.
HANDELMAN, DON, BRUCE KAPFERER
  1972 Forms of joking activity: a comparative approach. *American Anthropologist* 74:484–517.
HYMES, DELL
  1967 Models of the interaction of language and social setting. *Journal of Social Issues* 23:8–28.
MC HUGH, P.
  1968 *Defining the situation.* Indianapolis: Bobbs-Merrill.
ROSE, A. M.
  1962 "Editor's introduction," in *Human behavior and social processes.* Edited by A. M. Rose, 3–21. London: Routledge and Kegan Paul.
SCHEFF, THOMAS J.
  1968 Negotiating reality: notes on power in the assessment of responsibility. *Social Problems* 16:3–17.
SCHEGLOFF, EMANUEL A.
  1968 Sequencing in conversational openings. *American Anthropologist* 70:1075–1095.
SPEIER, M.
  1972 "Some conversational problems for interactional analysis," in *Studies in social interaction.* Edited by D. Sudnow, 397–427. New York: Free Press.
WILSON, THOMAS P.
  1970 Conceptions of interaction and forms of sociological explanation. *American Sociological Review* 35:697–709.

SECTION FIVE

Language and the Science of Man

Analysis of a Culture Through Its Culturemes: Theory and Method

FERNANDO POYATOS

CULTURE AND CULTUREME

If we consider culture as a series of habits shared by members of a community, learned but biologically conditioned, such as the means of communication (language being the basis of them all), social relations at different levels, the various activities of daily life, the products of that community and how they are utilized, the peculiar manifestations of both individual and national personalities in their cultural context, its patterns and prohibitions, and their ideas concerning their own existence and their fellow men; if we think of culture in these terms, we realize that culture is made up of a complex mesh of behaviors, and of the active or static results of those behaviors.

No matter how much our world is shrinking, no matter how many common goals are recognized as personal and mass communication media develop, cultures, we must agree, are still different worlds in themselves, both physically and intellectually. In order to communicate we seek linguistic fluency, but around that core of language we need to build up other fluencies as well: kinesic, paralinguistic, proxemic, chronemic, to name only the broader categories (Poyatos 1972). We need, in sum, to attain "cultural fluency," and for this we must analyze a culture with a high degree of accuracy, decide what is universal and what culture-bound, contrast it with our own, and decide also which kind of observation, or acculturation, process we wish to go through, which type of communication we seek, how deep we want to probe into that culture, or whether we only aim at its general style. In fact the strategies depend on the specific goals of each particular field, since the study of a culture is an interdisciplinary enterprise, and any attempt at conducting serious fieldwork or research through only one channel, say, social psychology, would be most unrealistic.

On the other hand, we should choose, I believe, the cross-cultural approach, for comparison is, at any rate, inevitable. But before we try to discover even the general style, composed of the many distinct patterns that give it shape, we must take a bird's-eye view of a culture as a preliminary step, and then zoom through a progressive microanalytic process in which we need to categorize, hierarchize, carry out a real vivisection of that culture, establish zones where social life develops certain boundaries, systematize.

In carrying out this approach we realize that, at different points, we are, more or less strictly, adhering to the three dimensions of semiotic analysis: the pragmatic one, in which we observe the behavior of the individual and of groups in terms of signs with symbolic values; the semantic one, which concentrates on the cultural expressions and behaviors from the point of view of their signification; and the syntactic one, in the last stages of our analysis, by which we investigate the relationships between those behaviors or signs and how they are combined to form systems and classes.

First, however, I would like to propose a unit for the analysis of a culture, without which a systematic study becomes a very problematic and precarious endeavor. Adopting the linguistic structure, as has been done in some specific fields, such as kinesics — kines, kinemes, kinemorphemes, etc. (Birdwhistell 1954) — would unnecessarily complicate the development of the approach I am proposing. On the other hand, applying the cultural units suggested by Hall (1959) — isolates, sets, and patterns — which in some ways precludes the progressive analysis I intend to follow, is perfectly valid and we do certainly acknowledge this validity in the course of our study of culture.

I have called the proposed unit CULTUREME, and I would define it as any portion of cultural activity sensorially or intellectually apprehended in signs of symbolic value, which can be divided up into smaller units or amalgamated into larger ones.

This analysis of a culture through its culturemes consists of several phases or stages, through which a progressive analysis is carried out from a broader view of culture to an exhaustive and minute study of features.[1]

---

[1]   It has been argued by Amos Rapoport and other colleagues that one could not make the dichotomy urban-rural universal, nor could one establish a clear-cut borderline between those two cultural settings. I wholeheartedly agree, and I am grateful for such comments for they give me an opportunity to explain that I am applying my scheme, in a case-study fashion, to Western cultures, specifically to Spanish culture. However, I believe that the lack of such a dichotomy in many other cultures does not invalidate the proposed

PHASE ONE

Any systematic observation of man must take into account his environment. Most cultural patterns are not the same in the URBAN society as they are in the RURAL one. Not only as a social being — because of the number of rules, tasks, and levels he may represent — but simply as a living organism, man functions differently in each of these two environments, behaves differently and, therefore, shapes culture differently, communicating differently and displaying different styles. But, besides man himself, as a living being engaged in social interaction, what sets apart the urban and the rural worlds — both man-shaped — is their sensorial manifestations, the sometimes radically diverse ways in which the observers perceive them.

Both of these aspects, the living, organic one, that is man, and the static but highly communicative one, involving environment, offer the student and the observer of culture two domains: the EXTERIOR and the INTERIOR, the latter always more difficult to explore and scrutinize in a microanalytic way, because it takes a high degree of familiarity, never reached in the first stages of observation or acculturation.

Phase One, then, is carried out according to four BASIC ZONES: urban-exterior, urban-interior, rural-exterior, and rural-interior, which at the same time constitute the four BASIC CULTUREMES.

Through them a given culture identifies itself, although in a rather impressionistic way and more sensorially than intellectually, because patterns in social attitudes, certain ideas concerning the handling of time in the various personal relationships, or the deep cultural background of the display or restraint of emotions, are not so easy to discern at this early stage under normal circumstances. In other words, the newly-arrived fieldworker in Spain, for instance, will soon detect visually, the blending of offices and homes in downtown buildings, the abundance of peculiar signs attached to balconies (*veraneas, gestoría, oposiciones*), gigantic film placards above theater entrances, sidewalk cafés, open-door bars, black taxis and many small cars, heavy traffic and white-helmeted officers, proxemic behavior characterized by frequent physical contact; through olfaction, side streets will offer him the old crafts and trades (the smell of leather, wine, esparto, carpenter's wood and glue, etc.), fish markets and

---

fieldwork methodology, as one would adapt it to his specific culture and strategies. Within the urban physical setting we find, of course, the rural population drawn to the cities, not only as an outskirt belt, but mingled with the downtown urbanites. In that case we should decide whether we are interested, for instance, in their rural nonverbal communication repertoire, or in their new urban behavior, regardless of social status. By the same token, we can analyze the life of urbanites residing in the rural areas.

butcher shops, bakeries and dairy shops, etc. These sensorial manifestations, however, when observed in an orderly way, will prepare us for a deeper understanding of that culture by revealing basic features of a national personality and a specific life-style (*gestoría*, the agency that can expedite matters in a highly complicated bureaucratic system; *oposiciones*, the competitive examinations for a limited number of posts in specific areas; the concept of, and the attitude towards, bars, etc.).

PHASE TWO

After differentiating four distinct basic zones by means of an approach that still takes a broad view of culture, it becomes apparent that any culture that has reached a certain degree of complexity offers to the most novel observer two more broad domains in each of the four preestablished basic zones. These have to do with man himself, on the one hand — that is, the individual functioning in daily relations as a biologically based being — and on the other the environment, which not only shapes his behaviors, but is in turn shaped, "culturized" by those behaviors which become more and more complex as the number of social functions in a culture increases. These two large subdivisions of each of the four basic zones or basic culturemes, I have termed NONHUMAN and HUMAN, thus constituting eight PRIMARY CULTUREMES.

An analysis in terms of those eight still basic categories allows for an intermediate level of study between the comprehensive basic zones and the progressively finer presentation of the more specifying stages, already offering a deeper understanding of culture, beyond which, depending on concrete strategies, certain studies may not have to proceed any further. We might want to deal with urban-human-interior culture in Spain, without specifying the various settings (Phase Three), but concentrating on all those cultural or pancultural characteristics displayed by the people themselves, that is, the more "active" manifestations of a culture, in contrast with the more "static," man-shaped ones: proxemics in closed spaces, loudness of voice and other obvious paralinguistic features, the personal perfumed space, etc.

Here we feel the need to seek some kind of structural framework. We concentrate on man, but man utilizes different communicative modalities, behaves according to certain rules, and we can, for the sake of methodological organization, classify those human manifestations in several groups.

While it is true that we could apply the linguistic framework adopted by Edward T. Hall — isolates, sets, and patterns — we would not require units below PATTERNS (relationships between customer and waiter in side-walk cafés, the social function of the porches in the small-town square), although we would recognize certain SETS (the clapping, or hissing, for a waiter in a sidewalk café), but hardly any ISOLATES (the position of the hands in clapping for a waiter). In other words, at this stage we do not want nor are we prepared to focus on individual cultural patterns trying to categorize them and analyze them against a conditioning background, but we simply want to make a broad distinction between human and non-human elements. This stage can be experienced as part of the accultura-tion process, whether through systematic learning or through observation. However, we can apply two methodological arrangements:

1. The first one is the CLASSIFICATION BY TOPICS, either referring to set-tings (the street, the park, the bus stop, the sidewalk café), or to the social techniques (general proxemic behavior, dressing).

2. The other one is the SENSORIAL-INTELLECTUAL APPROACH, which I favor. We perceive culture sensorially (smells, sounds, kinesthetic ex-periences) and intellectually (use of time, employer-employee relationship).

As soon as we initiate a process of aculturation (a term applicable not only to an immigrant, or a diplomat, but to a traveller and to the serious fieldworker) we are also starting a process of sensorial involvement — which, as we find in a finer analysis, may vary considerably from one cul-ture to another — an involvement that develops in this order: visual — a-coustic — tactile (kinesthetic and skin senses) — olfactory — gustatory. At first we do not acknowledge any hierarchy or classification of sensory perceptions, but we simply "sense" them in a sort of cultural amalgam. At the same time our culturally shaped intellect begins to discern cultural patterns (after Hall's sets, of course), such as the customer-waiter rela-tionship just mentioned.

PHASE THREE

Phase Three offers a much finer analysis by breaking down each primary cultureme into as many SETTINGS as we can find in a given culture (the home, the church, the school, the bar, the restaurant, the square, some lacking in the less developed cultures) for individual study. Each one of them constitutes now a separate cultureme, called a SECONDARY CUL-TUREME, which, naturally, can also be approached, as long as it is feasible to do so, through the various sensorial channels and intellectually. At this stage, however, those areas of cultural perception are still viewed more impressionistically than analytically, that is, not as isolated provinces.

I hope that the rationale of this approach to culture is somehow justified so far. It is intended to work as a systematic progression toward a finer and finer apprehension of various systems (the home, the school, etc.), similar to the also progressive development of learning, or observation, in the acculturation process. To deal at the very start with smaller units would not only be unrealistic, but would hinder further analysis in many ways, because we would not consider broader areas first, and then, in a logical way, work through more specific compartments as our needs and particular strategies would demand. Certain studies of, say, the home (under urban-interior-nonhuman) would outline the layout of the rooms, the proxemic arrangement of formal and informal space, etc. Later, of course, at the very end of "visual perception," for instance, we could discriminate between foveal, macular, and peripheral vision, as perceptual modalities of one single cultureme, "visual culture in the home"; while still later, as a derived cultureme, an even more critical analysis could deal exclusively with peripheral vision as related to spatial arrangement, also as a separate cultureme in itself. In other words, I would not recommend the type of fieldwork that would bypass secondary, tertiary, and derived culturemes, for instance, in order to carry out a minute analysis of eye contact at the table between upper-class hosts and middle-class guests, without progressively studying first their kinesic behavior in such a situation (derived cultureme 1), their general kinesic repertoires (derived cultureme), the other visually perceived systems, such as proxemics (tertiary cultureme), and the urban-interior-human behavior of those two groups in the home as a setting (secondary cultureme).

It is at this level of secondary culturemes, however, that we begin to identify certain interrelationships among different cultural SYSTEMS and SUBSYSTEMS (paralinguistic, or kinesic, behavior in face-to-face interaction, proxemics and sex values, etc.), while some borderlines between various SUBCULTURES within the same culture, geographically as well as socially, begin to show themselves more distinctly. Both cultural systems and subcultures can be analyzed competently after Phase Four.

PHASE FOUR

Phase Four, in this progressive probing of cultural layers in search of signs — we must not forget that we are carrying out a semiotic exploration — is a breakdown of each secondary cultureme into smaller units; naturally, as we limit the span of our analysis we substantially gain in depth, and later both span and depth will be combined in the regrouping of culturemes belonging to each class.

Culturemes in this phase are TERTIARY CULTUREMES, and here the sensorial-intellectual approach allows for an even more systematic classification, because each sensorial or intellectual compartment is analyzed as a separate unit, e.g. urban-interior-human-acoustic: the home; or chronemic behavior in the urban home in Spain.

It is at this stage, when we have gone as far as isolating not only the various settings against which men develop a great number of behaviors at different levels, but also those behaviors — as we acquire more and more elements of judgement — that we, according to our specific aims, may identify, with a reasonable amount of accuracy, two important elements:

1. CULTURAL SYSTEMS. After observing, for instance, the urban-interior-human-VISUAL culture as reflected in the home, the school, the church, the cafeteria, the university, the theater, the funeral parlor, the barbershop, the supermarket, etc., we have enough material to deal with systems such as furniture, or proxemic arrangement of interior spaces across one whole culture. But this knowledge, let us not forget it, comes only after working through Phases One, Two, and Three.

2. SUBCULTURES. Consequently, the recognition of certain systems permits us to differentiate some subcultures, both geographically (horizontally) and socially (vertically). After studying urban-interior-nonhuman-visual culture in the home as one cultureme in different areas of the country, the differences and similarities will usually stand out quite clearly. At the same time, we will differentiate the interior of the upper-class home from that of the worker, or the richer and more harmonious kinesic repertoire of the urban classes from that of the farmer. If we acknowledge Hall's categorizations of cultural units, we realize that sets and patterns become more obvious: the types of chairs, or pictures on the walls, etc. (sets) that constitute certain rules in upper- or middle-class homes (patterns), while isolates (i.e. the material — brass, silver — of the typical "Last Supper" hanging in many dining rooms) would not generally be identified until later.

DERIVED PHASES

Derived phases come after this point, when, continuing our progressive analysis, we can once more break down the last unit we isolated, that is, a tertiary cultureme, such as urban-interior-nonhuman-visual, the home, into smaller ones, now focusing on each manifestation of that communicative modality, that is, visual. Following the above example, we will break it down into: clothing, kinesics, proxemics (previously included

Table 1. Analysis of a culture through its culturemes

Phase One		Phase Two	Phase Three	Phase Four	Derived Phases		
Basic Zones Basic Culturemes		Primary Culturemes	Secondary Culturemes	Tertiary Culturemes	Derived Culturemes	Derived Culturemes 1	Derived Culturemes 2
Urban	1 Exterior	1 Nonhuman	Home, School, Office, Classroom, Theater, Restaurant, Bar, Park, Church, Square, etc. (according to specific cultures)	Visual, Acoustic, Tactile (Kinesthetic, Skin Senses), Olfactory, Gustatory, Chronemics, Social Attitudes.	Clothing, *Kinesics*, Proxemics	*Kinesics at the table according to social class* Derived	*Kinesics at the table according to social class* Derived
	2 Interior	2 Human					Culturemes 3
	3 Exterior	3 Nonhuman					*Eye contact at the table*
		4 Human					
Rural		5 Nonhuman					
		6 Human					
	4 Interior	7 Nonhuman					
		8 Human					

Sensorial–Intellectual Approach
Visual–Acoustic–Tactile–Olfactory–Gustatory–Soc. Attitudes

PROGRESSIVE ANALYSIS

Synchronic—Diachronic

Cultural Systems and Subcultures discernible here

Conditioning Background

Biophysicopsychological									Sociogeographical				Socioeconomic				
Sex	Age	Hereditary Somatogenic	Physiology	Health	Psychology	Physical Medium	Socio-economic	Individual	Married Couple	Family Clan	Social Group	Geographical Variety	Refined	Educated	Modest Employee	Pseudo-Educated	Rustic

Note: Italicized words indicate sample culturemes broken down further into successive culturemes.

within a tertiary cultureme), each one being an individual DERIVED CUL-
TUREME. But kinesics, for instance, would specify the behavior in the living
room, at the table, etc., thus offering the possibility for finer further analysis.

DERIVED CULTUREMES 1 concentrate on specific areas of each derived
cultureme, as, for instance, kinesics at the table, which would refer to informal meals, or formal ones, according to the social status of both hosts
and guests. So, should we require more critical distinctions, we would go
into:

DERIVED CULTUREMES 2, as, for instance, kinesic behavior of upper-class
hosts and guests, or upper-class hosts and middle-class guests (a most interesting situation), or middle-class hosts and guests, or lower-class hosts
and middle-class guests; or vice versa. Formal and informal encounters
around the table would also display characteristic social techniques. In
addition, within each of the situations mentioned, we may want (backed
at this point by solid and systematic terms of reference), to concentrate on:

DERIVED CULTUREMES 3, such as upper-class eye-contact behavior at the
table.

For the sake of orderliness, within the area of human behavior, all D1's
may deal with clothing, all D2's with kinesics, all D3's with proxemics, all
D4's with chronemics, and so on.

It was pointed out before that each time we deal with a different cultureme, such as eye contact, it is possible to build up a whole CLASS,
including in this case: eye-contact behavior in exteriors as well as in
interiors, in urban as well as in rural environments, made up of carefully
and progressively analyzed segments at different levels.

All systems and subcultures can be exhaustively described. In addition,
the relationships between different systems, which began to appear after
the analysis of tertiary culturemes, can now be studied in great detail, as,
for instance: relationship between eye contact and proxemic behavior at
the table according to social status, in a given culture; relationship between
proxemics and architecture; relationship between kinesthetic involvement
and architectural style; relationship between peripheral vision and architectural style, etc.

Finally, any study of behavior and communication within the context of
culture must consider at all times, but very particularly in the last stages
of microanalysis, what I have outlined elsewhere as the *biophysicopsycho-
logical and socioeconomic conditioning background of the speaker-actor*,
shown in Table 1, against which each individual or collective behavior
must be weighed. Certain factors, such as age, sex, socioeconomic
medium, geographical location, etc., will present elements for finer and

exhaustive analysis, revealing, as they become discernible, individual, family, community, and national features within each communicative modality, from speech through object language to chronemics.

I trust that the validity of this methodological approach, particularly from the cross-cultural point of view, has been demonstrated, that this type of analysis — susceptible of being applied with logical and systematic flexibility — will be deemed practical for fieldwork and research at different levels, and, above all, realistic, because it is based on a gradual knowledge of human behaviors and environments.

REFERENCES

BIRDWHISTELL, RAY L.
   1954   *Introduction to kinesics: an annotation system for analysis of body motation and gesture.* Louisville: University of Louisville.
HALL, EDWARD T.
   1959   *The silent language.* Garden City, New York: Doubleday.
POYATOS, FERNANDO
   1972   The communication system of the speaker-actor and his culture: a preliminary investigation. *Linguistics* 83:64–86.

Sociolinguistic Considerations on Psychosocial Socialization: The Beginnings of a Theory of Verbalization

RUTH LEODOLTER and MICHAEL LEODOLTER

The central issue of this report is concerned with the category of the "speech situation." It provides a common framework for adequate presentation and analysis of social links and interactions from the point of view of the spoken language. This is discussed in the first short section. The development of the social and cognitive capacity of the small child (socialization), considered to be determined within the family by the specific structure of speech and interaction situations prevailing there, will be enlarged upon in the second section of this report.

1. INTERPENDENCE BETWEEN SITUATIONAL INTERACTION AND SPOKEN LANGUAGE

1.1. Critical Comment on the Concept of "Codes"

The term "speech situation" was purposely chosen in place of the more frequently used terms "codes," "style," or "register." For many reasons we do not think that the Bernstein concept of "code"[1] is appropriate as the central category of a sociolinguistic theory of interaction and socialization (c.f. Bernstein 1970; Bernstein, ed. 1970: 117–133). "Codes" refers to the speaking capability of the individual. However, in theory it also characterizes, on a psychic level, a verbal planning stage

---

[1] In a programatic manner, Oevermann (1972: 329) indicates some chances for developing Bernstein's (1970) code concept further. He prefers to differentiate between two versions of the concept of code: a "universal" concept to analyze the code-transcending situation which is characteristic of the individual's life story, and an "elementary" version for the purpose of investigating single codes relevant in one situation only.

determined on the one hand by the social structure of the situation, and on the other by the individual's perceptual capability in its cognitive aspects. Since assigning an individual code type to a single social level (in this case most likely the manner of speech) proved to be too general, Bernstein decided to modify his concept by making the development of the code dependent on the family structure, i.e. certain family structures are characteristic of certain social classes. Thus, in accordance with structure depending on status, the lower-class family uses a restricted code while the middle-class family, with a more elaborate code, corresponds to an individual-orientated social structure. However, how the development of such a code — which extends beyond the situation — comes about within the framework of socialization is merely implied. In individual-orientated families, decisions are based on language and thus can be questioned and discussed later. In status-orientated families, this is not the case: decisions are adopted in accordance with the power potential assigned to each role. Reasons for the decisions are not stated and decisions must be complied with unconditionally. Thus codes are to be regarded as a specific result of each particular social structure, arrived at through the socialization process.

Although we accept Bernstein's idea that social structure within the lower class is more likely to be characterized by status-orientated interaction and within the middle class by individual-orientated interaction thus rendering socialization different — we nevertheless maintain (a) that the differentiation between "status-orientated" and 'individual-orientated" interactions with regard to the interrelationship between the structure, the socializing familial interaction, and the psychosocial development of small children is too general and not sufficiently detailed; and (b) that, accordingly, the concept of two class-specific codes cannot properly be applied to socialization as a dynamic process taking place in dialogue interaction, nor has this abstract-cognitive standardization of codes been successfully applied to the analysis of other present-day interactional speech processes.

For these reasons we prefer the category of "speech situation" which is designed especially to describe and analyze interaction within the family. Cognitive, social, and speech developments are dependent on the structure and peculiarities of these multiple socializing interactions within the family nucleus.

1.2.   *Situational Interaction and Definition of Situation*

In our definition of the term, "situation" does not, as it might according to common sense, simply and vaguely imply "position" or "condition," i.e. "simple existence." Rather, we believe that this concept serves as a general paradigmatic category (just like the concept "interaction") for a preliminary standardized, but sufficiently specific, classification and systemization of social interactional processes. The term "situation" permits classification of interpersonal social action and interaction, i.e. of structures and functions of interrelated events in accordance with important characteristics. The conceptual definition "situation," therefore, comprises potentially interacting individuals. It does not refer in a reductive manner to general monologic or individual psychic processes in individuals. Rather, we visualize a model in which social exchange and interaction take place only when the potentially interacting partners ACQUIRE a common general view of the social situation relevant to action. This, however, is not assured beforehand. The interacting parties actively share (with regard to their social activities) certain dispositions to act with regard to situations and perceive the situational aspects of important and specific circumstances for joint action in the same manner.

The metascientific question now arises of how such a socioscientific classification of social action relations actually taking place can be tested and validated. We assume as a paradigm that the units which arise from the scientific work of classifying social interaction according to situations exist not only (as in the case of the natural sciences) for scientific observers and theoreticians, but we assume also that the participants themselves (i.e. in a manner of speaking, the objects) of this scientific (linked in social interaction) endeavor likewise perceive their actions with a uniform and classificatory attitude in accordance with typical interactional situations, and that each actively applies this approach in an individual manner. At the same time we share the metascientific understanding of the social sciences of Weber (1964: 15), Cicourel (1970), and Habermas (1969: 178).[2]

Therefore, people act under the impact of a situation which they themselves perceive. For them, as well as for the social scientist analyzing the situational interaction context, the social world is broken

---

[2] Typing and hypothetical assumption as advanced by social scientists have to be *sinnadäquat* [the quality of adequately conforming to the meaning of a concept]: "... that concepts in sociology have to be drafted by classifying the meaning possibly intended, i.e. as though action were in fact determined by such meaning" (Weber 1964: 15). Weber and the *verstehende* school of sociology make special reference to Dilthey (1970: 235). In this context Habermas' (1969: 178) interpretation of Dilthey is also of interest. Schütz (1962: 267-270) and Cicourel (1970) have paid special attention to the *Sinnadäquanz* of sociological models.

down into situational experience and interactional units: the specific perception of the situation by the participants influences their mutual interaction. In the case of successful interaction and communication, understanding of action situations (the "situation definition") must be in adequate agreement among all parties involved. Should the definition of the situation by the participants diverge in important aspects, we speak of problems in communication,[3] or else of failure of the attempt at interaction (Watzlawick et al. 1972). Definitions of situation [4] can only be adequately homogeneous if they represent GENERALITY, i.e. if they are conceived according to (social) principles transcending the individual and thus possess a validity and existence independent of the individual, and if they are generally sociocultural in nature.

This universal validity of communication symbolism and the culture-specific interaction pattern is not, as with animals, species-specific, fixed organically and physiologically in instincts, but is rather based socioculturally on the general medium of human language. In human speech the characteristic and essential principle of independence prevailing between a designated object (referendum) and a language sign (designatum) offers a potentially independent sphere of communication and interaction. This is how the forms of human speech can have an existence *sui generis* in various native tongues, imparting, on the one hand, the nature of a universally exchangeable possession and, on the other, of a sociocultural social phenomenon in the more implied sense of the term.

The general, sociocultural inherited speech and interactional forms can be broken down into various analytical dimensions: (a) grammatical functions and language structures; (b) the semantic-cognitive dimension of designation in communication; and (c) the emotional-motivational and, at the same time, value-defining and pragmatic dimension of communicational interaction (Morris 1970: 6).[5] Sociolinguis-

[3] Even though the analyses of communication by Watzlawick et al. (1972) are rather vivid and interesting, the authors confine their description of relational conflicts to the dimension of logicoabstract paradoxes (for instance "double-bind").

[4] "Situations" are generally regarded to be accumulations of environmental data. However, these data have to be interpreted SUBJECTIVELY in order to be perceived as "situations" by the individual: "I take a social situation to be a complex of objective data within a social frame of reference, a spatial and temporal structure delimited by a horizon of concomitant facts; this complex constitutes the situation to the extent to which it refers to the subject acting in a specific situation" (Dreitzel 1968: 152). The concept of "situation" thus refers to the manner in which the acting individual subjectively perceives the objective data of a social structure.

[5] In sociolinguistics, however, we never consider linguistic signs outside of their situational context (without which they do not have any meaning at all). We are establishing a link to "analytical philosophy" and to the concepts of Wittgenstein.

tics normally is involved with these latter two dimensions of language.

To sum up briefly, we have proceeded on the assumption that for interaction to succeed, participants must essentially agree in their social situation definitions. The premise for such agreement lies in the possibility of using human colloquial speech, verbally irrespective of the situation. This is done on the basis of the supraindividual and social universality and validity of their inherited culture-specific symbolism of language.

1.3. Interaction, Social Standards, and the Development of Identity

We now wish to develop these conditions of "coverage" for situation definitions as they are applicable to interacting individuals further and in greater detail. The interaction role theory provides a suitable schematic taxonomy[6] for adequately describing social action within situations and for an analytico-hypothetical understanding. Moreover, the interaction perspective is also useful for a theory of socialization as will be demonstrated in Section 2.

Situation role-acting is characterized by the fact that the acts of interaction actually occurring in situations are consolidated in a normative manner.[7] This means that observance of or deviation from standardized social patterns of action is subject to an emphatic and effective social evaluation. Individual behavior in accordance with the prevailing

---

Words acquire meaning only through regular USE. In none but scientific language is an attempt made to convey unequivocal meanings irrespective of context (Wittgenstein 1967: §§ 340, 419, 616; Kamlah and Lorenzen 1967: 64). In this context sociolinguistics could be regarded as the science (or the paradigm) of linguistics with the objective of investigating the *Sprachspiele* (as Wittgenstein interpreted it).

[6] Symbolic interactionism refers to the social relationships of the individual in a symbolic environment. This forms part of the tradition of Schütz (1962) and the *verstehende* sociology. A good summarization of the goals of interactionism is presented by Krappmann (1972: 20) with many data on literature leading further afield.

[7] Dahrendorf has delved into the normative nature of roles: "Social roles constitute pressure exerted upon the individual ... those who do not play their role are punished, those who do so are rewarded or, at least, not punished" (1970: 36). Interactionism contradicts the Dahrendorf concept by stating that society demands not only role-conforming behavior, but also requires that the individual be able to advance his identity in spite of the role played. The possibility of joint agreement on the interpretation of norms forms the focus of interactionist analyses (cf. Turner 1962: 21). In the empirical analysis of the descriptive capacity of defendants facing a court, R. Leodolter (1975) proved that the definitions of situational roles even of judges differ significantly even though it could have been expected that in such an institutionalized speech and interaction situation the playing of roles would be regulated in a normative manner.

rules for action is subject to positive sanction, whereas deviations will be subject to negative sanction.

The question as to which normative interaction pattern is selected by an actor from a socioculturally determined set of alternatives depends on the situation definitions of the interacting parties; if we reverse the argument, for situation definitions to be in agreement implies that a definite pattern is common to the participants and that they will, in fact, behave accordingly in their situational interaction.

From the point of view of the individual, the possibility of his encountering certain situation definitions and introducing them into interaction is in itself socially determined. This means that the possibility depends on his status, the positions he has reached, and on the — also normatively sanctioned — social expectations connected with this.[8] For associated with social position (e.g. class, age, sex, religion, race, occupation, family status), there are the social prerogatives of individuals, the prerogative to advance certain definitions *vis-à-vis* other individuals in interaction or to recognize these definitions and to establish a corresponding interaction relation. Therefore, status and position are characterized to a varying extent by only partially codified social rights. This means that they are equipped with a certain degree of power and the potential for levying sanctions against the other interacting partners. For example, with regard to interacting situation definitions within a factory, a plant manager has greater power and potential for sanctions than an ordinary worker and he has this power with respect to many other interaction situations in our society as well.

Individuals are not "social machines" who, due to the combination of their status and position roles (social identities), will AUTOMATICALLY determine situation role definitions. To varying degrees each role permits individual shaping, i.e. it has a certain "role latitude." The individual can only acquire a separate identity if, while following the standard rules of intercourse in his actions, he makes individual use of role latitude at the same time. In this way, he himself realizes, and makes clear to the other interacting partners, that he is not completely

---

[8]   Gerhardt distinguishes between status, position, and situation roles. Status roles are acquired during primary socialization, are subject to stringent social evaluation and cannot be renounced (e.g. sex, race, social levels). Position roles determine persistent and frequently repetitive relationships and have a firm place within organized society. Situation roles characterize typical normative modes of behavior in topical brief interaction stuations. The initial premises for situation roles are frequently formulated in terms of status and position (e.g. women must not smoke on the street!) (Gerhardt 1971: 167)). The fact that the style of speaking depends on the combination of status roles was proved in an analysis of bilingualism in Britanny, France (Dressler and Leodolter 1973: 45–58).

identifiable with a single situation role. Contrary to the concepts of well-known theoretical systems which describe role expectations as well-defined, with each situation delimited adequately by a single role, it appears that in a normal case the individual is exposed to various partly CONFLICTING normative behavior expectations. The capacity mentioned above for developing an individual identity consists of creating a certain detachment from a role, thus establishing an individual synthesis between the conflicting expectations of a normative social pattern.[9] Juggling his roles continually, the individual has, in his actual behavior, to opt for one or the other conflicting normative rules. At the same time (through awareness of other role possibilities) he has to detach himself in some way from the currently assumed action role. Possibilities for such overcoming of conflicts, "role distance" (detachment from one's role),[10] and other important strategies for developing an individual identity depend, among other things, on the primary socialization processes of small children. (Section 2 will deal with this aspect.) As far as the power gradient between participating interacting partners is concerned, the more powerful one has greater "role latitude." This means that he may deviate further from the prescribed normative rules of conduct without having to fear sanctions. As it is, the individual who is most powerful socially is the one who dictates the situation definitions. Not only can he behave more spontaneously, but he can also shape the playing of roles in a more individual manner. Therefore the person relatively more powerful socially, as well as the person who has absolute social power, has fundamentally better opportunities to develop an individual identity (even if in many instances this chance is not used and is only expressed diffusely in greater self-esteem and a sense of power).

We now claim that the capacity for dealing in a meaningful manner with conflicting interaction expectations in accordance with individual

[9] Krappmann's concept of identity appears particularly useful in this context even though it does not go into detail on the linguistic aspect of socialization: "He (the individual) should consider divergent expectations in his approach while maintaining consistency and continuity. He should agree to a preliminary consensus on the interpretation of the situation while clearly stating his reservations. He should strive for joint, unequivocal orientation in action through an identifiable presentation of his own expectations and indicate at the same time that complete agreement is not feasible. He should take his part in the interaction but express by this participation that he is also engaged elsewhere. He should make an impression of being reliable as a partner in interaction and demonstrate at the same time that he is also capable of different action, has acted differently and will again act differently in the future" (Krappmann 1972: 56–57).

[10] The identity-advancing strategies, particularly "role distance," are best described by Goffman (1971: 141).

needs is tied to their VERBALIZATION. In turn, this means that only to the extent that the individual's normative behavior expectations are verbalizable and can in fact be verbalized by him, can he actively come to terms with these expectations. On the one hand, a meaningful compromise is produced between conflicting expectations; on the other, normative expectations are differentiated individually and a certain detachment from them is established. In such a manner the possibilities for overcoming conflict, establishing detachment from roles, and discovering individual identity depend directly on the ability to verbalize.

1.4.   Interdependence Between Verbal and Nonverbal Forms of Communication: Concept of Verbalization

In the following we should like to develop the argument about this thesis and establish the connection between verbalization and the acquisition of an individual social identity.

Human colloquial speech comprises three levels of communication: (a) the cognitive verbal; (b) the action normative; and (c) the bodily expressive level of communication behavior (Habermas 1969: 204). In concrete interactive and communicative behavior, the contents expressed on various levels are INTERPRETED mutually (i.e. corrected, modified, delimited, and supplemented). However, the level of verbal expression is distinguished as one which is best elaborated in its cognitive aspects and the one most suitable for progressive cognitive differentiation and structuring of communicative contents. By verbalization as a mechanism for a meaningful discovery of identity and for resolving conflicts in the above-mentioned sense, we understand a process in which the motives of social action with respect to interaction are raised to the level of verbal speech; that is to say, they are made explicit. They are thereby developed from the dull, semiautomatic forced form of behavior control to a conscious, controllable, relatively flexible motivation and value hierarchy, subject to scrutiny in the individual's psyche. To put it more simply: only through a multitude of verbalizations can individuals become aware of their present motives for actions, of other possibilities for action, and of the consequences of their implementation. In addition, the possibility exists of actually deciding between alternative actions. This awareness of one's own motives for actions thus depends on whether the individuals are in a position to verbally express their motives for action. Table 1 outlines briefly the types of verbalization; their application represents the individuals' presuppositions for solving conflicting expectations and developing individual identities in interactions.[11]

Table 1.   Types of verbalization

Role or action	Expressions	
Personal desires	I hope I want to I should	I wish I expect
Social obligations	I must It is necessary I must not	I consider it important I am obliged to
Insights and attitudes	I know It is clear to me I believe I assume I am convinced	I understood it in this way I put it up for discussion I did not know I am in doubt I am not sure
Evaluations	I am in favor It is my right It is good (bad)	It is better (worse) It appears more important to me

As may be seen, the ready availability of such performative verbal expressions implies the following conditions:

a.   A comparatively constant and not very contradictory personal system of motivation and values is established, a process which generally takes place within primary familial socialization. It provides the basis for any meaningful resolution of conflicts and for discovery of an identity in the concrete interactions of the adult. In the real sense of this concept it therefore identifies him as an emancipated partner in interaction.

b.   The individual motives for action remain subject to critique and differentiation from the cognitive and ethical points of view, and this holds true of both the individual and his counterpart in interaction. (This is what we meant by "progressive cognitive differentiation through verbalization.")

c.   Since the performative expressions are especially well suited for striking balanced compromises as to situation definitions between interacting partners, they help the individual create comparatively rational and only slightly repressive social interaction conditions.

---

[11]   These types of verbal expressions do not coincide with Habermas' classification (1971: 109–114) since our paper does not deal with the classification of speech acts but rather with the verbalization of role and action elements. An act of speech is regarded as a social performance (Searle 1971: 38). However, such an act is only monologic in nature and applies solely to the constituent elements of a situation or a dialogue and not to the interaction within a situation as such. In addition, Habermas' categories are not attributable to important communicative situations in socialization. Within the framework of a theory of verbalization, performatives have great significance; this is due to the fact that these performatives make an understanding of a situation possible while at the same time acting as constituent elements in such situations.

1.5. *Verbalization and Interaction Situation*

Let us proceed one step further. The actual process of verbalization, like every social event, takes place in social situations in which the opinions and attitudes of the individual (who defines the interaction situation) are explicitly stated. In this case we are not simply talking within the context of a situation the way we undertake many other things within the scope of social environment; rather, through verbalization the socially normative conditions as such in which one acts or speaks are created or altered. Thus, in a semiparadoxical manner we ourselves, by speaking with each other, influence situational conditions.[12]

For this reason sociolinguistic theory has to analyze the conditions of spoken communication both within socialization and within actual situations of interaction; it also has to clarify to what extent the forms of verbalizing interaction may affect the initial social conditions of a normative situation-defining pattern. The theory must examine which social structures (i.e. interaction relationships and forms of communication) support or inhibit the important process of rational agreement on situation definitions by promoting or impairing interactive processes of verbalization.[13] The theory thereby supports the objective that communication and interaction be such that all normative elements of social situation definitions are verbalized by the interacting participants, and conflicts are synthesized into meaningful compromises. Thus the aim is the ideal of social relationships, based upon unrestricted verbal communication and free of coercion and repression.

2. SOCIALIZATION AS COMMUNICATIVE INTERACTION

2.1. *Arguments for a Sociolinguistic Theory of Socialization*

We will now discuss the various sometimes dissociated and implied

[12] This also holds true for verbalization in soliloquy, i.e. without an interacting partner. Psychologically speaking such communications are addressed to fictitious partners; thus only fictitious interaction situations are defined. This may, for instance, be observed in child play. During this phase of egocentric thinking children may play in a fictitious, self-designed environment with no one but themselves as company. The children's objects of nonverbalized imagination are externalized and projected into the external objects of play and into play as such.
[13] Lorenzer has defined speech processes within the psychoanalytic situation where the patient is relieved of his neurosis: this is done by verbalizing repressed drives involving a heavy load of conflict. However, the author does not associate his model with the "normal" interaction processes in socialization (1970: 72, 104).

opinions about the processes of socialization scattered throughout the first section more systematically and in an abbreviated form. Generally we have the impression that theories of socialization recognize language in the general sense as an important phenomenon in socialization. However, a theory of socialization as a communicative process and as LANGUAGE socialization has not yet been developed in detail. This section is designed to outline a preliminary theoretical premise for these important questions.

One often finds the term "socialization" used to designate all processes connected with the acquisition of basic qualifications for social action and communication. Opinions vary as to what is relevant to such basic qualifications of social action. This is not surprising in view of the fact that opinions concerning the prerequisites for individuals to act in a social manner are closely related to the various — partly mutually contradictory — paradigmatic categories of structure and function of interaction and social systems in general. A further complication in dealing with events from a sociolinguistic point of view arises from the fact that due to the nature of the subject matter the scientific disciplines of sociology, social psychology, psychoanalysis, and linguistics necessarily overlap.[14] Perhaps one single discipline of socio- and psycholinguistics, being developed now, will be capable of adequately conceptualizing a theory of socialization in connection with language and speech.

It seems to us that the theoretical system for analyzing socialization processes attempted by T. Parsons (cf. Parsons 1951; Berger and Luckmann 1966: 67, 127–135) is important in general; so is the apprehensive acceptance through symbolic interactionism and the interacting role theory linked primarily to E. Goffman (1971) and more recent authors. Therefore, the two contributions will be discussed briefly to the extent that they seem to be important for our research.

2.2. *The "System-Theory" Approach and an Interaction Critique*

From the very start of his life, the infant is engaged in various social interactions with the people who relate primarily to him. At first these people involve the infant as a passive participant in social action. In

---

[14] Stampe's models of generative grammar and of natural phonology uphold inherent concepts of the socialization theory. However, within the scope of this paper it is not possible to discuss the relative significance of these concepts.

Bruner, a protagonist of the genetico-cognitive action theory, tries to link his concept of the origin of language with the syntax theory of Chomsky (Bruner, Olver, and Greenfield n.d.: 55–95.

this way the child learns in specific phases to understand and accept the various behavior expectations of his parents. At the same time the child tries to set up (normatively evaluated) behavior expectations of his own; this takes place partly in continuity (i.e. by imitation) and partly by sudden identification (i.e. by identification in the more limited sense, as a consequence of highly affective conflict assimilation [M. Leodolter 1972]). As a result of the child's identification with the normative parental behavior expectations, a system is established in the psyche of the growing child based on forms of drive control, forbidding, on the one hand, certain behavior, and encouraging, on the other, forms related to ideal parental models (superego). There also exists a definite individual need and a motivation system which, in a complementary sense, is related to the psyche, to drive control.

T. Parsons (1951) maintains that there exist: (a) the unequivocal nature of role expectations; (b) the complete agreement between the interpretations of role expectations by interacting parties; and (c) the absence of conflicts and lack of contradiction, on the one hand, between the role interpretations of the interacting partners interindividually and, on the other, within the pattern of personal motivaion intraindividually (this is something Parsons considers necessary for a stable functioning of social systems). This constitutes the main point of the interactionist critique: the interactionists claim that the majority of social interactions are neither characterized by stereotyped or clearly-defined role expectations, nor are they normally characterized by identical role interpretations and need-structures that are operative as the result of the processes of socialization. To be sure, there are a few culture-specific normative behavior expectations (prohibitions and commandments) which determine very clearly, emphatically, and in a stereotyped manner the socially enforced behavior expected by parents (e.g. with respect to cleanliness, eating habits, force, property). However, this does not apply to most of the behavior patterns and traits induced in the growing child during socialization.

2.3. Structure of Interaction and Language Processes in Primary Socialization

2.3.1. The concept of "open interaction." We believe that even interaction relations of primary socialization in the family are particularly characterized by what may be called "open interaction."[15] This holds

[15] "The actor is not the occupant of a position for which there is a neat set of rules — a culture or set of norms — but a person who must act in the perspective

true for several reasons. In analyzing the interactional dyad mother-child during the initial years of the child's life (Spitz 1969: 140), we find that from the abstract and theoretical points of view the continuous multiple, interrelated, and socializing familial courses of action can hardly be related to reasonable, rigid rules and patterns. This is because social interchange, initially averbal in many instances, is strongly affective in nature on both sides and extremely flexible on the part of the mother. This interchange is oriented towards the needs of the infant, needs perceived by intuition. The infant's growing sensory perception of objects in the environment and the experience gained with these objects are based on this very important affective parental relationship during early infancy. In the case of a major disturbance in this relationship, severe retardation or even complete arrest of all cognitive and social development may ensue; extreme cases even result in retarded physical maturation, a phenomenon for which the term "hospitalism" has been coined (Spitz 1969; Bittner and Schmid-Cords 1970). Generally, during this period of life socialization implies rather spontaneous, flexible, intuitive joint actions characterized by a multitude of variations in momentary situational conditions, actions in which the infant increasingly assumes more active social situational roles.

2.3.2. *Language and socialization: types of verbalization.* Language has a special place in this process. On the one hand, language learning (development of language understanding and speaking ability with the corresponding cognitive and social results) is greatly advanced by a positive affective interaction with mother and father, proved among others by the work of Irwin, McCarthy, Bellugi and Brown, Lewis, and Flavell, among others.[16] On the other hand, it appears probable and

---

supplied in part by his relationship to others whose actions reflect roles that he must identify. Since the role of alter can only be inferred rather than directly known by ego, testing inferences about the role of alter is a continuing element in interaction. Hence the tentative character of the individual's own role definition and performance is never wholly suspended" (Turner 1962: 23).

[16] Irwin (1948: 320–323) proved that after the sixth month (depending on socialization) differences in the total number of phonemes a child uses will occur, and that after the eighteenth month there are even differences in the number of different phonemes within a unit of behavior. McCarthy (1966: 305–343) was also able to prove empirically the interrelationship between language learning and the mother-child relationship. In their observation of Eve, Bellugi and Brown (1972: 139–172) were able to determine to what extent the child's pivot sentences in terms of meaning depended on the speech situation. Although they did describe the continuous affective interaction between Eve and her mother, they did not, in our opinion, adequately stress the relative significance of these pivot sentences in obtaining successful speech socialization. Flavell (1966: 246–271) was able to prove that

plausible that the rate acquisition of this comprehensive, logically discursive system of symbols used by the infant depends on the extent to which the mother (or both parents) verbally articulates the various actions and situations as well as the objects and contexts, both factual and ethical, contained in them. To put it simply: It depends on HOW MUCH AND WHAT is discussed with the child during the continuous process of socializing interaction. Both conditions, affective warmth and verbal attention, are frequently found to prevail at the same time; however, this is not always the case and, depending on the social level, this may be expected to vary (e.g. in families of the lower social strata verbal attention in interaction seems to be slight compared to the affective warmth offered (Oevermann n.d.: 53).

Beyond these general considerations we should like to draw up a more detailed model of the linguistic processes of socialization. This model is then to serve as the premise for a theory of verbalization, as a structured and meaningful system for coping with speech situations. a.   The manifold socializing interactions between parents and child as mentioned above are generally accompanied by speaking. In addition to demonstrative actions, speech also has the function of denoting objects, initially simple ones. This applies particularly to objects which the child cannot handle directly because of distance in space and time and because of the resulting impossibility of acquiring sensomotor experience. Basically, however, this verbal conveyance holds true for all objects, the properties of which are transmitted to the child by the verbal denoting utterances of the mother and leading to the formation of a simple cognitive structure in the child. Thus, in the child a latent understanding for the simple predicative symbolic words of the mother is developed.[17] On the one hand, the child's cognitive relationship and the structure of the objects in his environment are centered around the verbal expressions; on the other hand, these simple symbols are then available for the child's own phase-conforming speech and for more sophisticated patterns of the language.[18]

---

greater linguistic differentiation leads to an increased capacity of a person to anticipate in a sophisticated manner the expectations of others. However, he denies a direct context.

[17]   Man's species-specific capacity may greatly expand perceptional latitude (i.e. the ability to differentiate almost indefinitely, depending on specific cultural aspects and on the symbols available in each language). Man's capacity of memory (i.e. the number and differentiation of structures) is also remarkably expanded by association with verbal language.

[18]   In symbolic play the child first develops a "private" language: he transfers verbal expressions and interaction patterns he has learned to elements of play. The child does so in a manner only he can understand (e.g. building blocks represent

b.   In addition to the simple denoting use of language the child, when addressed by the parents, experiences the verbal expressions as part of a certain logical and conceptual system. The more frequently parents render the logical and conceptual context explicit (i.e. the more often they apply verbal classification and hierarchical systematization) the better and more differentiated become the logical and conceptual understanding of the child as well as the corresponding abilities he acquires. The capacity for developing abstract thinking and for gradually progressive abstraction also depends on the afore-mentioned factors. In any event, it takes about eight years until this system of abstract and logical classification conforms to reality.

c.   This also holds true for the various cognitive types of relationships: temporal, causal, final, conditional, and consecutive (Bruner, et al. n.d.: 135–222). In every language specific to a culture, these relationships are structurally linked to certain words and grammatical patterns. The more often the mother uses these words or patterns and presents the environment to the child couched in terms of these relationships, the sooner will the child understand these environmental relationships in their cognitive significance and establish them actively as part of his own cognitive processes. Thus the child does not experience the environment simply as an object acting upon him. The explanations conveyed enable the child to use the intellect as an instrument for perception and action, and the child is thus provided with an active, subjective potential to comprehend these relationships and events. In addition, explanations of such relationships tend to relieve major symptoms of severe anxiety and insecurity.

d.   The world surrounding the child in the process of socialization is not merely structured according to physical and logical patterns, but, in a more restricted sense, is also structured according to emotional and social elements, i.e. from the motivational point of view. This implies that the mother conveys to the child, verbally as well as in other ways, her motivations for different types of actions which are more or less standardized by society and approved by society to varying degrees. From these communications the child develops an image of likely social motives for action as related to interaction and for needs to be fulfilled. What we have termed the SOCIAL SET OF VALUES is character-

---

persons of the environment). Once the rule replaces the symbol (i.e. play proceeds according to rules), the child has been socialized into the adult world. The "private" language becomes "public." Play according to rules still imparts sensomotor and intellectual satisfaction but this satisfaction has become legitimate and is subject to a system of values, to a set of ethical rules (Piaget 1969: 151, 207).

istic of these verbal presentations and explanations of parental intentions and motives; depending on their nature, these values are assigned to desired, sanctioned, or prohibited courses of action. Using averbal means of communicating the rating of values,[19] but also — and this is important — verbal manifestations of emotional and social values and classifications,[20] the mother confronts the child with a more or less constant system of values and motivations, a system consistent and flexible within its own frame of reference. The child accepts these manifold action-motivating assessments and their assigned rating and, by identification, establishes part of his own motivational pattern.

However, there is an important difference between the consequences of verbal and of averbal forms of communicating values. Whereas the verbal ones are potentially subject to cognitive processing and classifying on the part of the persons in the process of socialization (i.e. they are subject to critical approach, modification, refutation, and checking for inconsistencies), the averbal types of sanction have a directly affective impact: as they need not be explained, there is no reasoning and no cognitive process required on the part of the recipient. The more motivations and social duties (including their emotional impacts) are conveyed verbally by the reference persons, the more we may expect the structuring and development of a consistent hierarchy of values by the young people which is subject to verification and rather specific and flexible in its application. Moreover, the young person is expected to set up in his own mind a corresponding control system regarding his own actions.[21]

2.4.   *Reflexive Family Communication and Formation of Identity*

In specific verbal socializing interaction, the levels differentiated analytically in points a to d above constantly interact. If we assume the considerations about verbalization in section 1 constitute the individual premise for detachment from roles, coping with conflicts, and formation

---

[19]   Positive expressions include expressions of joy, satisfaction, love, tenderness, affection, and actions with corresponding symbolic values while negative expressions include anger, despisal, abomination, and sanctioning acts of punishment in the limited sense of the term.

[20]   Positive expressions include "you may," "you should," "that is good," "you are good (pretty, nice, etc.)," while negative expressions include "you mustn't," "that is prohibited (bad, evil, mean)."

[21]   Miller and Swanson (1966) demonstrated that averbal sanctions inhibit the ability to cope with conflicts later in life.

of individual identity, we have to discuss which of the parents' inter-action and language structures advance the development of the ability to verbalize. So far we have primarily considered the family speech situation a socializing factor from the point of view of the specificity and structure of the speech interaction patterns of the primary reference persons. Now we should remember that every communication and inter-action takes place basically in a dialogue situation: the children's language socialization pattern does not merely constitute a more or less perfect image of the language structure of the mother (or parents) but, starting with the earliest stages, the child is a potentially inde-pendent individual in his interaction with his father and mother, even though no one but the parents socialize the child.

The more this independence, particularly from the emotional aspect, is accepted by the parents, the more the child will have the chance to develop a reasonable individual identity. Such acceptance of the child's separateness and individuality must be expressed in conversational in-teraction. This is manifested in a sympathetic and relatively tolerant attitude toward spontaneity, individual modifications and deviations on the part of the child, and, equally important, in the ability of the parents to practice METALINGUISTIC COMMUNICATION in their joint interaction with the child. Thus, time and again they have to establish a verbal consensus in defining the specific interaction, and these defi-nitions must be designed so as not to impose parental superiority on the child. In these metalinguistic REFLEXIVE COMMUNICATIONS the child, guided by the parents, assumes a fundamentally independent and indi-vidual role. No one can force the child to accept a consensus in the proper sense of the term, and agreement depends upon the child as an individual. In this metalinguistic communication in interaction situa-tions, in many instances the reference persons doing the socialization use expressions and questions that we have already mentioned in the section about types of verbalization. It is important to once more present a summary of these expressions, this time not so much from the point of view of individual definitions of situations but rather from the aspect of SOCIALIZING interaction and communication (see Table 2). We should like to term the expressions in Table 2 "identity-promoting expressions" or "reflexive performatives." It is to be noted that the reflexive use of such expressions has three consequences with respect to socialization.

First, they serve to define the various interaction situations existing between parents and child without applying pressure. They serve to verbally establish a temporary specific situational interaction structure

Table 2.   Socializing expressions

Are you sure that	But I have told you that
I know already that	If I have understood you correctly
I do not doubt that	Just think
You may be sure that	I guess you just did not feel like it
I understand you	Don't you want to
I believe you	Shouldn't we
I trust you	Unfortunately we have to
Just imagine	Why didn't you
It will work out	You should have done it

with certain goals and purposes. If such metacommunicative information refers to communicative interactions already past, it may be used to define more closely its structures and norms for both partners in the interaction process (i.e. for the child and the parents) and reveal misunderstandings, differences in approach, criticism, etc.

Second, at the same time the use of such metalinguistic communication methods, first by the parents, imparts to the child an instrumentarium which may be used independently and individually with respect to all interactions, even the socializing ones. The child may make use of them depending on his own stage of cognitive or linguistic development. The child is thus able to develop an individual identity through subjective relativization even of his own actions and the child also develops a new cognitive dimension in establishing social relations and social situations.

Finally, on the level of social ACTION, mastery in using performatory reflexive idioms acquired through adequate socialization is demonstrated by (a) greater flexibility in performing interactional roles; and (b) expansion and better individual utilization of the latitude allowed by these roles, through the process of detaching oneself from the roles manifested in the capacity of relating an interactional role adopted through communicative reference to other possible roles. Furthermore, (c) it was precisely the interactionist critique of the metatheoretical model which demonstrated that, in general, role expectations do not agree clearly or without conflict; nor do they at first coincide with the motivational patterns of those involved. Rather, the individuals involved are permanently faced with conflicting role expectations and inter- and intraindividual conflicts within interaction-wise definitions of situations. The child in the process of socialization learns and practices these types of communication precisely by means of reflexive performatives used within the scope of socialization — as part of the multitude of metalinguistic family communications.

Thus the child continues to acquire greater capacity to cope with conflicts and to reach meaningful compromises in situational definitions — between individuals without force or repression as well as within himself without the need to develop neurotic defense mechanisms.

2.5. *Some Observations about the Significance of Play in Childhood for the Purpose of Language Learning and Socialization*

In conclusion we should like to set down a final programmatical assertion for which, however, we are within the scope of this paper not in a position to state a well-conceived argument. We believe that simple linguistic socialization as well as metalinguistic verbalizing socialization can only be achieved in a specific interaction milieu, i.e. in an atmosphere of play interaction.[22]

In playing the emphasis is placed on imagination, spontaneous desires and decisions, as well as on the voluntary action of those engaged in playing. Reality recedes into the background: it is typical for play that decisions adopted and actions taken during play are valid only within the scope of playing. Generally we differentiate between "play" and "reality." In principle it is quite possible for the individual to interrupt play through outside metalinguistic communication, provided he or she has a mastery of these metalinguistic forms.

Many authors assume that play constitutes an important anthropological root of language[23] and that from the ontogenetic point of view play is an important medium of language development (Piaget 1969). In addition, the babbling of the infant is regarded as the first type of active play on the part of the child (Lewis 1970: 25–26). We are also of the opinion that uninhibited and pleasant playing activity, based on voluntary action, satisfaction, and spontaneous imagination, lends itself particularly well to socialization by means of spoken language — also as far as the formation of metalinguistic communication symbols of

[22] The inspiration for this section was derived from Wagner's "Die Grundlagen des 'forschenden Unterrichts' " (1973).

[23] Gehlen considers play one of the basic forms of human expression: "The attraction of play consists in persisting, spontaneous interest as long as interaction continues. It is quite wrong to consider the motivation for play solely an interest in the above-mentioned 'serious' achievements, such as learning of movements, etc. Play is unhampered in its possibilities and the joy of playing is the joy of creative development, of manifesting different incentives of changing context and goals, and without defined necessity" (1971: 207).

agreement on definitions of situation is concerned. Successful linguistic socialization with respect to the category of the speech situation implies that in appropriate speech situations and social conditions the child will, while playing, acquire a rich and flexible vocabulary skillfully designed in its cognitive aspects, which will also enable the child to verbally define social interaction situations and to cope with social conflicts by verbalization. Thus, rigid interaction relationships may be transformed into quasi-play speech situations which may then be raised by the subjects to a level of communication that is free from repression and coercion, to a "genuine" social consensus.

REFERENCES

BELLUGI, U., R. BROWN
   1972   "Drei Prozesse beim Erwerb der Syntax durch das Kind," in *Neue Perspektiven in der Erforschung der Sprache*. Edited by E. Lenneberg, 139–172. Frankfurt: Suhrkamp.
BERGER, R., R. LUCKMANN
   1966   *The social reconstruction of reality*. Harmondsworth: Penguin.
BERNSTEIN, B.
   1970   "Some sociological determinants of perception: an inquiry into subcultural differences," in *The sociology of language*. Edited by J. Fishman. The Hague: Mouton.
BERNSTEIN, B., *editor*
   1970   "Familiales Rollensystem, Kommunikation und Sozialisation," in *Soziale Struktur, Sozialisation und Sprachverhalten*. Amsterdam.
BITTNER, G., E. SCHMID-CORDS
   1970   *Erziehung in früher Kindheit*. Berlin: Luchterhand.
BRUNER, J., R. OLVER, P. GREENFIELD
   n.d.   *Studien zur kognitiven Entwicklung*. Stuttgart: Klett.
CICOUREL, A. V.
   1970   *Methode und Messung in der Soziologie*. Frankfurt: Suhrkamp.
DAHRENDORF, R.
   1970   *Homo sociologus*. Cologne: Fischer.
DILTHEY, W.
   1970   "Erleben, Ausdruck und Verstehen," in *Der Aufbau der geschichtlichen Welt in den Geisteswissenschaften*. Frankfurt: Suhrkamp.
DRESSLER, W., R. LEODOLTER
   1973   Sprachbewahrung und Sprachtod in der Bretagne. *Wiener Linguistische Gazette* 3:45–58.
DREITZEL, H. P.
   1968   *Die gesellschaftlichen Leiden und das Leiden an der Gesellschaft*. Stuttgart: Klett.
FLAVELL, J.
   1966   "The development of the two related forms of social cognition: role-taking and verbal communication," in *Perceptual development*

in children. Edited by A. Kidd and J. Rivoire, 246–271. New York: International Universities Press.

GEHLEN, A.
1971   *Der Mensch.* Frankfurt: Suhrkamp.

GERHARDT, U.
1971   *Rollenanalyse als kritische Soziologie.* Berlin: Luchterhand.

GOFFMAN, E.
1971   *The presentation of self in everyday life.* Harmondsworth: Penguin.

HABERMAS, J.
1969   *Erkenntnis und Interesse.* Frankfurt: Suhrkamp.
1971   "Vorbereitende Bemerkungen zu einer Theorie der kommunikativen Kompetenz," in *Theorie der Gesellschaft oder Sozialtechnologie.* Edited by J. Habermas and N. Luhmann, 109–114. Frankfurt: Suhrkamp.

IRWIN, D.
1948   "The effect of family occupational status and the age on sound frequency. *Journal of Speech and Hearing Disorders* 13:320–323.

KAMLAH, W., P. LORENZEN
1967   *Logische Propädeutik.* Mannheim: Bibliographisches Institut Hochschultaschenbücher.

KRAPPMANN, L.
1972   *Soziologische Dimensionen der Identität.* Stuttgart: Klett.

LEODOLTER, M.
1972   "Psychosexuelle Differenzen in der Geschlechtsrollenidentifizierung." Unpublished manuscript. Vienna.

LEODOLTER, R.
1975   *Das Sprachverhalten von Angeklagten bei Gericht.* Kronberg: Scriptor.

LEWIS, H.
1970   *Sprache, Denken und Persönlichkeit im Kindesalter.* Dusseldorf: Schwann.

LORENZER, A.
1970   *Sprachzerstörung und Rekonstruktion.* Frankfurt: Suhrkamp.

MC CARTHY, D.
1966   "Affective aspects of language learning," in *Perceptual development in children.* Edited by A. Kidd and J. Rivoire, 305–343. New York: International Universities Press.

MILLER, D., G. SWANSON
1966   *Inner conflict and defense.* New York: Schoken Books.

MORRIS, C.
1970   *Foundation of the theory of signs,* volume 1(2):6. Chicago: University of Chicago Press.

OEVERMANN, U.
n.d.   "Schichtspezifische Formen des Sprachverhaltens und ihr Einflusz auf die kognitiven Prozesse," in *Sozialisation und Sprachbarrieren.* Edited by H. Roth and U. Oevermann. Private edition.
1972   *Sprache und soziale Herkunft.* Frankfurt: Suhrkamp.

PARSONS, T.
1951   *The social system.* Glencoe: Free Press.
PIAGET, J.
1969   *Nachahmung, Spiel und Traum.* Stuttgart: Klett.
SEARLE, J.
1971   *Sprechakte.* Frankfurt: Suhrkamp.
SCHÜTZ, A.
1962   *Der sinnhafte Aufbau der sozialen Welt.* Vienna: Springer.
SPITZ, R.
1969   *Vom Säugling zum Kleinkind.* Stuttgart: Klett.
TURNER, R.
1962   "Role-taking: process versus conformity," in *Human Behavior and Social Processes.* Edited by Arnold Rose. Boston: Houghton Mifflin.
WAGNER, I.
1973   "Die Grundlagen des 'forschenden Unterrichts' im kindlichen Spiel." Unpublished manuscript. Vienna.
WATZLAWICK, P., J. BEAVIN, D. JACKSON
1972   *Menschliche Kommunikation.* Stuttgart: Huber.
WEBER, M.
1964   *Wirtschaft und Gesellschaft.* Tübingen.
WITTGENSTEIN, L.
1967   *Philosophische Untersuchungen.* Frankfurt: Suhrkamp.

The Contribution of Romanian Cultural-Linguistic Anthropology to the Complex Study of Modern Populations

ION OPRESCU

During the period when classical anthropology investigated small communities of savage people, it inevitably viewed them from the outside and, at the same time, approached them as whole phenomena, which is a very important point of view. The ascertained facts were placed almost entirely outside the sphere of the "habitué," ranging from the physical constitution to the social organization and language. The novelty of the material led to very vivid interpretations and to comparisons, all the more interesting since correlations could usually be established between the obtained results. This way, starting from mere information, one could reach a thorough knowledge of those communities.

Present-day anthropologists investigating the so-called modern cultures and the peoples belonging to these cultures are, in fact, standing apart from their own cultures and populations. At the same time, these cultures and populations constitute an object of study and investigation for the social and human sciences; these sciences, due to their extremely diversified and specialized character offer an endless amount of INFORMATION about man, and are even able to mislead the anthropologist. Numerous data, having also the value of specialized information, may be obtained by the anthropologist thanks to his own investigating activity, which often doubles the effort of the social and human sciences, thus increasing the amount of information and, at the same time, rendering more difficult the handling of extensive material. The confusion seems to be accentuated by the fact that this information is very often contradictory (some people may characterize a man as silent, since he was silent when they saw him; other people, on the contrary, may say he is restless, as he was restless when they met him). This is the so-called anthropological paradox (Săhleanu 1971).

If we also take into account the rapid changes, which are sometimes very deep, taking place nowadays in all forms of human existence in the whole world, we then understand better the necessity for drawing the entire amount of information existing into a systemic prospect (Săhleanu 1970). This implies assimilating the information from an anthropological point of view, which means a significant integration of the results of the research on:

a.   human formation and evolution;

b.   the dialectics existing between the biological, the social and the cultural;

c.   the abolition of the borders separating the scientific domains and an opening of the no-man's-land zones between the disciplines.

It is in this way that the accumulated INFORMATION is converted into KNOWLEDGE — one of the fundamental aims of anthropology. We must also stress the fact that there are certain aspects of the human which only anthropology is able to set forth, because:

a.   it is an interdisciplinary science and a science of synthesis;

b.   it significantly integrates the results in the above mentioned areas.

Man's knowledge means that he at the same time creates and continuously improves a certain language of organization which can be used as efficiently as possible in a medium of dynamic changes (Jantsch 1970). What then is the territory of cultural-linguistic anthropology, what is its working material, what are the problems and the questions this discipline must elucidate, what is the contribution this science is expected to make and, finally, what is it generally expected to produce?

Cultural-linguistic anthropology is a branch of anthropology; it aims at investigating all the communication tools by means of which the human reality is transmitted from childhood to death, from man's appearance on earth through his evolution. The questions then are: how these tools correspond, develop, deteriorate, alter, improve; how they are used, adopted, eliminated, invented; and why?

Human means of communication are either a system of specifically human elements (language, mime, etc.) or a system of elements created by man, having a cultural value (which is implicitly social), with a large sphere of action in time and space, expressing directly or indirectly certain meanings (with cultural-historical value and variability) useful for establishing contact between individuals or human groups at the same time and in the same space, as well as for establishing contacts in a different time and space (near or remote). The human means of communication convey the most usual and current meanings in daily life; however, at the same time they convey the cultural significance of events, either through folklore, legends, and popular productions, or through less spontaneous means such as history, science and art.

A funeral stele, a cult object, a monument or a work of art had a certain meaning for those who created them, but may have another meaning for us. We do not always know exactly what the creator wanted to transmit; we do not know if some part of the meaning got lost; but anyway, in such cases we tend to extract much more significance than was perhaps intended by the creators.

The meaning round which human means of communication are centered is the DESIRE to communicate and to cooperate. Human society would not have appeared, existed and developped without interhuman communication. Human means of communication are a human creation and a specifically human domain of manifestation. There is a perpetual communication between epochs and between generations. The human means of communication act like a nervous system within human culture and society. They establish both synchronic and diachronic connections, direct or crossed relations between near or remote epochs and places, achieving an immense dialogue on different planes, in time and in space. The human means of communication maintain and develop the cohesion of the entire human culture. They appeared with man; they evolve and develop more rapidly or more slowly, adapt themselves, change, becoming increasingly complex along with man and his evolution. The interaction and the cooperation within social life mean a continuous process of adaptation and revision, hence a permanent dynamic of the human means of communication.

Disorder of human communication occurs either spontaneously (as if being taken ill) or deliberately (an artificial change of the meaning of events, of the behavior of words) as a flagrant interference in the social metabolism or as a result of the wish to dominate, by a false communicational conditioning.

Communication means diversification. Communication does not depend only on the capacity of verbal expression, but it also depends on the ability to hear, to perceive (strictly or figuratively speaking), and the capacity to receive and decipher the intercepted signals and messages.

The transfer of meanings from one man to another, from one group to another, from one region to another, from a time remote in the past to a present one, achieved through communication, signifies the personal imprint of the individual group, place and/or time of the transferred meaning, which usually undergoes certain changes and receives new touches while preserving its essence unaltered (but not always).

Every man is a unique and inimitable individual. Nature's effort to create individuals is evident in the elements by which we can characterize and single out one person: hair, eyes, palm prints, lip prints, voice (sonogram), writing (graphology), chemical signs (having a biological value). Man, integrated into society since birth, aims consciously or unconsciously to distinguish himself within the society too. As if the genetic marks he was given were not enough for him, he continues his play of the infinite diversity in nature by means of what society has put at his disposal, in our case the means of communication. Each man speaks in his own way. Each family speaks in a certain way (a "language"). Slang is a whole complex means of communication proper to a particular social-moral category.

The means of communication are the intersection between the individual and society. Thus certain sociocultural processes may be understood, as the achieving of the means of communication depends both on the individual and on the society, their manifestation being a social activity. The means of communication are a social organism and an individual one as well. Eric Buyssens says that language is the asset of the whole world and of no one in particular. This assertion can be applied to the other means of communication as well.

It is also worth noting and stressing the fact that individuals are perpetually changing in time and space. At an individual level, subtle factors, depending on the person, operate as well as factors of an external sociocultural nature. Similarly, human groups change perpetually due to certain characteristics and at the same time due to certain conditions existing outside the group. The populations, the nations, also undergo a permanent dialectic formation-evolution and transformation. A cultural enrichment, a growth of the communicational patrimony results from this permanent movement of the means of communication.

Social integration depends on the means of communication too. By continuously developing and improving the means of communication from the time they emerged till today, man tried to master time and space. He will never stop trying to annul time and space by means of new inventions and conquests, by discovering the significance lying inside the human creations, starting from the spoken language with all its component parts and finishing with a stone cut by a man some tens of thousands of years ago. This happens because all human creations are full of explicit or implicit significance which asks only to be brought to light.

The problems regarding interhuman communication are extremely complex and numerous. They cannot be entirely treated in a work whose aim is to outline the theoretical and methodological concerns of anthropology in the study of modern populations. That is why certain problems regarding communication are either omitted or only mentioned; the stress is laid upon the way we understand the means of communication and upon what their investigation and analysis can offer.

TERRITORY

The investigation of the means of communication by cultural-linguistic anthropology imposes a systematic, hierarchical, correlated, and comprehensive approach. Without going into detail, we point out that the means of communication are divided into two large categories: verbal and nonverbal. Verbal categories are represented by the spoken language and the written one. The verbal sign, and the spoken language, could become the object of exhaustive consideration. We mention that the conditions of interhuman communication are very diverse and independent of the language system. More accurately, the language system may be used as an instrument meant for achieving the interhuman communication to which it is subordinated.

The written language is approached in terms of its general evolution from the magic and intuitive phase of the primeval epoch up to the present-day written language of the advanced civilizations.

Nevertheless, cultural-linguistic anthropology confers a central place on the spoken language of every man, on the language spoken in the street, at home, and at work, with its mistakes of expression, stumblings, turns, unexpected interruptions and redundancies. Spoken language is one of the most genuine and spontaneous human manifestations; it precedes by far the emergence of the written language, it is by far more prevalent, accompanied by a whole scale of elements, nonexistent in the written language, which complete, color, blend, dissolve, or strengthen the message orally expressed.

Interhuman communication is not only verbally achieved. Among nonverbal elements, we mention first the kinesic aspects: the movements of the body which form a system directly comparable to the spoken languages (Birdwhistell 1970). As a matter of fact, correlations between certain syllables and movements were established in some neurotic patients. Then, the gesture and the mimic follow. Other nonverbal elements are: lack of fluency in speech, pauses, certain sounds which do not belong to language such as laughter, yawning, grunting, or other specific sounds which we would call "sonorous gestures of the vocal apparatus." We can also add as factors of communication: clothes, state of cleanliness, smell, cosmetics used, make-up, body hair, and facial hairiness. Nonverbal behaviors express specific cultural forms (Duncan 1969). They determine the role and status of the communication. The alcohol smell emanating from a man transmits a certain kind of information, and all the other elements of the means of communication will be interpreted in terms of this specific of the moment. Finally, other nonverbal elements are: the timbre, the vocal intensity, the frequency of the tone, the speed of speech, and other qualities of the voice itself. All these elements have well-defined values which cannot be left aside in the study of the means of communication when the communicating contact takes place in the same space and at the same time. Certain nonverbal elements of the means of communication are based on the proper language constituted of words (verbal signs). Other nonverbal elements are spontaneous expressions, conscious or not, having a significant impact which is sometimes preponderant as we have seen above.

WORKING MATERIAL

The investigation of the means of communication must be performed from the "outside," on the basis of material and with theoretical and methodological equipment which we shall present later on.

To investigate the psychological and sociocultural universe of a specific human individual and of the group he belongs to, we must first collect language samples. In our research, each subject first gives his identity data: he answers, during a conversation as casual as possible, a series of questions regarding his legal status, professional standing, etc. The investigator then explains that he will pronounce a word which the subject must define. For better understanding, the researcher gives one or two examples. We stress the fact that each subject is dealt with separately, under exactly the same conditions as every other member of the group. We may use a macrosample (for instance a long talk) but we can also use a microsample, as we showed above. The microsamples we have worked with so far are answers given to the simple enunciation of a word which is recorded on tape. We obtained twelve language samples from each subject, corresponding to the set of twelve words we used during all our investigations. The words are: Habit, Mind, Love, Town, World, Sport, *Obşte* (Romanian word designating an old socioeconomic form of organization), Language, Fate (a sign of the zodiac), Thought, Longing for, and Fight.

The language sample is somewhat analogous to a blood sample collected from an individual for certain biochemical analyses. We add that the total language sample registers both the sonorous aspects (by means of a tape recorder) and the visual-kinetic ones (on film). The language sample is afterwards analysed in the laboratory of cultural-linguistic anthropology; the analysis aims to set forth multiple aspects of the investigated person or group. The parameters which may be followed are 100 at present. Their list is not definitive and must not be wholly applied to all the language samples. Depending on our aim, we can use the parameters to illuminate the areas on which the investigation is focused (as is the case with a biochemical analysis of a blood sample which can be oriented in a certain way to give information pertinent to the aim of the investigation).

AREAS OF ANALYSIS

The large areas of analysis are:
1. To establish whether or not the subjects are willing to answer; that is, if the communication and the language sample collecting are possible.
2. The way of addressing which is used (egocentric or sociocentric; thus, the social cohesion of the group).
3. The way in which the subject begins to answer.
4. The way in which the subject formulates his answer (definition, explanation, examples, tautology, etc.).
5. The correctness of the answer or, more exactly, the mistakes made.
6. Logical analysis.
7. Lexical analysis.
8. Semantic analysis (the establishment of a significant axis).
9. The volume of the given answer.
10. The speed of speech.
11. The capacity for being explicit.
12. Timbre, intensity, frequency of tone.
13. Pauses (mute, sonorous, masked).
14. Diverse reactions (laughter, yawning, grunting).
15. Clothes.
16. State of cleanliness.
17. Cosmetics, make-up.
18. Body hair or facial hairiness.   } By means of film
19. Kinetic aspects.
20. Proxemic aspects.

The list remains open for changes or additions. Among the aspects which we intend to set forth we may also mention: the inclination towards the abstract or the concrete, the fluency of speech, and the ratio between verbal means of communication and nonverbal ones.

We consider that the material we obtained consists of two main parts: one of CONTENT, with a value of the expressed, and one of FORM, with the value of the expresser, of the individual or of the group he belongs to.

Content Aspects

Each language sample which we obtain by offering the subject the twelve word-notions outlines the particular ideas showing exactly the value of these ideas in the minds of the members of the group, in the investigated culture, which they express by means of language. It is evident that one of the fundamental elements of cultural-linguistic anthropology appears, namely, the connection between language, thought, and culture. Irrespective of the way in which the subjects express the content of the particular word, whether by definition, examples, synonyms, explanation, or tautology, this content is far from that of dictionaries and encyclopedias, which use literary texts as a starting point. As we study each word-notion, we begin to see from the language samples the meaning which it has in the investigated culture, having a concrete communication value which is attributed to it in everyday life by the speakers belonging to that culture. Moreover, we mention the informational character of the investigated collectivity as being a system or an organism in which the parts organize in a compensatory way, that is they are distributed as informational wholes, well defined and articulated. For instance, the word Fate (sign of the zodiac) got its meaning completely outlined thanks only to the participation of the whole group. The task of the researcher is to discover and establish the SIGNIFICANT AXIS existing in each obtained sample and/or observe the hierarchy of the "meanings" which the subject and the group, respectively, establish in the investigated culture.

Aspects of Form

The lexical inventory offers numerous data both on the investigated culture and on the group itself, that is, it has a value of EXPRESSED and a value of EXPRESSER as well. The lists of full words, i.e. nouns and verbs, extracted from the language samples are considered as a variant of the content (constituted by words) or of the meaning given by the members of a culture to certain notions. These lists result from samples representing different cultures or subcultures. They become extremely significant when examined side by side. Thus, after eliminating the common terms, i.e. those which appear in all the lists, only the terms used exclusively by the members of one culture remain. These edited lists of terms let us see typical features of the particular culture to which the examined subjects belong. The comparison of these lists, as well as the analysis of the classes and semantic categories of the words (terms) proper to the investigated cultures, is in fact an analysis of the specific features, the analysis and the comparison of certain components, of the studied culture. We are shown the sphere of interests, mentality, cares, and aspirations existing implicitly in the spoken language which are set forth by cultural-linguistic anthropology.

The examples given here illustrate in part the investigations performed on four groups:

Group A: urban-industrial environment;

Group B: rural-agricultural environment I (prosperous settlement, with multiple connections with the town);

Group C: rural-agricultural environment II (also a prosperous settlement, but an isolated mountain village); and

Group D: student environment (teenage pupils, living in a boarding school in a provincial town).

The lexical inventories were made on the basis of the language samples obtained by means of the word-notion HABIT. The four groups are differentiated first according to the number of terms used exclusively by the members of each culture for explaining the word Habit (Table 1).

Table 1. Terms exclusive to each group

Group	Nouns	Verbs
A	42	27
B	57	23
C	16	14
D	24	15

We now write out twelve nouns (Table 2) and twelve verbs (Table 3) of these lists of terms used only by the particular group for explaining the same notion Habit, as an illustration of the connection between language, thought, and culture.

It is evident that in group A, the dynamic verbs connected with the activity in a factory are predominant while the nouns represent varied

Table 2. Nouns

Group	A	B	C	D
	folklore	baptism	gentleman	book
	reel	money	peasant	classroom
	vice	present	walk	pupil
	philanderer	bride	smoking	geography
	countryside	ancestor	cigarette	mind
	blood (fig.)	film	tea	sex
	plant	orchestra	parable	sport
	years	radio	gift	aim
	century	T.V.	age	future
	period	hunt	brandy	speech
	moment	stupidity	state	football
	nation	wickedness	stare	monkey

Table 3. Verbs

Group	A	B	C	D
	to produce	to run	to hear	to learn
	to perform	to run away	to look at	to show
	to maintain	to practice sports	to see	to read
	to apply	to lead	to spray	to confound
	to actualize	to educate	to send	to imitate
	to determine	to participate	to talk	to impress
	to make concrete	to spend	to quarrel	to use
	to exert	to have fun	to discuss	to play
	to perpetuate	to ask for	to congratulate	to eat
	to transmit	to organize	to give birth	to rest
	to analyse	to get drunk	to yell	to follow
	to compare	to finish	to translate	to live

preoccupations and interests. In group B, the noun list reveals a preoccupation with diversion, with family life and events; the verb list contains many verbs which express movement, while others confirm the semantic color of the nouns. Group C has a predilection for dialectal terms, for archaisms; dynamic verbs are almost nonexistent; a passivity specific to a closed culture of a rather isolated mountain village is evident. Finally, in group D (teenage pupils in a boarding school) both nouns and verbs underline the range of concerns specific to the pupils' age and condition.

The whole test sets forth the fact that the same word-notion was described differently by each of the representatives of the respective groups, that in the sphere of individual and collective consciousness the notion has a communication value and presence in the culture, which the speakers in daily life attribute to it.

Our research covers twelve word-notions, which means that the table of results offered by the lexical inventory should be extremely expressive for the investigated cultures. Joining the other results of the language samples and correlating the data, we obtain very complete and precise indications on the investigated groups and cultures.

We give another aspect as an example: we work out the percentages for the verbal substance of the language samples, putting together all the words given for the notion of Habit (Table 4).

Table 4.   Total number of words in the sample

Group	Number of words
A	1190
B	1224
C	882
D	483

The frequency of the full words is represented in Table 5, in absolute figures and in percentages (as against the total number of the full words).

Table 5.   Frequency of full words

Group	Total number of words	Full words		Nouns		Verbs	
		abs.	%	abs.	%	abs.	%
A	1190	108	9.07	58	4.87	50	4.20
B	1224	115	9.39	68	5.55	47	3.83
C	882	64	7.25	28	3.17	36	4.08
D	483	188	38.92	114	23.60	74	15.32

A rather ignored dimension of the spoken language is its development in time. One of the aspects which one may determine is the measuring in seconds of the spoken language samples (which we have done here only for groups A, B, and C). Out of the ratio between the total number of the spoken words and the time expressed in seconds we obtain the speed of speech (Table 6).

Table 6.   Speed of speech (in words per second)

Group	Number of seconds	Number of words	Speed
A	873	1190	1.36
B	867	1224	1.41
C	600	882	1.47

The significant density results out of the ratio between the full words (nouns + verbs) and the total number of seconds: the substantive significant density and separately, the verbal significant density are given by the ratio between nouns and, respectively, verbs, and the time expressed in seconds (Table 7).

Table 7.   Density

Group	Number of seconds per sample	global	substantive	verbal
			Density	
A	873	0.123	0.066	0.057
B	867	0.132	0.078	0.054
C	600	0.106	0.046	0.060

Understanding and describing the human individual and the group he belongs to, looked at from our standpoint, takes account of context in a very broad sense in collecting the material as well processing and interpreting it. This means that both the grammatical context of the word and the ethnic, social, cultural, and biological context of the investigation are taken into account.

Cultural aspects are evident in the use of the human means of communication (hence the denomination of cultural-linguistic anthropology and not linguistic anthropology) but there are also biological, temperamental, and pathological aspects which vary from one case to another.

The character of cultural-linguistic anthropology, which is as objective and systematic as possible, is shown both in the processing of the material — the recording by means of magnetic tape and film is objective — and in the way in which the material is analysed. Using the same parameters, we satisfy the comparability criterion too. The investigation is as quantitative as possible. We calculate the statistical indices and the correlation existing between them.

PROBLEMS CONCERNING CULTURAL-LINGUISTIC ANTHROPOLOGY

Our methodology is open. In addition to psychology, sociology, and medicine, we are also interested in the concepts and methods of the science of information. One example is redundance. For the telecommunications engineer, the extra signs and communicative signals as against what would be considered as strictly necessary, i.e. the redundance, must be reduced to a minimum. But it is just the redundance that interests us. Because it plays a prominent part in the individual's utterance, it may show which is the main object preoccupying the individual or the group he belongs to. At the same time, the presence or the absence of the redundance may become a defining feature for the culture or subculture anthropologically investigated.

We draw attention now to two types of connections outlined during the investigations on the language samples.

The first one is the connection between cultural-linguistic anthropology and stylistics ("Style is man," Buffon). Stylistics, as the word is used by social and cultural anthropologists opens our way towards a person. Of course, this is not only a matter of verbal stylistics, but also of kinesic stylistics and of other ways of expression, those of the person and of the group, which means the style specific to the studied culture. It goes without saying that there is a certain style in any modality of concrete existence: dressing, perfuming oneself, etc.

The second connection is that established with psychopathology. The notion of "normal" is very lax, just as the norm of grammatical correctness in oral expression is one of important gaps or mistakes. Within the pathological phenomenon there is a "bursting" of the biological into the social, which reveals certain aspects of the dialectics of the biological and the social. Psychiatric research offers some materials setting forth certain "caricaturing" manifestations of some current tendencies. But there are still very few psychiatric works investigating the means of communication of the patients other than from a symptomatic point of view, with concern for diagnosis. The dialectics of the normal and pathological have an importance which may be compared to that of the dialectics of the individual and social. Investigations of this type are extremely significant for anthropology.

THE CONTRIBUTION OF CULTURAL-LINGUISTIC ANTHROPOLOGY

How could cultural-linguistic anthropology contribute to the knowledge and study of complicated and complex processes such as the permanent human formation and evolution? This is in fact one of the objects of anthropology, as we showed at the beginning, consisting in setting forth the biocultural dynamics lying at the basis of the human formation and evolution, by correlating the classifications, hierarchies, and categories.

The characterization of human groups gives conclusive evidence about man, about the group he belongs to, and about his culture. Based on the exploration of certain indices, we can perceive the local or ethnic specific features. In this way, we follow the processes and values which support the life of a particular group and which, at the same time, change it. Such research satisfies both the exigency of a synchronic investigation and that of a diachronic one.

Cultural-linguistic anthropology contributes to the explanation of the significant detail, blends the known data, and brings to light the implicit factors and fineness of the objective observation. The language sample, as the rough material, constitutes an extremely rich source as far as objective data are concerned, able to be processed with mathematical precision, permitting us to obtain exact and comprehensive results, confirming or invalidating, changing or completing certain impressionistic researches, and offering its data for correlation with other disciplines, as if they were some free valences.

Cultural-linguistic anthropology does not accumulate data for accumulation's sake, does not illustrate already known schemas, but it aims at discovering the biological and/or social factors supporting and changing the different aspects of life, man, and culture.

REFERENCES

BAUMGARTEN, F.
  1966   Der Werkgebundene und der Lebensgebundene Typus. *Arbeit und Leistung* 7–8.
BIRDWHISTELL, RAY L.
  1970   *Kinesics and context: essays on body motion communication.* Philadelphia: University of Pennsylvania Press.
CASSIRER, E.
  1923   *Philosophie der symbolischen Formen*, volume one. Berlin: B. Cassirer.
COHEN, YEHUDI
  1969   *Man in adaptation* Chicago: Aldine.
DUMITRU, N., VICTOR SĂHLEANU
  1969   "Obiectul şi specificul antropologici ca ştiinţă despre om [The objects and characteristics of anthropology as a science of man]," in *Dialectica metodelor în cercetarea ştiinţifică*, volume two. Bucharest: Ed. Ştiinţifică.
DUNCAN, STARKEY, JR.
  1969   Nonverbal communication. *Psychological Bulletin* 72(2):118–137.
FTHENAKIS WASSILIOS, E.
  1971   *Probleme und Ergebnisse der Sozialanthropologie.* Munich: Acta Antropologica.
HEUSE, GEORGES, A.
  1953   *La psychologie ethnique.* Paris: Librarie Philosophique.
JAKOBSON, ROMAN
  1967   "Linguistics in its relation to other sciences," in *Actes du Dixième Congrès International des Linguistes*, 75–122. Bucharest: The Academy Publishing House.
JANTSCH, E.
  1970   Inter- and transdisciplinary university: a systems approach to education and innovation. *Policy Sciences* 1:403–428.
OPRESCU, ION
  1970a   "O metodă de cercetare antropolingvistică cu aplicabilitate în studiile

sociologice" [Anthropolinguistic research which can be applied in sociological studies]," in *Metode şi tehnici ale sociologiei*, 249–261. Bucharest: Didact. Ped.

1970b "Cercetările de antropolingvistică în studiul minorului infractor [Investigations of anthropolinguistics in the study of teenager delinquents]," in *Metode de cunoaştere a personalităţii minorului infractor*, 38–58. Bucharest.

1971a Cercetarea mijloacelor de comunicaţie interumane [Investigation of the interhuman communication means]. *Forum Ştiinţe Sociale* 2: 113–121.

1971b "Diagnosticul prin metodele antropologiei cultural lingvistice în urmărirea eficienţei procesului de educare [The diagnosis performed by the methods of cultural-linguistic anthropology in following the efficiency of the educational process]," in *Modernizarea procesului instructiv educativ*, 105–125. Bucharest.

OPRESCU, ION, VICTOR SĂHLEANU
1972 Antropologia cultural-lingvistică: principii, metode, probleme [Cultural linguistic-anthropology: principles, methods, problems]. *Studii şi Cercetări de Antropologia* 9(1):97–123.

SĂHLEANU, V.
1970 "Omul ca sistem: o încercare de antropologie abstractă [Man considered as a system: an essay on abstract anthropology]," in Symposium *Cybernetics in biology and medicine*. Bucharest.

1971 "Asupra unor paradoxe antropologice [On certain anthropological paradoxes]." Unpublished lecture, Psychiatric Department, Institutul de Medicina, Timişoara.

SAPIR, ED.
1921 *Language*. New York: Harcourt, Brace.

SAPIR, ED.
1966 *Culture, language and personality*. Los Angeles: University of California Press.

SCHAFF, A.
1966 *Introducere în semantică* [Introduction to semantics]. Bucharest: Ed. Stiinţifică.

SLAMA-CAZACU, TATIANA
1959 *Limbaj şi context* [Language and context]. Bucharest: Ed. Stiinţifică.

TAX, SOL.
1964 *Horizons of anthropology*. London: George Allen and Unwin.

WEINREICH, URIEL
1964 *Languages in contact: findings and problems*. The Hague: Mouton.

WHORF, B. L.
1956 *Language thought and reality*. New York, London: John Wiley and Sons.

1971 *Le comportement verbal*. Paris: Dunod.

SECTION SIX

Discussion

Summary of Discussion

S. A. WURM

The central issue emerging from the totality of discussion of language in anthropology, and in fact one of the major subjects to which much of the discussion was devoted, was the importance attributed to the study of language in its social and cultural setting and the recognition of the paramount role of sociolinguistic approaches both in studies involving language in its function as a means of intercommunication and also in studies dealing with the nature of language itself. Approaches widely regarded as valid, especially transformational-generative approaches, came under severe criticism. Their artificially restrictive nature in dissociating the subject matters which they study from the social and cultural background in which these subject matters function was regarded as a severe drawback which made the value of their findings questionable. It was argued that these subject matters of study have a real existence only in the social and cultural settings in which they appear and against the background of these settings, and it was pointed out that approaches to the study of language which ignore these settings and backgrounds in the light of their orientation can only produce results of doubtful validity, or at least results which lack relevance. In other words, they indicate WHAT is going on in language, but not HOW it relates to the world.

Other views put forward admitted that a distance exists between the transformational-generative approach and sociolinguistics (which was increasingly being hailed as THE linguistics), but it was suggested that the transformational-generative approach could be extended to include sociolinguistic factors in its system of description. This was countered by holders of the opposite view who felt that the sociolinguistic approach involves the utilization of methods which belong basically to realms lying outside the field of linguistics.

In general, there was wide agreement that it is necessary to include a fundamental tenet of sociolinguistics, that of the study of variation and sociocultural setting, into the study of language, but there was disagreement as to the nature of the approach. The essence of the opposition was the view that (a) such an extension requires the utilization of methods which come into linguistics from other disciplines, whereas (b) the adherents of the transformational-generativist schools argued that it could be achieved from within linguistics through an application of linguistic methods to the study of social factors impinging on language.

In the subsession on "Language and Man," opening discussion was provided by three formal discussants, Dr. Adam Kendon of the Project on Human Communication at the Bronx State Hospital of New York City, Professor Thomas A. Sebeok of Indiana University, and Professor Tatiana Slama-Cazacu of the University of Bucharest.

Kendon started by saying that the theme suggested for this section, "language capacity and acquisition as paradigmatical for man as a species," entails the question of what language IS, how it contrasts with other modes of communication, and how far the properties of language are indeed specific to man. Language acquisition also constitutes a central issue. He said that several of the papers in this session dealt with how the individual person acquires language as he grows up, and he pointed out that we might perhaps also be concerned with the question of how the human species acquired language. He mentioned that though only a few of the papers in this session touched directly on this question, several of them had important implications for any discussion of it.

He then turned to the question of what language IS. He admitted that he was struck by the number of authors who were dissatisfied with the conception of language which linguistics had worked so hard to establish. The notion of language as an abstract system, as a "thing in itself" to be studied apart from the utterances of live individuals in interactional situations no longer appeared tenable to many of them. Ever since linguistics has sought to distinguish itself as a branch of study, it has sought to purify itself and to sift out from the complexities of communication some apparently stable system whose structure could be described. What many writers whose papers were included in this session bore witness to was that this process of purification had reached the point of diminishing returns. This was because they were turning from texts to talk — indeed they were turning to talk and regarding it as such and not, as has sometimes been the case, to talk regarded as imperfect or fragmentary text. In turning from text to talk, investigators were finding that substantial changes in linguistic theory were going to be necessary.

Kendon continued by quoting the papers by Crystal, Poyatos, Slama-Cazacu, and von Raffler Engel as being all quite explicit in their dissatisfaction with the scope of linguistics as currently conceived. The essence of their criticism seemed to be that linguists treated any information they could not describe with their present theoretical and notational apparatus as nonlinguistic. Kendon added, without intending to discuss this definition, that one new definition of language could be that it is a communication system which is capable of transmitting new information. He said that attempts are now being made to define language in terms of its function or functions, e.g. by Halliday, rather than in terms of its structural properties. This is becoming necessary because, as soon as one begins to observe closely the patterns of behavior that people in face-to-face interaction engage in, one finds very quickly that what might be called "linguistic work" is being done by behavior whose structural properties seem, on the surface at least, to be very different indeed from what is usually thought of as language.

Kendon remarked that this point is being made with particular clarity by those who are beginning to look at kinesics. The papers by Crystal and Poyatos, each in its different way, point out that what has hitherto been disregarded by linguists in the vocal output of people has as much structural and functional claim to be incorporated into language as words do, and von Raffler Engel and, particularly, Slama-Cazacu make the same point for body motion. Kendon mentioned that for his own part he was particularly interested in Slama-Cazacu's paper, "Nonverbal components in the sequence of the message," for in it she demonstrates how usual and commonplace the use of gesture is both as an alternate and as an addition to speech, that body motion is not a mere modifier of what we say, adding in the emotional overtones, but that it is a fully incorporated party to the business of doing the work of language. He said that he thought this work demonstrates conclusively that any attempt to construct theories of language based on speech alone, or on written texts alone, must be regarded as attempts at SPECIAL language theories and not GENERAL language theories.

Kendon continued by saying that one important conclusion that he, at least, drew from all this was that earlier definitive pronouncements on the nature of language and so, by implication, pronouncements on the nature of language as a property specific to *Homo sapiens*, had been at best premature. What we need, he said, and, judging from many of the papers in the session, what we appear to be getting, is a recognition that we must reimmerse ourselves in the complexities of behavior. He maintained that for further progress on certain key issues of linguistic theory a meticulous examination of occasions of human interaction is necessary. Some of the papers included in this session do make beginnings in this direction. For example, Duncan's paper constitutes a careful study of the signalling systems that serve to coordinate utterances in conversations; Handelman's paper gives a demonstration of the concept of frame and a further demonstration of the integrated functioning of behavior in interaction, the paper by Bullowa and her colleagues demonstrates how interaction is founded in the synchronization of bodily movements: it shows convincingly, Kendon asserted, how vocal utterances are already fully embedded within an established interdependence of bodily behavior. Her techniques, using the analysis of sound films of mother-infant interaction point the way research has to go, Kendon felt, to understand how linguistic interchange emerges in development.

Such close studies of occasions of interaction are beginning to demonstrate how, when people interact, they enter with one another into highly complex systems of behavioral interdependence, systems which are inextricably interwoven. If we are to be able to get at the question of how *Homo sapiens* acquires "language" we have to look at how he acquires the complex of behavioral systems of which language appears to be a part. This means that we have to come to grips with the systems of behavioral interdependence that comprise the phenomenon of "face-to-face interaction." As yet, Kendon said, we lack the theoretical framework for this. He added that he thought that at the moment what was needed were more descriptive studies. He felt that the theory would emerge gradually, as our methods of analysis developed and as the languages we used to provide the systematic descriptions became more refined and comprehensive. He added that he thought that language evolves in interactional events: it is the study of interaction that will provide us with the illumination we need.

Sebeok started his remarks by saying that he saw the papers of the session as surprisingly and excitingly focusing around two very general themes. The first of these, which he also noticed in papers written for other sessions, could be summed up by the word "semiotics." Semiotics, Sebeok said, had a complex history, and he wanted to allude only to the two dominant traditions in Western thought for which the papers had relevance, though the word "semiotics" was not much mentioned in them. One of these was what he called the Locke-Pierce-Morris tradition which began in English philosophy in 1690 when John Locke injected the term into English philosophical discourse and elaborated on it. Locke spoke not only about human semiotics, but also, for instance, about birds and he did not draw the distinction between humans and animals very sharply. His successor Charles Pierce developed semiotics beyond Locke and did not distinguish between the human use of signs and the use of signs by animals. Charles Morris explicitly said that he did not distinguish between the semiotic mechanisms of humans, animals, and the computer. While the tradition of Locke, Pierce, and Morris was elaborated in the Anglo-Saxon, Germanic, and Slavic traditions, another tradition prevailed in the Romance countries. It went back to Ferdinand de Saussure, and linguists in general had adopted the Saussure model more than the other model. These linguists paid lip-service to semiotics but they considered linguistics to be a special kind of semiotics, the chief among the contributors to it, and it was even maintained that semiotics was a subdiscipline of linguistics. Sebeok added that Soviet scholarship was similar to the Anglo-Saxon tradition rather than to the French one.

The second of the two themes which Sebeok felt the papers had focused on could be summed up by the word "ethology." The term was introduced at the beginning of the nineteenth century and it came to to the fore with the work of Charles Darwin. The communicational interest of ethology had focused on the term "ritualization" and the effect of this in semiotic studies was that it introduced a diachronic dimension — it focused on the phylogenetic aspects of semiotic events. Sebeok continued by saying that in 1963 he had coined a term "zoo-semiotics" which had been widely diffused. He said that he had meant by this a mediating concept in order to reconcile two seemingly antithetical spheres of discourse: semiotics and ethology, ethology being the realm of nature, and semiotics the realm of culture insofar as the emphasis of linguists was concerned.

Sebeok remarked that, if time permitted, he could make an analysis of terms which are on the borderline between semiotics and ethology which he felt would play a great role in future research in this field. "Ritualization" is one of these. Another would be "ethogram" which corresponds to what we call "code" — the total species-specific code of an animal — and "display" is another one which is used very vaguely by animal behaviorists. This is what semioticians call "signs," and a semiotic analysis of what displays are and how they are used is very important. Sebeok argued that every sign which has been subject to close study such as a signal, symptom, syndrome, name, symbol, emblem, etc. could be traced both in human and animal behavior, and he said that it is quite untrue that there is a complete distinction between man and animal in this respect.

Sebeok added that one aspect of all this work has not really been explored in detail except by a few scholars. This is that we have a great deal to learn especially at the interface of man's communication with animals. In all relations between man and animal, the communication system is absolutely decisive. What is involved here is a phenomenon called code-switching, i.e. the animal has to learn a part of man's code and *vice versa*. This leads to such developments as taming and training, and if a diachronic perspective is imposed then it results in domestication.

Sebeok pointed out that semiotic analysis would be of enormous profit in ethology. He felt that ethology would have to be very carefully informed of semiotics, and that semiotics would have to be fully aware of ethology, especially if interactional analysis were stressed. Sebeok pointed out that ethology had failed to solve the one problem that linguists worry about, i.e. the evolution of language. If looked at as a problem in ritualization, this has not been solved, because ritualization works on the assumption that behavior unfolds with morphological growth and differentiation, and the comparative method has to be applied — but this cannot be applied to a sample of one. One cannot study language by ritualization, because there is nothing to compare it with.

Sebeok concluded by saying that it is already possible to envisage the outlines of a semiotics that avoids anthropocentrism, together with an ethology that avoids parochialism, and we can hope that a full synthesis may be achieved before long. This would offer a new paradigm and a methodology for the comparative analysis of semiosis in its full diversity — with semiosis, independent of form and substance, seen as a universal, criterial property of animate existence.

Slama-Cazacu began her comments by saying that the reading of the papers included in the session had given her the opportunity of feeling what she called the "pulse of our time," and to feel, at many points, in unison with the rhythm of the future. Some of the papers clearly express a dissatisfaction with what linguistics and its models have offered up to the time of her speaking, and an idea that is implicit in many of the others — and which she also has long maintained — is the necessity of modifying the traditional patterns of linguistics, of thoroughly knowing what language is in reality, i.e. in its functioning, and in consequence the need for collecting facts through field research.

Slama-Cazacu said that the formalizing models of the linguistic trends influenced by information theory, as well as some structuralist models and those of transformational-generative linguistics do not seem to be more satisfactory than the traditional ones. They are not validated when applied to practical needs such as machine translation and language teaching; they generally do not hold up when confronted with reality. There are some scientific fields that demand thorough knowledge of how language functions in real life; among them are the anthropological sciences, psychology, sociology, and pedagogy. During the past ten years many linguists have lived through a dramatic situation: the linguistic theory they had learned, created, or taught, did not seem to be very useful when they had to answer questions in applied linguistics, such as language teaching, and they turned against their ancient credo and criticized it. Considering language only *in abstracto* and *in vacuo* brought us to a deadlock, hence it should be also considered in its very existence, that is, in connection with man, who created it, who uses and transforms it. Slama-Cazacu said that she sees in this confrontation the germs of future development for the scientific study of language itself. Whether linguistics will or will not enter this stream, whether it will or will not accept this trend, is no longer the important problem. The important fact is that language will be studied in its very functioning *nolens volens* by those sciences which endeavor to study real life communication directly, where language is to be found in a hypostasis that is far from being that imposed by the above-mentioned models, i.e. language in an oral form, especially in dialogues intermingled with nonverbal cues, with paralinguistic forms that are not yet well known, profoundly influenced by the context — and especially by the social context that influences the physical state of the partners and which determines the switching of the registers, the selection in the mnemonic stock. She warned that we should not forget that we still do not know exactly what "language" is and how it functions. In consequence, we still cannot answer the question of what is innate in it, or whether it shares features in common with animals.

She continued by saying that these papers mirror an *état d'âme* which is symptomatic of the present crisis as well as of what are thought to be its remedies. She enumerated the symptoms as follows: FIRST SYMPTOM The need for observing reality, where what is then noticed is not a code as a single phenomenon, but a communication or, better still, a situation of communication (involving the act, its performers, and their context), a human communication, species-specific, because in no other animal do we find such a complex and complete phenomenon of communication through several channels and various means. Observing the most frequent key words in such a symposium might become a method for discovering the dominant trends. Some key words encountered in the papers are: real situation, communication (instead of language), human communication, interaction, oral or face-to-face communication, study of dialogue (for instance in the papers by Duncan, Handelman, Martirena, and Slama-Cazacu), and total communication, including paralinguistic and nonverbal events (a leitmotif in the papers by Bynon, Crystal, Duncan, von Raffler Engel, and Slama-Cazacu).

SECOND SYMPTOM   The need to modify or completely renounce previous theories; the necessity of searching for a more comprehensive theory, largely humanistic; the search for a solution to the problem of the existence and the extent of innate capacities and of the role of social context in answering the question of species-specific *versus* phylogenetic continuity up to complete similarity; the need to understand the process of language acquisition and the multicode switching operation.

THIRD SYMPTOM   The necessity of stressing the collection of facts (in the papers by Bullowa and coworkers Halliday, and Slama-Cazacu).

FOURTH SYMPTOM   Trends toward defining adequate methodologies for these aims (in the papers by Bullowa and coworkers Duncan, Oksaar, Poyatos, and von Raffler Engel).

However, Slama-Cazacu continued, symptomatological analysis is not sufficient. An etiological treatment is difficult, and she proceeded to summarize some general pitfalls involved in the very solutions that are now proposed as a counterbalance to the ancient ones, and which run the risk of themselves becoming new idols in both senses, of dogmatic image, and of fallacious expedient.

She felt that true knowledge adequate for the description and interpretation of communication will never be achieved, and nonverbal as well as paralinguistic aspects will not be adequately studied if communication is not envisaged as a whole act in its situation and as a product of concrete men. For this, large teams should undertake the recording of what is yet unknown, i.e. how we communicate in various tongues, in the reality of oral communication, of dialogue, where nonverbal cues intermingle and even fuse with the verbal ones, as is pointed out in the papers by Slama-Cazacu ("Mixed syntax," "Syntax of dialogue") and Duncan. She added that this is why she thinks that "nonverbal communication" or "kinesics" as separate fields where facts other than the verbal ones are studied, are not appropriate; there are nonverbal cues in any so-called verbal or oral communication and a proper nonverbal communication only occurs in special cases as with deaf-mutes, for instance, under very special conditions.

As far as the theory is concerned, Slama-Cazacu felt that a theory is necessary, but the danger is in theorizing before sufficient facts are collected. She thought that the paper by Halliday was a brilliant demonstration of the ability to make a classical linguistic-theoretic analysis. What is however needed is not merely a theory *ante factum*, but theory AND facts, facts AND theory, both linked together with no sharp chronology dividing them, facts constructing little by little a theory whose germs are born from observing prior facts. She said she saw the struggle to find truth in science as a battle where a strategy has to be defined: when people are too much captivated by their theory, facts begin to be lost from view or only those facts are seen that fit the theory.

Slama-Cazacu said that facts are necessary, and that we still have very few. We certainly cannot pretend that many facts could be given in summarized papers such as those presented; but in reality they were even BASED on very few facts, some did not even report any, and some just used the future tense when speaking about facts. On the other hand, a pitfall threatens when the collected facts reflect a partial, or even unilateral and fallacious aspect, because they are not integrated into the whole, relatively, synchronically, or diachronically speaking, as is the case with the paper by Halliday. The danger also lies in the following: facts connected with the newborn must not only be recorded, but also compared with OTHER FACTS in the language of the environment, so that we may know what is really inborn and what is acquired. The same could be said when present studies invoke nonverbal facts which are not connected with the whole of the communicative act.

Slama-Cazacu remarked that we are arriving, through this objection, at the proper problem of the method itself. Integration is a methodological requirement and she herself called the method which she uses and advocates a "contextual-dynamic method" (involving also integration in the sequence of the events, of life, of activity, of age, etc.). She said that the demonstration by Halliday did not convince her because it omits the starting point: his study begins at the age of nine months: it takes its departure from a point which is SUPPOSED — but not proved — to be the point in time at which the child begins to learn language from adults. While this study should begin from the first days, when the impact of social environment is really active, the problem is also connected with what is understood by the term "language learning" itself, hence an integration into a larger theoretical interdisciplinary approach is also necessary. On the other hand, the necessity of a multimethodological approach looms high. Last, but not least, said Slama-Cazacu, she wanted to mention another methodological complaint: the lack of information given about what has been done before in this field, especially by American scholars about European studies.

In conclusion, Slama-Cazacu asked what was the diagnosis offered by these papers. She said that one of the points of consensus between the papers concerns the problem of paralinguistic phenomena, which has the value of an argument and not only of mere description. In his paper, Crystal shows that there is no discontinuity between linguistic and paralinguistic signs, that they are arbitrary signs, motivated by the system of a certain language, culturally varying, hence socially determined; hence we would no more see the the necessity of separating them from the "other" linguistic facts. In trying to summarize what she had been suggesting concerning various crucial problems treated in the papers, she said it would be hard to find many points of consensus in the results, or even firm and consistent statements in the various parts of the same papers.

Regarding the very difficult problem of inborn and acquired aspects in language behavior, contradictory statements were put forward. Crystal considered that, at least as far as concerned paralinguistic phenomena, there was no real similarity between human and animal vocalization. Bullowa, et al., and von Raffler Engel spoke about a very early interaction between adult and infant, while Halliday stated that there was no early language learning, imitation, and true interaction.

Slama-Cazacu said that in fact, reality is contradictory in itself, or, more correctly, its thorough study shows how unilateral and extremist each theory is, because one can find facts supporting each theory. Aspects certainly exist that are inborn. They do not pertain, however, to language as a code, but to its functioning and to the cognitive structure specific to humans as well as to the process of learning. In this respect one should notice not only that the impact of social life begins very early, but also that social life is necessary in order that the native capacities become actualized. The optimistic conclusion about the possibilities of social life, in particular of education, is justified, and the paper by Söderbergh which talks about educating children to read at the age of two years is also an argument for this conclusion. Many contradictions and deadlocks may disappear when the problems are analyzed in their various aspects. Slama-Cazacu added that she would conclude her remarks by referring to an example concerning the coexistence of various codes, especially in bilingualism. She said that one should distinguish the problem of elicitation based on memory, which very probably operates by selective switching between two separate — but also partially overlapping — stocks, from the other problem of learning, which involves the accumulation of a basic code as well as of the other linguistic systems on the basis of common learning principles or "universals of learning." Kessler, in her paper, speaks about a "common pool," about linguistic universals, while Oksaar operates with the concept of an "overall code" formed after acquiring two languages. Slama-Cazacu felt that this last concept did not necessarily imply the adoption of nativistic explanations. She said that a third aspect should however be mentioned as well: that of learning a first metalanguage (the grammatical code), which helps afterwards in the acquisition of other languages and of other metalanguages.

She ended by saying that it would be desirable for scholars to thoroughly separate aspects that they are confusing, and, on the other hand, to integrate, or study as a whole, many aspects which they are inadequately relating.

Because a few papers in the present volume on *Language and man* were included for discussion in other subsessions of the General Session on "Language in Anthropology," three received notice from formal discussants in those subsessions. Dr. Valerie Makkai, a discussant for the subsession published as *Approaches to language*, referred to the papers by Miller and von Raffler Engel as examples of papers which emphasized the need to look at the extralinguistic contexts of language itself. Dr. Michael A. K. Halliday, a discussant for the subsession published as *Language and society*, spoke about the paper by von Raffler Engel as demonstrating that kinesic behavior was more closely associated with culture than with language. He remarked that Oprescu's paper underlines communication as a means of transmitting and conserving what is human in the sense of the social semiotic.

General discussions on the papers in the present volume, both during the subsession on "Language and Man," and at other subsessions of the General Session on "Language in Anthropology," turned partly on the issues set forth at the outset of this Summary of Discussion, and accommodated also the following.

Victor Yngve remarked that we are at a turning point in linguistics, particularly in linguistics as it relates to anthropology, sociology, psychology, and the many other disciplines with which linguistics shares a frontier. He mentioned that many people are dissatisfied with the existing approaches to the description of language and that the development of a new set of basic concepts is needed. However, he cautioned that it might take a long time to develop a new set that was more satisfactory for the present much broader area of interest, and that there would be many false starts in trying to develop a new set of basic concepts. Concepts of language in any new schematization should not be primary but secondary or derived concepts.

David Crystal, unable to attend the Congress from England, was afterwards sent a copy of this Summary of Discusssion, and responded as follows:

A pity there's no reference to the notion of CRITERIA — I don't much like this bald fact *versus* theory opposition, or some of the black and white positions that are suggested. . . . [There is] need for methodological explicitness if some of the theoretical differences are to be resolved. The notion of criteria of analysis is particularly crucial *re* the Sebeok argument (p. 363).

I share the leaning towards socio-etc. perspectives, but I get the feeling that participants were a mite too ready to reject formal linguistics outright. . . . It would be sad indeed if the good in Chomsky, et al. was jettisoned along with the bad. And in fact sociolinguists are extremely indebted — sometimes more than they know, I think — to Chomskian principles, e.g. in using notions of productivity, etc.

Finally, one informal discussion subsession which constituted itself entirely around the problem of language acquisition yielded views which Wurm reported at formal subsessions and which for the reason of close pertinence are summarized not only below but also in the Summary of Discussion in the volume *Language and society*. At this informal subsession, discussion very quickly concentrated on the question of what was referred to as nature *versus* nurture, i.e. the question of innate *versus* learning, nativism *versus* environmentalism. This led to some confrontation between adherents and opponents of the transformational-generativist school, and it was pointed out the environment had a very strong influence and was responsible for much that could not be explained through this innate approach. It was largely agreed that both factors were vital, though there was disagreement as to which of the two was more vital. It was mentioned that in grammatical descriptions, for instance, the issue was not only whether sentences were linguistically acceptable, but also which of these were culturally acceptable.

It was argued that the issue revolves on the opposition of universals on one side and the question of cultural acquisition on the other, but it was quickly stressed that there are universals which are not based on genetic factors, and the existence of linguistic means of addressing a group was mentioned as an example. This led to the question as to how nature affects nurture an vice versa, and it was accepted that our knowledge as to what belongs to which of these two is inadequate. It was agreed that while language certainly depends on both nature and nurture, it is possible that some feature which has been thought to depend on nature, i.e. to be innate, might depend on nurture instead. It was also stressed that it is important to keep apart the phylogeny of language, its ontogony as based on nature and nurture (or environment), and the history of language as a cultural product.

Biographical Notes

JOHN G. BORDIE is Professor of Linguistics and of Curriculum and Instruction at the University of Texas at Austin. He received his B.A. from the University of Chicago in 1949 and his Ph.D. in Linguistics from the University of Texas in 1958. His special interests are the languages of the northern Middle East and Pakistan, language acquisition and teaching, and applied linguistics. He is currently Director of the Foreign Language Education Center of the University of Texas at Austin.

MARGARET BULLOWA (1909–   ) was born in New York City. She earned an A.B. from Barnard College, an M.S. in Public Health from Columbia University, and an M.D. from New York University. She is now retired from the practice of psychiatry. Her interest in failure of communication, especially in the language sphere, led to initiating research, at first directed to language acquisition. Studies were based on weekly longitudinal recording of infant vocalization and behavior from birth to thirty months in the infants' own homes. Pilot work was started in 1959 and a research project was begun at the Massachusetts Mental Health Center in 1960 and continued in the Speech Communication Group at the Massachusetts Institute of Technology since 1965. A number of linguists and social scientists have collaborated in the studies from time to time. As the thinking and writing about the data appeared to be converging with the work of ethnologists working on issues of child development, she is spending a year (August 1974–August 1975) in the laboratory of N. Blurton Jones at the Institute of Child Health of the University of London.

JAMES BYNON (1925–   ), after studying Berber and Maghrebi Arabic at the Institut des Hautes Études in Rabit and at the École Nationale des Langues Orientales Vivantes in Paris, obtained his Doctorat en Linguistique from the Sorbonne in 1963 and has since 1964 been Lecturer in Berber at the School of Oriental and African Studies of the University of London. Although his activities are primarily directed towards North African dialectology, oral literature, and traditional art, he is also involved in such wider issues as first language acquisition and Hamito-Semitic (Afroasiatic) comparison. Two areas of special interest are the ethno-ornithology and the ethnobotany of the North African and Saharan regions.

DAVID CRYSTAL.   No biographical data available.

STARKEY DUNCAN, JR.   No biographical data available.

JAMES L. FIDELHOLTZ (1941–) received his S.B. in Mathematics (1963) and his Ph.D. in Linguistics (1968) from M.I.T. He has been in the linguistics program at the University of Maryland since 1969. His major interests include Micmac and English phonology, and generative phonological theory. He is editor of the *Conference on American Indian Languages Clearinghouse Newsletter*. Recent publications are on mathematical linguistics, language teaching, English orthography, and Micmac verb morphology. Recent research is in semantic organization of the lexicon, English vowel reduction, and a Micmac lexicon.

MICHAEL A. K. HALLIDAY (1925–   ) was born in Leeds, England. He took his B.A. in Chinese at the University of London and studied linguistics at Peking University and at Lingnan University, Canton, before receiving his Ph.D. from Cambridge in 1955. In 1965 he became Professor of General Linguistics at University College, London; he is now Professor at the University of Illinois (Chicago Circle). His publications have included works in Chinese linguistics, general linguistic theory, applied linguistics, machine translation, stylistics, child language and sociolinguistics; his name is particularly associated with a social-semiotic approach to the study of the linguistic system and of language development.

DON HANDELMAN (1939–   ) was born in Montreal. He received a B.A.

and M.A. from McGill University and a Ph.D. in Social Anthropology from the University of Manchester in 1971. Since 1972 he has been Lecturer in Anthropology at The Hebrew University of Jerusalem. He has held a Postdoctoral Fellowship in Anthropology at the Institute of Social and Economic Research, Memorial University of Newfoundland. His research interests include the study of shamanism, expressive behavior, face-to-face interaction, and bureaucracy.

EVELYN HATCH (1930–   ) was born in Cedar Falls, Iowa. She received her B.A., M.A., and Ph.D. from the University of California. She is an Associate Professor at UCLA, teaching classes in applied linguistics. Her special interests are in second language acquisition and in reading a second language.

ADAM KENDON (1934–   ) studied biological sciences and experimental psychology at Cambridge University and received his Ph.D. from Oxford University for a study of face-to-face interaction using the techniques of Eliot Chapple. He was associated with Cornell University from 1959 until 1962 and was a member of the Social Skills Project at Oxford University from 1963 until 1966. After a year at Pittsburg and a year as a Visiting Assistant Professor at Cornell University, he joined Albert Scheflen at the Project on Human Communication at Bronx State Hospital, New York, where he remained until the end of 1973. He is now Senior Research Fellow in the Department of Anthropology, Institute of Advanced Studies, Australian National University, Canberra, where he is extending studies of communication behavior to various cultural areas in the Pacific region. He is the author of several scientific papers.

ALLAN R. KESSLER (1941–) is on the research staff of the Center for International Studies and the Research Laboratory of Electronics at the Massachusetts Institute of Technology. He received his S.B. in 1964 and his Ph.D in 1972 from M.I.T. in Political Science. His present research is in the area of computer-based information management systems and their application to longitudinal records of human behavior.

CAROLYN KESSLER (1932–   ) is a linguist on the faculty of the University of Texas at San Antonio in the Division of Bicultural-Bilingual Studies. She received her B.S. (1954) in French from St. Mary of the Woods College, Indiana, an M.S. (1967), and Ph.D. (1971) in linguistics from Georgetown University. She had studied at the University of Grenoble and was a Fulbright Lecturer in English as a Second Language at the University of Rome, 1967–1968. She has also taught at Stanford University (Lecturer in Linguistics/English for Foreign Students) and conducted research in child language at the Institute of Childhood Aphasis, formerly associated with the Stanford University School of Medicine. The primary area of her publications is that of psycholinguistics, first and second language acquisition.

MICHAEL LEODOLTER (1949–   ) was born in Vienna, where he attended primary and secondary school. In autumn 1967, he began a study of medicine at the University of Vienna where he received his degree as Doctor of Medicine in 1975. He received the distinction of the Republic of Austria "Sub auspiciis praesidentis rei publicae Austriacae," for his achievements in his studies. In 1970 he became a candidate of the Viennese Psychoanalytic Association, passing his training analysis, and, since 1975, he has been working as a clinical assistant in the Psychiatric Department of the University of Vienna. His main interests are psychoanalysis, clinical psychiatry, and social psychology. His unpublished works include "Sexual differences in the psychosociological socialisation resulting in role finding — men and women"; "Primary socialisation in respect to language development from the psychoanalytic point of view" and "Remarks on the metapsychological theory concerning personality structures: critical reviews of Jurgen Habermas' position."

RUTH WODAK-LEODOLTER was born in London. She finished her Ph.D. in Linguistics at the University of Vienna in 1974 and is presently Assistant Professor at the Linguistic Institute of the University of Vienna. Her main interests are socio- and psycholinguistics and her present research interest lies in neurotic and psychotic language, especially in cases of schizophrenia, as well as language behavior in specific situations, such as behavior in courts, schools, hospitals, etc. Among her most recent publications are *Die Sprache van Angeklagten bei Gericht. Ansätze zu einer soziolinguistichen Theorie der Verbalisierung* (Kronberg, 1975); "Gestörte Sprache oder Privatsprache: Kommunikation bei Schizophrenen," (*Wiener Linguistiche Gazette* 10/11 1975, pp. 75–95); and *Language Preservation and Language Death in Brittany* (with W. Dressler; forthcoming).

NGUYEN DANG LIEM.   No biographical data available.

ANA MARÍA MARTIRENA (1943–   ) was born in Buenos Aires, Argentina.

She studied linguistics at Cornell University, where she received an M.A. degree, and at the University of Chicago. She is now an Associate Researcher at the Sección Lenguas Indígenas, Instituto T. Di Tella, Buenos Aires, and has a grant from the Consejo Nacional de Investigaciones Científicas y Técnicas, Argentina. She is at present working on the grammar of Toba, a South American Indian language.

WILLIAM C. McCORMACK (1929–   ), a Canadian, is Professor of Anthropology and Linguistics at the University of Calgary. Born in the U.S.A., he received a B.A. in Liberal Arts from the University of Chicago in 1948, a B.A. with distinction in Psychology from Stanford University in 1949, an M.A. in Anthropology from Stanford in 1950, and, after also studying at the University of California (Berkeley, 1950–1951), a Ph.D. in Anthropology from the University of Chicago in 1956. Having studied linguistics, he took part in a Summer Institute at the University of Michigan (Ann Arbor, 1956), then taught and researched in linguistics during 1956–1958 at Deccan College, Poona, India, with special reference to Kannada ethnolinguistics and sociolinguistics. He is author of *Kannada: a cultural introduction to the spoken styles of the language* (1966) and of many articles on language in relation to society, religion, and identity in India. Since his fieldwork in Friesland and Scotland in 1967–1968, his research orientations have been comparative over forms of religious communication among Lingayats of South India and selected Calvinists of the West.

MARY R. MILLER (1920–   ) was born in Williamsburg, Iowa. She received her B.A. from the University of Iowa, her M.A. from Denver University, and her Ph.D. from Georgetown University (1969). She is presently Associate Professor of Linguistics in the English Department of the University of Maryland. Her research interests include language acquisition, marginal languages, bilingualism, place names, and the linguistic analysis of literary style. She is the author of a number of publications in these fields.

ELS OKSAAR (1926–   ) was born in Estonia. She received her academic training in Sweden and in Germany and took her Ph.D. at the University of Stockholm in 1958. She taught German Philology and Linguistics at the University of Stockholm until she was appointed Professor of General and Comparative Linguistics at the University of Hamburg in 1967. She was also Visiting Professor at the Australian National University in Canberra. Her publications include works on synchronic and diachronic semantics, socio- and psycholinguistics, poetic language, child language, languages in contact, and various aspects of German, Swedish, and Estonian grammar. She has done fieldwork with Estonian immigrants in Australia, the USA, Canada, and Sweden. She is co-editor of *Zeitschrift für Germanistische Linguistik* and *Semantische Hefte*. In 1975, she was elected President of the International Association for the Study of Child Language.

ION OPRESCU (1932–   ) was born in Bucharest, Romania. He studied at the University of Bucharest and is now Research worker in Cultural and Social Anthropology, Executive of the Laboratory of Cultural-Linguistic Anthropology to the Central de Cercetari Anthropologice, Bucharest. Initiator of studies and field researches of cultural-linguistic anthropology in Romania (by language sample), his principal research interests include: (1) the knowledge of man (and culture too) by means of the investigation of human means of communication (including spoken language, kinetics, proxemics, nonverbal elements) and (2) applied cultural-linguistic anthropology in the study of doctor-patient communication and interaction, in the study of teenagers, following the efficiency of educational processes, and in sociology.

FERNANDO POYATOS (1933–   ), Professor of Romance Languages, received his doctorate in Modern Philology from the University of Madrid (1966). His work (often assisted by the Canada Council) pursues an integrative, interdisciplinary approach to verbal and nonverbal systems of communication (centered around "the basic triple structure," language-paralanguage-kinesics), particularly within the total mechanism of interaction and in a cultural context. Among several other applications of his theoretical and methodological ideas are: "Nueva perspective de la narración a través de los repertorios extraverbales de los personajes" (1976), "Cross-cultural study of paralinguistic 'alternants' in face-to-face interaction" (1976), "Gesture inventories: fieldwork methodology and problems (1975), "Language in the context of total body communication" (1976), and *Man beyond words: theory and methodology of nonverbal communication* (1976). He has lectured in North America and in Europe.

THOMAS A. SEBEOK (1920–) is a native of Budapest who has lived in the United States since 1937. After studying literary criticism, anthropology, and linguistics at the University of Chicago, he earned his doctorate at Princeton University in Oriental Languages and Civilizations. He has been a member of the Indiana University faculty in linguistics since

1943, since 1967 with the rank of Distinguished Professor. He also serves as Chairman of the University's Research Center for the Language Sciences. He has held fellowships from the John Simon Guggenheim Memorial Foundation (1958–1959) and the Center for Advanced Study in the Behavioral Sciences (1960–1961), and was Senior Postdoctoral Fellow of the National Science Foundation (1966–1967). In 1973–1974 he was, successively, Senior Fellow of the Culture Learning Institute, East-West Center, and Senior Fellow of the National Endowment for the Humanities, and, coincidentally, Fellow of the Netherlands Institute for Advanced Study. In 1964, he was Director of the Linguistic Institute of the Linguistic Society of America which he served as Secretary-Treasurer (1969–1973), Vice-President (1974), and President (1975). He organized and, until 1963, was Chairman of the Committee on Linguistic Information. Beginning in 1968, he became Editor-in-Chief of *Semiotica*.

TATIANA SLAMA-CAZACU, born in Bucharest, is Professor of Psycholinguistics and Applied Linguistics at the University of Bucharest. She received an M.A. in Philosophy (Psychology) and M.A. in Modern Philology at the University of Bucharest and her Dr. in Psychology and Doctor-docent in Sciences. An initiator of psycholinguistics and of child language studied in Romania, she has published *Langage et contexte* (1961, Rom. ed., 1959), *Relationship between thought and language in ontogenesis* (1957, Rom. ed.; German ed., in press), *Dialogue in children* (1961, Rom. ed.; Czeck. ed., 1966; Engl. ed., in press), *Communication in the process of work* (1964; Rom. ed.), *Introduction to psycholinguistics* (1968, Rom. ed.; 1963, Engl. and Ital. eds.), *La psycholinguistique lectures* (1972), *La psycholinguistique appliquée* (in press), etc. Organizer of various sessions on psycholinguistics in international congresses, Chairman AILA Commission on Applied Psycholinguistics, Editor-in-Chief *International Journal of Psycholinguistics*.

RAGNHILD SÖDERBERGH (1933–) is Docent at the Institute for Scandinavian Languages, University of Stockholm. Her Doctor of Arts (F.D.) was obtained in 1964 on a study called "Suffixet -mässig i svenskan" (English summary: "The suffix -Mässig in Swedish: an historical-semantic study in word-formation"). Currently she is heading Project Child Language Syntax at the University of Stockholm. Besides numerous journal articles she has written two books, *Svensk ordbildning* (1968) and *Reading in early childhood* (1971).

WALBURGA VON RAFFLER ENGEL (1920–   ) has been working on the

384 *Bibliographical Notes*

relationship of verbal and nonverbal elements in first language acquisition since the early sixties. She is presently doing research on the kinesics of bilingual children and is Chairperson of the Anniversary Film Committee of the Linguistic Society of America. Her other interests include child language (Secretary of the International Child Language Association) and sociolinguistics. Her most recent book presents a critical survey of language enrichment programs for the socially disadvanced. She was born in Munich, Germany, and studied Classical Languages at the University of Turin, Italy, and at the Italian Institute of Archaeology (Dr. Litt., 1949, University of Turin); and then General Linguistics at Indiana University (Ph.D., 1951). She is presently teaching at Vanderbilt University and is Chairperson of the Committee on Linguistics of the Nashville University Center, an interinstitutional program in Linguistics involving Vanderbilt University, Fisk University, Peabody College, and Scarritt College. Professor von Raffler Engel, who joined Vanderbilt in 1965, is currently President of the Tennessee Conference on Linguistics. She has taught at various American and European universities and held a visiting professorship at Ottawa University in Canada.

STEPHEN A. WURM (1922–   ), an Australian, studied linguistics, anthropology and Oriental languages at the University of Vienna where he received his doctorate. He held teaching and research posts at the University of Vienna, the Central Asian Research Centre (associated with St. Anthony's College, Oxford University), Sydney University, and the Australian National University, and visiting appointments at Northwestern University, Indiana University, and the University of Hawaii. Since 1958, he has been in charge of the extensive research program in Pacific Linguistics at the Australian National University and was appointed to the Chair of Linguistics in the School of Pacific Studies of that University in 1968. He has been Editor of the serial publication *Pacific Linguistics* since its inception in 1963. His major research interests are concerned with the Papuan, Australian, South Western Pacific Austronesian, and pidgin languages of the Pacific as well as with sociolinguistics (formerly he studied Turkic languages as well). He has published widely in these fields.

Index of Names

Index of Subjects